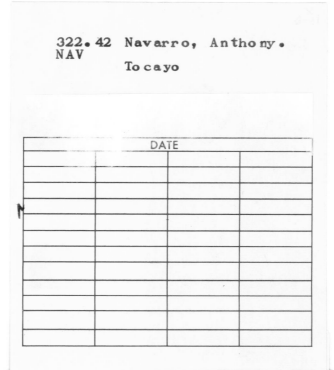

322.42 Navarro, Anthony.
NAV
     Tocayo

DATE			

TOCAYO

TOCAYO

ANTONIO NAVARRO

SANDOWN BOOKS

A Division of Shamrock Publishing Co. Inc.
Westport, Connecticut

DEDICATION

To Avis, my wife, and Louise, my secretary, who, in very different ways,
made the book possible.

To the late Malcolm Reiss who first encouraged it.

To those who died in the action.

SANDOWN BOOKS
A Division of Shamrock Publishing Co. Inc.
Westport, Connecticut

Arlington House Publishers
333 Post Road West
Westport, Connecticut

Library of Congress Cataloging in Publication Data

Navarro, Anthony.
  Tocayo.

  1. Cuba—History—Revolution, 1959.   2. Cuba—History
—1959–   .   3. Navarro, Anthony.   I. Title.
F1788.N37   972.91′064   80–27938
ISBN 0–87000–508–1

Manufactured in the United States of America
9   8   7   6   5   4   3   2   1

AUTHOR'S FOREWORD

THIS IS NOT a political book, although it is inevitably a book *about politics*. And about politics' unfortunate companions: violence, terror and death. It is the intensely personal story of an ordinary man, unprepared by training or inclination, turned revolutionary by force of circumstances in post-Castro Cuba. There is no spoon-feeding of any political position, no diatribes. As a reader you are simply exposed to the events and left to experience them and to draw your own conclusions, if any.

The book was written to provide a backdrop for a better understanding of an important and controversial event in our century: the Cuban Revolution. Those readers who wonder why the Cuban Revolution was so different from the typical Latin American upheavals of the past and present may find an answer in the book. And they may find answers to other questions. What was Cuba like before Castro? What were the hidden forces and resentments which Castro tapped? How could the Cuban people and the U.S. State Department have been so wrong about Castro? Was Fidel always a Communist? What was Che Guevara, the legend, like as a human being? Did the U.S. in fact "drive Castro into the hands of the Soviets" by refusing to help him at the outset? How could the gay, carefree Cubans turn into sullen doctrinaires? What was the mood before the Bay of Pigs invasion? What was the role of the CIA throughout it all?

The events recorded in the book actually happened. Some names have been changed to protect the guilty. Cuba is still a police-state. For the same reason, or to aid comprehension, some sequences are composites of separate events and characters, and chronology is occasionally altered. Key situations, however, are faithfully recorded. All persons who died during the action, or since, are called by their real names. The book is intended as a tribute to them.

1

I WALKED INTO my great-aunt's sickroom. She was dying all right. Nanita waved weakly without lifting her arm. A broken hip at eighty-nine made things nearly hopeless. My doctor friends had told me that what appeared to have been a fall was really the fragile age-worn bones of the hip and thigh finally giving way. After that came immobility and bedsores, and the end from pneumonia or kidney failure or whatever.

All my life I'd loved this old lady—my "Nanita." I never knew my real grandmother, and my mother was a beautiful woman but intense and driven. All the quiet warmth I ever knew came from Nanita.

I walked out onto an upstairs terrace off Nanita's room and looked over the golf links of the Havana Country Club spreading before me, and beyond them toward the big, beautiful tree-lined houses which bordered the fairways. They were all empty now. The owners, wealthy members of the Havana community, had left Cuba many months ago. The Clubhouse, at a distance, was deathly quiet, nothing moving in or around it, and the usual specks of white-clad golfers no longer broke the green expanse of the fairways. It was December, and the weather reflected a winter of sorts, a Caribbean winter; the wind was less oppressive, cooler, and it had the smell of the ocean about it, the nearby ocean, ever-present around the narrow island. It all made me thoughtful and nostalgic. Well, no sense being sad about the inevitable—not any more.

And yet, I found myself being objective about it all. Nanita's illness, her approaching death, the whole damned tragedy, I realized, was my fault if indeed it was anyone's. She was after all just a pawn, a tragically useful pawn in my work. So be it. We are all expendable in the end.

I moved quietly past Nanita's room to a large window which fronted the approaching road and glanced at my watch. It was time. Sure enough, a block away I could see the little figure of a man walking toward the house with short rapid steps. He wore a white tunic, carried a black bulging satchel, and looked like a doctor or a male nurse paying a house call, which was exactly what he was supposed to look like. I let him in.

1

"Go ahead," I nodded to him. "I'll be up in a minute. And be careful."

Contact time was almost on us, and preparations, in our special circumstances, were time-consuming indeed. Still, I took a minute to come downstairs into the library and look in on my "partner" Maria, who was scanning the day's newspapers with a look of obvious boredom. She looked up, happy to see me, a pretty girl, petite, with lots of dark hair and big green eyes.

I bent over her just long enough to tweak the nipple of her right breast and move quickly out of her reach. My aim must have been good. "Ouch." She said a soft "ouch," devoid of pain, responding lovingly to the brusque caress—the reaction of a woman who has known a man's intimacy and feels secure in his affection. It was tough on Maria, I thought, the whole thing.

"Frightened?" I asked, stroking her hair lightly and holding it in my hands for a moment.

She nodded. "Sometimes I wish I could just go back to painting."

"Sometimes I feel like taking it up." I leaned down and kissed her. She responded instantly, her lips full and moist, and I lingered for a quick minute, then left the room.

I went back upstairs and looked in on Nanita.

"How are you feeling, *viejita?*"

"Just fine, *mi amor.* I'm feeling so much better every day." She was lying. I knew her bedsores were extremely painful.

"Carlos came by a little while ago and helped me sit up," she added, closing her eyes from fatigue. "He's been such an angel . . ."

Carlos was a refugee from the G-2—the Cuban police—who was "burned out," in the underground jargon, and was hiding in my house until he could be taken off the island. He and I took turns lifting Nanita up from bed and helping her sit by the window for short periods of time. These periods were getting shorter each day, however, and we had all given up hope. Nanita knew it too and accepted her fate. Being near me was all she seemed to care about any more.

I stayed for several minutes until Nanita fell asleep, then walked into the hall where the little "physician" was sitting quietly, very straight, waiting for me. He looked a lot like a doll dressed up as a doctor, all white, short sleeves, trim haircut. I had never been able to get close to this small, efficient, exasperatingly silent man, and I never tried any more. After all, he was risking his life with me, and that was surely enough.

The operator's black valise was lying by his side. In it, I knew, there would be an assortment of medicines and hypodermics, as anyone would expect. However, under the first tier, neatly tucked away, there was a Morse telegraph key, shiny and polished like its owner. No doubt somewhere on his person he would also have a spare battery, as the ones at the house were wearing out.

"Better start getting ready," I said. "The boys up in Miami must be desperate by now. How long will it take you?"

"A few minutes," he answered quietly.

I looked at my watch. 3:45 P.M. We went into a small room around the corner from Nanita's. It was dark and soundproof enough to muffle the penetrating bip bip bip of the radio-telegraph key. While the little man was setting up his equipment, I went into my bedroom and to the telephone extension there. "Number One" would be waiting for my call, I knew, always efficient, always a jump ahead of everyone.

I picked up the receiver, waited for the dial tone, and dialed the number. Instead of the ring, I heard:

". . . Long Live the Maximum Leader . . . Fatherland or Death —We Shall Conquer . . . Socialist Cuba, Free Territory of America . . ."

There *was* no ring, only a litany of slogans, rhythmical, unending. It was a recording, a recent stunt of the government in the new Cuba. It went on, following the patterns of a normal telephone ring, pounding the captive caller's ear. I should have been used to it, but it annoyed me every time.

"Every invader will die on our glorious shores . . . Long Live the Maximum Leader . . ." It went on and on, mechanically, with a young woman's voice full of holy fervor. Suddenly it clicked, in the middle of some deathless slogan. Someone on the other end said a cautious hello.

"Hello, Max," I said. "This is Tocayo." In the Spanish-speaking countries, if someone bears your same given name, you often acknowledge that fact by referring to him as "Tocayo." It means literally "namesake." This custom often adds a warm quality to a relationship, a camaraderie, by the mere accident of a first name in common. I had picked Tocayo as my code name in the underground, and whenever I used it over the tapped telephone, the intercepter would conclude that my real name was the same as that of the person I was calling. It made for some interesting and welcome confusion.

"I know. What's new, Tocayo?"

"Not much, Max," I said as casually as I could. "Nothing since last night. I've got to put in a call to the tinplate suppliers in France tonight. Anything on your end?"

"No, no change. Tell 'the friends' that unless the tinplate is delivered on schedule, the factory may have to shut down by the weekend, unless another of the local factories comes to the rescue, and that's not likely, is it?"

"No, I'll do my best to *insist* on delivery, Max. What else?"

"One more thing. Don't forget my boots. I need them to go hunting."

"Yes, Max. Moreno already told me. I'll try to see you tonight. Otherwise, I'll talk to you tomorrow. Adios."

"Adios, Tocayo," Max said, and then added, "Good luck."

I made a mental note that, indeed, I had to telephone France and push for the delivery of that tinplate. That would close the circle for the eavesdroppers. It was part of my cover, my "front," and it had worked well. I did in fact represent a French tinplate supplier, Fer Blanc of Paris, and Cuba, cut off from the United States, was in desperate need of tinplate for its canning operations. So Max and I used "tinplate" when we meant weapons, ammunition and supplies for the guerrillas. The part about the boots was straight. Our anti-Castro men in the hills were literally going barefoot, and Max was anxious that the next airdrop include an assortment of sturdy footwear.

Always before radio contact my nerves were on edge. Ever since a major raid last November (led by Castro himself) had destroyed our Movement's main radio station and sent a flock of our people to the firing squad, all radio transmitting was done from my house. Our broadcasts were being monitored by the Central Intelligence Agency, but immediate contact was with our co-partisans in Miami and only through them with the CIA which, amongst us, was known simply as "the friends," and never mentioned by the familiar initials, not even in private conversation.

Although it was early in the afternoon, I walked down the hall to a little parlor looking for a drink. I poured myself a sort of daiquiri without frills: white rum, lemon, a little sugar and ice. It was good, cheap, and available. A poor man's daiquiri, I thought. God bless it.

I looked at my watch again. Almost 4 P.M.—contact time. I checked that the operator was ready, and that Nanita was alive, and then tackled the job of getting the transmitter/receiver equipment from its hiding place to the room upstairs where the actual transmission took place. It was a well-worn and laborious routine, but it was always exciting, flavored with that odd titillation which motivates revolutionaries everywhere. During the time the radio gear was actually out and operating, there was always great danger. Under normal circumstances, a surprise visit from the Communist government's G-2 police could probably be handled with a good snow-job. If the intelligence they had was not too solid, there was a fair chance that my "front" and my history of sympathy with the regime would carry us all through. Of no small help would be my photograph with Castro, clipped from *Life* magazine and posted in a conspicuous place near the front door. More discreet but visible too was a picture of me sharing a smile and a handshake with Anastas Mikoyan, Deputy Premier of the USSR. If all else failed, there was also the possibility of a quick exit through the back door via the golf course. However, if the actual radio gear was spotted, if we were caught with the transmitter blazing, it meant nothing less than a swift one-way trip to *El Paredon*, "the Wall," where executions were performed with summary dispatch and no questions asked. The Communist regime was extremely sensitive about its inability to wipe out the anti-Castro guerrillas in the hills and knew that our lifeline was a radio communication with the Miami groups of exiles—and the well-aimed airdrops which followed, with food and ammunition for the fighting men. Possession of an unauthorized transmitter, therefore, was as high on the treason list as you could climb.

I walked into our home elevator at the second floor level, pushed the button marked "cellar" and started the slow ride down, passing through the main floor where I cast an anxious look outside through the little round elevator window. Nothing unusual, I noted with only mild relief.

The elevator continued down until it clunked softly to rest on the cellar floor. I got out, turned on a small light, and looked around. As I peered into the damp gloom, I thought nostalgically how I had always meant to turn this room into one of Havana's few wine cellars, complete with air conditioning and automatic humidity control. The Cuban climate was unkind to wines, and Cubans were not generally wine drinkers. The delicate Bordeaux reds and even the sturdier Spanish wines quickly soured in our heat, and as a result many Cubans had never really tasted a sound bottle.

I thought fleetingly about my ancestors—Spanish-speaking Basques whose appreciation of wine I shared as much as their history of rebellion against repression. They would be disappointed to see my would-be wine cellar containing nothing but a few bottles of the Spanish claret *Marques de Riscal,* all I could salvage from the Revolution. Some day, I thought, I would finish the cave and stock it with the best—some day.

The door to the elevator cab had been allowed to close. After quickly surveying the premises, I walked behind the cab and into the tight little area which housed the guts of the elevator's mechanical system. I tripped a special switch, using a wooden pole left there for that purpose; the cab shook a little and started to rise to the main floor. I peered down into the elevator well, a black square five feet deep with a huge grease-covered spring in the middle. Arranged around this spring were several metal boxes, five submachine guns, a half-dozen Browning automatic rifles, and several .45 caliber handguns, all in plastic bags. I jumped into the well, carefully avoiding the springs and the grease, reached for two large metal boxes, and then got up and out.

Back to the elevator machinery, I triggered the switch again, and the cab returned, covering up the hole, the perfect concealment. I had in fact sealed off the only other entrance to the cellar, and anyone searching the cellar would have to use the elevator and would himself cover, with the cabin, that for which he was looking. Or so I hoped.

Carrying the metal boxes, I climbed into the cab and punched the button for the second floor. As I ascended, I caught a glimpse of Maria through the little window. She had given up her newspaper and was nervously pacing the room. The elevator continued to the top floor; at the landing the radio operator was waiting.

The little man took both metal boxes from me and went back into the transmission room. The room was quiet and could be tightly closed off to muffle the sharp, high-pitched electric sound. He opened the boxes. One contained the transmitter/receiver, a set of headphones and a Morse key; the second held the batteries to operate the transmitter. He took everything out but the Morse key, which he refused to use. He had his own. He went about efficiently and briskly setting up the equipment. I watched him, fascinated, as always. He didn't look much like a revolutionary or even a man of action; he was a technician doing his job, efficient, nondescript. Yet his life was as much on the line as mine. Not unlike myself, I thought, not totally unlike . . .

"Ready," the operator whispered. "Let's connect the antenna." He finished his own connections and handed me the crocodile clip fixed to the end of the transmitter's long wire. I took it with the wire trailing through Nanita's room onto the adjoining corner terrace. The old lady didn't stir. On the terrace, I looked out toward the golf links and the quiet houses. I had not been much of a golfer, but I loved the wide grassy fairways which blended with my own backyard without any sort of boundary. It gave me the opulent feeling of owning a vast green world. But all that was, as they say, B. C.—Before Castro. I reminded myself I was now looking for militia men or policemen on their rounds, or for next-door servants eager to turn in one of the masters, or for low-flying helicopters. There were none.

The terrace had a wire clothesline strung across it which ran perpendicular to a line drawn from the house to the receiving station somewhere in south Florida. The next move was critical. I did a few fake push-ups and violent arm-spreads for the possible hidden gallery, quickly snapped the crocodile clip to the center of the clothesline, and walked unhurriedly back into the house. The operator was already bipbipping away when I reentered the radio room. It was a steady signal at the agreed frequency: 7.42 megacycles. One or two minutes of monotonous bipping elapsed and, finally, acknowledgment—contact with Miami was established.

"Commander Augusto," the head of military operations for our anti-Castro Movement, would be waiting at the other end. Waiting eagerly. The guerrilla warfare in the mountains was going badly. The Communist Government, expecting and fearing the announced invasion, had mounted an all-out offensive on all approaches to the highlands, crushing the poor frightened farmers in the area into submission, not stopping short of on-the-spot executions of the head of any family caught aiding the enemy. It was thus becoming increasingly difficult to get supplies by land to the men up in the hills; air drops of food and ammunition from outside the island soon became the only practical way to sustain the war.

For this reason, Commander Augusto, on this day in mid-December 1960, was anxiously awaiting information that would enable him to at least try to get food, ammunition and medicine to the men before their democratic fervor, or whatever drove them to action, was beaten down. Some had been up there since Castro had come to power, not wanting to join in a political movement they had come to distrust while helping it to succeed. They were fatigued, disillusioned, war-weary.

For indeed it was a war in those days before the Bay of Pigs invasion—an open, skirmishing war in the mountains, but a quiet, pervasive, sullen war in the cities where the mention of the word invasion brought fear to the eyes of some and hope to the eyes of many.

The radio operator looked to me for this afternoon's message, and I handed him a piece of paper with writing on it that looked as if a child had been playing with a typewriter: L/R MXUAV GZ YOKXXG XUYGXOU . . .

Drawing on my engineering background, I had come up with this code by a simple trick of the engineer's slide rule, and my well-seasoned comrades had looked on it with interest and perhaps admiration. It was the development of this code, I suppose, that helped them accept me, that told them I had *something* going for me, even if I wasn't much with plastic dynamite or a sharp knife.

The technique was simple but effective. I had pasted an alphabet, twice repeated—A to Z, then A to Z again—on the moving section of the rule, and had done the same thing on the standing part of the rule. I could then slide any upper-series letter over any lower-series letter, say L over R, and I had a code. The operator would transmit the key L/R, and the receiver on the other end would fix his slide rule to this combination. All the letters would then fall into place. The code, moreover, could be readily changed in the middle of a message by simply transmitting a change of key.

The operator took the paper from me and began tapping. The message in its decoded form read:

L/R GROUP AT SIERRA ROSARIO EXPECTING DELIVERY TO-NIGHT OR TOMORROW NIGHT STOP SITUATION DESPERATE STOP APPROXIMATE COORDINATES NOW LONGITUDE 83 DE-GREES 22 MINUTES 11 SECONDS LATITUDE 22 DEGREES 13 MIN-UTES 03 SECONDS ABOUT 20 KILOMETERS FROM BAHIA HONDA EAST OF THE GUAJAIBON MOUNTAIN PEAK STOP LAND SUPPLY ROUTE NOW VIRTUALLY CUT OFF STOP WILL YOU DELIVER STOP ANSWER ON FREQUENCY NUMBER 2 OVER . . .

Carlos, the refugee who had been in hiding with us, opened the radio room door and stuck his head in. It was hard being a man on the run, I knew. He had nothing to do, and was fully aware that he was only added danger for me.

"How you guys doing?" he whispered with a raspy voice that showed signs of disuse.

"We've just made contact," I said, a little impatiently, and then, more gently, "Carlos, I think we may be taking you out to Miami next week. Probably through Cardenas or Varadero. So don't worry." I smiled. "I know it's tough, old boy, but try to take it easy."

"Oh, it's okay," Carlos lied, and closed the door softly behind him.

The operator changed his crystal to the new frequency, 7.48 megacycles, and prepared to receive Miami's answer. As he worked I gradually became aware of a faint but horribly persistent noise, clearly audible now that the radio was silent. I was on edge all right, but the sound was no hallucination. It was a feathery, staccato noise: faff faff faff faff faff. Before I had fully opened the door and rushed through Nanita's room to the terrace I knew damned well what it was.

"Get that message," I said, returning quickly to the radio room, trying to appear unruffled. "We *have* to have it. Then sign off immediately and let's put the gear away." I wondered why he hadn't heard the noise outside, but I was glad he hadn't.

The operator, it turned out, had already received the message and was finishing the decoding. So far, it read:

C/T TOCAYO WE WILL DO OUR BEST TO DELIVER TO RO-
SARIO WITHIN NEXT THREE DAYS DEPENDING ON MOON CON-
DITIONS STOP TELL THEM TO LIGHT FLARES OR FIRES IN SHAPE
OF CRUCIFIXION TYPE CROSS IN CLEARED AREA STOP SEVEN
LIGHTS HIGH BY FIVE ACROSS ALL WELL APART STOP REPEAT
FOR NEXT THREE NIGHTS FROM 2200 TO 0300 STOP GOOD LUCK
FROM AUGUSTO STOP SHIFTING TO FREQUENCY . . .

"Never mind the boots!" I almost shouted. "Just shut the damned thing off
right now. There's a tracer helicopter outside."

I didn't stop to see the look on the operator's face. He knew the penalty. It
was his fault, too, dammit. He'd taken a lot of time making contact and had
stayed too long on the same frequency.

The helicopter would be one of two radio tracer stations, one fixed on land,
the other mobile up in the air. Between the two, with direction-finding antennas,
they could pinpoint the location of a clandestine transmitting station down to
a small area, even a house on a golf course.

I rushed out to the terrace. As I moved past the sleeping Nanita the sound
was growing, faff, faff FAFF FAFF FAFF. Outside, the craft was hovering over
the fifth fairway, within shouting distance of the house. I thought of doing my
push-up routine but decided it was absurd in the circumstances. You just don't
ignore a helicopter in your backyard, especially in Castro's Cuba. I glanced at the
crocodile clip and the antenna lead on the clothesline and wondered if *they* could
see them, too. I was scared. Very scared, and sick to my stomach, and, at the
same time, very excited—that fearful titillation again.

The helicopter hovered, and there was no mistake, the pilots were both clearly
looking at *me*. Nothing else, no one else around—*Me!*

Deciding on nonchalance, I looked straight at the men and waved, my two
hands clasped over my head—a sign which in Cuba means anything from "Good
luck with that girl tonight" to "God save the Queen." Most importantly, it meant
you were on that person's side.

No response. Nothing. Just the anonymous stare of two dark faces. Cold quiet
scrutiny from the vague eyes in the distance. A landing on the fairway was the
simplest thing in the world. I thought the radio gear would still be exposed, and
the elevator gimmick took minutes, too many minutes.

I should have shown the operator how to hide the equipment. I should have
trusted the man. What an ass I can be! This, then, was it. What will happen
now to Nanita, poor soul? She adores me and I put her through this. And Maria?
Had she had the good sense to get out? Probably not, being loyal. No question
about Carlos; he would shoot it out. That was it, of course.

Shoot the pilots. The idea welled up like an eruption. I'm a good shot, and
I could hit them both at a hundred yards. But not with a handgun, good Lord,
not with a pistol . . . Then I knew the whole idea was preposterous.

Even if I had the guts, which I didn't, and the radio operator did not panic, which he would, a missing helicopter wouldn't be missing long. I just stood where I was, motionless, with images of execution by firing squad dancing in my brain. An odd fact ran through my mind. I recalled that all prisoners were medically bled immediately before facing the squad in order to save the blood for later use in hospitals. I wondered who would get mine . . . type O.

I was one big, pounding heart standing on the terrace. Then, slowly, came that curious calm of the truly inevitable. I would just draw my gun and chance it . . . At that moment the pilot waved at me! The helicopter made a frightening little dip toward the green carpet below, and immediately began rising fast, very fast, in that odd way helicopters move, as if they were falling sideways, FAFF FAFF FAFF faff faff faff—each faff a little weaker, like the fade-out ending of a popular song. I watched the helicopter until it disappeared, a black speck in the clear Cuban sky.

I walked back into the house in a daze, the adrenalin swirling. I looked at the operator, our eyes communicating for the first time, and told him almost dreamily that everything was all right, that he could leave the radio gear and take off.

I picked up what was left of my daiquiri and walked back to Nanita's side and slumped down on a chair near the dying woman. The drink felt warm and sweet going down. I could hear the tortured croaking breath nearby, and I could feel my own heart still pounding. The room and the house were very still.

I sat there for a long time, spent, as my mind looked back, almost as a stranger, on the events which had led to this crazy mess which seemed to be propelling me inexorably toward a violent end.

2

THE MORNING OF December 30, 1958, was beautiful and clear. It had almost
been promised to the group of notables who came from New York by chartered
plane to the Cuban Isle of Pines. They had been brought there by Colonel Ben
Finney to inaugurate the relatively small but plush resort hotel Los Pinos, where
there were all sorts of fun and games and, not at all incidentally, a brand new
casino. In fact, the New York travelers had been selected, among other reasons,
for their substantial interest in the games of chance and their substantial ability
to indulge in them. There were several old New York families, including the
Gimbels, the ubiquitous Prince Obolensky, and a coterie of wealthy Canadian
miners. To look after their needs in the way to which they were accustomed, two
headwaiters from the "21" Club had been smuggled in with them, presumably
with the acquiescence of the Kriendlers who ran the exclusive New York restaurant.

Out to greet the visitors was an equally wealthy Cuban contingent, composed
primarily of the young, the handsome and the beautiful, many of them personal
friends of the hotel owner. This group, mostly couples, had been seduced away
from Havana by promises of a merry New Year's Eve celebration in the relative
peace of the Isle of Pines, although some had voiced misgivings about fiddling
while their particular Rome was burning. The Batista government which had
ruled Cuba so long and so ruthlessly was about to fall—but they still came. There
was nothing much they individually could do about it, anyway, and this could well
be the last gay New Year's celebration. And, in any case, revolutions surely wait
for New Year's to be over, don't they?

I sat by the side of the pool, worn desert boots propped up on a chair, a beach
umbrella from a nearby table protecting me from the late morning sun. I felt
comfortable as I looked over the girls by the pool and, beyond them, to the sand
and the waters of the Caribbean. The small waves lapped lazily at the wet sand
which sparkled like a scattering of sequins under the bright sun. If you kept going,
I thought, you would reach Mexico, Merida maybe, or perhaps one of the Central
American republics. It was difficult to get that geography straight with all the

10

pretty girls in bikinis around. There was one little blond in particular whose bikini hugged the curves and the creases nicely, very nicely. She must be one of the *Americanitas* with the New York group, I thought. No Cuban girl would flaunt her beauty quite this way.

Soon my wife Avis and our friends would be joining me at the pool, and that too made me happy. They were not only our friends, but our best friends. I couldn't think of any other people I'd rather be with on New Year's Eve.

Avis and I had left Havana early that morning on a small private plane, leaving behind our two young children, Tony and Avis. Naming them after ourselves in the standard bid for self-perpetuation had ended up causing more confusion than immortality. We used the company's Beechcraft piloted by Manuel, the family's chauffeur cum valet cum pilot. Avis' father, Burke Hedges, was owner-operator of Textilera Ariguanabo, one of the largest textile factories in Latin America. With a fleet of private planes, he saw to it that one was available to us. Burke Hedges was even then headed for Mexico on board his personal airplane, a Lodestar.

The small plane took off into the cool morning air, bearing south, and was soon beyond the outskirts of Havana. The land below was bright green and red, the unique red earth so typical of Cuba. The patches of land appeared neatly laid out, with trim edges, somewhat belying the carefree nature of the farmers who worked it.

After a few minutes over the center of the narrow island, we reached the southern coast of Cuba. Beyond that stretched the light-into-deep blue of the Caribbean and, in the distance, the Isle of Pines. From the air, the whole scene looked like a map in a geography book, a deep green island on a field of blue, surrounded by a sprinkling of keys. It made one think of Blackbeard and gold doubloons, and the Isle of Pines had, in fact, been reputedly the setting for Stevenson's *Treasure Island.* Today, however, the island contained nothing but a sleepy port capital, a few scattered retreats of the wealthy, the so-called Model Prison—*La Prision Modelo*, where Batista kept political prisoners—and lots and lots of pine trees which gave this wonderful island its name.

The aircraft passed over the seagoing ferry, which traveled between the main island and the Isle of Pines twice a day, then over Nueva Gerona, the capital town. A short distance from here was the prison, a solid austere circular building with a large center patio. Manuel instinctively lowered the nose of the plane to see better, and Avis and I leaned hard against the windows, looking down at the prison. No word was spoken, but for a minute there was between us a feeling of concern, of involvement, of something wrong which both of us wanted to sweep under the rug.

Then came the lifting of the eyebrows, the shrugging of the shoulders which clearly said, "What *can* one do in our position?" Burke Hedges, after all, was a personal friend of Batista. Even though he did not approve of Batista's politics, the relationship was nonetheless an important one. No one in our family would rock the boat. That's the price you pay for riding it.

Toward the far end of the island the new hotel came into view. It was everything the best Caribbean resort postcards could claim. No wonder the *Americanos* came all the way down from New York for the inauguration. It had a central building with wings and *casitas* or villas spotted around. The focal point was the beautiful swimming pool which shone crystal-like from below, occasionally reflecting a flash of sun toward the plane and contrasting with the slightly darker and rippled waters of the ocean nearby. The outstanding attraction, the Casino, was not immediately visible, but one could be sure it was there somewhere, waiting to blossom the moment the Caribbean twilight was upon us, bringing its manufactured risk to the tourists.

Around the buildings there was a large area of land clearly meant to become a golf course and, somewhat removed, a fenced area with a small stand which I recognized with pleasure as the shooting range where the promised live-pigeon tournament would take place.

We circled the hotel once, waving the wings and making the motors roar for the sheer joy of it, and landed on the strip near the big DC-6 from New York which stood parked importantly to one side. We went through registration and the amenities of greeting the owner, an old personal friend. It was then, while Avis went off to look for our friends who had preceded us from Havana, that I went to the pool and settled into the pleasant pastime of people-watching.

"Oh, there you are." I heard the voice and looked up. It was Avis, leading our group of friends in my direction.

"No, I'm not here," I shouted back. "I'm over at a quiet bar in Merida somewhere. Or maybe it's Nicaragua. I'm not sure myself."

Avis smiled with affection. "Well, come back, honey. We're all here."

Avis had been born in Cuba of Irish-American parents who had settled on the island. She was petite and decidedly pretty and, if one accepted a miniature, she could also be called beautiful. She had a full quota of freckles, a warm winning smile, and hazel eyes which, though exquisite, were not always happy; there was a certain sereness in them which occasionally lapsed into melancholy.

"Always the philosopher, Navarro!" This came from Clelia, married to my best friend, Julio Batista ("No relation to the Dictator," Julio made sure to tell everyone). Actually, Julio was one of my *two* best friends, the other being Alberto Fowler. We three were inseparable. I was the oldest of the three, and constantly reminded of that fact by the others. Clelia Batista was a vivacious girl with an Italian background and Mediterranean good looks. Endowed with a great deal of insight and wit, she enjoyed being the cynic of the group, and wouldn't let any of us get away with anything even *slightly* phony.

"Okay, Clelia," I said with a touch of resignation. "You guys won't let me talk about religion, so I talk about philosophy. I have to meditate, become one with the Great Dynamo in the sky . . ."

"Let you talk about religion?" Clelia laughed. "Listen, Tony, you have said everything that has ever been said for and against religion. Twice. You've shocked the hell out of enough poor God-fearing girls already."

"Maybe I shocked you all when I first came down from the States," I replied with a straight face. "I kind of hoped I could disabuse you of all the fairy tales and the silly fears of my own religious upbringing. But I learned better. You don't want to be disabused. No one does. Not even me, damn it. You get branded with the stuff, and then it hurts to pull the cooled iron off the seared flesh. How do you like *that* for a metaphor?"

"You and Fidel Castro and your rebellions!" Clelia dismissed my comment.

In fact, Castro and I had both attended the Jesuit high school in Havana, four years apart. I thought of myself now as an agnostic of sorts, when I wasn't bold enough to be an atheist or scared enough to return to my faith. Castro, however, was then an unknown quantity in such matters. I had always maintained that the Jesuits specialized in making either rebels or saints. Since I wasn't quite certain which way Castro had turned, I didn't want to get into the subject again, certainly not with the formidable Clelia.

Alberto Fowler, just coming within earshot, laughed out loud. "For Christ's sake, are you two at it again?" he said. "Look, you guys, we're down here to have fun, get it? F-U-N. So, cut it out. Let's have a drink and discuss something non-controversial—like politics."

"Politics," I said, rolling my eyes. "How materialistic."

"Yes, but how important, Tony," Alberto shot back. "How *important.*"

Alberto underscored the last part of the sentence with a facial expression calculated to be meaningful and slightly furtive. He was the hedonist of our group, anything for pleasure, always reliable for a good time, whether he had to swallow benzedrine tablets wrapped in rose petals to shock the old ladies (which he often did), or let a live frog jump out of his mouth to scare the young ones (which he did once). Withal, he was far from superficial. He was artistic and sensitive, and lately had become involved in politics—as he put it: *very* involved. Having a strong sense of drama, as one might have guessed, he made much of his involvement, and Julio and I had repeatedly warned him it could mean anything from a reprimand to a handful of lost fingernails if one of Batista's boys wandered by when he was onstage. Physically, Alberto was the Latin of the group, his Anglo-Saxon name notwithstanding. He had nearly the archetypical Latin good looks, and he managed somehow to keep a perennial suntan when it wasn't tinged with a greenish hue from too many daiquiris or rose petals. His family, descended from English stock, had been in Cuba for several generations. It was rumored, more often than not by Alberto, that the Fowlers were helping Castro guerrillas in the area of their sugar mill.

Since Alberto had become a Castro partisan, he expected everyone else to follow suit immediately. From my point of view this made no sense. Though perhaps a political animal at heart, I had become disenchanted with government through repeated disappointments, and had settled down to enjoy the easy life in our precarious society while it was still there to enjoy. Alberto did not understand this attitude, and therefore he regarded my disillusionment as abandonment.

The minute Alberto mentioned drinks, the group stirred, remembering that noontime was upon us and that lunch would soon be served. I looked for a waiter and spotted one shifting in and out of the American contingent. The Americans, of course, had discovered noontime much earlier, and were sampling all kinds of pre-lunch delicacies and crazy rum concoctions. Watching them trying the various drinks, I remembered the wild combinations of alcohol I had once had in Honolulu and wondered if the Hawaiians really drank them. I decided then that they probably didn't, any more than the Cubans do.

The waiter emerged from behind a small cloud of terry cloth, which turned out to be a chubby Cuban lady. When I caught his eye and made that unmistakable sound which is a cross between a long kiss and a sucking whistle, an aspiratory burble which brings waiters instantly in Havana but would get only the haughtiest disdain in the most modest U.S. coffee shop, he rushed over to us.

"Your order, please," the young man said, obviously harassed. I noted that I had not seen the two waiters from "21" anywhere, and I guessed they were being reserved for the big blast the next night, New Year's Eve.

"How you doing, chico?" I asked.

"All right, sir," the waiter answered. "A little rushed with all the *Americanos.*" He managed a quick smile.

"And how is the situation?" I inquired. Everyone knew what "the situation" meant.

"Everything's quiet here, sir, so far," he lowered his voice slightly, "but I don't know if it will last the year out. I don't know." He shook his head.

Alberto, who was listening intently, immediately put on his meaningful look which was meant to say, "What did I tell you?"

I ignored it and ordered sherry and vermouth for the girls. Alberto and I both had daiquiris; we would settle down later in the day to more reasonable drinking. Julio, predictably, was reasonable from the start: he ordered Scotch and soda.

"Apropos politics," Alberto's wife Paulette said, "Alberto and I drove by the prison coming in today, and I felt a little scared when we passed it. Things are really getting awful." Paulette was a Belgian, the only one in the group not born in Cuba. A healthy-looking creature with an attractive Nordic face, she had met Alberto during a trip to Havana and had fallen madly and instantly in love with him. She had a reputation for being able to out-wrestle a man and, indeed, her friends had seen her do just that. For this reason, she tried to act soft and feminine, and to take a back seat to Alberto's assertiveness. She carried it off well, but just the same the boys prudently avoided horseplay around her. She was, however, soundly European in mind, and most of these Cuban goings-on were quite beyond her.

Still, I knew Paulette was right. The situation *was* awful. Batista was acting like a damned fool or a madman. While it was said he was the prisoner of his staff, this same thing had been said about many dictators and didn't ring true, especially for a man like Batista who was not about to let *anyone* dominate him. Government reprisals for terrorist activities had been exaggerated, especially where it involved the thrill-seeking university students. And it *was* true that the leaders of Batista's army were accepting bribes to look the other way and thus keep the "war" going so that money from Uncle Sam would keep pouring into Batista's coffers.

Batista, meanwhile, had repeatedly been asked to step down for the sake of the country, but had stubbornly said no. Instead, he announced and carried out national elections which were flagrantly fraudulent. His handpicked candidate had, of course, won by a wide margin, but no one was taken in. As late as mid-December, the U.S. had again asked the Dictator to agree to leave and make room for a provisional junta acceptable to all. The message was conveyed by a respected American industrialist and by U.S. Ambassador Earl Smith. Again, the proposal was turned down. Now, in the last few days, I had heard Castro was advancing toward the second largest city on the island, Santiago de Cuba, and that Che Guevara's men were threatening the provincial capital of Santa Clara. The Central Highway, the single cross-country road on which all transit depended, had been cut off at various places. Batista's soldiers, from privates to colonels, were said to be defecting in large numbers and accepting Castro's promises of forgiveness. Yes, there was no doubt that "the situation" was awful and, it now appeared, hopeless.

"I know, Paulette," I said. "Avis and I flew over the prison this morning, and I swear you could feel the tension all the way up there. Something's got to give. What bothers me is Castro. What the hell do we really know about him anyway?"

"You may not know much about him, for obvious reasons," Alberto chimed in, referring to my standoffish attitude and my family's involvement, "but I do. And you have my personal guarantee he's what this country has been waiting for."

"Your personal guarantee, Alberto?" I whistled long and low. "If I'd known that, I wouldn't have been so worried."

Alberto brushed off the dig. "Democracy and decency," he said. "We're tired of being a brothel and a gambling joint for the Americans." It sounded rather peculiar with the Casino right next to us, but there was no question that Alberto was in earnest. I didn't know then—no one did—how deep that feeling of shame and resentment over American domination ran in the Cuban bloodstream.

"Well, he may be all those wonderful things now," I came back. "Most revolutionaries are great in the beginning. But what about later, that's what I want to know, when this 'man of the people' has his little taste of power? Power, Alberto—you know what it does, don't you?"

Alberto listened quietly. I was surprised he didn't try to interrupt.

"Look at our history," I continued. "Even before Batista, there were these so-called democracies. Corruption, friends and family in juicy jobs. Officials on the take. Quotas imposed for collecting fake taxes from the rich—just like now. Nothing's different. Nothing will be different."

I paused, looking around to show I involved everyone in my harangue.

"Your cynicism's articulate, as usual," Alberto said, "and wrong, as usual."

"We don't all think it has to be that way, Tony," Julio broke in. "We don't all feel the way you do about it."

"You know, Tony," Alberto mused, "you would make a good *Fidelista* after all . . ."

I ignored Alberto. "More to the point, Julio. Look at Batista himself . . ." I looked around, suddenly aware that my voice was a bit too loud. A waiter was coming, and I shifted into English, asking the group to "hold it a minute." The whole conversation had now become "bilingual," an indulgence native to the educated Cuban, with no affectation or snobbishness attached, although the more chauvinistic Cubans didn't approve.

The waiter brought the second round of drinks in answer to my long-range kissing sound and a circular motion of my right hand. When he was gone, I continued, making sure that no one would grab the platform. In that group, with the exception of the very proper Julio, you could divide the number of people by two and you would have at least that many conversations going on at the same time. This time I was lucky; the subject was dangerous enough to keep the others conservative.

"More to the point," I repeated, "look at Batista himself. Have you seen those 1934 photos of him, just after the Sergeants' Revolt?" No one answered, which meant no one had.

"Well, I have. There he was, the hero sergeant, saving his country from chaos, giving the little people hope for the first time in their dreary lives. At the time, maybe he really *did* mean it, really *did* want to help Cuba. Christ, look at him now, twenty-odd years later. Rich, flaccid, bourgeois, insensitive from so much violence, corrupt, maybe even stupid. Oh, no, Alberto, I am totally disenchanted with leaders. Castro, or *whoever*, will be just the same."

"Castro *won't* be like that, dammit! Jesus, can't you tell the difference between him and the others?" Alberto shouted intensely.

"Do you know Castro personally?" I asked quietly.

"No, I don't. You *know* I don't," Alberto answered. "But I know Camilo Cienfuegos, and *he* knows Fidel. That's enough for me."

"Commander" Cienfuegos was one of Castro's principal lieutenants, carrying on his military campaign near Alberto's mill in central Cuba, and it was no secret that Alberto was helping him and that they were "friends." I had seen Alberto's treasured black-and-red armband several times, a symbol of the "26th of July" Movement founded by Castro after the aborted attack on Batista's barracks on July 26, 1956.

The conversation was getting out of hand and obviously into dangerous territory. At this time the moderator was heard.

"I wish you two would cut this out," Julio said with a certain degree of authority. "I thought someone said we're here to have fun . . . F-U-N. Remember, Alberto? So let's have it, huh? I don't know about you guys, but we're having a pigeon shoot tomorrow, and *that's* something worth getting worked up about."

I welcomed the interruption. I'd said all I wanted to say, anyway, and probably more than I should. The thought of the pigeon shoot diverted me in a pleasant way. I looked fondly at my shotgun, sitting inside its case by the side of the table.

"I'll second that," I said.

"I'll third it," Avis added, relieved the argument was over.

Alberto said nothing; he just sat quietly. Julio looked a little surprised that his brief admonition had had such an effect on his two friends, and he smiled happily as if he had done something marvelous.

Julio was in his early thirties, pink-complexioned and boyish-looking, and fun in a restrained sort of way. Like many Cubans of old wealth, he tended to underplay his social and financial position, sometimes to a degree that, in the case of the latter, his two friends would call him just plain stingy. This was especially true at that painful slow-motion time when the dinner bill had to be picked up. And his sense of propriety was keen, although at times it was a struggle with his own imagination.

"Come on," Julio said in an attempt at spontaneity, "it's getting to be lunch time, even for us. Let's have a last one."

I stood up. "Not for me. I'm going to wander over and see what the Americans are up to."

A waiter just then swept by and left a spilling bowl of *mariquitas* on the table, delicious wafer-thin slices of green cooking bananas, fried in deep fat, and tasting like nuts. I stopped to take a bunch of the crackly things and found that Julio was going to start things all over again.

"I'll say one thing for Tony's side," Julio said, munching away with the rest of us. "Mr. Castro's credentials aren't all that great. Not after his performance in Bogotá some years ago, eh?" Julio said it calmly enough, but this particular accusation, the time Castro and his cohorts allegedly turned a political meeting in Bogotá into a Communist-led massacre where priests and children had been killed, had gained him a lot of bad press. The reminder made Alberto go into a slow burn.

"The trouble with you two guys," Alberto answered back, "is that you listen to rumors like that. You're ready to believe the worst and go on living in this sad thing called Cuba and not do anything about it. You, who handle industries and wheel and deal in banks, you're willing to deal with corrupt officials rather than fight."

Alberto was going a bit too far now, but he was also hitting home. Julio and I looked at each other. We had discussed this particular matter between ourselves before, and it was true that we'd come to the sad conclusion that we would have to play ball with the venal functionaries in order to survive. Not that it was only a matter of paying the proper taxes. We would have done that more or less gladly. It was a matter of being *over-assessed*, officially and without appeal. And this the government would do unless you paid off the tax collectors. Alberto knew of it also and was taking advantage of privy information.

"You're privileged people, you two, by training, by upbringing, by your responsibilities. You should be running the government, or at least *helping* to run it, because it's *you* who are the most vulnerable when it isn't run properly. But do you? Of course not!" Alberto was getting inspired. "You'd rather buy off a public servant than become one!"

He stopped, stupefied, aware that he had unwittingly come up with an absolutely brilliant, lapidary phrase, a capsule definition of the Cuban problem. The others, including Julio and me, were aware of it, too, and our silence was testimony. Some of the girls started to applaud.

"Oh, good God!" I finally said in mock disgust, as I got up from my chair. I smiled at the group, gave Avis a kiss on the nose, and announced that once more I was headed toward America. I wandered over to the pool, grabbing a rum-and-soda as I went by a passing waiter's tray, mumbling something about my bill being "back there."

The daiquiris and the sun and the early morning plane ride had taken their toll, and I walked a little dreamily into the midst of the merry Americans. By this time, a crowd of *regular* U.S. tourists had arrived from Havana. I could see the buses outside as I passed in front of the main entrance. They were apparently coming to the new hotel for lunch as an added attraction of their tour. Most of them were dressed in slacks and loud skirts and straw hats and carried the inevitable cameras, and soon they blended in with the New York contingent, the bright clothes contrasting with the bare skins by the pool. As I made my way through the crowd, I found myself being stopped, as I moved a bit hazily, by people anxious to talk with a *real* Cuban.

"You mean to say you don't *know* Juan Romero? Why, I thought *everyone* knew him. I suppose Havana *is* a big place, though, isn't it? Well, you can't know everyone, can you?"

"No, I don't know Mr. Romero, sorry. No, I don't suppose you *can* know everyone . . ."

"Young man, you must be Cuban. Wher*ever* did you learn English so well? I'm amazed."

"Thank you. In school in the States, I guess . . ."

"Mister . . . ah . . . *Nav*arro?"

"Navarro, ma'am. That's right."

"Oh, yes, *Nav*arro. Are you married, Mr. *Nav*arro? I suppose that's a silly question, isn't it? It doesn't *really* matter to Cubans."

"Sometimes it does."

"Why, Mr. Navarro, how very nice to see you. We're having a *very* good time. We hope we're not imposing at a difficult time for your country."

"It *is* a difficult time, Mrs. Gimbel. I appreciate your concern . . ."

"Young man, I don't recall seeing you on the plane from New York. But I overheard you talking to the waiter. Wher*ever* did you learn Spanish so well? I'm amazed."

"Thank you. At home, I guess . . ."

"My, my, these are the best whatchamacallit banana things I ever ate. Does your mother make them for you, Mr. Navarro?"

"No, my mother is allergic to bananas. And to cooking . . ."

" 'Como esta usted, Señor Navarro?' That is Castilian Spanish, of course. You speak a sort of dialect here, don't you?"

"Very good accent. No, sorry, no dialect."

"My church auxiliary, Baptist y'know, is planning to finance sending a missionary to bring the Word to the natives here in the jungles. Tell me frankly, Mr. Navarro, do you think the timing is just not right?"

"Not right, I'm afraid. And no jungles."

"You know, Mr. Navarro, if I were that fellow Batista, I'll tell you exactly what I would do. I would get myself some old P-38s and I'd bomb those yellow bastards out of those hills . . . or whatever color they are. That's what I would do. It worked for us in Guam, I'll tell you."

"It may be a good idea. The bastards, by the way, are Cubans."

"Mr. Navarro. Tony, I believe. I heard you talking to Mrs. Gimbel. Tell me, Tony, between us men. I've heard a lot about this Casa Marina, the house of . . . ah . . . ill-repute, y'know. I don't want to be taken for a fool. You know how these things are. Do you know the people who run it? What does it take to get a good in?"

"Money. And the usual equipment." My patience was thinning.

"I watched you watching us, Mr. Navarro. Distant-like." It was the small blond in the small bikini. I woke up instantly.

"I assure you," I said, "that the distance was not a matter of choice."

She told me that her name was Louise and that she lived in Connecticut with her family. She had prepared for college at Rosemary Hall, where she had known some Cuban girls—maybe I knew them?—and she was struggling at Radcliffe. Right now she was on Christmas vacation with an older female cousin.

I listened carefully and gave my instincts free rein. I told her about the live-pigeon shoot the next morning and she said she would be there, of course, after making a slight moue in defense of the poor pigeons. I said goodbye, holding her hand a little longer than necessary, with that special heightened awareness of the sense of touch. I then moved on around the pool. At the end of the mass of people, still in the group but yet discreetly separate and not in swimsuits, I found the two headwaiters from the "21" Club, Walter and Mario. They were chatting away with an old black Cuban waiter whom I knew very well from Havana—probably, I thought, about matters related to their shared trade.

Walter was a solid man all around, strong, but it was his head that really stood out. It was massive, and it gave him rather a menacing look, somewhat like a giant whose body had not quite kept up. The impression was quickly dissipated on contact with what was a kind and warm human being and a very able "captain" as well.

"How are you, Mr. Navarro?" Walter addressed me first, to show he remembered, in the age-old waiter tradition. "And your father-in-law, Mr. Hedges? We haven't seen him at the Club since about last January. Or you either, sir."

"We're both fine, Walter." I could play the memory game, too. "Mr. Hedges is in Mexico right now. He should be coming back soon," and I added, "if nothing happens to discourage him . . ."

"Oh, nothing will, Mr. Navarro," Walter said. "Revolutions just don't happen on New Year's Eve."

"Is that an Italian tradition or a Cuban one?" I asked, laughing, and looked questioningly at the old black Cuban waiter who was standing there, listening. Don Pedro, as I always addressed him deferentially, had known and looked after me at one of Havana's best restaurants since I was a child, and we had a special relationship.

"What do you think, Don Pedro?" I asked in English. He had learned the language from years of passing tourists. "Will there be big trouble soon?"

"I don't know much about these things, Tonito," he replied, his large, sad eyes glancing at me with affection. "I have enough problems making my grandchildren behave." He paused while we laughed. "We poor people, Tonito, have nothing much to win or lose, whatever happens. I don't bother with politics and I hope it doesn't bother with me. But I'll tell you one thing: from what I hear tell, you rich boys won't have it so good any more if this man comes to the power. This Castro. Not so good any more, Tonito." He said it without any malice whatsoever, but he knew the point would not be lost on me. We looked at each other for several moments.

"Perhaps so, Don Pedro. Perhaps so," I finally said and, to Walter and Mario: "Hasta luego. I'll see you fellows later."

Moving away from the three waiters, and still smarting from the remark, I walked over and greeted a group of men whom I knew to be Canadians, led by Duncan MacMartin of the mining family. They were wearing what looked like cotton kilts over their swimming trunks and berets on their heads, and thus were by far the most picturesque of the New York group. One of them had a reputation for chewing and *swallowing* champagne glasses, a skill which certainly impressed me. Someone had told me the Canadians liked shooting, so I mentioned the match the next day and urged them to join us. They already knew about it, had brought their guns and, yes, of course, they said they would participate. I said goodbye and returned to my friends via the long but uncrowded way around the large amoeba-shaped pool. I was still thinking about Don Pedro.

I found my group finishing their third "last drink before lunch." "Why not?" I said. "Might as well splurge. It won't go so well for us rich boys come the revolution. And, anyway, maybe there won't be a New Year's Eve." It was the first time the possibility had been mentioned, but everyone understood. The news of "the situation" was getting worse, or better, depending on the listener's viewpoint. At any rate, the possibility of open fighting in Havana was certainly there. The mothers of the group, Avis and Paulette, undoubtedly thought of their children back home, but nothing was said.

I toasted the gathering, wished all a premature Happy New Year, and tried the mildly fruity, rosin taste of the wine we had brought, nodding approvingly. The Spanish "Monopole" never failed you. The waiter then brought the single dish we had ordered collectively: a steaming casserole of *arroz con mariscos,* all kinds of seafood in yellow rice. It very much resembled the Spanish *paella,* but *paella* also had in it fish and chicken and even Spanish sausage, and it was reserved for important occasions. After the main dish, the girls had the typical Cuban-Spanish custard called *flan* for dessert, and the men had coffee.

After, or rather *with,* the strong Cuban coffee, I asked the waiter for cigars, and the choice as usual was overwhelming: *Upmann, Montecristo, Partagas, Larrañaga, Romeo y Julieta, Cuatro Vegas.* I selected the lesser-known *Cuatro Vegas,* a wonderful cigar which traditionally came without any band at all, implying that a *real* connoisseur should recognize it without any pedestrian help. If, as I sat blissfully puffing my cigar, I had known just what a furor the lack of these little treasures would soon cause among American smokers, I would have savored it the more. Still, I enjoyed it immensely.

"What luxury, eh, Tony?" Clelia said. " 'Come the Revolution' there will be only one brand, and you'll like it, Tony, you'll like it."

"Now you're spouting politics too," I said. "I always thought you were above it all . . ."

"Go to sleep or something, huh, Navarro," Clelia interrupted and we both laughed. Nonetheless her remark also reflected a growing awareness that was closing in on us. We all pretended to ignore it, and the girls deliberately engaged in inconsequential talk. I puffed my cigar, more pensive now: "You rich boys will not have it so good any more."

I got up and invited Avis to come and take a nap with me, announcing that I wanted to be rested for tomorrow's shooting match. I was feeling my wine, and we left for our room, saying *hasta luego* to our friends. Back in the room, I threw the safety lock on the door, unusual for Cuba and a familiar signal for Avis. There was something about a strange room that almost always led to making love. I was more intense than usual this time, the wine and the worries spending themselves finally into passion. I insisted on watching Avis nude for a while, and she was not shy about complying, enjoying my look of anticipation.

I had been an only child, no sisters, no peer females at all in my infancy or early adolescence. This feminine deprivation was followed by the all-boys Catholic school. I had never seen a totally nude woman, one at least I could hope to touch, for many, many young years, and women still remained an enigma. That was not altogether unusual, really, for young Cubans of my generation, except for relations with prostitutes, and I had never been much for that. I had always been too young-looking when growing up, and my friends told me I would never make the grade at the local training ground. Girls, the next-door variety, remained a tantalizing mystery for a long time. Now I could not get enough of it and hoped it would never become commonplace. I had a lot of lost time to make up. Avis, a product of a different culture, never understood my emotions entirely in this sensitive area, but she pleased me in every way out of simple, uncomplicated love, and she enjoyed my wonderment.

I held her by her hands at arms' length and enjoyed her simple girlish beauty.

Her womanly body looked just a little odd under her very young face, as if, I thought, it had its own independent personality which had to be acknowledged. No doubt about it, nature put that innocent face there to bring you to terms with a body which has its own demands and, ultimately, its own urge to preserve the human race. At this point, I was more than willing to help nature out.

When it was all over, we lay back, content, and listened to the faint rumbling of the waves through the open windows facing the ocean. It reminded me of our honeymoon, not so long ago, really. We compared notes on our respective reactions to that nostalgic and sometimes funny first night four years before, part of which we had been forced to share with our persistent, irreverent friends.

Avis and I laughed at the pleasant recollections, snoozed a while, and decided we would not go down for dinner that night; we would send for soup instead, maybe garlic soup, and perhaps some cold beer. The soup, which sounds menacing at first blush, was delicious. It is just broth into which cloves of fresh garlic, cut and deeply browned, have been tossed along with lots of broken-up French bread. The garlic loses most of its bite and the whole thing is surprisingly mild and very tasty. Just before serving, the cook drops a raw egg into each bowl, and by the time Avis and I got the soup, the egg looked as though it were poached. Avis scooped out the gooey thing, but I ate it with relish. The Spaniards swore by the soup; it was supposed to be a hangover remedy and an aphrodisiac, but neither one was of great interest to us at the moment.

We called our friends on the house phone to say goodnight. Alberto was somewhere listening to the radio and making telephone calls, but Julio was there and I reminded him that the next morning the great pigeon shoot was on, blew a loud trumpet fanfare over the telephone, and bid him goodnight.

Through the window we could hear music playing at the pool area. It was old Cuban music without the pounding rhythms of the modern versions, a blend of negro slave laments with the happier Spanish airs plus occasional touches of nineteenth-century ballroom dance music mixed in . . . a funny blend, maybe a *contradanza*, I thought, something by Lecuona or Roig, names famous to the older Cubans . . . almost anything good of the period was composed by Lecuona . . . it certainly was beautiful . . . good that the tourists should hear it, that they should know about our music, our culture, our world . . . almost midnight, December 30, 1958 . . . a long, strange day . . . should tell Avis, but she has already started her tiny little snore . . . almost midnight . . . rich boys . . . not any more.

3

I GOT UP EARLY on December 31, trying not to awaken Avis, but she stirred anyway and we exchanged sleepy "good mornings." We agreed to meet at the shooting match scheduled to start at ten that morning or, being Cuba, "about ten." I put on slacks, a polo shirt, my old reliable desert boots, and a new shooting jacket from Abercrombie & Fitch in New York with small pockets for shells and large hopeful pockets for dead birds. Julio and Alberto would love that jacket and would rib me about it, of course; that was part of the fun.

I had a quick breakfast by the coffee bar. Juice, coffee, a piece of Cuban bread with butter: more or less a typical Cuban breakfast. I added a glass of milk, a hangover from my American schooldays, since most Cubans—in fact, most Latin Americans—don't drink milk past the age of seventeen.

I walked the short distance to the "Gun Club" with pleasant anticipation and a mild case of nerves which I would hide successfully. The Club showed signs of new construction. There was a trap court which looked functional, a skeet field still being built, and a live-pigeon court ready for today's action. Behind the pigeon court was a small, rather makeshift stand with a roof.

Most of the Americans were already there, sitting around unpacking their guns. Julio was there, too, methodically cleaning his gun, a Spanish-made "Zarrasqueta," two-barreled side-by-side, one of the "Cadillacs" of the gun trade. Frugal in everyday things, Julio would nevertheless spend money generously on his major pleasures. Thus, he owned the best Ferrari sports car, the best skis, and, probably, the best gun. I kidded him a lot, but I basically approved of indulging where it counts. Alberto hadn't arrived yet; he would make a last-minute entrance, of course, in the latest togs.

"Hi, Champ," I greeted Julio.

"Hi, Killer," Julio said. "Seen the pigeons yet?"

"No," I answered, "and I don't want to. I don't want to strike up any friendships."

I got my gun out of the case and started to put it together. Mine was a Belgian Browning, an over-and-under, or "superimposed," as Europeans called it to distinguish it from the more traditional side-by-side double-barreled gun. The stock was beige in color, probably bleached mahogany, with a fine glossy polish, not unlike a woman's silky blond hair. So I called it my "Blond" and, to tell the truth, I was deeply involved with that gun. And though Avis pretended to be jealous of it, I wouldn't have changed it for any other. I assembled it with a series of pleasant clicks, and brought it up to my shoulder to get the feel. The combined smell of burnt powder and gun oil filled the air, bringing me even closer to hunter's heaven.

The others were also "gearing up," and some were already practicing at the trap court at the far end. I could hear the cadential cries of "Pull!" followed by the distant guns' reports. The Americans had all kinds of guns: American-made Brownings, Remingtons, Winchesters; and one of the Canadians owned a Franchy, a beautiful Italian shotgun and the lightest one on the market.

By this time the spectators were beginning to fill the stand. "Our" girls were there, and so were Louise and Mrs. Gimbel and the man from Guam (looking authoritative), and the Baptist lady (soon to look horrified)—even Walter and Mario. There weren't really many shooters participating, maybe a dozen or so including us, if Alberto ever arrived. And *we* would be the only Cubans present, even though there were many excellent "guns" in Havana. This shoot was a small private event and, presumably, most people had other plans for the New Year's weekend. This was certainly true, but not the real reason. I walked over to Julio.

"This is a lot of fun, Julio," I said, "but it really isn't right, is it? I mean, the way things are." I had heard part of the news while having breakfast. Castro had taken Santiago de Cuba and at this very moment was negotiating with Batista's general there. The "Rebel Radio" was calling for a general strike in support of the Revolution, and was cautioning that Batista would try to flee and escape punishment. The radio said several of the major social clubs in Havana were canceling their New Year's Eve parties, so some of our other friends would have to forego their *own* brand of fiddling while Rome burned. It sure looked like the end, and I just had to share my feeling of guilt.

"It probably isn't right, Tony, no," Julio said seriously. "But we are here, and we probably couldn't get back if we wanted to. So let's try to enjoy it and quit worrying."

That made sense. I was quiet for a minute and then changed the subject.

"Did you see those guys with pump-guns? They're *crazy* to go after pigeons with those." The old-timers didn't approve of automatics or pump-guns for Club shooting, but some of the men participating were hunters and preferred field guns.

"You'd be surprised," Julio said. "Some guys are faster with a pump than you would be with an automatic."

"Okay," I argued, "but you can't beat a double barrel for speed. It's simpler, and it doesn't have all that machinery to move around." The subject having been changed successfully, we went over to the stand to greet the girls, *all* the girls.

Alberto was just arriving, "at the last minute in the latest togs." He eyed my new shooting jacket and made the expected snide remark. It was time to start.

A live-pigeon shooting court consists of a stretch of concrete walk, running forward from the stands about twelve to fifteen yards (that distance is not important except for the eardrums of the spectators). Beyond the walk is a fan-shaped area surrounded by a low wire fence. The radius of that semicircle is about fifty yards, or roughly three times the length of the cement walk.

The shooter stands at the end of the walk and a "dead" pigeon must drop within the enclosed area ahead of him; a pigeon falling on the outside of the limiting fence is a "miss." The gunner may shoot forward or to the sides, or even straight up in the air, but never behind him, for obvious reasons. The pigeon cages are buried in the ground about twenty-five yards ahead of the shooter.

The released pigeons may fly to the far end, take off to the sides or straight up, or not fly at all and just sit there (though not for long). The shooter has two shots at each bird in flight, which is right for a double-barreled gun and probably the genesis of the rule. If a pigeon is released and just sits there, it may be killed with a *second* shot, but not with the first one. So, the shooter can wait until the pigeon decides to fly, or be sneaky and fire a shot into the air (guaranteed to make the poor thing fly) and then nail it with the second shot even on the ground. (In Philadelphia, the cradle and still the authority of live-pigeon shooting in the U.S., rules are slightly different.)

In other words, it's fair to kill a sitting bird with the second shot. Cruel? Yes, probably. But, as they say, it's okay if you eat the birds, or *someone* eats them. Julio was fond of saying that it was gruesome, but "that's the way the pigeons crumble." Julio's humor was always of the Chaplin era.

So that all contestants get the same breaks, or as much as luck will allow, the locks on the five cages are connected to a sort of roulette wheel at the end of the cement walk. Before calling for his bird, the shooter will twirl the wheel which will determine which one of the cages will open when the call is made.

The hotel owner was scheduled to start the contest, but was nowhere to be found. I took note of the fact, and it was *my* turn to look meaningfully at Julio.

Someone announced that the shooting should begin, and one of the contestants asked to see a bird. The pigeon popped up from the far-left cage, fluttered in the air, dazed (a good time to get it, I noted), and a second later took off toward the side and away. Like people, some pigeons are lucky.

Someone else asked for a second bird. This one was fast—what is called a "deer" in the jargon. It went straight from the cage toward the fence, no more than three feet above ground, and was gone in seconds. The crowd cheered, always for the underdog. In the big leagues, fifteen birds per person are released, in groups of five, but here it was judged that ten birds, two sets of five, would be enough.

Some of the Americans were very professional. They were told to shout *"Pajaro"* for bird, and *"Pajaro"* they yelled in their best Spanish. They would walk up the cement path with all the poise they could muster, twirl the wheel lightly, stand at the end of the walk, gun at the shoulder in the accepted ready position for live pigeons, and shout *"Pajaro!"* The crowd would hush. The bird might be killed cleanly, instantly, and the crowd would roar approval. Often, however, the pigeon would be only wounded by the burst of pellets, and would lie there, fluttering and bleeding. If it had been the first shot, the bird could be mercifully finished with the second. If both shots had been fired, then it would have to die the long, natural way.

In such instances, Clelia and Paulette could be heard assuring the other ladies in the audience that the dead pigeons were turned over to an orphanage run by nuns, to feed the children. At one such point in the shoot, the Baptist lady gasped audibly and opted for a quick exit, probably convinced that a missionary was indeed an absolute necessity in these parts.

We performed reasonably well. Julio's style was professional; Alberto at least had flair; I was aggressive, but I knew I lacked Julio's grace, and I was really outclassed. The girls cheered us on, no matter what, and Louise and her cousin were also part of our private claque. At the end of the first set of five pigeons, seven of the twelve participating guns, Julio and I included, had five kills out of five, and Alberto had some sort of a record: zero.

The second set of five pigeons started, and I drew the last position, an advantage of sorts. Tension increased with the imminence of the end, and the nervous shouts of *"Pajaro,"* followed by deafening blasts of the 12-gauge shotguns, went on and on.

On Alberto's tenth and last bird, with the frustration of a blank score behind him, the pigeon rose and promptly sat back down right by the cage. Alberto properly shot into the air, hoping to get the sitting bird with his second, but the blast was too much for the poor bird and it took off wildly over Alberto's head in the direction of the stands. That, in turn, was too much for Alberto on his very last chance. He spun around and was about to fire into the top of the stands when a shriek from the crowd brought him back to his senses and he pulled the gun up, firing at the heavens, which were probably responsible for his bad luck anyway. There was a ripple of nervous laughter from the crowd, and then an open roar—which eventually Alberto joined.

When composure was restored, the second round continued. This round was more difficult, for no rational reason, since the birds certainly didn't know the difference. By the time Julio, Mike Wormer of Time-Life, New York, and I were up for our second five, none of the contestants still in the running had scored more than seven kills out of the possible ten.

Julio killed the first two birds of his five cleanly and with admirable form, drawing a round of applause from the audience. The third pigeon popped up from his cage; Julio somehow missed the first crucial shot, and the bird, dazed by the noise, sat down a few yards from the cage. Julio, good old Julio, always the proper sportsman, chose not to kill the sitting bird and, instead, made noises to make it fly. Suddenly it did fly, very fast and very low, and Julio missed it. After that, a little nervous and over-anxious, Julio missed the last two birds by not "leading" them sufficiently, for a final score of seven kills, which was not good enough.

Mike Wormer was a marvel of poise and determination. He was by far the best shot in the group. I was lucky to have reached this point with him. He took his first three birds of the second set for eight kills, establishing himself as the leader at that point. The last two birds were both "deer," taking off to the sides at a tremendous clip. He missed one entirely, and the second fell beyond the regulation fence. Wormer thus stood at eight, the winner so far.

It was my turn at "the walk." If only my luck would hold out. I was nervous and keyed up, with the feeling of being "onstage." As I twirled the roulette wheel, the fact that I was about to kill a living creature never entered my mind. I killed my first three pigeons quickly, efficiently, almost mechanically, placing myself on a par with the leader. The crowd was hushed.

The ninth pigeon came up at my slightly shaky cry of *"Pajaro,"* feinted toward the right and then took off to the left. I shot at it out of sheer instinct. The blast raised a cloud of feathers behind the bird, definitely a hit, but not a kill. The pigeon, mortally wounded and dazed, managed to land on the court's fence less than thirty yards ahead and to my left, and perched there obviously dying. I froze for an instant. The second shot could easily topple the bird outside the court for a miss. As I hesitated, a cry of "Kill it, Tony, kill it!" from somewhere in the crowd only added to my confusion. At that moment the pigeon closed its eyes and fell over backward, a lifeless feathery lump, on the *wrong* side of the fence. The crowd shouted its disappointment.

I lowered my gun. Eight out of nine. One definitive bird to go.

I twirled the wheel, more with resignation than determination, and shook my head visibly as if to ward off unwanted thoughts of defeat. The crowd was silent. I moved to the very end of the cement walk. All of a sudden it was no longer a game. My whole being, every nerve, every gun-worthy muscle, for that moment at least, had the single purpose of killing that last bird. I took a deep breath in, and out, then in again and held it. I brought the gun to the ready position.

"Pajaro!" I shouted, louder than I wanted to and much louder than any time before. The middle cage sprung with a crack which startled the tense audience. The pigeon didn't hesitate. As if it had been waiting inside the cage, poised, with a preconceived pattern of escape, it came straight toward me like a feathered dart. I didn't lose a tenth of a second. Instinctively, I swung the gun up, covered the bird and fired. The pigeon was hit full. It closed its wings and plummeted heavily in a perfect ballistic curve, landing with a soft thud at my feet, a sort of tribute to the surprised winner of the first—and the last—live-pigeon shooting tournament ever on the Isle of Pines.

The crowd surged back to the poolside and the bar, and there was a noisy celebration to toast the shooters. Alberto was proclaimed "Defender of the Pigeons" and took it in good humor. The ex-combatant from Guam told me he sure could have used us "back in those days," and Walter and Mario gave me a bottle of Dom Perignon, which we all shared. The Baptist lady, on the other hand, was reading a book at the far end of the patio, her face sternly showing her determination to stay away from "all those murderers."

Alberto, always a sucker for "omens," came over to me and said, "Congratulations, Tony. Fine job. But let me tell you. One of the old men around, one of the 'islanders,' said a pigeon dying that way, y'know, falling at your feet, was bad luck for sure. *'Peligro de muerte,'* he said. I don't believe in such things myself," Alberto lied, "but I thought I should tell you." And he was quite serious.

"Well," I said, "it was certainly bad luck for the *pigeon,*" and I laughed, but took note of the remark. I always respected old wisdom. It wasn't old for nothing.

Anyway, it had been a lot of fun, but the news from the radio was bad, and everyone realized that the time was not right for merrymaking. Let's face it, while the sportsmen were killing pigeons, somewhere in Cuba men were dying, brother against brother. We all knew it, and now, with the excitement of competition over, we were painfully aware of the unhappy contrast.

It was beginning to look as if the New Year's celebration, despite all the preparations, would be at best a quiet affair. Our women had planned to go to Nueva Gerona for lunch and shopping. They were more than a little apprehensive because of the mounting trend of the news but decided to go anyway, just being sure to return as soon as possible. A group of New Yorkers offered to accompany them into town, but the trip didn't suit my mood. I was still excited from the shoot.

My thoughts turned quite naturally from one primitive drive to another—and the name for that right now was Louise. I could see her at a distance, fresh and attractive as ever, and decided, what the hell, this could well be my last opportunity for a slightly wild and irresponsible fling. And who would be hurt, anyway? No one, really. *"Ojos que no ven, corazon que no siente."* ("What the eyes don't see, the heart doesn't feel.") Or so I thought then.

I told Avis and the girls that I was tired, worn out from the excitement of the match, and suggested that they go ahead. I would just sit by the pool or, most likely, take a long nap before tonight's party. They left, dragging Julio and Alberto under protest. Alberto pulled me aside, muttered, "You bastard," and rushed to join the others.

I was left alone, and just for a second felt a touch of anxiety at the separation. I walked slowly to the bar, a little removed from the pool, and sat down for a drink and to get my thoughts in order.

The usual noontime Caribbean breeze came up; in Cuba you could set your watch by it. You could feel it and smell it, and I enjoyed it. Also at that time the sea began to ripple under the wind and the little bits of foam looked like white legions forever marching onto the beach. What had been a crystal-smooth surface, with the bottom clearly visible, to be plumbed trustingly, became cloudy and a little menacing, hiding who knows what creatures. I again felt the vague, indefinable anxiety. It was definitely a day for martinis.

"On the rocks, very dry, lemon peel," I said to the barman, who nodded comprehension. It was a good martini. It had that elusive, mellow taste that is at once so simple and so difficult to duplicate at will—something to do with the amount of dissolved water; after all, "the ice is not *just* for cooling," the wise men say.

I drank it faster than it deserved and ordered another. Almost immediately I felt the expected warmth and the buoyancy, like Popeye getting to his can of spinach. Dangerous things, martinis, but at times nothing else will do.

Casually then, probably too casually, I asked the bartender: "Do you happen to know if there are any empty rooms left in the hotel?"

"Yes, there are, sir," the barman replied quickly, almost as if he had expected the question. Bartending is a worldly profession.

"Thanks," I said.

Just in case.

I really did not consider myself constitutionally unfaithful; I knew I felt uncomfortable in adultery. The one time I cheated on my wife I had been taken by the devastatingly beautiful daughter of an ambassador, and the fact that I knew that, for her, it was far from the first or last experience did not deter my ardor. I worried for days and planned the time and meeting place like a commando raid. It was wonderful and wild and naughty. I even found I was freer with my wife after it, less inhibited, making decidedly better love to *her*. One day I told my lover about this wonderful side-effect, this bonus of our clandestine relation. Shortly thereafter, strangely, the affair ended. And I had been a fairly good boy since that day.

But of course Louise was different, wasn't she? Here I was, probably witnessing the end of an era; and a few yards away there was a pretty young American girl, perhaps willing to give herself to me. The martinis were *definitely* working.

"Don't forget how you made those wonderful martinis," I said to the barman. "I'll be wanting more of them."

As I walked over to the table where Louise and her cousin were sitting, sipping some tall concoctions, I felt again the reassurance I had come to expect from a drink. It got me over an initial shyness that only my most perceptive friends would have ascribed to me.

Louise was wearing a different bikini, equally revealing, and some sort of beach cover-up, flimsy and tight enough to do very little for modesty. She looked good enough to eat—which certainly was not foreign to my fantasies at that very moment.

I said hello and sat down with them as if it were the most natural and unplanned thing in the world. Louise was obviously happy to see me, and we exchanged pleasantries with just enough embarrassment to make the encounter simply delicious. The cousin made up some untranscendental excuse and left us alone.

Walter, the kind giant, saw us together, grasped the situation immediately with the experience of years, and came over with a chunky serving of grey, pearly caviar which was brought down, he said, for the DC-6 group from New York.

"Courtesy of Mr. Kriendler," Walter said, "or say it's just Mario and me." He put down small servings of chopped egg, chopped raw onion, and a lemon wedge wrapped in a little cloth jacket.

"Thank you, good friend," I said sincerely, pleased that Louise would be impressed with the attention. Inconsequential chitchat followed, as a lunch of some sort of Cuban fish, probably *pargo*, red snapper, was served to us along with Spanish white wine.

The alcohol, the sun, the caviar, the pampered feeling and, most of all, my honest flattery made the atmosphere heady and exciting for Louise and, of course, for me. Long before I had learned that, for whatever reason, women tend to be more responsive after they've been fed. I was sure it was something atavistic, and I could visualize the successful Neanderthal rogue feeding his lady a choice morsel of broiled dinosaur and then collecting for his efforts.

"Honestly, you know," I said quite dishonestly, in the age-old courting tradition, "I'd just love to kiss you. Nothing more." Louise looked at me, half-flattered, half-disappointed.

"Oh?" she said.

It was clear to her and to me, and certainly to the waiters milling around and enjoying it all, that my intentions were not *quite* that pure.

However, my exposure to American ways must have dulled the edge of my daring, because somehow I couldn't bring myself to go as far as I had to, to say what was needed, or to do what the wise barman was expecting me to do.

It was just as well.

"Mr. Navarro?" A bellboy ran in, a little breathless.

"Yes?"

"Mr. Navarro, your friends are here. I was asked to tell you. They're just getting out of the car."

The establishment was protecting me from myself. I gave the boy a tip and Louise the most chaste kiss ever.

One of the waiters who had served us came closer to me and whispered:

"Don't worry, señor, *una menos*, that's all—one less."

"One less!" I thought. "Come on, dammit, I haven't had that many!"

"Honey, it was horrible," Avis said, rushing in, hugging me and giving Louise a wife-like nod. I felt guilty, but virtuous. Louise excused herself, saying something about having to meet her cousin, and somehow no one objected.

"Where is everyone else?" I asked Avis.

"I don't know, Tony. I think they went up to change, but I'm scared and I wanted to be with you. That trip was ghastly!"

"I can imagine, but let's not talk about it. Nothing's going to happen to you."

It was beginning to get dark, and Avis and I decided to join the crowd clustered in groups around the radios in the inside bar. Radio Rebelde was now on many of the main stations, asking people to be calm and await further news, and to join the general strike if it became necessary. There was no word from Batista

or the government, and the so-called official stations kept broadcasting uninter-
rupted music, a sure sign that something was *very* wrong.

I got myself a Scotch and water and sat down to listen. Outside, near the casino
structure which could be seen through the picture windows, a team of croupiers
was adjusting the slot machines for this evening's activities. A group of Americans, who weren't particularly interested in the news and couldn't understand the
Spanish anyway, were watching the croupiers with a great deal of interest. The
machines were open in the back and the "guts" were exposed: apples and oranges
or whatever they were, on those little wheels, and of course the bells.

"Fix 'em so they pay off *once in a while,* will you?" I heard one of the
Americans crack, and they all laughed.

In the dining room adjoining the bar, tables were being set up—the usual New
Year's Eve decorations, with a bottle of Scotch whiskey and a bottle of Bacardi
rum on each table. The gay *serpentinas,* the serpent-like papers streamers, were
already weaving their way around glasses following some decorator's fancy, and
the bass fiddle and bongo drums were already on stage.

Clelia walked into the bar, followed by Julio, both fresh out of the shower but
obviously distraught, especially Clelia.

"We drove by the prison," she cut in, "and there was the scariest noise—like
a drone from an angry beehive. It scared the hell out of me. Naturally the
prisoners are hearing what you guys have been listening to here, and that place
isn't going to hold out very long."

At that moment Louise came into view around the pool area, apparently to
take a last dip before dressing for the party. I saw her instantly and our eyes met
briefly as she walked past the bar toward the lighted pool. Avis noticed the
exchange, or at least I felt she had. I was not wrong.

"You like her, don't you, Tony?" Avis said quietly, moving close to me.

"Yes, I do, honey, but it isn't important. I like crepes suzette, too." I tried to
make light of it and kissed her on the nose.

"I hope so, darling, for our sake," she said seriously.

Alberto and the others came in and became glued to the radio. The announcer
was reading a prepared message to the nation from Fidel:

"Compatriots, the glorious day has arrived at last. We shall soon be rid of the
hated tyrant. But he will not escape the people's justice. We shall see to that.
A general strike has been called and it should be obeyed. If you are not involved
directly in the struggle, be calm, stay off the streets, stay at home and we will
keep you informed. Do not act individually. Remember, this is a *different* Revolution. Fatherland or death. We shall conquer."

The announcement electrified all of us, including the Americans who were
struggling with translations from several Cubans at the same time.

Alberto called me aside and said: "Tony, let's skip the party. We should start
thinking about getting home."

It wasn't necessary. At that very moment the owner of the hotel came into
the patio and asked for our attention.

"I have to advise you," he said, "that the hotel's help have notified me that they are joining the general strike. For this reason, and because it does not, in any case, seem appropriate to have a celebration in the circumstances, which I believe are known to you all, we have regretfully decided to call off the New Year's party. I am very sorry. It should be obvious that the problem is totally beyond my control, and our country must now undergo, rightly or wrongly, one more upheaval in a long history of turmoil which has been our sad fate.

"The bar will be open for your convenience at no charge, the very least we can do, and sandwiches will be brought in shortly. You are welcome to help yourselves; I will personally be your very willing bartender for whatever time I shall remain with you tonight. Thank you very much."

He stopped, and then added: "Oh, I forgot. Before you ask me, I should tell you that I have been officially advised that all aircraft are grounded until further notice. You will not, therefore, be able to return home by plane from this island, at least for the present. You may, if you wish, decide to travel by ferry to the capital, Havana, where, I feel sure, convenient transportation may be arranged. Meanwhile, I very sincerely hope you will enjoy whatever facilities we have. The sun and the ocean are still with us." He tried to manage a smile, but it didn't quite come off.

No, it was not a laughing matter for anyone. The owner repeated the little speech, more briefly, in Spanish, and walked away, signaling me to follow him.

"Look, Tony," he said, "the planes are grounded, yours included. I am very worried." The hotel owner had been a friend of Batista—not a political ally, but very much a friend. The Dictator had welcomed such friendships; they gave him an aura of respectability and, after all, he was the country's head of state. And, for those friends, being *near* power also had its satisfactions. I could understand that.

"I've got to get out," the owner said. "Everyone knows Batista was my friend. I'm thinking of using my yacht, if they'll let me. Serge Obolensky is trying to help me. Where's your father-in-law? How will he get out? He sure as hell *has* to."

"Burke is outside the country, thank God," I said, "probably somewhere in Mexico. He was stopping there on his way back to Cuba, and should get the news soon. As for us, we'll probably try for the ferry tomorrow. Avis and I have youngsters to think about. The best of luck to you—we're all going to need it, I'm afraid."

It was a very quiet bunch indeed which gathered at the bar, staying together, sensing security in proximity.

One of the all-music radio stations was playing a fast, loud Cuban rumba. Someone quietly reached over and turned it off.

It was seven-thirty in the evening of December 31, 1958. The New Year's Eve celebration for the year 1959 had ended before it started.

4

NEW YEAR'S DAY at Los Pinos was quiet, at least outwardly. Small groups gathered by the pool around portable radios while finishing a mass breakfast of scrambled eggs and bacon and Bloody Marys. The on-strike Cuban help had left the premises, and Mrs. Gimbel, in a *simpatico* gesture, had volunteered to make breakfast for the entire group, provided that everyone agreed on scrambled eggs. Everyone had. Julio and I had prepared large pitchers of the tomato-and-vodka drink and all were enjoying it, albeit with a certain reserve which the circumstances seemed to impose. Walter and Mario were sitting by the pool's edge in their swimming trunks, with a plate of eggs each, staying to themselves and looking just a bit uncomfortable. They would certainly have a story to tell when (and if) they got back to "21." We had decided that it might not be the right thing to have the American waiters cater to us; it might be construed as strike-breaking or something. So the roles were reversed, and the guests were serving *them.* Julio and I found the whole thing very amusing. Alberto, of course, was glued to the radio.

The news came both from clandestine broadcasts, such as Radio Rebelde, and from the regular stations. Dictator Batista had fled during the night by plane with his family, his immediate staff and some of his cronies. A number of followers who wanted to resist at the heavily fortified Camp Columbia, the Army's headquarters in Havana, were disappointed. Other prominent members of the regime had left from airports all over the island, and some had departed by sea in private yachts. Finally, many had taken refuge—"political asylum," it was called—in various Latin American embassies which honored the Southern Hemisphere's Right of Asylum Pact.

Commander Cienfuegos, under orders from Castro, was about to enter Havana with the taking of Camp Columbia as his objective. Castro himself was preparing to leave the eastern city of Santiago de Cuba for a triumphal march to Havana. There were reports of mass executions of *Batistianos* in the east by younger brother Raul Castro, already possessed of a reputation for ruthlessness, and of looting and sacking, in Havana and elsewhere, of the houses of the former regime's notables and of the heads of Batista's repressive forces.

At that point in the broadcast, I had looked over at Avis and found her quiet, her eyes wet. She was obviously thinking of our children, alone in that big house in Havana, a pretentious house which could be a temptation. I wanted to say something comforting, but thought better of it. Perhaps telephone connections would be reestablished during the day.

Meantime, incessantly, the announcers asked the people to trust the Revolution and refrain from taking justice in their own hands . . .

Finishing my coffee at the poolside table, I looked thoughtfully at Alberto who was listening in a sort of trance to the news—news which marked the end of the cloak-and-dagger era of underground operations which Alberto had so thoroughly enjoyed. I knew it was both a good and a bad time for my friend. He had taken his red-and-black 26th of July armband, which had been hidden in his luggage, and was wearing it prominently around his hunting cap.

"What are we going to do with him *now?*" I asked mockingly of our friends, pointing to Alberto by the radio. "He will be *insufferable.*" Alberto heard the friendly insult, but understood my half-joking reflection very well. He turned from the radio and assumed the look and stance of one about to make an important revelation.

"Not at all, my friend," he said, louder than necessary. "I can assure you— not speaking only for myself—that we shall be noble in victory."

"Oh, God, no!" I shouted. *"Two* lapidary statements in one weekend is too much!"

Everyone laughed at the exchange, including Avis and Alberto, who then protested he was deadly serious and *knew* what he was talking about.

We then turned to the more immediate business of how to get back to Havana. The Americans had been told officially by the local 26th of July representative that planes would be grounded for an indefinite period to prevent the escape of "war criminals" sought by the Revolution, and they had the choice of waiting the time out at Los Pinos or trying to make it to Havana by ferry. They were assured that the Revolution would not harm visitors from a friendly nation and that as good an escort as could be managed would be provided. The Cuban group knew without being told officially that at least the Hedges plane could not leave the island, and they, too, were considering the possibility of a trip back by ferry. There were frightening rumors that the political prisoners from the Model Prison might decide to take over Los Pinos and its guests, which of course affected the departure decision. The alternative chosen was the ferry. I told Manuel, the pilot, to wait with the Beechcraft until he was allowed to fly back, and we all withdrew to our rooms to pack for an early start the next morning.

We left the morning of January 2 in the car that Julio had driven to the small island. Fortunately it was a regular stock car, where all fit without strain—Julio had wisely chosen not to risk his sleek but unroomy Ferrari on the ferry. On the way to Nueva Gerona, the small capital town, we drove by the prison but did not stop. It was relatively quiet; apparently the prisoners had been released by the Rebel Command and, except for emergency flights to bring the leaders to Havana, the men were being "repatriated" by ferry.

Nueva Gerona was a beehive of activity. The main square was crowded, as if there were going to be a town meeting. The atmosphere was tense. Officials from the 26th of July Movement (to which all the rural guerrillas and Castro and his lieutenants belonged), as well as young men from the students' underground group, the Directorio Estudiantil, were scurrying around Nueva Gerona wearing their respective armbands, self-appointed to sudden prominence. They were especially in evidence around the City Hall and the police station on the Square, which had been commandeered. With few exceptions, they were all very young and they carried, as prominently as possible, all sorts of handguns. A full beard was regarded with admiration, but there were very few around since they were immediately associated with the guerrillas. One such "beard" told us we could ride the ferry. And that at least was a relief.

The bearded man turned out to be a Captain Fernandez, a regular Army officer who had rebelled and joined the revolutionary movement months before and, being older and trained, had been appointed to leadership. Alberto exchanged a few words with him and was told the automobile could not go; all room in the ferry was needed for people. Julio could leave it parked by the police station and hand over the keys. It might be used, but for official business only, of course. Julio would be given a receipt and could claim the car when matters quieted down. The Captain looked us over closely and, quickly grasping our situation, cautioned us to try to *pasar desapercibidos,* meaning to try to pass unnoticed. Unfortunately it was not easy to keep *that* group unnoticed; Julio and I tried to meld as best we could, but Alberto was beginning to look a little awkward in his headband, and the girls were a little too chic for the circumstances. About that time the owner of Los Pinos came by.

"I'm in real trouble," he said to Alberto and me. "They won't let my yacht sail. Besides," he lowered his voice, "I'm afraid I'd fare worse in Havana. I don't know what to do. I'd send my wife to Havana, but she won't leave me. I guess we'll wait it out here. Are you going back?"

"Yes, I think we will," I answered. "We're not quite as important, I guess." We both knew I was trying to be kind. The owner *was* more important than anyone in my group, and he would not be allowed to leave so easily. We shook hands, and I wished him good luck, leaving behind a troubled man.

"I have some friends," Alberto promised in parting. "I'll try to help." We watched the hotel owner walk slowly back to the improvised police headquarters on the town square.

We finally managed to get on board the ferry and found a quiet corner on deck, away from the shouting and singing amidships, and I convinced Alberto that this was the best policy for him too. The ship was overloaded but there was no general cargo, only people. There was a lot of rum passing around, and we men took a swig whenever it was offered. The singing was limited, at first, to what was evidently the *new* Cuban national anthem, *"Adelante Cubanos,"* although the *real* one, *"Al Combate Corred Bayameses,"* was also sung. With time and rum, the floating party got down to the old nostalgic songs, which all but the very young managed to remember. We were left pretty much to ourselves. One time, a youngster, armbanded and slightly tipsy, tried to strike up a conversation and ended up asking what we were doing on the Isle of Pines in the first place, seeing that we were not prisoners as he had imagined. We managed to get rid of the boy, but we realized more and more that our position was dangerous. In due course, the combination of the rum, the now subdued singing, and the rocking of the ship brought a little sleep to us, and the voyage, while trying on the nerves, was not really too long or tiring.

We arrived at Batabano, on the southern coast of Cuba, late in the afternoon. The picture at the town square was identical to what we had seen at the little island. There were, perhaps, more people, and the radios were, if anything, more blaring. Castro was progressing slowly on his march toward Havana; the speed was both militarily cautious and politically calculated. Meantime, more *Batistianos* had been discovered to have left during the few previous days, and torture chambers within the several prisons now open to official inspection were beginning to be found and reported on in profuse detail by the written press—some newspapers already under revolutionary "supervision" and some merely trying to gain favor with the new power of the land.

We managed to get ourselves and our luggage to the bus station, the girls puffing a little but realizing that this was no time for exaggerated femininity. At the station there was a large crowd, and no buses in sight. I thought we should try to rent a taxi, and the men started on that alternative which appeared no more unlikely than waiting for an over-committed bus that wasn't even there. We walked into the station house, conscious that we were being observed with curiosity and, maybe, slight hostility because of our clothes, the number and style of our bags, and the fact that we would frequently lapse into English despite our earlier agreement not to do so. In fact, everything about us was patently alien to the surroundings and betrayed wealth or position or something that, in a few short hours, had gone out of style. I took in the situation and asked the girls to go into the ladies' room and please, please come out looking like normal people. It was hopeless. The girls probably tried to blend with the surroundings, but the kerchiefs around their heads somehow had just the right—in this case, the wrong —tilt, the bows had a certain flair, and naturally they had not resisted the temptation to touch up their make-up. I sighed and walked outside to see what success my buddies might have had with the taxi search.

I found Alberto talking to a young man who looked official and wore a prominent 26th of July armband. Alberto was saying, "No, I belong to the Movement in the province of Las Villas. Our leader is Rufo Lopez-Fresquet . . . and Commander Cienfuegos."

"But you're not there *now*, Señor Fowler, when you're probably most needed. What are you doing in the Havana area?" the young man asked.

Alberto was getting visibly more and more nervous. "I had business to attend to in Havana," he managed to say.

"But you were not *in* Havana, were you?" the young man insisted. The situation was clearly deteriorating.

"No, I wasn't," Alberto admitted with a slight lowering of his eyes.

"All right, I understand," the young man said. "I suggest, Señor Fowler, that you take that band from your cap and put it away. There will be opportunities later on to help the cause and claim your rights. Someone on the road might not understand." The young man smiled and walked away.

A very quiet Alberto went back to the station house, with me following. Neither of us spoke. Alberto took the 26th of July band from his cap and put it in his pocket. The girls were sitting on the luggage, beginning to show signs of weariness. At that point Julio showed up with a slightly beat-up but very welcome taxi, just in time for the anxious women inside the crowded waiting room. People, somehow, were beginning to realize that long-standing resentments against the privileged classes could now be vented. So far it was only furtive looks and whispered comments, but it would go beyond that. It would go beyond that very soon.

Our group managed to fit somehow into the one taxi, bags and guns in the trunk and the excess crammed in between legs and feet. There was little conversation as we took the road between Batabano and Havana. We passed many little hamlets on our way. Most of the *bohios,* the typical countryside Cuban huts roofed with dried, bushy palm fronds, were flying little Cuban flags and improvised red-and-black 26th of July emblems. In the small towns we rode through, there were groups of people marching down the main streets, singing and shouting, with cries of *Viva!* and *Muera!* applied, respectively, to revolutionary heroes and members of the fallen regime. At the entrance and exit to the small towns there were impromptu checkpoints, with groups of young men who would search people and cars leaving the town, no doubt looking for notable *Batistianos* hoping to escape from the "people's justice." Occasionally, small-arms fire could be heard at a distance. In revolutions in the past, there had been some frightful scenes of mob revenge on members of the deposed regimes. Once caught, they were shot and hacked by the frenzied crowd, then tied to the backs of automobiles and dragged around the main square while people cheered. Sometimes the unfortunate man was not quite dead during the gory performance.

After about an hour of traveling, the taxi went through the larger town of Quibican and, at the exit toward Havana, encountered a more organized checkpoint, with a larger group of men armed with submachine guns. A young man with the inevitable armband asked us to please get out of the car so they could inspect it. They looked under the seats, checked the men lightly for weapons, and asked to have the trunk opened.

The young leader immediately spotted the two gun cases amongst the luggage and looked up at us. "Shotguns?" he asked, "or rifles?"

"Shotguns," I answered. "Hunting guns."

"I'm sorry," the young man said, "but we'll have to take them. I'll give you a receipt in the name of the Movement, and you may have them back when matters settle down. You shouldn't go around with guns in these times unless you have a reason. You might get into trouble."

Alberto started to interfere, but I stopped him with a look and an outstretched arm. The group of revolutionists moved closer.

"Yeah," another young man in the group said, looking around at his comrades, "we have more important game to look for than birds, don't we, boys?" They all laughed.

I saw my "blond" leave with genuine sadness, and I knew that I would never see it again. Silently I murmured, "Goodbye, old friend."

The leader handed Julio and me each a slip of paper with a blurry rubber stamp and a signature at the bottom as a receipt for "one hunting gun, 12 gauge," bade us goodbye, and motioned us to move on.

As we were getting into the car, one of the men shouted derisively, looking straight at me with a cocky smirk: "Adios, oligarcas, que tengan buen viaje" ("Goodbye, oligarchs, have a good trip"). It was the first time I had heard the word "oligarch" actually *spoken* rather than reading it in books about Marxism, and it had been said with venom and scorn. I looked back at the man aggressively, but he had turned and was already on his way back to the makeshift guardhouse. I sat down in the back seat, smoldering with anger for failing to react quickly enough to the provocation.

The taxi continued on to Havana, the afternoon rapidly turning into night. No one spoke during the ensuing half-hour, each lost in personal reflections, each trying to understand what was happening to our world, the small world which had somehow changed so much in so little time. What *was* going on, after all? I could have understood animosity, even overt hostility, toward the members of the "opposite party," whoever they might be. But why our group? To be sure, Avis' family could be said to be on the side of the ex-Dictator. But no one knew us personally on this road to Havana. And what about the others? Surely they were not identified with the Dictator at all. If anything, Alberto was making an effort to be just the opposite. Why, then, this hostility, now openly articulated by that man at Quibican? Could it be that it was a matter of *classes*, rather than parties? On the other hand, wasn't it the middle class, after all, that had fought the Dictator most vigorously, while the "true poor" remained indifferent or even sided abjectly with the government? It was too much for me. I always wanted to understand motivations, to pigeonhole people neatly, and I decided that I would worry about it later, and would now concentrate on the road, which was turning decidedly dark as we moved swiftly toward Havana.

Despite the dimming light, it was obvious that the excitement along the road grew in direct proportion to the proximity to Havana, and the little towns on the way got closer and closer to each other as we approached the pre-suburbia of the big city. At the approach to one such town, the taxi suddenly confronted two large Greyhound-type buses parked across the road, blocking it completely, and, just ahead of them, the now familiar group of men with guns and banners and armbands. A tall middle-aged black approached the stopped automobile and pointed a gun through the windshield. The driver instinctively ducked below the level of the dashboard. Julio got out, and I followed. The black man carried an old one-shot shotgun with a long, rusty barrel which he held in front of him as he and others advanced toward the car. These men were less professional than earlier groups and obviously uncertain and frightened, which made them dangerous.

"Where you going?" the black said, a meaningless question addressed to a car on the approaches to Havana with no connecting roads between that point and the city.

"To Havana, of course," Julio said, annoyed but cautious.

"Where you coming from?" the man insisted.

"From Batabano," Julio answered, and then volunteered, "from a weekend outing . . . for New Year's."

"How many in your party?" the black man asked, and to his men he motioned toward the car: "Search it."

Alberto got out and joined us. Some members of the search group looked inside the car and, seeing no one but the girls and the frightened driver, turned away to frisk the men for guns. One young man asked me to open the trunk. He held a revolver in his shaky right hand. The gun was cocked, his index finger *inside* the trigger guard, and he waved the revolver around, using it to point and to signal. It was clear that the boy had never handled a real gun before. He pointed the weapon directly at me as he prepared to open the trunk. I love guns and had been trained to respect them. The incredible performance of the youth thus angered me to the point that I forgot my delicate situation. Besides, dammit, I had nothing to hide from these awkward jerks.

"Look, young man," I said, standing away from the trunk and right in front of the menacing revolver, "either you take your finger away from the trigger of that gun, or you shoot me and get it over with." I was as mad as I could get, and the danger only made me more reckless. "If you can't handle a gun responsibly, you shouldn't be allowed to have one." The boy was shocked by the authority of my words, and his self-assurance crumbled. He looked down at his index finger with something like perplexity and slowly removed it from the trigger. Totally broken, back to the little kid he was, he tried to regain his composure, but he was interrupted.

"What's going on here?" An older man, with an air of command, joined the group behind the car.

"Nothing," the younger man said, his eyes and his gun down toward his feet. "They're okay."

I seized the opportunity, although I didn't want to embarrass the boy any further. "Look, mister," I said, "we've been checked before, on the way from the coast." I produced the little slip of paper with the blurry stamp. He looked at it approvingly, then glanced at me.

"Go ahead," he said. "Skirt around the bus on your right. You can get through. Sorry about all this trouble. I'm sure you'll agree it's not too high a price to pay for our liberation." It was a rhetorical question, but he still looked at me, obviously expecting an answer.

"Of course it isn't," I said, and the thing was that I wasn't sure I didn't mean it, not sure at all. In fact, I wasn't sure what I thought about the bewildering process into which we had been plunged.

"Good luck to you," I said honestly to the leader of the improvised squad, and he waved back. Back in the car, we continued our drive toward Havana, the lights of which we could already see reflected back from an overcast sky.

We ran into a few more checkpoints, but the posses were more sophisticated, recognized us as harmless, and readily acknowledged the little slips of paper with the now all-important rubber stamp: *Movimiento 26 de Julio.*

No old city has attractive approaches from the outskirts, and Havana was no exception. A city grows from the center out, and the immigrants from the provinces settle around it, as if testing the water before plunging in. Industry also chooses that area for economic reasons. In time, the growing amoebic city engulfs both people and industries, and commerce appears, the garish neon signs and the rest, all geared to the low income and high tolerance of the inhabitants.

"My, but it's ugly, isn't it?" Alberto said, coming out of his depression. "Somehow it didn't seem that way on the way out; maybe speed demon Julio didn't let me have a close look." Looking around the practically deserted streets, he added, "I sure hope these people haven't decided to take over *our* neighborhood . . ."

Avis didn't need that remark. She had been so terribly quiet that I knew she was worrying about the children. Beside her in the front seat, I squeezed her hand. "They're all right, honey," I said gently, and she nodded.

"You know," Clelia joined the conversation, going back to Alberto's comment, "coming into the city this way is like meeting someone for the first time from the back, y'know, from the *popo.*"

We all laughed a little, as much as the circumstances and our weariness allowed. Even the taxi driver came out of his stupor and grinned.

Clelia, as usual, was absolutely right. Havana was, and had always been, oriented toward the sea, from which the good and the bad always had come to a city as old as the discovery of America. To approach her from behind was just not fair: dreary neighborhoods, small rundown movie houses, and dozens of little kiosks with their zinc-plate roofs and single bare light bulbs, selling over-cooked hamburgers.

We drove swiftly through the area, strangely quiet in comparison with the towns we had passed only a few miles before, and moved through the older sections of La Vibora and Santos Suarez. Here the sprawling mansions, once stately residences of the wealthy, now bore the signs of neglect and the enforced proximity of many families living under one roof.

Streetcars used to run here, but now there remained only rusty lengths of steel forever imbedded in brick and asphalt. The undulating tramways had been replaced by speedier, clattering buses which carried a louder, less inhibited crowd to and from their modern jobs in industry. On this day, probably following official directives or just common sense, few buses were in fact running.

The taxi finally emerged from the "backside" of the city and reached the ocean front only a few blocks away from the "colonial city" of cathedrals and cobblestones and courtyards and brothels. It was dark and quiet, with no signs of sacking or looting. I was privately grateful for the sake of our children, although I knew intuitively that this was not the section of town where this type of action was likely to take place anyway. At my direction, the driver skirted the center of the city and followed the Malecon, the drive which borders the Atlantic Ocean, starting on the environs of the famous Morro Castle. We passed, however, near enough to the Presidential Palace and to the long and central Prado Avenue to be able to see and hear the excited crowds at a distance. Avis heard the menacing rumble of the mob and gave a little sigh of despair.

Two blocks later, after we passed the Morro Castle on the right, the level of the mob noises increased, and cries of anguish blended in with the anger. I asked the driver to speed up, but we still couldn't avoid coming frighteningly near the crowd—there was nothing but the ocean on our right. Through the crowd, we could see bodies strewn over the road and sidewalk, some wearing the "revolutionary" fatigue uniforms and some the blue of Batista's police force. Women were shouting "Asesinos!" and waving clenched fists. We managed to get away fast, fearful of a wild, irrational attack on the car. At the next barricade, I asked a guard, "What happened back there? There were bodies all over the place."

"Just part of the revolution, Compañero," the guard said. The word "compañero" immediately identified him as a member of the right side, the winning side. I looked over toward Julio for recognition of that fact, and he acknowledged it with his eyes.

"But why all the bodies?" Alberto asked, still feeling more a part of the goings-on than the rest of us.

The guard looked angry, and he had angry words to say: "One of Batista's policemen in our barrio, a son-of-a-bitch he was, was killed by a group of our boys." And then, as the most natural thing, he added, "God rest his soul. He was killed on the street and left there, because there was nothing else to do."

"I'm sure the man deserved it," Alberto said.

"He certainly did," the guard agreed, "but what happened is that some of his buddies placed a bomb, a booby trap, under his body."

There was an audible gasp from the women in the car.

"Yeah," he said, "the dead man lay there for most of the day, in the heat and all, y'know, people just blessing themselves as they hurried past him."

"Oh, my God," someone said.

"Well," the guard continued, "just before sundown, as you might expect, a patrol of our boys tried to move him to a kind of morgue they had set up nearby. It was a terrible thing. The bomb exploded, mixing the live with the dead. God, the screams . . ."

The group was silent.

"Naturally, the people are yelling for revenge and, believe me, they'll get it. Three of our best boys in the barrio were killed. We think we know who did it, and when we get them . . ."

"Please, please," one of the girls said. "I don't want to hear any more."

The guard shrugged his shoulders and waved us on. The car started again, no one speaking for a while as it headed, as fast as possible, down the broad drive toward home.

The Malecon hugged the coastline for miles of developed waterfront, but there was no sandy beach within sight, only sharp rocks worn into razor-like filigree shapes by the waves, and then an ocean which looked and *was* disquietingly deep.

I looked down the Malecon as we moved through the lighted ocean drive in the direction of the suburbs and the big hotels. It might be a trite concept but, I thought, it certainly does look like a string of pearls winding off beyond sight. We passed several monuments and the large Hotel Nacional, for many years the only really luxurious accommodation available to tourists and somewhat of a landmark. I looked at Avis in the dark and again squeezed her hand; it was at the Hotel Nacional that we had first met.

The taxi left the Malecon at the entrance to the suburb of Vedado and shifted over to one of the long main avenues. At one of the largest and most attractive mansions in this sector of the city, we left Julio and Clelia, who still lived with his parents while their future home was being built. Vedado was probably the first plush suburban area to be developed, and although it had been superseded in desirability by suburbs farther out from the city, it was characteristic of Julio's family that they aristocratically refused to allow changing fashions to affect their established way of life. Julio's parents had heard the taxi and were waiting at the door. We said hasty goodbyes, the rest of us anxious to get to our own homes.

The taxi moved on beyond Vedado, taking the tunnel under the Almendares River, thus reaching the famous Fifth Avenue (La Quinta Avenida) of the resolutely residential and rich suburb called Miramar. We followed Fifth Avenue to the end and then veered to the left to enter the Country Club section, known simply as El Country. The suburb, almost rural in its lush verdure of trees and bushes, was perhaps the most exclusive of them all. It featured the Country Club itself, surrounded by large homes and estates dotted in a continuum of green made up of the private gardens and the fairways of the golf club. Alberto and I both lived in houses bordering the links, with tree-filled back patios extending uninterruptedly into the fairways. Alberto and Paulette shared their home with the elder Fowlers, and Avis and I lived in a handsome English-style home which had been willed to Avis by her grandfather. The Fowlers were dropped first and disappeared quickly into the large house, hugging their baby boy whom a nursemaid had brought to the door. The house, the whole area, was quiet—almost too quiet.

Avis and I approached our home and we both looked around anxiously. There were no crowds, however. There was nothing at all, thank God. We were home.

I paid the driver what seemed to be a huge bill, but was certainly well worth it. It was late, but young Tonito and Avisita were awake and excited and happy to see us. Avis hugged them both together and then held them, one by one, quietly, for a long time.

The children, jumping around, could sense that something out of the ordinary was going on, but it was all good fun to them. Nanita, good old Nanita, almost ninety years old, had nevertheless managed to get over to our home from her little room in a semi-nursing home in the center of Havana. The maid, Gisela, and her husband, José, who lived in and helped with the housework, were also there. I thought I noticed something strange, something different in the way José greeted us, the way he looked at us, but decided it was my imagination.

Gisela handed me a long list of telephone calls from family, friends, and the textile mill. It included several long-distance calls from Burke Hedges, undoubtedly anxiously sitting around in Mexico City.

When we arrived, Fidel Castro was on the radio from somewhere on the road leading to Havana from the eastern provinces, and while Avis and I greeted everyone, he could be heard continuing his long speech. I decided, however, that I was much too tired to hear him out. Besides, somehow I had the feeling that there would be many opportunities ahead to learn what Castro was all about. I kissed Nanita and the children, told Avis I was going to bed, and started upstairs to our room. Tomorrow would be time enough to think it all out.

As I moved up the stairs, I could hear Avis talking to Gisela about something I, too, had noticed.

"Gisela, what happened to the Christmas decorations?" Avis asked, trying to sound casual. "I don't see the tree, and the big star on the door. The children loved it."

"José and I took them down, señora," Gisela answered. Then, in quite a different tone, with an odd note of authority, her husband by her side, she added: "After all, señora, we shouldn't have celebrated the holidays this year. You should have known that. José and I didn't think it was right."

5

THE DAYS WHICH FOLLOWED our return from the Isle of Pines were exciting times for us. Burke Hedges decided, wisely, not to return to Cuba, and flew directly from Mexico to Miami. I was therefore left as the chief representative of the family at Burke's headquarters in Havana and the textile mills in the westernmost province of the island. Burke's brother, James, and his sons, Dayton, Mike and Jimmy, very young at the time, would look after the other half of the Hedges' family interests.

Everywhere in Cuba, there was a feeling of elation and relief in those early days. The vindictiveness, the daily persecution of members of the deposed regime, and the summary executions of the most notorious "criminals of war," as the press referred to them, were regarded as necessary elements of the cleansing process, an unavoidable quid pro quo for previous "atrocities." It was also, unfortunately, the typical aftermath of *all* Cuban revolutions in the people's memory, and everyone just hoped that the violence would end soon.

Fidel Castro was on radio from somewhere on the island every single day. And everyone listened:

"I believe this is a decisive moment in our history. The tyranny has been cast out. Joy is immense, and yet, much remains to be done. Let us not fool ourselves into believing that in the future everything will be easy. Perhaps in the future everything will be more difficult . . ."

That was Castro, at the very beginning, already calling for austerity and sacrifice from the people, new words in the modern Cuban lexicon.

On January 8, Castro arrived triumphantly in Havana and addressed the nation on TV from the Presidential Palace on his way to Camp Columbia, the former Army stronghold, the surrender of which was for Cubans the symbol of total victory. It was there that Batista's men might have resisted the Rebel Army, but chose not to do so. Camilo Cienfuegos, who reached Havana two days ahead of Castro, took it without a casualty on either side. At the Palace stopover, Castro made a brief speech. It was the first time the people in Havana had seen him in the flesh. He wore the fatigues, the beard, and the "telescopic-sight" rifle which were to become the ubiquitous symbols of power. On that day he also wore strings of rosaries around his neck, given to him on the road by pious women who already saw evidence of divine guidance in the young leader.

"Above all, we are fighting for a democratic Cuba and an end to dictatorship . . . And because the Rebel Army had Commander Camilo Cienfuegos in the province of Santa Clara, and because it also had Commander Ernesto Guevara in the same conquered area, I was able on January 1 to order Cienfuegos to advance on Havana and just tell him 'to take Camp Columbia.' "

The crowd roared its approval. A simple man like Cienfuegos had performed a heroic feat simply because he was told to do it. Castro then asked the huge mass of people gathered before him at the Palace Square to separate and form a lane for him to continue his journey. They complied, displaying an incredible discipline which Cubanologists of the time might have profitably noted, and Castro walked through to his caravan, slowly, without any protection. The crowd went wild, and Avis and I, glued to the TV, hugged each other in teary-eyed excitement. Castro moved on to Camp Columbia, where Cienfuegos had obediently taken the fortress and was awaiting his master. At Camp Columbia, Castro displayed for the first time the speech format, in both style and in length, which was to become his trademark, and to both astound and amuse the world. Six million Cubans listened:

"How did the Rebel Army win the war? By telling the truth to the people. How did the tyranny lose the war? By lying to the soldiers. Because the people are invincible. And it was the people who won this war. Because we had no Army; we had no Navy; we had no tanks, we had no aeroplanes, we had no cannons. We had no military academies. We had no training camps. We had no divisions, no regiments, no companies, no platoons, we did not even have squads!" The thunder of applause brought on a pause; then he finished, like the closing of a sonnet: *"But, who won the war? Who? The people; the people won the war."*

At the end of his speech, the cheering and the applause of the people who had just discovered *they* had won the war went on for minutes and minutes. It seemed to the viewers at home that it would never end, and that that was all, in fact, the Cuban people would ever do from now on—cheer its leader.

At one point two white doves came down, seemingly from nowhere, and landed on Castro's head and shoulder. A hushed murmur ran through the crowd, and there were a few seconds of almost devout silence. The next day the press reported the incident and offered discreet suggestions of divine guidance and the incarnate presence of the Holy Ghost. It had been, of course, a good publicity stunt. The poor birds, released at street level, simply found the highest perch on the square: Fidel Castro's army cap and epaulets. Unfortunately, the birds were less conscious of their historic role than of nature's call, and there were some unseemly accidents recorded for posterity by the TV camera.

Castro's oratory, our friends noted, was decidedly different from that of the traditional *politicos* to which Cubans were accustomed. He didn't shout and strain his voice to reach a manufactured crack at the end of a telling point. He wasn't declaiming in the good old Spanish theatre style. There were no erudite quotations from the past. Castro simply talked to the people, to the cook and the intellectual in a single language and in deceptively simple terms, with the repetitive style that approaches a point from every conceivable angle. Castro's speech format, in fact, was more reminiscent of Roosevelt and Churchill, speaking on war and courage and victory, than of a multitude of bombastic Latin American speechmakers who had preceded him. By contrast, Fidel appeared unpretentious and modest. And he managed to assume occasionally a hurt look, with sad, closely knit eyebrows converging upward, seeming to ask heaven *why* these terrible things could have been done. He projected at one time the father image that was inherent in his role of deliverer plus that of the helpless youth questioning the selfishness of an uncomprehending and incomprehensible world—an irresistible underdog characterization that Chaplin might have envied. Add to that an eastern-Cuba accent so that no one would forget the origins and credentials of the Revolution, and it was a winning formula that confronted the crowds and the viewers on January 8. Yes, Castro had charisma, that indefinable but instantly recognizable set of qualities which, simply, enable a leader to lead.

If the format was effective, the content was no less so. To a bone-tired people, tired of violence and terror, tired of corruption in government, feeling somehow unclean and unworthy beneath the glitter of Havana night life, to hear someone talk about honesty and appear to mean it . . . talk about human dignity and make it sound as if the pleasures of life could be given up for the sake of it . . . and to have it all come from this giant of a man . . . was more than anyone dared to expect. It was, perhaps, at last, the light at the end of the long tunnel. Alberto Fowler had not been wrong when he cautioned that the depths and possibilities of the Cuban soul had not been plumbed, but even Fowler did not imagine what hardships would be willingly assumed by the people in pursuit of an illusion that appeared within reach.

Avis and I sat riveted to the television screen and drank in every concept, every contrived repetition.

"Look, Avis," I said when it was over and the cheering finally died out, "you know I don't know this man well, so I can't really tell. He was four years behind me in school. But I have to say that so far he's done everything right. He's named the right people to his cabinet—decent people, people we know, committed to democracy. So what if they *are* for social reform? Who the hell can say we don't need it? Don't you agree we need it?" My look demanded an answer. I knew I was overreacting; I had been for days. Avis knew it, too, but she understood. It was my country, after all.

"Tony, of course I agree we need a change of *some* kind. It's obvious the country couldn't stand the situation any longer; we all know that. Maybe Castro *is* what we need, what we thought we'd never get. I'm sorry, dear. I'm just a little overwhelmed by . . . by everything."

"I know, Avis," I said as gently as I could. "The thing is that people are telling me that this is a *Leftist* revolution. So what if it is? Can't we make *any* sacrifices for this damned country? The measures this man is talking about all seem reasonable. Elections in eighteen months; doing away with a large regular army which we don't really need; a reasonable agrarian reform to put the land to work and to redistribute the wealth; Christ, even Batista was for *that,* a break for the little people . . ." I stopped, aware that my intensity was frightening Avis.

"Go on, honey, go on," she said. "I don't mind."

"Look, darling," I said, more composed, "I know I'm supposed to be the cynic. But I really have always wanted to help. I ignored it because I thought it was useless . . . so often it *has* been useless. But maybe there's a chance." I paused. "Do I dare believe this man?" I asked myself as much as Avis. "Avis, honey, I don't want to be taken . . ."

In fact, I was already taken, and there were good reasons for it. My childhood and adolescence had been difficult financially and socially, and I readily identified with the underprivileged. It was an attitude we all liked to regard as "social emotion," but which was rooted in much deeper personal frustrations and resentments. Another reason was that I had lost my faith after a too-intense Catholic upbringing, leaving a great, aching vacuum which my soul was eager to fill with anything my *intellect* would accept. Nothing through the years had met the requirements. This Cuban revolution unfolding before me had all the mystical qualities and the selfless dedication to the weak, the humble and the deprived of which a faith is made up. And it was a "this world" faith, to be touched and acted on. In Fidel Castro's words:

"It is the people, the little people who count. They have the peace they wanted, a peace without dictatorship, a peace without crime, a peace without censorship . . . Elections will take place in a period of eighteen months; and, to make it possible, political parties will be reorganized in between eight and ten months . . . This is a government which respects the rights of the people. The press is not censored; it is now free and it has the assurance that it will always be. And the people may gather freely when they want to . . . The people want to know, they want to know very badly, if we are really going to make this a revolution, or if we are going to fall into the same errors of the last revolution, and the one before that."

I remembered the last revolution, and the one before that. My parents had been the victims of one of the earlier revolutions against another dictator, General Machado, in the early 1930s. The Navarros, fearing for their lives, left for exile in Miami with me, their only child, leaving behind everything they had. Matters went from bad to worse, and my parents divorced and eventually returned separately to Cuba when it was safe to do so. My father lost whatever drive and energy he had, settled for anonymity and a subsistence level of life, and provided little material support for us. My mother, with Nanita and me, moved to a decrepit house on the fringes of the suburbs. She sold smuggled imported dresses to her wealthy friends and took in boarders. Nanita, already an old woman, took in sewing. All the time, by a heroic pretense my mother sponsored, I kept up my association with the rich boys who earlier had been my peers, and who displayed the same artless kindness and cruelty of children everywhere. Fraternization at the vastly different income levels was traumatic in many ways for me; and it was a painful daily experience, after school, to leave my friends when they gathered at the very social Havana Yacht Club while I went home alone.

Forever fresh in my mind was the day when Nanita, probably using up weeks of sewing money, had surprised me with a bicycle—without doubt my fondest hope, for it was a way to join friends, a means to get away a little. All that Nanita could afford, however, was the kind of second-hand bicycle used by the *mensajeros,* the myriad of messenger boys who daily, ant-like, crisscrossed the city delivering groceries and medicines and bills. The work-bicycles shared one unique characteristic, a very functional one: the handlebars had been bent close together so that the messenger and his vehicle could dart between the tramways and the buses and cars in the narrow Havana streets. My bicycle was like that. I was mortified but would not for the world offend Nanita, and so I faced the embarrassment of joining my friends and their shiny bikes with their broad handlebars. The inevitable taunts of "Hey, Tony, go deliver your stuff!" and "Hurry up, you'll get fired!" were good-natured enough, but they hurt—they hurt a lot. It is perhaps difficult to understand today, in our work-oriented, middle-class American society, the stigma attached to being a delivery boy in the essentially aristocratic social structure of the Cuba of those days. Finally, I would ride my *mensajera,* as I called it in self-defense, mostly alone through the quieter streets of my own neighborhood.

My mother, aware of my humiliation at the innocent slights, tried to compensate by making much of the family ancestry, which was a direct line from Spanish nobility transplanted to Cuba. My great-grandfather, a member of the Zuazo family, was the Marquess of Almeiras. It impressed me, but I soon found out that it didn't impress anyone else without the more material evidence of rank. It certainly didn't buy the fun things important to a boy's life. Right then and there I had decided I would make it on my own.

When the time came for high school, my mother somehow managed to get me into Belen, the leading private school in Havana, run by the Jesuit Fathers. I guess I was considered intelligent, and my mother had dedication enough for both of us. It was expensive, but for me there was no tuition. Although it might have qualified as a scholarship in more sophisticated times or places, it was really charity on the part of the good Spanish priests.

I did well in school (I *had* to), outdistancing more affluent classmates with lesser pressures on them, and I drank heavily of the religious indoctrination that permeated life in and out of the classroom. I graduated with high honors and a large tuition bill that no one expected to collect.

Four years behind me at Belen was a boy from the provinces, big for his age, who excelled in sports and had a reputation for a bad temper. His name was Fidel Castro. The year I graduated, young Castro had been turned down by the school's debating society for failing to pass the society's requirement to prepare and deliver a *three-minute speech!*

Success at high school gave me the grounds and courage to literally cajole my passingly wealthy uncle, José Ramon Bandujo (Uncle Joe), into paying my way through engineering school in the U.S. on a year-by-year, "we'll-decide-if-you're-going-back" basis. It wasn't the most secure way but, still, it gave me a crack at it, and I graduated from Georgia Tech in chemical engineering without great distinction except for involvement in campus politics. I worked for a major oil company for several years in California, did well enough at it, and eventually returned to Cuba a fairly successful young engineer with a good job in Havana in the sugar industry. During my absence, freed rather drastically from the womb-like religious atmosphere that the Jesuits had provided, I had moved away from faith toward doubt and finally into a militant agnosticism that was as passionate as my religion had been. But I never again had the peace of mind of either the faithful or the truly emancipated.

It was in this mood that I had confronted my friends in Havana—a mood that Clelia Batista had joked about on the Isle of Pines. Mine was not a popular stance either with the girls who treasured their sheltered religious position or with the men, many of whom practiced a respectful and convenient indifference. In politics I arrogantly considered myself extra-national, a citizen of the world, who could not be overly concerned with the petty politics of Cuba. In any event, it was clear that those politics had proven *ad nauseam* to be nothing more than the periodic repetition of a pattern: dictatorship, revolution, a starry-eyed, inept attempt at democracy, followed by a military coup d'état and another dictatorship —each system sooner or later permeated by an ever-higher level of corruption. In this area, I found little argument since—with a few commendable exceptions —everyone *agreed* that it was hopeless. This attitude explained the surprising lack of Cuban political awareness that permitted Fidel Castro to reach Havana on January 8, 1959, as a virtual stranger to most people, even though there were bulky dossiers in many embassies of his strongly radical activities.

Because of my job with Julio Lobo, the most respected industrialist and merchant in the sugar world, and because of my education and childhood friends, I was more or less accepted as a member of Havana society quite naturally. I guess the girls found me interesting enough as a friend, or even as a suitor if the girl was content with the prospective rewards of nothing but a promising career. Some apparently were. Before I met Avis, I went through a few romances, one a very bruising affair which had ended abruptly and left me heartbroken. Avis was warm and understanding, even when I foolishly declared my continuing love for the former sweetheart. That's a tough role for any woman to play convincingly. But Avis was made of special material.

"I'll wait, Tony," she had said. "But don't take too long."

I didn't take long. The "Americanita's" disarming warmth was a quick healer, and we were married after a short engagement.

I was lucky to find Avis because she had the special qualities of personal character we would need in what lay ahead for us, when the money, the security and the power would no longer be there. While I didn't work for her father until some years later, I was of course associated with a family known to be friendly with the Dictator, although without financial profit therefrom—the Hedges clan didn't need it. The situation was perfectly all right with me. After all, nothing could be done; nothing had ever been done. With my social conscience repressed, I found my life, my family, and the company of my friends comfortable and agreeable.

This, then, was my background—the backdrop against which a man who barely knew I existed, Fidel, was to play such an important role.

So the Revolution fell on fertile psychological ground as far as I was concerned. They say there is no stricter disciplinarian than a convert, and I was no exception. I embraced the Castro cause with all the pent-up fervor I had stored for so many years. And I had plenty of company, inside and outside Cuba. About that time, *The New York Times,* which was again available in Havana, editorialized:

". . . One other thing must be said and this is an acknowledgment of the extraordinary young man, Fidel Castro, who fought against such heavy odds with such tenacity, bravery and intelligence . . . The American people will wish him and all Cubans good fortune."

The *Times'* wishes were surely representative of those of the entire hemisphere and, in fact, the world.

The young leader meanwhile kept addressing his people almost every day and outlining his program in the simplest of terms:

•suppression of graft, sinecures and subsidies;
•distribution of idle government land to farmers who would work it;
•the breaking up of large, improperly cultivated estates;
•tariff protection to encourage the formation of new industries;
•tax reform to correct loopholes and ensure collection;
•suppression of prostitution, gambling and narcotics;
•reduction and reorganization of the armed forces.

Who could possibly argue against such a program? No one but prostitutes, pimps, gamblers, dope pushers, dishonest public officials, tax evaders, militarists, foreign exporters, monopolistic industrialists and selfish land-owners!

One mildly dissident voice was heard from afar. The Vatican sounded a note of caution. *L'Osservatore Romano* commented: "Observers are still cautious in predicting the final turn of events and whether the victory of the Fidelistas really marks for Cuba the start of a working democratic order."

I, and many like me, immediately discounted those words as the Church forever siding with the establishment. For an "antiestablishmentarian" it was rather fun, in fact, having the Church against you.

And then, of course, there was my friend Julio, always cool and objective—and reserving judgment. I would telephone Julio after a Castro speech and ask him excitedly, "Did you hear him?"

"Yes, I did," Julio would answer, and from the tone of the "yes-I-did," I could tell Julio was not thrilled.

"Aw, come on, Julio," I would keep pushing, "you know it's better than buying off those gangsters who call themselves fiscal agents. Remember? You can't deny that."

"Yes, I do remember, and no, I don't deny it. Frankly, I just find it too good to be true. I hope he means it all. I also sense an animosity against anyone who was *anything* in the past. Not all the rich people were criminals, Tony."

"You're overreacting, Julio," I said.

"Maybe." Julio was unconvinced. He hesitated, and then went on, with uncharacteristic heat: "And, dammit, we are *not* the poor, hungry and illiterate people we are now claimed to be. You know that as well as I do, and so does Castro, *caramba!*" Julio never used *coño* or *carajo* if he could help it, but this time he came close.

"We have the highest per capita income in Latin America. Who the hell are we supposed to compare with? Did you ever hear of a Cuban starving to death? And if you want to measure the so-called distribution of wealth"—a sore point with Julio—"we have more television sets than any country in Latin America." Julio laughed as he added, "Unfortunately, as it turns out."

By and large, however, everyone inside Cuba went along with Castro. Some didn't—some were directly involved with the deposed Dictator, and for the most part were in hiding and trying to get out. Others constituted the minute percentage who knew Castro from "before" and had some honest forebodings. Still others were people who simply had something to lose. They knew that the process would require them to share their wealth if it was to work at all, and they, or their ancestors, had come by it honestly. (They were the ones who might some day turn out to have been right, but for the wrong reasons.) On the other hand, some who by definition belonged to the same privileged group went beyond the call of duty the other way. A number of Cuban industrialists, men of commerce, and even prudent U.S. firms such as the National City Bank, the Bank of Boston, International Harvester, United Fruit, and many sugar mills spontaneously *advanced* their estimated 1959 income taxes to help get the new government back on its financial feet—a remarkable move for businessmen to make anywhere in the world.

At the textile mills, cooperation was enthusiastic—everyone looked forward to revitalizing a depleted national economy. Jesus Soto, the labor leader of the Hedges industries, was becoming a leader in the national federation of textile workers; he would go far with the revolution. Soto had been an active force, combative but reasonable, during the difficult Batista years, keeping the Communists at arm's length in the labor movement. He and I found that we worked well together—a great help to me at a time when office gossip was more a clue to my own basic chances of survival than to who were the troublemakers on the job.

Running a business for someone else is always difficult, and to do so at a distance and in the middle of a revolutionary process is damned near impossible. I did my best, and Burke Hedges called me every day from Miami. Hedges was not always pleased with developments, but the system seemed to be working and there was no other way. Everyone knew Burke had left because of his personal friendship with Batista, not because of political involvement.

"Do you think I should come back?" Burke asked me on the telephone. There was no serious fear of phone-tapping yet, although talk about it was beginning.

"I don't think you'd better, Burke. I wish you could—I sure need you. But the situation here is far from clear. The factions even within the Revolution don't seem to agree on everything, or with Fidel even. It's hard to tell who controls what. It isn't very organized, but I guess revolutions aren't."

"No, I guess they're not," Hedges cut in bitterly.

"The thing is, Burke," I went on, "no one accuses you of political involvement, but everyone knows you were a personal friend of the Dictator [I said the *Dictator* on purpose, just in case] and they might just need a good scapegoat at some point. Giving comfort to the enemy, collaborating, that sort of thing . . ."

"Tony, my relationship with *President* Batista [Burke was not about to follow suit, and he was in Miami, after all] was purely personal. And, I might add, he certainly disappointed me. As for the future, Tony, who can say? We've done business honestly and successfully for two generations in Cuba, under four or five governments. If, as he says, Castro makes it an honest government—well, we'll do even better, and so will the country."

As time passed, the Revolution became a sort of religion for me, and if I had reservations, I managed to suppress them.

On a trip to the States to discuss business with Burke, I found opportunities to argue in favor of the Revolution with Cubans whose telescopic view of the situation, plus the natural prejudice of their own unfortunate situation, made it impossible for them to see any good in social changes no matter how justified or beneficial they might have been. I was discouraged, and perhaps even a little shaken by their attitude, but I persevered.

The reactions of Americans were a mixed bag and, as is natural when the only information comes from the newspapers, they tended to oversimplify the situation. Batista had been bad; Castro was good but he *might* be a Communist and he had to be watched.

"But he's *not* a Communist," I would argue. "He's too undisciplined to be a Communist. He just has a vague, unjelled social philosophy about helping the little people, the common people. And, to quote Lincoln, God sure made lots of those . . ."

"Speaking of Lincoln," someone cut in once, "I read that Castro said his government would be 'of the oppressed, by the oppressed, and for the oppressed,' and that just isn't very reassuring, Mr. Navarro."

"That was just a good phrase. He picked up good rhetoric from the Jesuits. There's not a damned thing oppressed about Fidel, you may be sure. The point is that the U.S. shouldn't push him into the other camp by refusing to recognize his good points. Rather, it should help him try to reconstruct the country."

The argument about "not pushing Castro toward Russia" was an impressive one, and many Americans embraced it. I defended it out of hope, but I knew that Fidel would never accept help and friendship from the U.S. He *could* have done it and eventually have become a sort of Caribbean Tito, but it wasn't in his makeup. He despised Americans, or the image he had of Americans, with a hatred rooted deeply, atavistically, in his Spanish soul—and Fidel's soul *was* Spanish. The Spanish Jesuits of our childhood years had transmitted to the young Castro their own poorly disguised disdain for the predominantly Protestant, Anglo-Saxon country, a giant in *material* things, as they said, and so had unwittingly added fuel to the irrational anti-Americanism of the Castro brothers. No, the U.S. would not "push" Fidel anywhere—he was well on his way unassisted.

While I was in the States, the National Broadcasting Company decided to do a "balanced" documentary on the Revolution, and I helped them make the right connections back home. NBC had wanted to use Che Guevara as a lesser-known, somewhat mysterious personality. Typically, however, Guevara turned us down, and Castro did the interview. It was only more *Fideliana*, except that it gave millions of Americans a closer look at the living legend with a beard who seemed ready to challenge them and the world if necessary.

I returned to the family business in Cuba with a wider perspective than I had before the trip. I found that a number of my friends, mostly from the older generation, were beginning to leave the island "for a while." I had to understand what was going on, so I paid a visit to my aunt and uncle. Uncle Joe was a man very different from me, but I respected his judgment because, behind a conservative facade to the right of the Pope, there was a spark of progressiveness and pragmatism that had to be reckoned with.

I found Uncle Joe preoccupied with some of the laws of "social content" being enacted or rumored. Uncle Joe was a bank manager, and a sort of financial genius. He respected work while deploring the idle rich and dishonesty in government, and he and I could have agreed on many things if either of us ever listened long enough. But "these little laws," as he called them that day, were getting out of hand. "These *leyecitas*, Antonio, are simply ignoring that there is such a thing as private property. And, mind you, not everyone inherited or stole what he has; some worked very hard for it. It isn't right."

"Aw, come on, uncle, you know some of those laws were needed." Typically, we were at it. "This is a very rich island and you know the concentration of wealth is just too much. No one's starving, sure, but the distribution's unfair. It simply isn't right for a rich friend to tell me he's very sad about the Agrarian Reform because one of his larger farms in the provinces he's *never seen!* I don't care how rightfully inherited it may have been!"

"It is a man's privilege, my dear Antonio, and an incentive, to leave something to his family," Uncle Joe said. "As for the distribution of wealth, it's bad all over the world, and always will be as long as some men are brighter than others, or work harder."

"Yes, I know," I said patiently. "That's the theory of 'divine injustice.' I invented it myself. But you can at least give people equal *opportunity* . . ."

I was cut off by my uncle, who wasn't in the mood for philosophy: "As for the so-called Agrarian Reform, I have yet to see any of the poor farmers actually owning the land, with titles and the right to do with it as they will. They've just changed bosses, that's all, and the new one looks pretty demanding to me."

"You *know* that's supposed to be only a step in the process . . ." I began.

"That's exactly the problem. Everything is a step, a 'bad but necessary' step," said my uncle, mimicking the government spokesmen, "and in the end it will all be well; but we won't be here to see that end, Antonio—not me, not even you."

Uncle Joe paused; he hadn't yet mentioned his most recent worry.

"What bothers me now," he said, "is the latest in the litany of reforms. We've had the Agrarian Reform and the Education Reform, and could you believe the Tax Reform, with those stupid provisions to levy a tax on the *social columns* of newspapers on a 'per mention' basis? My God, who gives a damn about those vain fools in the first place. Anyway, now they come up with the Urban Reform, which is no more than legalizing the stealing of your real estate in the cities. And you know what they're going to pay you for it?"

"No." I didn't know. I hadn't paid attention; and besides, Uncle Joe couldn't wait to tell me.

"Well," he said, "they're going to pay you in bonds; but that's not the worst part. The value will be the value assessed for the purpose of paying real estate taxes, and you know what that is in our country!"

I wasn't getting the point. I didn't know "what that is in our country." I had never owned any real estate, let alone paid real estate taxes.

"You mean they put an artificially low valuation on your land or whatever it is?" I asked.

"Right. They use the self-assessment declaration and only pay you *that,*" the uncle explained.

I was beginning to catch on. "Wait a minute, Uncle," I said. "You mean to say that they propose to pay you what you yourself said it was worth for the purpose of paying taxes?"

Uncle Joe didn't like to have it put quite that way, but he said, "Yes, nephew, that's correct. Can you imagine doing that in this country?"

"I'm sorry, Uncle, but I think that's the funniest thing I've ever heard." I burst out laughing, while Uncle Joe got madder. "That Fidel sure is a smart bastard," I said. "He's going to pay you what *you* said it was worth, when you were . . . ah . . . cheating the government. How the hell can you argue against it? Boy, that's just too clever—the wages of sin . . ." I broke up. Uncle Joe had had enough.

"It's easy to see that you know nothing about our country and our ways—and even easier to see that it's not *your* property. Just wait until they take on your rich in-laws, as they sure as hell will. You won't be laughing then, and I ask you out of respect that we end this conversation."

Things were getting out of hand, and Aunt Maria Elena intervened.

"Don't upset your uncle, Antonio, please," she said. "He has a lot on his mind these days. I don't understand these financial matters, but I can tell you this: I don't like the way Fidel allows the Communists to run things. Those people are treacherous and they are Godless. He must be a Communist, too, or else he's a fool who thinks he can use them. You can't *use* the Bolsheviks." Aunt Maria Elena was of the old school, and she still referred to the Communists as Bolsheviks.

"Look, Tia," I answered, "Fidel has not been a Communist and he is not one now. And I doubt that he's a fool."

Uncle Joe snorted audibly, and it was hard to tell *which* statement he disagreed with.

I continued, "I'll admit I didn't know as much about his pre-Revolutionary history as I should have. But the American Embassy has shown me his dossier, and I'll still bet he's not a Commie. It happens that he *needs* the Communists. No doubt they're the best organized, the hardest working. I know from our own labor problems at the mills. You could always count on the Communist members of the union leadership; they were *responsible*. Alberto had the same experience."

"Sure," Uncle Joe cut in, "they're responsible all right—responsible to Russia!"

"Responsible to the Devil," Aunt Maria Elena dared to contribute, for her the strongest cut of all.

"Okay, you're right," I said, "but when they're *told* the party line is to cooperate, you couldn't ask for better allies. Everyone knows the Commies worked with Batista and only changed over to Castro weeks before he took over. But he still needs them to help run the bureaucracy. They're trained and they're dedicated. But he won't let them take over; I honestly believe that."

"I hope you're right, Antonio," my aunt said. "God help us if you're wrong," and she gave me a kiss on the cheek.

"I hope so, too, Tia," I answered. I got up to go and Uncle Joe followed. I was already outside in the hall when he said, holding the door ajar, "Just remember, my dear Antonio, that we property owners had to pay *another* 'tax' to the tax collector for his own pocket. I was not a thief, Antonio. Goodbye." Then he closed the door.

I went back to my job, determined to do my work despite a growing sense of something like confusion. And Castro went about *his* work with a developing sense of something like absolute power.

Fidel continued to run the country from the city squares, by the sheer acclamation of the frenetic crowds, whose collective vocabulary was limited to "Viva Fidel!" and "Sí!"—all that was needed to justify what Castro called his "Athenian Democracy," a sort of "government-by-roar" reminiscent of the mass meetings conducted some years back by Adolf Hitler.

Ever more frequently the mass vocabulary began to be peppered with slogans manufactured on the spot from Castro's phrases. It had started at the Camp Columbia speech. At one point Fidel had turned to Commander Cienfuegos who was standing next to him, and had said, in an aside loud enough to come clearly over the microphone: "How'm I doing, Camilo?" The next day the Spanish equivalent, *"Voy bien, Camilo?"* was a byword all over Cuba.

Yes, Castro was doing very *bien* indeed. From then on his phrases became slogans; in fact, they often became the law of the land right then and there.

A rival faction, the Student Directorate, which felt left out of things by Castro, started hoarding weapons at the University campus which was still "off limits" even for Castro's police. Fidel, during a timely speech, asked the crowd: "Weapons? Weapons for *what?"* The huge crowd booed and carried on, and possession of arms was made illegal by acclaim that very night, with transgression punishable by death. The weapons were turned in the next day by a contrite group of student revolutionists. Many other "laws" would follow in the course of the revolutionary process.

It was, perhaps, an odd way for a democratic government to behave. It left little room for opposition or even a minority opinion, but, then, maybe there weren't any. And the people—at times more than a million people gathered in the main square—simply loved it. Without doubt, everything was going well for Fidel Castro and his Revolution. Everything, that is, except the executions.

In the area of "revolutionary justice," arrests of persons accused of close collaboration with the ousted regime continued. No one was safe from a hasty or ill-intentioned denunciation. The executions were now a matter of common practice and also were beginning to reach beyond the "proven" cases to cases that were not quite so clear in the public's eye—the Cuban public and those watching from abroad. The mass execution of a group of seventy-five in Santiago was reported by the local press and carried by the wire services. The executions were carried out, the press reported, "by automatic weapons, in two groups, and the bodies buried in a trench dug behind them. Some men protested that they were members of the rebel movement; others stood at attention; still others prayed. The coup de grace for each man, with pistols, took a little time to deliver."

There were protests from all over the world, and the U.S. Congress officially deplored the news. After all, hundreds more, maybe thousands, were reported awaiting execution. Castro, for the first time, was unhappy and lashed back. He accused the wire services of lying, blamed the reactionary forces for a deliberate campaign of defamation, challenged the United States, and confiscated the guilty local newspapers. It was the beginning of something not quite understood:

"We are executing those whom the people would have punished had we not asked them to have faith in the justice of the Revolution."

"We will shoot every one of them, and if we must oppose world opinion, we will do so."

"If the Americans do not like what is happening in Cuba, they can land the Marines and then there will be 200,000 Yankees dead."

Castro later publicly regretted the last statement, "made in anger," he said, but it had been *made,* and it showed the thin skin of the leader where criticism was concerned, a revealing clue to his character. The American ambassador, Earl Smith, a political appointee but an able man who had witnessed the entire process, was removed and a career diplomat named to the post.

At the mass meeting called to approve of the executions, the calls for "Yankee, Go Home" began to take hold of the crowd. Soon there was a singing slogan which would be around for a long time: *"Fidel, seguro, a los yanquis dale duro."* It would be sung in unison, by hundreds of thousands of voices, and repeated for minutes at a time, gathering momentum and decibels as it went: *"Fidel, do it well, and send the Yankees to hell."* Soon it was all over the land, and from then on the "Yankees" were no longer officially friends, if they ever were . . .

". . . I am responsible, in the first place, to my people, the Cuban people, and, in the second place, to all the other peoples of America."

Castro was already making a subtle bid for the hemisphere he wanted to conquer.

The theme for that night, among others, was the righteousness of the executions and the unfairness and hidden motivation of the criticism.

". . . The executions are not a crime. Where there is justice there is no crime. Where there is crime there is no freedom of the press. Where there is crime, what is done is hidden from the people. We hide nothing."

". . . Batista would have fallen with a campaign such as is now being mounted against us, against the Revolution. And who is behind it? The monopolistic interests, the oligarchs who have lost their power, the foreign companies who enjoy the great concessions of our natural resources . . ."

The crowd chanted, "Justice, yes! Criticism, no!" and ended with a few minutes of "Fidel, do it well, and send the Yankees to hell."

After the speech I called Julio, perhaps with just a little less zest than usual.

"Hello, Julio? Did you hear him?"

"Yes, Tony, I heard him. And before you ask, I didn't like what I heard."

"Are you worried about the executions?" I asked, hoping for an opening.

"Tony, please, I will not discuss the executions, not even with you," Julio answered sharply, "but it wasn't just that."

"What, then?"

"I don't like the eminently personal approach." Julio was precise in thought and in speech. "We were supposed to get away from that. I don't like the servile, the abject way the press is behaving. No one can be right always; life just isn't like that. I think he is also fanning the flames of class hatred. And, my dear Tony, we are on the *wrong* end of that lollypop. Finally, I don't like to talk on the telephone. I'm beginning to think it's tapped, and that makes me feel paranoid or something. Do you think it's tapped? 'Say, sir, inside there, are you tapping us?' "

"Very funny," I said. Then I decided to go along. "I understand your worries, Julio, and I have to say I share some of them. 'Did you hear that, sir, whoever you are?' "

"Paranoia is contagious, I see," Julio laughed.

"Honest, though, Julio, I think the guy is trying to do a job. I don't like everything he's doing either, but he needs help. Do you remember how old Alberto said it was people like us who should get involved, quit looking at the bullfight from the stands and get in the arena? Have you thought that this could be a second chance for us?"

"Look, Tony. I wasn't even sure I wanted a *first* chance. And as for now, do you honestly think they want *our* help? Sorry, that's a silly question; you know damned well they don't. They want the support of a much different group. What they want from us is . . . oh, forget it."

"No, come on. To hell with the frigging tape if there is one," I came back. "What *do* you think they want from us?"

"Absence, Tony. Absence."

I was silent for a moment. Then I said, very seriously and very slowly: "That is the *last* thing we should give them."

After another awkward silence, Julio changed the subject: "Have you heard from Alberto?"

"Not a word lately," I answered. "His reaction should be very interesting."

"I'm sure it will be," Julio said, "and, knowing Alberto, we'll get it someday. In Technicolor."

We laughed at that, made plans to see each other over the weekend, and said goodbye.

6

THE EARLY DAYS of the Revolution were much easier for Alberto and Paulette Fowler than they had been for us. Alberto adapted readily to the process, conditioned by his underground activities of many months with the guerrillas in the mountain ranges near his sugar mill, Narcisa, in the center of the island.

Despite his less than satisfactory treatment by the revolutionary groups on the way back to Havana, Alberto felt that he had a stake in this revolution. The year before, as Alberto told it, he had confronted his father with his decision to work with the guerrilla fighters in his area and to join the clandestine 26th of July Movement. Alberto's father had the poise and the wisdom of years lived out as owner of a sugar mill on an island where sugar was king; divorced and available, he was a sought-after social lion in Havana.

"Look, son," the older Fowler had said, "I understand your reasons. Believe me, I do, whether or not I agree with you. But there's something you must consider. The Fowlers have never intervened in politics—by design, mind you, not through lack of opportunity. We have survived by minding our own business, which is making and selling sugar. And we have all lived very well—including you."

"Father, I know that," Alberto answered. "And I respect it. But the point is that the sidelines approach won't work. Not this time. We're involved whether we want to be or not. Take my word for it, Batista has had it—and we've got to be on the winning side. And I intend to be, with or without your permission."

"If you feel that strongly," said the older man slowly, "then of course I won't stand in your way. You're running the business and you know what you're doing. But, for God's sake, be careful. The mill is important, Bertie, but you're more important."

"Thanks, Dad. I'll be careful," Alberto agreed. "And nothing has to change for you. In fact, it *shouldn't* change. Accept any invitations by government people—go to any of their parties. It'll be a good cover for me."

The older man laughed. "Bertie, you know I never turn down a party."

Alberto then met with the hard core of the 26th of July movement, mostly

59

middle-class men—lawyers, doctors, economists. From Havana, these men directed the underground struggles in the cities while maintaining liaison with the guerrillas led by Castro and others in the mountain ranges. Alberto's closest friend in the group was Rufo Lopez-Fresquet, a well-known economist and a member of the highest policy-making body of the Movement.

"Welcome, Alberto," Rufo had said. "Glad you want to join us. We don't have many sugar mill owners in the Movement, and you can be a great help. A sugar boycott from the top down would finish off Batista just like that." Rufo snapped his fingers. "Anyway, we'll accept anyone who wants to fight the tyranny. Well, almost anyone," he added, smiling at Alberto. Alberto knew how Rufo felt about the Communists. "So why don't you tell our compañeros here" (the Soviet-related word "camarada" or "comrade" was avoided) "how you think you can help the Movement." The small group of men readjusted their seating and lit their cigarettes, prepared to listen.

Alberto had thought a great deal about the subject and was ready. "The way I see it," he said, "I can help in two ways. As a member of the Movement, I think I can influence others to join, and I have rich friends who might kick in with some money. They trust me. The other thing I can do is to help support the guerrillas. Batista's soldiers won't suspect the owner of a mill, and your men can work more freely if they know I'm with them."

"Sounds good to me," Rufo said. "Agree?" He looked briefly around, and the men nodded assent.

"One more thing," Alberto said. "The Communists at the mill hate my guts, and as usual they're playing their double game. But they'll try to take the credit for what we do. Their one objective is power, and Narcisa will be no exception. I want you to know that I refuse to work with them, as a matter of principle. I'm sorry, but that's how it is." Alberto spoke softly, but with a firmness which left no argument.

"We feel . . ." Rufo hesitated slightly. "Most of us feel the same way, Alberto. At this point, however, you understand that we have to accept any help we can get. *Our* main objective is to bring Batista down, and we'll worry about philosophy later. Anyway, we understand you perfectly and I don't think you'll have any trouble. You will represent the movement at Narcisa and we will notify our guerrillas in your area. They'll be discreet, I promise."

Alberto immediately went back to the mill and plunged wholeheartedly into the job of bringing down the Batista regime. He supplied the men in the highlands whenever he could, and he hid them, sometimes in his own home, when they were in trouble. He was proud to be doing his part. He and Paulette would drive to a party in a pick-up truck filled with food and medicines, and sometimes with ammunition, and leave it conveniently parked at some agreed point where the rebels could retrieve the supplies while they were at the party.

Two months before the downfall, when the denouement was clearly within sight, the small group of hard-core Communists at Narcisa, announcing by the usual pamphlets that they were openly joining the Revolution, left the sugar mill town or *batey* and set up a rebel camp of their own up in the neighboring hills. From there they sent threatening messages to the nearby landowners demanding provisions or money or else. Alberto was shocked when he received a note saying that if he did not turn over five thousand dollars, his young son would be kidnapped. He immediately protested to the leadership of his Movement in Havana that he was already helping more than enough and that he had no commitment to this maverick Commie-come-lately group, as he called them. But a week later, a young landowner who had refused to contribute was found in his own home with the back of his head shot away, and Alberto immediately moved his family to Havana.

He returned to the mill, typically ignoring the danger of being caught between the Batista forces moving toward the provinces and the rebels moving toward Havana. But Alberto was resourceful enough for two armies and got through with a few close calls, including being strafed and nearly hit by Batista's planes as he was approaching Narcisa on horseback over the hills.

At the mill his suspicions that the Communist influence had gained during his absence were confirmed. A few days later the rebel forces led by Camilo Cienfuegos arrived at the mill. Alberto was at the head of the contingent of workers, farmers, women and children who joyfully went to meet the mythical leader.

Cienfuegos was a tall, lanky man with sorrowful eyes, a sort of Biblical figure, part Jesus, part John the Baptist, except that his big, worn Texan hat made him look more like Gregory Peck. Only when you got quite close, Alberto noted, could you realize that behind the reddish-blond beard was the face of a very young man. He was soft-spoken and gentle, and immediately likable, but beneath it all he was an extremely able guerrilla fighter and tactician. His reputation had preceded him. He was known all over the island and was generally regarded as number two to Fidel and probably the only man whom Castro genuinely admired. Since he was considered anti-Communist, Alberto sought him out immediately. When the meeting finally took place—purposely delayed by the rebel chief to establish the new pecking order—Alberto was not terribly surprised to find the local Communist leaders, now wearing Commanders' insignia, sitting by Cienfuegos' side.

Alberto was bold, probably foolhardy. "Commander Cienfuegos," he said, "I must tell you that I am disappointed to see these men here with you. It isn't a matter of political philosophy. It's just that they didn't join the Revolution until two months ago. Their party line called for a different attitude before that. You know that I represent the 26th of July in our zone, and I cannot work with these men, who even went so far as to kill my friends and threaten my own family."

"Compañero Fowler," Cienfuegos said, "please calm down. There's nothing to worry about. I am truly sorry about those unfortunate episodes, and have ordered an investigation." He looked around for confirmation, but the men just stared at Alberto. "This is no time for differences," Commander Camilo continued. "Our objective is not yet accomplished, and that objective, for *everyone* who joins us, is to bring down the Dictator and establish a democratic government." He glanced at Alberto, and then turned to the others. "A government of the people," he added, wisely covering every front.

Alberto realized that his revolution had ended right then and that his life at the mill, both before and after victory, would be very difficult. Therefore, in early December 1958, he decided to take his case directly to the general headquarters of the Movement in Havana. A secondary but pleasant purpose was to join his two friends, Julio and me, to catch up on recent events and to share an enjoyable New Year's weekend. It was slightly irresponsible in the circumstances, Alberto knew, but what the hell. The fight was won and the future was uncertain, to say the least. And so it came to pass that Alberto and Paulette Fowler spent the last weekend of 1958—and of Batista's seven-year dictatorship—at the Isle of Pines.

One month later, the ill-starred weekend and the traumatic return journey behind him, the first thing Alberto did in Havana was to seek out Captain Fernandez whom he had met at Nueva Gerona and who was now awaiting assignment at Camp Columbia. Fernandez and Alberto had struck up one of those instant friendships. Captain Fernandez had every right to expect an important job with the Revolution. He had been a leader of an earlier uprising against the rampant corruption of the Batista regime—the conspiracy of *Los Puros,* the "pure ones," as it was known. The revolt failed, and Fernandez had spent two hair-raising years in the Model Prison at the Isle of Pines. With two purposes in mind, Alberto found the Captain at one of the barracks. The first purpose he dispatched quickly: would the Captain order the release of the owner of Los Pinos Hotel, being held as a "common" prisoner on the tiny satellite island? A promise was a sacred duty with Alberto, and he discharged it well. The Captain agreed, and Alberto's friend left for the big island that day and was off to Miami one day later, barely missing the persecution of "collaborators."

Alberto's second purpose was politically more sensitive, and the approach had to be just right.

"Captain," Alberto said, "I know your military record and your political trajectory, and I respect them both. You deserve—and I'm sure you will be offered—an important job with the Revolution. However, if you should care to try private life, for a while at least, I have a proposition to make you." The Captain said nothing, and Alberto was sure he was interested. "I offer you *my* job."

"Your job? Why would you do that?" the Captain protested. "What would *you* do? You can't be thinking of leaving Cuba. You're one of us, and we need you." Despite all the protestations, however, he did *not* turn Alberto down.

"No, no, nothing like that," Alberto said, "but I must be realistic, Captain. The Communists are trying to run their own revolution in my mill, and they're not going to give up easily."

"I see," the Captain said thoughtfully.

"There's no way I can control this move of theirs. I won't fool myself." Alberto plunged right in. "I need a strong man at the mill, someone who knows how to handle them. You have a record of anti-Communism and your position is unassailable. You take over the mill and I stay in Havana. We'll work as a team. The salary will be good—we can discuss that later—and you're free to leave any time Fidel calls you."

It was hard for Captain Fernandez to say no. The fact was that he had *not* been offered a job yet by Fidel. Castro was playing his cards very close to his chest, and it was obvious that he distrusted all but his "unconditionals." If nothing else, it might force Castro's hand if he consulted him about the sugar mill job.

"Would you mind if I discussed the matter openly with Fidel?" the Captain asked.

Alberto obviously would not mind; indeed he would love it. It was killing *all* birds with one stone—an Army Captain managing Narcisa with Castro's blessing!

"No, of course not," he said. "I'd *like* him to know."

"Would you come along, if I can arrange the meeting?" the Captain asked.

It was difficult even for Alberto to play the part convincingly. He tried to look pensive; then he replied, "Yes . . . I guess it would be all right," and he added, "if he will receive me."

It took days, but the Captain managed a meeting with Castro. It occurred at Camp Columbia when Fidel had a brief respite from scheduled speeches, impromptu speeches, news conferences, hiring, firing and rehiring all kinds of government officials and, somewhere in between, maybe, sleep, in one of the several houses and apartments where he would arrive unannounced and leave unscheduled, a modus vivendi he was never to abandon.

Alberto described that important meeting to me.

He and the Captain had waited in a room which would have shocked anyone who ever wore a uniform, shined a boot or clicked a heel. In the anteroom to Fidel's office, obviously an important room, an unseemly number of guards in dirty fatigues were lying, not sitting, on tables and benches, smoking or sleeping, rifles and automatic weapons propped up against the wall. The two men waited, literally, all of two days and part of the nights. Castro would go in and out, nodding to the Captain as he passed, but that was all.

Toward the end of the second day, the Captain, weary, and embarrassed by the slight, decided to leave for a while, urging Alberto to lie down in an empty storeroom which adjoined both the waiting room and Castro's office. Alberto was tired, too, and he fell asleep. Loud talking from a small room which he hadn't noticed awakened him. He couldn't resist the temptation to peek, so he carefully and silently opened the door a crack. In the middle of the room was Fidel Castro himself, a tall, roaring figure so large that he seemed to fill the entire room. He was screaming in anger at a small man cringing and crying at his feet. From his limited field of vision, Castro appeared to Alberto in globs of sight and sound, alternately growing and shrinking, balloon-like, as he moved in and out of view, producing the optical effect of the grotesque reflections in the convex mirrors of a horror tunnel. Alberto shrank from the unreal, Kafkian scene, but he didn't shut the door.

"You miserable little son of a bitch," Castro was shouting, towering over the weeping man, "you had to go and sell your worthless newspaper column to those bastards. You betrayed the Revolution and you betrayed me. Out of fear, you coward. You have no balls at all."

"I didn't mean to . . . ah . . . it didn't matter, anyway," the man was saying.

"Or was it money?" Castro was not listening. *"Was* it money? You dirty pig," Castro insisted.

"No, it wasn't. No, Fidel, I swear it . . . on my honor," the man pleaded.

"Never mind your honor," Castro said. "You will now write *for* the Revolution and make up for all your damage. You'd better thank God I give you that break for old times' sake. One wrong word and it will give me great pleasure to sign your execution. You have *my* word on that." Then he suddenly changed. "All right," he said in a normal tone of voice, "that's enough. Let's go."

Alberto knew he shouldn't have been there and it wouldn't do to be found out, so he quickly and quietly backed away and made his way out of the building. The sleeping guards didn't move. No one would threaten the Maximum Leader of the Revolution anyway.

The next morning Fidel Castro received Captain Fernandez and Alberto Fowler in his office. Alberto said he would never forget it. Castro was sitting at a makeshift desk, feet propped up, short wide-legged boots showing, behind a cloud of blue-grey smoke from the big cigar which had become part of his image. Castro appeared to be in a good mood. He was signing some papers in front of him and looked up, cordially.

"Good morning, Captain. Good to see you," he said cordially. "Sorry I've had to keep you waiting. Seems I never stop, day or night. It was never like this up in the Sierra. Trying to run a country is not easy. And there are things one must do oneself." He acknowledged Alberto with a glance. "Sit down please, Señores." Castro, oddly, was not terribly fond of the word compañeros in private; it did not come easily. "I hate to sign these things," he continued conversationally, "but, if I don't, I'm afraid Che will execute *me."* Castro was signing a small stack of death warrants, and "Che," of course, was Guevara. Che Guevara was in charge of the executions at the Cabana fortress, site of the Paredon, the Wall, and was fast gaining a reputation as the Avenging Angel of the Revolution, carrying out his duty without anger but also without remorse.

Castro finished *his* duty, seemingly unruffled by it, and turned to his visitors.

"Well, Captain, how does it feel to be out of prison?" Castro asked.

"It feels good, Commander, very good." The old career officer carefully acknowledged the new order of things, addressing his superior by his title. The highest rank in the Rebel Army was that of Commander, roughly equivalent to a regular army major. It just happened that Castro was first among peers.

"I'm glad," Castro said. "I know how it feels—in my own flesh, as they say." He paused briefly, then, "We're getting organized, Captain, restructured. Everyone should have a chance to help the Revolution do the formidable work that must be done. We haven't forgotten you . . ." Castro was a jump ahead of the Captain and had broached the subject first.

The Captain interrupted. "No, no, Commander, I'm not here for that . . ." he started to say.

"Captain," Castro cut in, holding a hand out in a friendly stop signal, "a man in your position should call me Fidel."

"All right . . . Fidel," the Captain agreed, but still he didn't use the familiar Spanish form of address. One can be formal in Spanish even on a first-name basis. "I want to introduce you to my friend, compañero Alberto Fowler."

Castro unpropped his boots, leaned forward and shook hands but remained silent, while Alberto said: *"Mucho gusto,* Commander. It's an honor." Then they returned to their original positions.

"Alberto owns a mill, Fidel," Captain Fernandez explained. "Central Narcisa. And he's been with the Revolution, with the Movement, for a long time."

"Reporting to Lopez-Fresquet, Commander," Alberto contributed somewhat eagerly.

"Yes," Castro said, pensive, searching his memory. "I believe someone told me about it. Maybe Camilo . . . you know, Commander Cienfuegos . . ."

"That's right, Commander," Alberto said. "I met Camilo at the mill in November."

"Isn't it amazing," Castro mused, shaking his head, "what kind of a revolution our Revolution is? What kind of a revolution is it that gathers illiterate farmers as well as sugar mill owners?" He held out his left hand, palm up, and glanced toward the ceiling, as if he expected someone up there to answer. It was an honest expression of surprise. It hinted at the fact that Castro, from his mountain stronghold, had underestimated the depth and breadth of the revolutionary feeling all over the island.

"It's *your* revolution, Commander," Alberto said, honestly and obviously moved.

Castro was silent, lost in his own thoughts for a few seconds, looking at but somehow beyond Alberto. "Well," he finally said briskly, "what brings you men to see me?"

"Fowler has offered me the job of mill manager, Fidel," Captain Fernandez began. "There are certain political elements at the mill . . . certain individuals . . ."

"The Communists, Commander," Alberto interrupted. He was dying to tell the story himself.

"Yes, the Communists," the Captain agreed. "Alberto says they have taken over, and he doesn't think he can handle the situation."

"Five weeks, Commander, five weeks before the end," Alberto broke in excitedly. "That's when they decided to join us and set up a separate camp up in the hills. Only five weeks and now they want to run their own revolution from my mill!"

"I understand." Castro looked serious. "Your mill has always been a stronghold of the old guard of the party. They used to call it 'little Moscow.' Perhaps you, or your family, did something in the past to provoke it." Alberto ignored the remark.

"Alberto believes I can help him, Fidel," the Captain said, "and I'd like to try it if it's all right with you . . . if you don't need me here." The real question was out at last.

"Captain," Castro said, "the Revolution needs *everyone*. And much more do we need those who served it bravely when others turned their backs or followed the easy route. You're a military man, an honorable soldier. We will use you. But first we must restructure the most basic elements of government. It will take a little time. You may use it profitably with Fowler." He looked briefly at Alberto. "Frankly, I find it all very intriguing. A soldier running a sugar mill, a private business. I tell you, this revolution is really amazing—even to *me*, and I should know it better than anyone."

"Then I have your permission to accept?" Captain Fernandez asked.

"Of course," Castro said. "Not that you need permission. This is a free country again, you know." He paused briefly. "How much is he going to pay you?" There was a mischievous twinkle in Castro's eyes.

"We haven't discussed that yet," Alberto put in.

"Well, whatever it is," Castro said to the Captain, "it won't be as much when you come back to us. The Revolution is not rich."

"I don't care about that, Fidel," the Captain said. "I could have gotten rich with Batista, and I didn't." It was a good point, and Castro recognized it.

"You're right, Captain," he said. "Well, you might learn a lot. Maybe how private business cheated the government." Castro looked at Alberto and added softly, "in the past." He thought a moment. "Or maybe how they took advantage of the workers? That must never happen again." Castro was dead serious, and Alberto remained silent.

"Thank you, Commander," the Captain reverted to the formal address. "I'm at your command at Narcisa whenever you need me."

"Very good, Captain," Castro said. "We won't forget you." Then, as an afterthought, "Remember, Captain, no excesses. But if revolutionary justice has to be handed out, I know you won't hesitate. After all, you were very near being executed yourself. Being 'pure' was not a good recommendation," he added in a half-joking way. Still smiling, he turned to Alberto.

"Goodbye, compañero mill owner," he said. "Good luck." Was there a touch of irony, of derision, in that smile half-hidden by the big cigar? Alberto wasn't sure, but it clearly was his cue. He was hurt by the generalization on private business, but not cowed. He got up to leave, nodded goodbye without offering a handshake, and said, looking straight at Castro:

"Goodbye, Commander. Thank you for receiving us and for allowing Fernandez to work with me for a time." Alberto paused, then added, stressing every word, "Remember, Commander, it's *your* revolution. Don't let them take it away from you." Fidel just looked at him. Alberto bowed slightly, and the two men walked out of Fidel Castro's office.

When Alberto called to tell me all this, he was obviously nettled by some of Castro's remarks but, at the same time, elated at actually having met for an hour with Castro, and proud of having stood up for himself.

"Tony—I've just spent an hour with 'The Horse!' " was the way he started out.

"Congratulations," I replied facetiously. Actually, I would have loved to spend an hour with Fidel, to ask him all the questions that kept torturing me.

"Okay, you jerk," Alberto said, "but let me tell you." And he did, ending with, "And I'm leaving for the mill tomorrow with my new manager, Captain Fernandez of the '*puros*,' appointed by Fidel." He lied a little, but only a little.

"I'm glad you got to see Castro," I said, "and I'm glad you're getting your mill problem straightened out. But I'm sorry I won't have you here to talk to. Talking to Julio these days is just asking for an 'I told you so,' and that's no fun."

"What's wrong, Tony?" Alberto asked, genuinely concerned.

"I'm worried, Alberto." I was so relieved to be able to say it at last that the words came rushing out. "I wouldn't tell Avis, and I can't tell Julio, but you and I have shared so many hopes . . ." I took a deep breath. "Things, Alberto," I said, "are not turning out the way I had hoped. It seems it's almost a crime to have been even modestly successful before. There's a stigma—and your friend The Horse is not discouraging that notion. He's *encouraging* it, Alberto," I was letting it all out, "and I'm running out of arguments for the Julios and the Avises of this world. I don't know, Alberto. Was I that wrong . . . again?"

Alberto was silent. After a few seconds, he said, "I know, Tony. I know," and I had never heard him speak so seriously or so sadly. He could have gone on to share his own disenchantment, but he chose not to. I was low enough.

"Okay, Alberto," I sighed audibly into the telephone. "Call me when you get back from the mill. Or before that if you need me. Good luck."

"Good luck to you, too, Tony. We're going to need it." Alberto held the receiver as if something had been left unsaid, then quietly put it down.

7

WHILE JULIO, ALBERTO AND I went our separate ways, the Cuban Revolution marched on, structuring its profile as it went, no one knowing what the ultimate goal was, or even if there was one. With time and events it turned more and more personalistic, wrapped around the figure of Fidel Castro. But, for the masses, this was easier to comprehend than having to deal with concepts. Cuba, after all, had always understood *caudillos*. Whatever Fidel approved of was right; what he decried was evil. Whoever opposed Castro's policies was not against *ideas,* he was against *Castro* and therefore against *the people*—which was perfectly in keeping with Castro's own psychological make-up. Love me, love my ideas; hate my ideas, hate me.

The Student Directorate had stated it quite clearly: "We are afraid that Fidel wants to run the show all by himself. He has reached a stage of exaltation where he won't accept criticism and can't stand people disagreeing with him. He wants to form the army his own way, and thus have the ultimate source of power at his disposition."

The world at large continued to criticize and at times condemn the continuing executions. What the world should have realized was that, given Castro's personality, open criticism was counterproductive. Such criticism only made him more determined to carry out the executions *and* to demand unqualified approval of them.

"If they doubt our sense of justice, if they question our procedures, if they want the trials to be public . . . is that what they want? Very well, then, we will have public trials."

So, public trials it was. The government selected three well-known army officers of the deposed regime to be the leading actors in the first drama. The principal defendant would be Lieutenant Colonel Jesus Sosa Blanco, who headed Batista's forces in eastern Cuba, scene of the worst part of the fighting.

A huge tent, set up at the Sports City Stadium, was jammed with 18,000 people, including some 300 foreign correspondents, embassy representatives, and thousands of farmers trucked in from the provinces to see the show, with straw hats and their cane-cutting machetes at their sides.

And it was, of course, a show. There were klieg lights and photographers' flashes, and hot dogs and ice cream vendors, and *mariquitas* and beer, and beards and uniforms and banners of all kinds, and a deep voice of authority from the over-loud public address system. It looked like a gathering of extras and film crews on location shooting *The Ten Commandments*. It was great fun for all, except for the defendants and for those sober-minded Cubans watching silently from their homes.

The accused Colonel Sosa, briskly military, stood at attention throughout, barely looking at the scores of witnesses on the stand testifying to crimes for which the death penalty was mandatory. It could have been a scene from the Nuremberg trials, which were, in fact, cited as a precedent:

"If the United States can try and execute war criminals from the Nazi regime, why are we criticized for exercising that same right?" the radio announcer would say, copying the why-do-they-do-this-to-us? approach that Fidel had developed to a fine art. "Are our dead Cubans less deserving than the German Jews? Since when is following a command an excuse for murder?"

Between such commentaries, the new national anthem, *"Adelante Cubanos,"* would be played both at the trial site and over radio and television stations. The whole scenario was intended to incite the mob to a righteous frenzy.

"Not guilty," the ramrod-straight colonel snapped when it was time for him to plead his case. "I resent being subjected to a Roman circus. I am a career soldier. I have killed in combat. I have ordered houses burned when required. But I have never murdered anyone. I swear it."

His defense lawyer explained the extenuating circumstances of the colonel's actions, careful not to overdo it and gain for himself the wrong kind of reputation in this new society.

The predictable verdict came: "Guilty as charged"; the prisoner was condemned to be *"pasado por las armas,"* a Spanish anachronism which literally means to be "passed through by the arms," and today means execution by firing squad. There was a roar of approval at the big tent as the trial ended. For me, still trying hard to believe that some excesses were worth the reward, it was a little sickening.

World reaction to the "Roman circus" was so harsh, so exactly opposite to what had been desired, that the revolutionary leaders decided to annul that trial and hold a second one in private with the same three judges. One of those judges was Commander Sori Marin of the Rebel Army who, having been a highly respected lawyer, might have been expected to negotiate a lighter sentence. But the death sentence was confirmed.

There were scores of executions—announced and unannounced—every day in Havana and the provinces, but Colonel Sosa's highly publicized execution claimed all the attention. For two weeks, his trial had been the soap opera substitute for television watchers all over the island.

The execution was carried out at the Cabana Fortress immediately following the second trial. The next day, the leading Cuban weekly news magazine, *Bohemia,* ran a photographic sequence of the actual execution. It was carefully chronological and it was graphic. The colonel was dressed in white, a civilian hat on his head. You could see him standing there as the sentence was being read to him. The members of the firing squad wore fatigues, typical of the informality that had become the trademark of the Revolution. Colonel Sosa had refused the blindfold and stood straighter than the wooden post to which he was loosely tied, and straighter than the old wall which provided a backdrop behind him, the awesome Paredon. According to the captions, the colonel's last words were addressed to the squad: "I forgive you and I ask your forgiveness." A close-up of the commanding officer showed him giving the age-old command: "Ready, aim, fire." The last full-page picture captured the moment of impact. Although the photograph was slightly blurred, it still clearly showed the condemned man arched backward as if blown by a strong gale. Issuing from the back of his white coat were a number of irregular little spurts, which showed up black on the black-and-white print. The gun bursts had blown the hat off, and it could be seen in mid-air. Also in the air, near the hat, was a smaller, wedge-shaped object, defying gravity by the camera's shutter speed. The text was mercifully silent on that point, but it needed only the picture to confirm that it was a section of the condemned man's head, shattered away by the volley.

Life magazine picked up the execution sequence and printed it worldwide. Reaction to the article was mostly of shock, as it is every time man-made death is brought close to home. The magazine followed it, some time later, with an article entitled "What Is Going Wrong in Cuba?" replete with examples of alleged unkept promises by "the Revolution," of arbitrary laws, ill-conceived economic measures, vindictiveness, capricious decisions and general chaos. (Incidentally, my photograph at Castro's side from earlier days was there. It was to serve me well.) Cuba was becoming, the magazine said, a military dictatorship regardless of its ideological beginnings—and, for the few days it was allowed to circulate in Havana, we all had it all spelled out for us, in black and white, for the first time.

Castro reacted predictably. Enemies began to be spotted everywhere, inside and outside Cuba. The Communist-led newspaper unions started the novel practice of printing "notes" immediately following news items or editorials which appeared, even remotely, to attack the Cuban Revolution. Soon the notes were more interesting than the news, exposing the alleged counter-revolutionary motivations of the United Press, the Associated Press and the owners of the Havana dailies still in private hands.

"The workers of this newspaper, conscious of their responsibility, disagree with the expressions or interpretation of the news, printed immediately above, as they are obviously inspired by counter-revolutionary agencies bent on destroying our glorious revolution."

They were in bold type and became known as *coletillas* because they were a sort of tail or *cola* which followed the original article. Ironically, the notes were justified in the name of "freedom of the press," but, in fact, they signaled the end of the free written word.

Shortly thereafter the private Havana dailies were confiscated and Castro created his own international press service, Prensa Latina, to disseminate the Cuban "truth." The circle was closed. Cubans from then on would read only what the Revolutionary government thought was appropriate.

Fidel carried the "we are misunderstood" syndrome to a climax at yet another public square gathering, and the crowd roared approval. A law was passed by acclaim, right then and there, decreeing capital punishment for counter-revolutionary activities as well as for something as vague and judgmental as "actions considered damaging to the national economy."

This time Julio called me first. "So," he said, "what do you think?"

I had expected the call and the tenor of it. "I don't know what to think, Julio," I said. "I'm not sure I *want* to think. Why are people so damned *stupid?* Are we a nation of sheep? That just bothers the hell out of me . . ."

"In the first place," Julio, always the logician, cut in, "you're wrong that it's stupid. Those people out there on the square—the 'sheep'—don't really have very much to lose, do they? Except, of course, their freedom, and they don't have much of that anyway. Any attack on those who do have something, dear Tony," Julio said pointedly, "is fine by them. It's good clean fun and it makes 'em feel better."

"For a patrician," I said, "you're beginning to sound a lot like Alberto."

"Never," Julio said with mock pomposity. "It's very simple. These people— or some of them, I should be precise—would love to destroy the system, because they haven't been able to make it. But if the system rolls over and dies—there's no stigma of failure, see? The others, poor babies, happen to *be* sheep; they'd follow anyone anywhere."

Julio paused. I didn't answer, so he went on. "And before you say anything, *if* you have anything to say, let me tell you my second point. Some phones are definitely tapped. I don't know if yours is, or mine, but as far as I'm concerned this is our last carefree conversation . . . and I hope I don't mean that literally."

"Oh?" I said, waiting.

"Oh is right," Julio said. "Now let me introduce you to the latest gimmick, brand new today. Hang up and call me back."

"What?"

"Hang up, Tony, and call me back," Julio repeated. "You know, depress the whatchamacallit, listen for the dial tone, dial each number slowly, etc. Come on Tony, *viejo*, you can do it."

I didn't know what was coming, but I obediently depressed the whatchamacallit, waited for the dial tone and dialed Julio's number. There was the usual click but, instead of the expected ring, I heard a woman's voice, following the same rhythm: "The executions of war criminals are fair and just . . . Cubans are a merciful people . . . We are responsible only to ourselves . . . Long live our Maximum Leader . . . Fatherland or Death—We Shall Conquer . . . The executions of war criminals are . . ."

Julio finally answered. "Hello, Tony? How do you like that? Hello, is that you?"

"Yeah," I finally said. "Thanks a lot."

"You'll be happy to know that that is known as 'conscientization' in proper Marxist language. It's a sort of way of thinking for you. But that shouldn't bother you or Alberto; now, should it?"

"Okay, you win, Julio. That *is* a bit much. If you don't mind, I think I'll hang up now." And I did.

The following week, *Bohemia*, loyal to the Revolution and still in private hands for that reason, printed a feature article under an "artist's inspired rendition" of Castro. Fidel had the pinched eyebrows over the heaven-cast eyes, and a subtly insinuated aureola surrounding his large bearded head. One didn't need the shadow of the cross or a weeping Mary Magdalene to hear the implicit "Lord, why hast Thou forsaken me?" and feel the urge to rush in there and single-handedly right whatever wrongs were furrowing that noble brow . . . It embarrassed me, but it probably impressed a hell of a lot of the pious. And, come to think of it, maybe there *were* some similarities, except that I couldn't remember Jesus ever going around using violence unless you counted the whiplashing of the merchants in the temple, and then He probably didn't hit them very hard.

Meantime, Castro was not necessarily turning the other cheek. A group of Batista's army pilots were tried by a revolutionary court in Santiago for bombing civilians during routine attacks on Castro's troops. The court acquitted the pilots, but Castro wasn't satisfied. He went on television, violently denounced the pilots *and* the judges, overruled the so-called judiciary branch, and ordered a second trial. This time they were all found guilty and sentenced to thirty years of hard labor. The previous chief judge committed suicide, and the defense attorney disappeared forever. Both had been trusted members of Castro's revolutionary movement. The incident shocked me, but it was devastating for Avis. She had followed the entire process closely on television, and her Anglo-Saxon respect for justice and law could not countenance Castro's personalistic approach and his public defamation of even his own men. For her it was the last straw. When the guilty sentence was announced, she made a clearly rehearsed speech to me in a quiet-but-firm tone.

"Tony," she said, "this is a dictatorship. It is a vindictive and personal dictatorship. What's more, it looks very much like a Communist dictatorship." She stopped for my reaction, then continued: "I will not live under it and my children will not be brought up under it, and that is final. I won't leave right away, but I *will* leave eventually. I hope you'll go with me, but if necessary I'll go alone."

Avis was not given to idle threats. She was reasonable and she was tolerably patient; but once she gave up on something, or somebody, it was final. And, accustomed as I was to the more volatile passions of the Latin, her finality frightened me. At the time, I really didn't see the army pilots' incident as any particular milestone, but maybe Avis expected more of the Revolution than I did.

"Darling, I know you're upset," I said. "I don't like it either, and if things don't straighten out, we'll *both* go. But, honey, we have responsibilities here. We can't just walk out on them. I promise I won't let us get trapped." Avis just looked at me sadly, so I added, "Come on, honey, cheer up. We've got the Brazilian Embassy tonight. Let's enjoy it."

I had never spoken like that to Avis. It was meant to reassure her, but it hadn't been what I really meant. While it was true that I had increased misgivings, I was still involved with the Revolution. In a recondite corner of my soul there was still the hope that matters *would* straighten out, and that the Communists would *not* take over and defeat Cuba's last bid for democracy.

And I was in good company in hanging on to my hope. Only weeks before, Herbert Mathews, the leading expert on Cuban affairs for *The New York Times*, the most influential newspaper in the free world, had commented on events in Havana:

"The Cuban and American business communities were strongly pro-Batista and anti-Castro. They were the former because Batista favored them in every way he could, and the latter because they believed the stories being circulated about Señor Castro's radicalism and even communism."

"Hurry up!" I shouted to Avis from downstairs, setting aside my half-finished pre-party Scotch. "Even in *Havana* we can't be late for a diplomatic dinner."

"I'm coming, I'm coming!" Avis called back, making last-minute noises. It was standard practice in Havana's social life that ladies *started* dressing at the time they were invited to *be* at the party. Anything earlier would have found the hosts in the shower, anyway. But embassies were the exception, and the Brazilian Embassy was no exception to the exception. So Avis flew down the stairs, looking absolutely radiant, and off to the party we went in my dark gray Mercedes 220.

By the end of that first year of the Revolution, embassy dinner parties were becoming the center of Havana's social life. Many of the socially prominent families had already left Cuba and those still in residence were not in the mood for parties. Besides, large receptions seemed out of place in a climate of austerity, and could be considered in bad taste by the government if not downright counter-revolutionary. Embassy parties, however, were quite another matter.

Havana has always been known as one of the gayest cities in the world. An ambassadorship there was very much a social plum for foreign service officers, and the Heads of Mission in Cuba were historically drawn from the ablest or wealthiest available in the service.

So embassy receptions were both lavish and perfectly acceptable and, since they were neutral territory, the guest list posed no problem. Since that guest list could include anyone from members of Castro's cabinet to the old-guard socialites, the parties were always fun and provided a welcome respite from the stifling puritanism of the new order.

The Brazilian Embassy's reputation for such parties was well known, and we were looking forward to a gala evening. Ambassador Vasco Leitao Da Cunha had rented a beautiful home in the Country Club area. Making embassies out of large private residences was to become common practice, because it gave the diplomats the setting they needed while providing protection of sorts for the owners who hoped to come back some day.

Avis and I crossed the enormous front lawn of the mansion and were greeted by the ambassadors at the door. We were genuinely fond of them, and Vasco was certainly number one in the diplomatic corps as far as Avis and I were concerned.

"Thank you for having us," I said, and the ambassador smiled at us warmly.

"Our pleasure, Tony, you both know that," the ambassador's wife, Niniña, answered for both of them.

"You're sure going to outdo the Argentinians tonight, aren't you, you old devil?" I kidded, looking around at the crystal chandeliers, the well-dressed guests, and the white-jacketed waiters with their silver trays.

"Never, my dear Tony, never," Vasco replied solemnly. The competition between Brazil and Argentina was wide open and well known, and it was always good for a laugh.

We escaped into the throng, and I snagged a passing waiter.

"Etiqueta Negra, Black Label, of course, Señor Navarro," the waiter said in answer to my very improper question about the origin of the embassy's whisky. Avis settled for champagne.

As we approached the inner patio, we could see that there was only one orchestra, thank God, and even that was going to be too much if one was to attempt conversation. It was playing Brazilian music, and Avis and I exchanged a happy and sneaky look.

While the Cubans were good dancers in general, the particular Brazilian cadence was just different enough to be confusing. We had spent some time in Rio de Janeiro, and would have a little fun showing off the subtleties. Right at that moment someone else was showing off. Isabel, the Ambassador's beautiful daughter, was dancing with one of the barbudos from the government's guest list. She was young, tall, blonde and green-eyed, but any resemblance to a New York debutante stopped right there, somewhere around the hips.

There is something very sensuous about Brazilian women that defies polite description. It's in the way they look and the way they move. The easiest way to put it is to say that they grow to a womanly body very early in life—and they are very much aware of it. They seem to have the voluptuousness of the Latin without the self-consciousness which makes the well-bred girls of other Latin American countries keep it all under tight girdle-control. The Brazilians move with a certain abandon that cannot possibly be faked. At the moment Isabel was putting her abandon to music and was the object of much male admiration.

Avis and I danced, saying hellos with varying degrees of friendliness as we moved around the floor. There were many members of the government and of the Rebel armed forces in attendance, as was to be expected at the Brazilian Embassy. The Da Cunhas were old and dear friends of Fidel Castro. Castro's brothers and sisters had in fact been in asylum at the embassy at various times, and some were there when Batista finally fell. Srha. Da Cunha, Niniña, was a fervent *Fidelista* in her own right. So Brazilian Embassy receptions were "command performances" for the Revolutionary Government, and it was possible that Fidel himself might show up at some point. The number of guards and patrol cars around the house hinted at the probability. Castro's young sister, Emita, was already there, and we spent a few moments with her. She was pleasant and friendly, not at all impressed by her position and not particularly interested in politics.

"I guess you *have* to have been to Brazil to do it right." The words came from the couple dancing right next to us. He was no less than the Sub-Chief of Police of Havana, and he was not more than thirty years old.

Commander Raul Diez-Arguelles was very Cuban in looks, and very attractive. He had dark hair, a handsome face and the body of an athlete. Diez-Arguelles had in fact been a prominent sportsman and a friend, though not an intimate, of our group before his "involvement" with the Revolution. Bumping into him at one of the big bashes at the Country Club or the Yacht Club was a frequent occurrence, but finding him at the Brazilian Embassy, with a beard and fatigues and the number two job in Cuba's police, was quite another matter.

At any rate, Commander Diez-Arguelles was friendly, and we stopped dancing briefly and exchanged greetings. We men embraced in typical Cuban fashion while the two women put their cheeks together and kissed the air in that greeting ritual designed to protect each other from their respective make-ups.

Mariana was an intelligent, good-looking woman. We asked her if she had brought her guitar, for she was a consummate player and singer. She said, a little shyly, that yes, she had, and we all agreed to get together for some singing after the party eventually thinned down to the fun people.

We found another old friend holding court in a remote corner. Dr. Raul Mendez Pirez was a party perennial, a society doctor, and somewhat of a character. Probably in his middle fifties, skeletally thin, and with alert dark eyes, he was an irrepressible chain smoker. I don't think he was a great doctor, but everybody loved him and, as usual, he had a crowd around him to hear his funny and sometimes irreverent doctor/patient stories.

"Hello, Tony. Hi, Avis," Dr. Mendez interrupted his story to greet us. "Good to see you. Come and join us."

"Good to see *you*, Doctor," I said, "but it isn't entirely unexpected."

"Have your fun, Tonito," the doctor said amiably, "but don't forget. You have to be here to see *me* here."

I spotted the Batistas. Clelia and Julio were standing off to one side, and I waved to them vigorously. They hadn't been going out much lately, and it was good to see them.

I tried to pay attention while the doctor rattled on, but my glance was irresistibly drawn to a point beyond the patio and across the lawn. It was hard to see the garage at the end of the lawn—the house was too brightly floodlighted—but I was able to make out the outlines of the garage and the tall fence around it. Behind the fence I could see, as I knew I would, a number of faces peering toward the house. Somewhere to the side, at some distance from the gate, a *miliciano* guard was leaning against the wall, his automatic rifle by his side.

Those men behind the fence were in what is known as "diplomatic asylum," or protection by the host country from danger of physical harm, imprisonment, or death as a result of their political beliefs.

Admission to an embassy for asylum is usually a formal procedure, arranged through a series of high-level meetings and discussions—all very proper and official. But desperate men will take desperate chances, and more than one such had gained unofficial entry to the embassy garage.

One of the most daring of these had to do with a bus driver doubling as an underground anti-Castro agent who had run into serious trouble with the government's G-2 men. He simply drove his big bus through the embassy fence, barreling by the unbelieving guards and, once inside, claimed and *was granted* political asylum. Even more amusing, two of the unsuspecting passengers, when presented with the unexpected opportunity, also asked for asylum—and got it! Most of the men in the garage of the Brazilian Embassy that night, however, had arrived there in more orthodox ways.

"There are quite a lot of them, aren't there, Tony?" said Julio who had come quietly up behind me.

"Yes, there are," I replied, still looking at the men in the distance, "and we know some of them—good, decent people." I had always disliked the term "decent people," but that's the way it came out.

"From both sides of the fence," Julio added. "Some *Batistianos* are still in there, now joined by the new defectors—*Fidelistas* who have now turned against Fidel." He pondered the thought for a moment. "I wonder how they get along in there, cooped up together . . ."

I was lost in my own thoughts.

"I wonder if I'd have the guts to really fight this thing physically," I said suddenly, turning toward Julio.

"I don't know about you, old man," Julio said, "but I'm afraid that's not the role for me. 'Bootmaker, stick to your last,' or something like that. In fact, I was glad to find you here tonight. I hoped I would. That's really the only reason we came. I wanted to talk to you, and I don't trust the telephone any more." Julio hesitated for a moment, looking straight at me. "I'm leaving Cuba, Tony," he said, "for good."

I couldn't think of a thing to say, not even "Why?" Julio noticed and went on: "I'm very sorry, Tony. Truly sorry. But in the end you'll leave, too, and wherever it is, we'll be together again."

He turned away, took time deliberately to get a drink from the nearest waiter, and came back to me.

"My family has asked me to leave, and I agreed. We know from a good source that the Agrarian Reform, in a matter of weeks—a few months at the most—will be extended to include the sugar mills, and ours will be taken. We had hoped that Sori Marin from Agriculture would keep it from happening, but he's lost out to the radicals, or sold out. And since the mills are all that's keeping us here, we'll move on to the family interests abroad. My brothers have other ideas about what they want to do with their lives, but someone has to run or supervise those foreign businesses. After all, my father is getting old."

Julio saw that I was still digesting the sudden news and could guess at my thoughts, so he added: "But we're not quitting, Tony. You can be sure of that. There are other ways . . ." and he stopped there.

"I don't know what to say, Julio . . . unless it's bon voyage." It was a pathetically weak attempt at humor. Then I went on, seriously: "You know, Julio, my own family has very little, and everything my in-laws have is here. My first responsibility has got to be to keep the Hedges business going for as long as I can."

"I understand," Julio said, "although I wouldn't bet on your success, I'm afraid."

"Okay, maybe you're right, but I've got to try," I replied. Then I added, lowering my voice a little, "And besides, Julio, I have another responsibility . . . a more personal one . . . to myself . . . and to you, and many others like you. If Cuba does go down the drain—and I'm still not resigned to it—I couldn't just say 'Sorry about that, fellows' and take off for Miami. I couldn't live with myself, and I wouldn't deserve to live with you. I will have been *so* wrong, Julio. I would have to do something about it . . ."

"Aw, come on, Tony," Julio interrupted, expressing what I couldn't quite say. "Fidel just fooled you the way he fooled so many others—most of Cuba, in fact. Don't single yourself out for guilt. The bell tolls for all of us."

"Thanks, Julio," I said, grateful for his absolution, "but I can't sit still for it. We'll see what happens. Meantime, I'm terribly sorry to see you go, you know that, and I wish you well. When will it be, or can't you tell me?"

"I can tell you," Julio answered, "but you can't tell anyone, not even Avis, okay?" I nodded and Julio continued, also lowering his voice and glancing toward the absorbed dancers and Dr. Mendez's "court": "I'll send Clelia ahead in the next few days, and I will leave sometime next week, pretending it's a vacation or a business trip. The rest of the family will leave over a reasonable period. My brother Laureano will stay for a while longer. He'll be okay. He has a good anti-Batista record, still valid credentials with the Castro boys, and he has some . . . some business to settle before he goes. Other than that, we should all be out within a month."

"All right, Julio. I understand," I said.

"One more thing," Julio added. "I think, for your sake, that we shouldn't see each other again . . . in Cuba, I mean." That really made it final, and we both felt the impact. "Sooner or later they'll discover that the Batista family has left the island. There'll be investigations, and you can't afford to be mixed up in our arrangements for leaving—not if you're going to stay."

"I guess you're right, Julio," I agreed. "If you don't mind, I think I'll go home now. I'll tell Avis I'm tired."

"I don't mind, Tony," Julio said, softly. "Goodnight—and goodbye." There was no drama in it. Julio carefully avoided it.

I shook Julio's hand, keeping a tight rein on my own emotions, left him behind on the edge of the shiny, red-tiled patio, and walked over to where Avis and Clelia were chatting. I pulled Clelia to me and threw my arm around her in a somewhat unusual physical gesture for Cubans, particularly with other men's wives, but justified in the circumstances. To Avis I said: "Honey, I guess I'm more tired than I thought. Would you mind if we go home now? I have an early meeting tomorrow and . . . well, frankly, I'm just not in the mood."

"Of course I don't mind," Avis answered. "It wouldn't be any fun, anyway, if you're tired. Let's go." She gave Clelia the standard air kiss and started into the house.

I kissed Clelia on the cheek, realizing that it really was goodbye. Clelia was as flip as ever, although she must have known that it was no ordinary parting. "You're getting old, Tony. When you went out with me, we stayed out much later. Remember?" Good old Clelia.

I turned to follow Avis and spotted her approaching Vasco, but before I could reach them she had already taken care of our goodbyes. As we started for the door, we passed the small gathering around Dr. Mendez.

". . . I told the lady, quite honestly, that there was absolutely nothing wrong with her except her age," Dr. Mendez was rattling on amidst snickers from his audience. "Her age," he whispered in an aside, the palm of his hand at the side of his mouth, "*was* rather advanced." A little laughter, a few more listeners stopping by, and he went on. "She simply wouldn't believe me and insisted on medication. So I treated her for a year, and all during that time I gave her aspirin and only aspirin, green and pink tablets of aspirin which I had made up for her. And I didn't feel at all guilty, because she was happy. And besides, she *did* have a little arthritis."

His audience laughed and clapped as Dr. Mendez stood there, straightfaced but pleased as punch. The sound of the laughter followed us as, hand in hand, we walked out the front door and down the dark expanse of the lawn. At the gate we said a polite goodnight to the cluster of guards who were patiently awaiting the possible arrival at the Brazilian Embassy of the Maximum Leader of the Cuban Revolution.

8

J ULIO BATISTA'S SOURCES proved to be absolutely correct. In the fast-moving events of the following weeks and months, the Cuban Government extended the Agrarian Reform to include the previously spared sugar mills. By the time Castro took over, only 36 out of a total of 121 mills were in the hands of U.S. corporations, a much lower participation than that which the Communist press had been quoting all over the world to stress the alleged U.S. dominance of the island. U.S. ownership, in fact, had come down from 55% of production in 1939 as a result of the growth of nationalism and of the Cuban middle class. At that rate of "Cubanization," U.S. participation in the industry would become insignificant in a few years.

The take-over affected Julio's family, owners of half a dozen mills, and they left as scheduled—a personal blow to me. Also affected was the third member of our trio, Alberto Fowler, who would lose his one mill, Narcisa. It was clearly the beginning of the end, the dropping of any pretense that radicalism would be curbed. Even the *production* of sugar, Cuba's primary crop, which made the country the world's number one supplier, was denounced as the source of the traditional and despised dependence on the United States, and diversification of crops was encouraged.

In an unexpected move, Julio Lobo, my former boss and the undisputed sugar king worldwide, was offered the opportunity to run the newly statized industry with a free hand, provided only that he gave up the dozen or so mills he owned. Lobo listened, asked for a few days to think it over and, within a week, left the island forever, leaving an empire behind. He lost his mills anyway, but would not condone "legalized thievery" by collaborating.

Commander Sori Marin, Minister of Agriculture, resigned in protest against an extremism he did not support. He disappeared from the scene and, some months later, organized a conspiracy against Castro which was betrayed and squelched. A prominent revolutionary figure and a comrade-at-arms of Fidel, Sori Marin was caught, tried and summarily executed. There was poetic justice or at least irony in the execution, since he had been one of the three judges who, some time before, had condemned Colonel Sosa Blanco in the public trial to be shot at the same Paredon. It was a warning to those who felt that a distinguished record of rebellion against the Batista regime or even close personal ties with Fidel gave them any degree of impunity if they disagreed with the way Castro was conducting *his* Revolution.

A more notorious event, and certainly a more significant one to the Cuban drama, took place shortly after my meeting with Julio at the Brazilian Embassy, the last meeting we were to have for several years. Dr. Urrutia, the puppet President of Cuba, a respectable and honest but totally lackluster judge, had been appointed to his office by Castro on the pretense that not all the power resided with the Prime Minister. His major claim to fame was the fact that, in the dismal Batista days, he had had the courage, as a trial judge, to rule in favor of the right of the people to rebel against the Government in certain extreme circumstances.

Courageous, yes, but not perceptive, for Dr. Urrutia had now misread Castro and was openly opposing the rising influence of Communism. Dr. Urrutia— lawyers are called "doctor" in Spanish-speaking countries, which leads to some disappointments at cocktail parties—was smart enough to discern that Cuba was going Communist, but not smart enough to understand that Castro had already decided that playing ball with Russia was his only way out from economic catastrophe.

Fidel had to make a choice about the old doctor, and he did. He absolutely crucified the man. Castro mounted a complete show in the best Grand Guignol tradition, at which he excelled. Starting with the circulation of carefully manufactured rumors and continuing with an unexplained absence of The Leader from public events, it ended with an unannounced appearance of Fidel on national television. As expected, five minutes after the beginning of the "surprise" program, most of the six million Cubans were watching and listening.

Castro told the world that he could not go on, made a contrite confession of disagreement with the President, "a man he respected," and said that therefore he, Castro, was irrevocably resigning from his post as Prime Minister in the interest of harmony and the Revolution. With that, he went off to one of his hiding places to pout—and wait.

Predictably, the country went absolutely mad. All of Cuba, it seemed, begged Fidel not to resign, in hasty meetings improvised at every available public square. Even the National Association of Manufacturers, one of the last capitalist enclaves, decided at a special meeting to ask the Prime Minister to remain in office —a gesture, they were told, that the Revolution would not forget.

The denouement was not long in coming: Dr. Urrutia was shamed out of office and went into a sort of exile within Cuba. In fact, as it happened, he went to a relative's home at the Hedges mill of Textilera Ariguanabo. Meanwhile Castro "reluctantly" accepted the call of the masses to return to the thankless job of Prime Minister.

But what about the Presidency? Well, that was really no problem. The Cabinet, after some heated discussion, appointed another lawyer, Dr. Dorticos, equally lackluster, equally subservient but, alas, much more committed; he was an old if somewhat bourgeois member of the Communist Party. As a result of the obvious farce, several members of the Cabinet who were not Castro's "unconditionals" resigned, including Rufo Lopez-Fresquet, the President of the National Bank. At that point, fully two-thirds of the original Revolutionary Cabinet which took office in January 1959 had been executed or jailed, were in political asylum at various embassies, had fled the country to exile, or had resigned and were somewhere on the island, very, very quiet.

It was perhaps sad to reflect that these were at one time among the strongest supporters of the Revolution. Now they refused to follow Castro for ideological, emotional or religious reasons—the position which Alberto Fowler had so clearly stated at an earlier opportunity. Their absence, however, also was no problem for Castro, especially with respect to the National Bank post.

Fidel, with what had to be tongue-in-cheek, appointed Che Guevara as the head of the bank, a dentist turned guerrilla fighter who at least had the sincerity to admit at his inauguration that he "knew absolutely nothing about banking and was not too sure he wanted to learn." In fact, to show his disdain for the job, Guevara signed the Cuban currency, as the National Bank President must, with only his nickname, "Che," a disregard for elementary propriety which had Havana laughing for weeks.

From then on, there was no question which way the country was going. There is something about a Leftist Revolution in a developing country which, like a Greek tragedy, has the quality of inevitability; it has to commit itself eventually to a major ideological current and to the country which most prominently endorses it and has the resources to help the little brothers. To allege that it could have been the United States was simply not to understand Castro's psychological make-up. What he wanted, what he must have, was absolute power. It mattered not whether it came from the Left or the Right, but it could not be democratic, burdened as it is with a Congress and its checks and balances and all the rest. It could, however, easily have been Nazi Germany if that had been a chronological possibility. The guilt feelings of Americans about the fact that Cuba could have been saved, that the U.S. *pushed* her into Soviet hands, were totally unfounded. True, the U.S. did not conduct its dealings with Cuba at that stage in the wisest of fashions, but even if it had, the end result would have been the same.

The Communists, in their infinite wisdom, realized that the day had come, and they had won the day. Their years of sacrifice, when the choice was the underground or a pariah existence in the open, were over. To be sure, Fidel remained a maverick, to be handled with kid gloves, but to cope with that the Communists had dedication, they had discipline, they had tact, and they had a cadre of professional bureaucrats who had been training for years for just such an opportunity. Above all, they had a clearly defined ideal to which everything, including themselves, must be sacrificed. They had been groomed for years to do the dull but essential administrative jobs which a new bureaucracy requires and for which the fighters and the wild-eyed speechmakers were eminently unprepared. It was for Fidel the answer to a maiden's prayer, a way out from the bureaucratic morass into which he had stumbled, aided by loyal but totally inept lieutenants. If a price had to be paid, he was prepared to pay it.

The neighborhood Committees for the Defense of the Revolution were strengthened. Their function, absolutely essential to a Communist take-over anywhere in the world, was to police the neighborhoods. Every block or group of blocks had its Committee, made up of the most radical, the most committed. They had the power of surveillance over their neighbors and the right to violate their homes to investigate suspicious or unusual behavior at any hour of the day or night and to search and arrest in the name of the Revolution. Meetings of friends in a home over drinks or cards, a "foreigner" to the block who stayed overnight, any criticism of the Revolution, however mild—all were proper subjects for investigation by the neighborhood Committees. One can imagine the personal vendettas that were settled in this fashion. Suspects were hauled off in trucks, with that special vindictiveness which only the weak who ascend to power can display, and often the trip could lead to the unexplained disappearance and even execution of the victims. The system of neighbor spying on neighbor became institutionalized, and from then on terror was the law of the land.

In parallel fashion, official repression, that of the G-2, tightened its grip. Rebellion of any sort against the new order was treated as the Communists must treat it: those who oppose the system must be eliminated as a simple matter of social hygiene, with no room for compromise. The *official* executions also continued unabated. The shock which normally attended public announcements of capital punishment gave way to a public acceptance of a sort of standard operating procedure. If, earlier in the process, minor political transgressions were treated with a degree of tolerance, now young men in their late teens were condemned to the death penalty for distributing subversive pamphlets.

Commander Huber Matos, one of the heroes of the Revolution, whose grip on the people's imagination was perhaps too strong for Castro's comfort and whose loyalty to democratic principles was unswerving, asked at that point for permission to resign from his post as Army Commander of one of the most crucial outlying provinces. The immediate result was a well-publicized trial for conspiracy and treason, and it was only because his reputation was so well entrenched that the death sentence the Communists demanded was reduced to twenty years of hard labor. In 1980, hoping to gain world approval for the Communist regime, Matos was released, a broken man but still fighting.

Commander Camilo Cienfuegos, the understated hero of the early struggle who had taken and held Camp Columbia for Fidel Castro, made a trip to the provinces to "take the pulse of the nation," as he announced at the Havana airport. No one really knew on which side of the struggle between democracy and Marxism his true sympathies lay, but everyone loved the man with the Gregory Peck charm which placed him second only to Fidel in popularity.

It was easier to understand Cienfuegos' true persuasion when, as reported officially by the Government, the small plane on which he was returning to

Havana some days later disappeared in the midst of a tropical storm. Half the Cuban Air Force was deployed to search for the missing plane. It was never found, and the man to whom Fidel Castro had turned in the course of his very first speech and asked, with affection, "How am I doing, Camilo?" was gone forever. Most Cubans concluded that a major obstacle in the path of the Communization of Cuba had been removed in true Marxist fashion.

At that point, the Electrical Workers Union called a national strike, both in protest against the way the country was going and in support of what the Government called unrevolutionary wage demands. The Cuban Federation of Labor, which comprised all unions, was taken over by the military. Its legitimately elected leader, himself an electrical worker, was removed and imprisoned, and Jesus Soto, my old friend from prerevolutionary Textilera days, was appointed by the Government to replace him. I learned from Soto himself that he had been given the alternative of joining the Communist Party and assuming the top position, or of following the fate of his unfortunate predecessor. Soto had nothing to lose, really, but his principles; and so he became the head of the Federation of Labor. And the Federation, which was the last major force that could have tempered the drive toward Communism, became one more tool of the totalitarian regime.

There was a lesson there for labor leaders everywhere, if they cared to learn it. Certainly, the AFL-CIO in the U.S. knows it very well. And there was a lesson, too, for businessmen who should realize that a strong, democratic trade union movement is the best defense a free country can have against Communism.

And so it went, one step after another along a course that it now appeared had been charted long ago.

When I arrived at Textilera Ariguanabo's offices the next morning, I sensed immediately that something was not right. Aside from the normal greetings, no one spoke to me, and people tended to avoid looking at me. I ran up the stairs and went into the anteroom which served the executive offices. My secretary was there, and she caught my eye and silently motioned toward Burke Hedges' vacant office.

I opened the door to my father-in-law's office. Seated behind Burke's desk at the far end was a young man in civilian clothes, a trim, neat young man in his late twenties or early thirties, who looked back at me. I didn't expect this meeting, but I wasn't really surprised. I knew immediately who he was. The only thing that surprised me was that he looked almost embarrassed, though trying hard to hide it.

I approached the desk and said, "Hello." The young man stood up respectfully, returned the greeting, gave his name, and added, as if it were desperately necessary: "Mr. Navarro, I am the Interventor."

He was rather a financial type: serious, circumspect, and humorless at first blush at least. One could hardly imagine him as politically aware, and certainly not dedicated. I had heard that these were the young men the Government appointed to supervise companies which were under investigation. All that was required was honesty, and this young man standing before me simply overflowed with honesty.

Since I had said nothing beyond "hello," the earnest young man felt compelled to repeat his introduction.

"I am the Interventor appointed for Textilera . . ." he said, almost diffidently, "by the Government," he added.

I still said nothing, and he went on, "You know, for the Ministry, the Ministry of Recovery."

I knew quite well what the "Ministry of Recovery" was—the Ministry for the Recovery of Assets, created soon after the Castro take-over. What was left out of the official title was that the "recovery" referred to assets "stolen" by members of the Batista regime, and that they were to be recovered "for the State."

As with the executions, this Ministry had addressed itself at first to the investigation of the most obvious transgressors: Cabinet members of the deposed regime known to be involved in graft; the well-heeled Generals of the Army; Batista's long line of relatives; the head of the Customs Office and the Chief Tax Collector; the large, profitable construction companies where the Dictator had appeared as a "silent partner," and so forth. But, as time went on, the long arm of the Ministry extended beyond the obviously culpable. The whole process is known as "gradualism."

Also paralleling the reaction to the executions, the Cuban people had managed to rationalize the Ministry's actions. As the reasoning went, "so-and-so (who was confiscated) was obviously taking money on the side—who wouldn't, in his position?" Another one was a distant relative of Batista in a major political office, and "he certainly wasn't there to stay poor." Yet another one was a big industrialist and, "well, industries just don't get that big without some shenanigans, now, do they?"

And so the irresponsible complacency prevailed—the rationalization always stopping short of the rationalizer himself because he, of course, had done nothing wrong. No, no one would fight anyone else's battles, and the Ministry marched on unchallenged on a very well-marked course where, in the end, there would be no exceptions, and guilt was no longer relevant to the true objective.

"I have a letter for you," the Interventor said, handing me a sealed envelope. I opened it, glanced at the standard introduction addressed to the "Manager of Textilera," and read the beginning of the first meaningful paragraph: "This is only a precautionary measure. There is no intention in any way . . ." I put the letter in my pocket and looked back at the man behind the desk.

"This is only a precautionary measure," the Interventor said, and I couldn't suppress a grin. "We do not want to interfere with production or with the normal conduct of business," he continued. "The Government only wants to assure itself that the company's funds are properly safeguarded."

"I understand," I said, mentally adding, "only too well."

"My job will be simply to see that any income is properly booked, and particularly that any disbursements are justified. I will have to initial these transactions as a representative of the Government. Beyond that I will not interfere with the running of the company." The speech was well-rehearsed, but the tone was almost apologetic and I could hardly keep from smiling. It would have been easy to strike back at a son-of-a-bitch, but this poor puppet was almost pathetically abject, and I had to remind myself that, still, he *was* the enemy.

The introductory conversation obviously concluded, the Interventor said, "I must apologize, Mr. Navarro, for sitting at Mr. Hedges' desk, but I knew it was vacant and I did not want to make further inquiries or disturb anyone before your arrival. In point of fact, however, I can discharge my duties from any quiet office anywhere in the building."

"Oh, no," I said, "I think this office is perfectly appropriate for your job, since you're here to supervise our operations. If the Government has decided that Textilera has to be investigated, I wouldn't want to hide it from the staff."

"Of course not," said the Interventor, sounding a little miffed, as if he could be faulted for not giving himself as much importance as I seemed to have given him. "On the contrary, I think you may wish to call the key executives of the firm and explain the situation to them."

I was starting out to call the staff when the Interventor, still standing practically at attention behind the desk, said, as a casual afterthought: "Oh, Mr. Navarro, I should tell you, since I notice you did not read the whole letter, that only the normal working accounts of the company will be under surveillance, but Mr. Hedges' *personal* account is frozen as of today."

"And what, exactly, does that mean?" I asked, resentment rising for the first time. This was too much.

"It means," the Interventor said, "that Mr. Hedges is under personal investigation, as distinct from his position as President of Textilera, and the funds in his personal account are frozen and cannot be touched as of the close of the banking day this afternoon."

I knew my father-in-law had a considerable amount of money in a personal bank account, but it was all he had to draw on to exist in his self-imposed exile. His father, Dayton Hedges, an American who had founded Textilera, had become a naturalized Cuban citizen (a twist which his American friends found difficult to understand) and, instead of transferring any of his considerable wealth to the U.S., had invested every cent in his mills in Cuba.

Burke Hedges, therefore, would find it difficult to survive in exile, even with the help of American friends who considered the whole situation as no more than a passing storm. But even the help of true friends has a limit. With the freeze of his personal account in Cuba, Burke's financial situation abroad would become very difficult indeed.

The banks were powerless to do anything about it, themselves fearing government reprisals—including, down the road, the nationalization of their Cuban branches, which in any case seemed inevitable. The sad part was that while most American banks limited themselves to providing strictly the information on private accounts requested by the government for their list of "suspects," some banks unfortunately went so far in their cooperation as to *volunteer* a list of other accounts, under different names, which the bank suspected of being fake accounts linked to the persons under investigation. Such abject behavior "beyond the call of duty" availed them nothing except the scorn of some of their former clients, and, in the end, they were taken over with all the other U.S. banks.

I made a mental note that there must be some way to send Burke money, but this was certainly no time to think about it; I would discuss it later with Juan Viera, our First Vice President, now acting President, a smart and loyal man.

I asked the three top executives in the company to join me. The First Vice President who was also the Treasurer, the Assistant Treasurer, and the firm's Secretary and legal counsel, Pedro Villoldo, were introduced to the Interventor and were told of the new situation. There was no point in asking why, so no one did.

While the Treasurer and the attorney maintained a respectful but distant attitude, the Assistant Treasurer seemed to go out of his way to cooperate, almost as if he welcomed the intervention. I observed his attitude with almost detached interest. The intriguing part of it was that, of the three men, the Assistant Treasurer was the most notoriously pro-company, always the toughest and most uncompromising with the employees and with labor in general. He had, in fact, been declared persona non grata by the unions several times in past years, and his dismissal was a perennial part of the yearly demands. And here he was, already telling the young Interventor what documents he should initial and why they were important to his supervisory function.

Oh, well, I thought, that's the way it goes. You think you have a sterling employee and, instead, you have a small Hitler waiting in the wings. To such people law and order and discipline are self-justifying in any situation.

Having settled on a modus operandi in which the Interventor would function, the three executives left the room. I then turned to him and said, "I would like to ask you one question about the freeze on the accounts. May I?"

"Of course," he answered, eager to cooperate.

"How about *my* account?" I asked casually.

The Interventor broke his composure slightly. "No, not yours, Mr. Navarro. It . . . it was not material," and then he, too, smiled. The ice had been broken, and I allowed myself a little fun with this serious young man.

"Rather small, isn't it? I guess I'm not much of an oligarch yet."

He smiled again.

"By the way," I added, "you impress me as a dedicated Revolutionist, but also as a reasonable man. I suppose you've heard the saying that revolutions, like the spiders, eat their young?" It was a low blow.

"Very amusing, Mr. Navarro," the Interventor said, no longer smiling. "Yes, I have considered that possibility." He paused. "It was a good meeting. Thank you for being so reasonable. I will see you tomorrow." With that he left the office.

"I walked out onto a side terrace upstairs on the big house and looked over the links of the Havana Country Club and beyond them toward the beautiful tree-lined houses. They were all empty now."

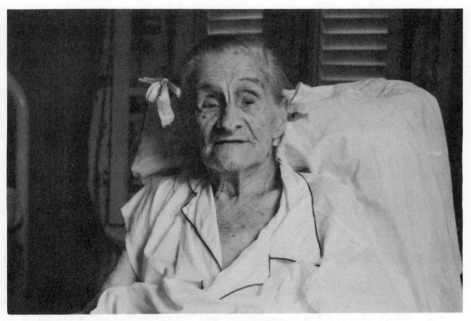

Nanita. A central figure to the very end. ". . . and all the quiet warmth I ever knew came from Nanita."

To Key West, Fla.
90 miles

Gulf of Mexico

Havana

Varadero
Beach

C U B A

Rosario
Range

SWAMP

BAY
OF PIGS

Escambray
Range

ISLE
OF
PINES

TRINIDAD

REVISED
LANDING SITE

ORIGINAL
LANDING SITE

Sierra Maestra
Range

Guantánamo
Naval Base

Caribbean Sea

THE ISLE OF PINES *"From the air the whole scene looked like a map in a geography book, deep green island on a field of blue, surrounded by a sprinkling of keys. It made one think of Blackbeard and gold doubloons, and the Isle of Pines had, in fact, been reputedly the setting for Stevenson's 'Treasure Island'."*

The ferry between the Isle of Pines and mainland Cuba, Isla Del Tesoro, *the fabled Treasure Island. "The group, increasingly, realized that our position was dangerous."*

(Above). General Batista, a witness at the wedding. "Hedges, after all, was a personal friend of Batista. Even though he did not approve of Batista's politics, the relationship was nonetheless an important one. No one in our family was about to rock the boat. That's the price you pay for riding it."

Avis (left). "She was petite and decidedly pretty and, if one accepted a miniature, she could also be called beautiful."

Readying the one-armed bandits for the New Year's Eve celebration. "Someone, without bothering to consult the group, reached over and turned the radio off. The silence was welcome. It was then seven-thirty in the evening of December 31, 1958. The New Year's Eve celebration for 1959 ended before it started."

Alberto (left) with his 26th of July band, and friends Sergio Veranes, Julio and Clelia Batista, in the harrowing return trip to Havana, two days after the Revolution. ". . . our appearance betrayed wealth or position or something that, in a few short hours, had gone out of style."

Barricades by young Revolutionaries. The "7-26" arm band reflects Castro's July 26th Movement. Very old weapons in very young hands. "A full beard was regarded with admiration."

A prepared message from Castro on his way to Havana: "Compatriots, the glorious day has arrived at last. We shall soon be rid of the hated tyrant. A general strike has been called and it should be obeyed. If you are not involved directly in the struggle, be calm, stay off the streets, stay at home and we will keep you informed. Do not act individually. Remember, this is a different Revolution."

A brand-new Castro on TV for the first time. Cautiously, he tests the waters. Thousands of speeches would follow.

Castro arrives in Havana.
"Divine approval" for the young leader: a great publicity stunt.

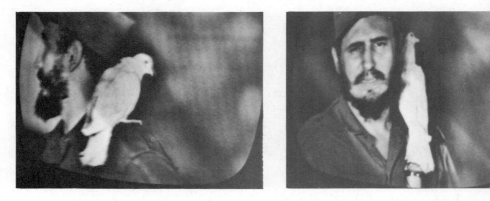

U.S. Ambassador Earl Smith warned the State Department. In vain.

Even "divine guidance" can be guided.

These Americanos don't understand us. (". . . *a hurt look, with sad, closely knit eyebrows converging upward, seeming to ask himself and Heaven why these terrible things could have been done.*") © *Andrew St. George,* LIFE MAGAZINE *c. 1959, Time Inc.*

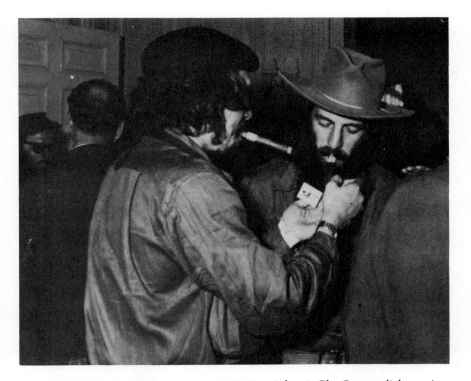

(Above). Che Guevara lights a cigar for Commander Camilo Cienfuegos on arrival to Havana. "Cienfuegos was a tall, lanky man . . . a sort of Biblical figure, part Jesus, part John the Baptist, and part Gregory Peck in a Texan hat." Cienfuegos, the only Revolutionary figure to compete with Castro in popular appeal, mysteriously disappeared with his plane in the fall of 1959 amid rumors, never confirmed, that Castro wanted him out of the way. © Jean Raeburn, N.Y.

Former Castro supporter, Alberto Fowler, and his family give up and choose exile in Florida. He would return on the Bay of Pigs Invasion.

Cuban farmers were trucked to the rallies by the hundreds of thousands. They discovered from Castro that they had won the war: "It was the people who won this war. Because we had no Army; we had no Navy; we had no tanks, we had no aeroplanes, we had no cannons. We had no military academies. We had no training camps. We had no divisions, no regiments, no companies, no platoons, we did not even have squads! But, who won the war? Who? The people; the people won the war." © *Joe Scherschel,* LIFE MAGAZINE *c. 1959, Time Inc.*

I called the Treasurer back into the office alone. After all, he was really Burke's number two man, and it was my father-in-law whom I now proposed to telephone to give him the bad news. I assumed that the conversation would be monitored or taped—now standard operating procedure for long distance calls—but the report to Hedges had to be made. When it came through, Burke took the news philosophically, as if he had expected it.

"I understand, Tony," he said, "and I know very well what it means. After all, it's happened to friends of mine, some of whom are here with me. The freezing of my personal account is quite a serious matter, of course. I don't suppose there's anything we can do about it?"

"No, not so far as the freeze is concerned," I answered, looking questioningly at the Treasurer, who nodded agreement, "but we're thinking of other possibilities and will let you know."

Hedges knew that was a subject we couldn't discuss on the phone, so he just said, "Yes." Then he added, "Well, Tony, you know how I've felt about it all along. This is only the beginning of the end."

"I hope not, Burke," I said, trying to be reassuring in spite of my own feelings on the subject. "I've decided to see the Prime Minister about this. It doesn't make any sense at all. If they were going to take Textilera, they'd have done it months ago. I don't understand it."

"You do that, Tony. After all, he's your friend," Hedges said ironically, "but I won't hold my breath."

"Okay, Burke, I get the point," I said. "I guess you're right. Maybe you always were. But I'll try anyway. Goodbye."

The Treasurer and I briefly discussed ways and means of getting money to Burke, but nothing looked too promising. The most popular maneuver, completely illegal of course, was to make a deal with a foreign supplier of materials needed by the mills—machinery, for instance—and arrange to be billed for something slightly above the real price, and deliver the overpayment to someone in the foreign country. It had to be absolutely secret, very modest in the overprice, and, of course, it was extremely dangerous. Discovery would lead immediately to a maximum jail sentence if not worse, plus, of course, immediate confiscation of the business. Could it be risked, with an Assistant Treasurer like ours? Probably not, we concluded, but we'd go into the possibilities again, once the extent and thoroughness of the Interventor's day-to-day supervision was determined.

I called Alberto at the Country Club and told him the news.

"Well, that's just the beginning, isn't it?" Alberto said. I just wasn't going to get any encouragement from anyone.

"Yes, Alberto, I guess it is," I said defensively, "but I've decided that the time has come for me to see Fidel personally. I've got to know where I stand."

"I could tell you where you stand," Alberto said, "but you wouldn't believe me, so I won't. Anyway, you can see The Horse tonight, if you want to, even if from a little far away. In any event, you'll certainly hear him. He's putting on his super-rally tonight. Even *he* needs reassurance, I guess."

"Yes, I know," I said.

Thus I attended my first mass meeting in the main public square. I wore appropriate clothes and stood on the fringes of the crowd which packed the square and looked like an ocean of heads, many wearing the typical straw hats of the peasants who had, as usual, been imported from the provinces.

Still, I could see Fidel and his entourage as they trooped to the dais about an hour after the appointed time, par for the course. I looked at them and thought, Jesus, look at those people on the dais. Look at the exposure. A fast jet fighter with an expert machine gunner could make one strafing pass and probably kill the whole damned lot. And the Revolution would be all over—if they got Fidel, that is. Come on, Tony, quit dreaming, I told myself. But, still, it *could* happen, you know . . .

The crowd was disciplined by Cuban standards. Official-looking men and women in fatigues and armbands subdued an occasional drunk or an overly excited soloist in the crowd. At Castro's appearance, the crowd intoned the now-traditional chants and slogans: against the U.S. imperialists, in favor of the biggest sugar crop ever, demanding execution for a number of counter-revolutionaries, etc. Fidel came to the microphone after a few preliminary speeches from the lesser luminaries, asked for silence, tolerated a few minutes of strident disobedience, and started his speech—which was to take four hours.

Toward the middle of the endless diatribe, Castro mentioned that voices had been raised recently asking for elections, and then he focused on the real purpose of the gathering.

"Elections!" he shouted. "What for?" He paused to survey the mob. "What for? To bring back a bunch of thieves to office? To delay the process of the Revolution with a sold-out Congress? To undo its achievements?"

As if predetermined, which of course it had been, the crowd began to chant, "Elections, what for? Elections, what for?" *("Elecciones, para que?")*, and kept it up for a full five minutes until Castro, both hands up in the air, asked gratefully for silence. The rest of the speech was routine. The point had been made. Cuba would have no elections. The earlier, highly touted provisionality of the Government went by the wayside. Forgotten was Fidel's categoric statement in the course of a speech in January, 1959, eight days after the Revolution:

"Elections will take place in eighteen months, and political parties will be allowed to reorganize."

The hastily prepared earlier laws, reducing the Presidential age to 30 so that Castro could run, and declaring Che Guevara a Cuban "by birth" so that he, too, could run, were never again mentioned. Cuba was to be a totalitarian Marxist state forever.

I didn't wait for the end of the speech but left for home, stopping by to see

Alberto on the way. I found him listening to the balance of the television broadcast. We turned off the TV, but there was no need for much conversation.

I just said, "This is it for me, Alberto. The end. I won't even say I'm disillusioned. It's just the end of a stupid dream."

Alberto was in no mood to provide comfort, but he tried anyway.

"Maybe it isn't, really, Tony," he said. "No one truly expected elections."

"I did," I said. "I did."

9

THE TIME HAD COME for me to see Castro, personally. The obvious, ostensible reason was that I had to defend my family's interests, but I harbored the hope that somehow I could influence the course of events, the process of the Revolution, if not the end results themselves. I knew it was an utterly naive hope, but I couldn't allow that to interfere with my immediate objective. I tracked Fidel like a camp follower, and I made myself obvious in the crowds which always accompanied Castro's public appearances.

The security forces soon came to recognize me, and the inevitable security check must have cleared me since I was never disturbed. Finally there was even recognition from Fidel, a glance or a wave.

I gave up my day-to-day work at the office and scanned the newspapers for those meetings where Castro was scheduled to appear and enjoyed guessing where he might make one of his now-famous "unexpected" appearances. The whole thing became a little bit of a private game I was playing with the Maximum Leader.

At one point a Castro visit was announced to Manzanillo, in the Oriente Province, the area where he himself came from. I learned of the trip ahead of time through my contacts, and I traveled to the lush eastern region, so geographically unlike the other provinces. I knew the area well from earlier days, so I was able to arrive in the little town several days ahead and get myself near the front in the cheering crowd. Of course Castro saw me and, disregarding his bodyguards, came to me directly.

"Look, Mr. Navarro, Tony," he said, "I know perfectly well who you are. We went to school together, but this is not a class reunion. I know your background, I know your family, and I know what you want. I hadn't intended to grant you an interview, but your persistence has impressed me. I didn't think persistence was an aristocratic virtue." Fidel smiled.

While the crowd around us jostled for his attention, I finally said: "You're right, Commander . . . Fidel, and I guess you're right about my purpose, too, or half right anyway. Will you see me?"

"I will, Tony," Castro answered, "but this is not the place. Go back to Havana and make a date through Conchita, my secretary. You know her, don't you?" I nodded. "Go see her at the Agrarian Reform offices. I'll be there . . . some time" —an obvious reference to his unpredictable schedule.

Then Fidel Castro shook my hand, and all of my better judgment, doubts and misgivings were not enough to stifle a flow of respect for the man. The crowd's emotionalism was indeed contagious.

I felt my mission, such as it was, had been accomplished, and I returned immediately to Havana ahead of Castro.

Conchita Fernandez was a tall, handsome woman. She had been the secretary and confidante of Eduardo Chivas, acknowledged as Castro's political mentor in the days when Chivas was a luminary and Castro presumably still had democratic ambitions for Cuba. Subsequently, Chivas, in a gesture probably unprecedented worldwide, went on the radio during the Batista days, at a very crucial moment in his own political life, warned the Cubans that this was his last call to them to join in civic action against the Dictator, and, right then and there, pulled out a revolver and shot himself in the stomach.

It will never be known whether it was one more dramatic gesture in the eminently dramatic career of that political figure but, whatever the intent, the wound was fatal. What influence this event might have had on a young Castro is impossible to tell, but it certainly inspired his secretary to follow a path which, in her mind, led to the unconsummated goal of her late boss. Conchita became Castro's secretary and displayed to him the same uncompromising loyalty she had had for Chivas.

The Agrarian Reform offices were located in a tall building somewhat removed from the center of Havana, in a new area which housed several ministries. It was not far from the public square used for most of the mass meetings. The building itself, still unfinished after months of occupancy, was in typical revolutionary disarray. It was one more example of a sort of general disdain for neatness, which probably had its psycho-political roots in the fact that neatness was considered a bourgeois virtue and therefore redolent of the old establishment, when almost every Cuban was a small private cloud of talcum powder.

It was as if the latter-day hippies had taken over the government and immediately banned ties, skirts and soap to dramatize their rebellion, a comparison which is not as farfetched as it might seem. That is not to say that most public offices are paragons of organization and discipline; they are not. But at the National Institute of Agrarian Reform, confusion was institutionalized, and over it all floated the aroma of strong cigars, strong coffee, and fatigues.

Fidel Castro's office was on the top floor, the whole top floor, with lots of empty rooms and halls with bare concrete walls and a few benches. There was really no reason why Prime Minister Castro should make his offices here, except perhaps that Fidel felt the central importance of land reform and wanted to distinguish the project with his presence. For whatever reason, this was Castro's number one office, among many all over the city, and it was where his official secretary, Conchita, held court.

I arrived at the Agrarian Reform office and mingled with the olive green fatigues, the shuffling peasants with bewildered eyes, the influence peddlers, the small lawyers, the milieu of any ministry anywhere. I looked for and eventually found what passed for an information desk, manned by a young woman in fatigue uniform, naturally, with an automatic rifle over the back of her chair, the proto- type of the mannish, aggressive female who was beginning to emerge as a product of the Revolution. I managed to ignore the irritating features of the set-up and asked my question. Fortunately for me, *everybody* knew where Conchita's offices were. Getting access to them was another matter.

For one thing, I stood out because I was wearing a coat and tie—definitely not a plus. On the other hand, if the coat-and-tie was no longer the symbol of position and was outranked by fatigues, it still could mean someone the Prime Minister *might* want to see, so the tomboy behind the desk was obliged to pay me some attention.

An understated remark to the girl about Castro's summons and a confirmation from the top floor on the intercom entitled me to a little piece of paper which, in turn, enabled me to have the elevator operator consider taking me to the top floor and even grant me, of all things, a military salute.

Conchita Fernandez did not make me wait long. I was ushered in to her desk, which was literally an island of order amidst chaos.

"Hello, Tony. I remember you," she said quite naturally. "I know Fidel told you in Manzanillo to come see me." She didn't say "Dr. Castro," and she was quite friendly and natural.

"I can't guarantee that I can get you to Fidel. You know how unpredictable he is," she said, "but if you tell me what you want with him, I promise to get you an answer."

Conchita was disarming in her openness. She certainly didn't reflect what some psychologists have called "the borrowed power syndrome" of executive secretar- ies, probably because Castro's power was so awesome, so total, that it didn't need to be flaunted. Whatever the reasons, she continued in the same vein:

"I know your in-laws. They weren't bad Americanos, really, and they did a lot for Cuba, a lot we probably couldn't have done for ourselves. But they befriended Batista. Maybe they couldn't help it, but they befriended Batista, and you know that will never be forgiven."

"I know it won't be forgiven," I said. "And I don't expect it to be. But that isn't really why I want to see Fidel."

Conchita went on as if my statement hadn't registered. "I don't know, Tony," she said. "I don't know that you'll be able to adjust. This is a new order of things. Let's put it this way: if I were in your place, with your background, I'd find it difficult to accept."

"Look, Conchita . . . may I call you Conchita?"

"Of course."

"Please don't judge me by my background. It wasn't much different from yours." And it *wasn't* much different. "And don't judge me by my in-laws. It wouldn't be fair to expect them to understand, and it doesn't matter anyway."

Conchita looked interested. "What do you mean, Tony?" she asked.

"I mean," I answered, "that I know the tools of production must eventually pass to the State. There's no turning back for us, for Cuba, any more."

Conchita was not prepared for that. She looked at me silently, and I could almost read her thoughts. Conchita, brought up as a Catholic and educated as an upper middle class young lady in the urbane, conservative Havana society, was already in the Marxist camp. Maybe I had hit pay dirt.

I went on, a little breathlessly: "Conchita, I'm not going to ask Fidel to spare Textilera. That would be foolish of me. All I'm saying is that the mill is working well. We don't have any production problems or labor problems. It's well managed, by people who understand the revolutionary process and wish the best for Cuba."

Conchita just listened.

"Textilera simply doesn't have to be taken right now, except for purely vindictive reasons, and that doesn't make any sense at all. The Revolution *needs* its management talent, and the mill isn't going to run away, so why take it now? Why not let me and my people run it? Run it *for* the Revolution, not against it." I ran out of steam.

"Tony," Conchita said, finally, "that makes sense to me, but maybe there are reasons I don't know about. I'm Fidel's secretary, sure, but I'm still a secretary. But I'll do my best to get Fidel to see you. If I can't do that, I'll talk to him and get back to you."

That was the best I could hope for, so I got up and kissed Conchita on the cheek by way of thanks and said goodbye. In the crowded elevator, I thought about what I had said to Conchita—could I have said it any better? and what she had said to me—had I read her correctly? Had I really convinced her? I did a lot of pondering on that short vertical trip.

Late that night, Conchita called me at home.

"Tony, Fidel is very busy—and that's not just a standard excuse. I really mean it. Things aren't going too well, you know."

There was no need for me to say anything.

"But I gave him your message," Conchita went on, "and he understood it."

With rising excitement, I said, "Yes?"

"He told me to tell you—and I'm giving it to you as faithfully as I can—that if you can convince Guevara that you're right, he, Fidel, has no strong feelings about it and will go along with whatever the Che decides."

I said nothing, thinking quickly what the obvious next step could mean.

Conchita continued, "And I'll add one more thing, Tony—confidentially, please. Fidel also said, 'You know, Navarro may be right. It could be a waste of effort and manpower that we can't spare.' " Then she said, "Goodbye, Tony. Sorry. I've got to go."

I said, "Thanks, Conchita, many thanks," but I was talking to a dead phone.

The next step was to try to see Guevara. I consulted briefly with my colleagues at the office—those I could trust, that is—and I got a few pointers from Alberto who, as usual, was a veritable encyclopedia of information about the man. I made countless phone calls, enlisted Conchita's help to open up the all-important secretaries' network, and after several days—probably part standard clearance process and part just plain disorganization—I received a call at my office. A curt, military type informed me that I had an appointment with Commander Guevara at midnight that same day—not an odd time at all, considering the Revolutionary standards for office hours which simply followed the working habits of Fidel Castro.

I collected Textilera's latest financial results, the contribution we were making to the general economy, and any other information that might help my case.

After a tense dinner which I didn't enjoy at all, I set forth in the middle of the night to meet Dr. Ernesto Guevara, a mildly successful Argentinian dentist who, as it happened, was also a Commander of the Cuban Revolutionary Army and the unlikely President of the country's financial policy-setter, the Cuban National Bank.

10

COMMANDER GUEVARA will see you now," a weary aide said. I looked at my watch. It read 5:30 A.M. I walked into a fairly large office with a desk at one end, parallel to the wall. Behind it, facing the room, sat Dr. Ernesto Guevara, known to friend and enemy as "El Che," a reference to his birth and early life in Argentina, where the meaningless but handy expression "che" was as frequent in popular conversation as "chico," or lad, was in my own country. Guevara motioned to me, and I sat on one of the several overstuffed chairs in front of the big glass-covered desk. With his large head and long hair, Guevara looked very much like a lion, a slightly uncomfortable lion in fatigues, clean and starched even at 5:30 in the morning. I took in the big, luminous eyes and the trim beard. He looked slim sitting back on his chair—one might even say frail; probably, I thought, the result of his well-known asthma—but the energy was unmistakably there. He sure as hell did not resemble the proper National Bank presidents I had seen on that spot in the old days, but neither did he look like most of his rumpled revolutionary comrades, Fidel included.

Guevara, in turn, looked me over silently. Seconds of silence spark rushes of thought. I imagined the man in front of me up in the mountains in the original guerrilla actions, tired and dusty and wheezing, trudging alongside the physical giant that was Fidel Castro—a mature, thoroughly committed Communist, counseling starry-eyed Fidel who was still being pushed by events, fumbling with vague notions of social justice and the rudiments of Marxism we all had learned instinctively to distrust in our Catholic schools. The large eyes kept studying me, and I squirmed slightly inside my business suit which suddenly felt too hot. I was conscious that I looked every bit of my thirty-seven years of age, my face creased with weariness after waiting several hours for the interview. Nevertheless, I managed to engineer a friendly smile by rearranging the wrinkles. And it was not altogether faked since, politics aside, I had always found Guevara a fascinating personality. Obviously, I had been thoroughly checked before the interview had been granted, and my credentials therefore were known, but I still had the feeling Guevara was trying to place me within his own personal memories.

I had, in fact, met Guevara before. Earlier in the Revolution, when my faith had not yet been shaken and I hoped that the United States would understand, I had helped the National Broadcasting Company try to get an interview with Guevara. Che had politely refused, telling me that sort of thing was more in Fidel's line. He used the South American word *"peliculina,"* a somewhat derogatory derivative of the word "film" in Spanish, implying a willingness, more often a burning desire, to be on camera. He said *that* was Fidel's specialty, not his. There was nothing openly derogatory, however, just a statement of fact: a division of jobs, the proper use of natural aptitudes. Guevara had said he was the *"guajiro"* of the group, the Cuban farmer, the guerrilla fighter and tactician, not the spokesman. Though I knew that Guevara could be eloquent when he wanted to be, I had known then that my effort was hopeless. And you certainly could not argue about Fidel being more articulate, not after six-hour-long speeches on almost any subject. So, Fidel it was. He accepted readily and NBC had its interview. I had seen the run-off and had been proud then of contributing to better relations with the "people" of the U.S. (the *government* of the U.S. was already a bad word). I wondered if Guevara remembered this episode over one year before—one hectic year for everyone.

Commander Guevara looked intently at me and said, nodding his head slightly: "It's good to see you, Navarro." He skipped the Mister and he used the familiar Spanish you, but still it did not quite have the easy warmth, the instant-friendship approach which comes naturally to Cubans and only with some effort at first to South Americans.

"I haven't forgotten our meeting a year ago. That interview with NBC didn't change anything after all, did it?"

"No, it did not, Commander," I said firmly, and added, "in either camp."

Guevara did not miss the subtle dig. He said: "I remember that you are with us in the Revolution, despite your father-in-law and your position. Or you were . . ." There was only the slightest pause, which I pretended to ignore, and Che went on quickly.

"You'll have to excuse me for the late hour. I find that I work better this way. The people who come to see me at this hour of the night, or of the morning," he grinned, "have a very clear purpose and are anxious to get it over with. There is no temptation for idle courtesies or long preambles. Most get right to the point. As I think I know *your* point, I will get down to it for you."

I made a sign meaning "Please go ahead."

"I know you are worried about your family business," he said. "And you are right. Your father-in-law is not our friend. He bet on the wrong horse. You think the Revolution wants to take your company from you. I will tell you this. I don't know if the Revolution wants to or should take it from you. I'm not the Revolution. I can only tell you how I feel about it. Your textile business is a respectable business, it is a hard-currency earner, or saver, and that is good. It's an old, established Cuban industry, and there is nothing wrong with that, either."

I waited nervously for the inevitable "but" and groped for my cigars in my breast pocket, offering one to Guevara with a motion.

"No, thank you. I can't take cigars too well; that's Fidel's department." He grinned, this time openly. "I try sometimes, even often, but they bother my asthma." Then he turned serious. Meeting my eyes directly, he said, "But don't forget one thing, Mr. Navarro, *'No se puede hacer tortillas sin romper huevos.'* ['You cannot make omelets without breaking eggs.'] The Revolution will not be good for *everyone.*"

"I fully understand that, Commander, I assure you," I said and, after a pause to let my remark sink in, I continued, "I was told your views on this matter were crucial . . ."

"I will tell you very frankly," Guevara cut in, "the textile industry is not strategic, it's not located in one of our ports, it's not absolutely essential to the economy, it's not a monopoly—not completely anyway. If it were any of those things, you can be sure we would confiscate it tomorrow, and we would find the reasons for doing it, or no reasons at all. But it isn't. So unless the Government wants to take it for political reasons or punitive reasons, I don't really care."

"May I convey this view to the other members of the Government?" I asked.

"You may," Guevara said softly, and there was a twinkle of sympathy in his eyes. I felt that the man liked me. And, to tell the truth, I myself could not help liking this eminently straightforward man, could not help admiring his sincerity, so unlike the double-dealing I had suffered recently. To be sure, Guevara would not hesitate one instant in having me shot if he half-suspected the rebellious ideas brewing in my head at that very moment. As the commander of the Cabana Fortress, in the early days of the Revolution, Che had ordered, or tolerated, the execution of innocent men whose guilt had not been established "beyond doubt" or who had merely disagreed with the new regime. And he was known for his readiness to deliver the coup de grace to the executed. Indeed, he had a reputation for ruthless dedication as the Avenging Angel of the Revolution. But, then, I too would, if I could, do away with this man who had so obviously and so importantly interfered with my dreams of a new, cleansed, democratic Cuba. Still Guevara would not be first on my list of candidates for elimination. After all, if there was a Maximum Leader, maximum guilt belonged to him. No, if it came to that, Guevara would not be the first on the list.

Ideological animosity aside and as yet unspoken, the human rapport had been established. I recognized, even envied, devotion to a cause, any cause. I wished I could offer Guevara *my* cause. He would be a good ally. But democracy had become diluted by complacency, had lost glamor by use and misuse, even if it was, I was sure, the only answer still. On the other hand, Communism, as an idea, had the charm of the untried, a philosophical beauty even if a practical unrealistic fraud. Guevara, in turn, probably saw in me someone willing to challenge the establishment whence I came and from which I had obviously profited materially. These thoughts were spoken, or half-spoken, between us after the business at hand had been transacted; and if Guevara was not much for preambles he apparently enjoyed an epilogue. He announced through the intercom to his aides that this would be the last appointment of the day, or night, and invited me to stay and offered to take me home.

Che talked, almost openly, about his early life, his own country, the injustices, and the great Cuban opportunity. He talked about Marxism-Leninism with great naturalness, as if he knew I would not be shocked. He even touched on his own ideological rebellion within the movement, which one day would lead to the Pekinese deviation, one of the modern-day schisms in the Left, and eventually to a confrontation with his former ideological pupil and friend, Fidel Castro. He mentioned the policy mistakes the Revolution had already made, some of them of Che's own doing. There had been the decision to cut down on sugar production, for instance, something like the Swiss quitting watchmaking, in order to reduce dependence on the great enemy, the United States. And then there had been infantile, dogmatic refusal to accept capable technicians and managers of somewhat conservative leanings, preferring over them a proven ideological loyalty, however inept, leading in the end to the brain drain which so hurt the struggling economy. His candidness was overwhelming, and flattering to me. I realized that Che thought I would be a good acquisition for the Revolution, if I could be made to see the light.

Intimacy breeds intimacy, after all, and I spoke at length about my own early traumas, my despair at injustice and discrimination, my disappointment with religion as a sometime treasured answer, the material superficiality of Cuban society as I had known it, the suicidal lack of concern, even contempt, for "politics" on the part of the wealthy and therefore the most responsible and most vulnerable sector, and the inane preoccupation with sexual mores while moral values more important to the survival of the country went ignored. I finally, cautiously, touched on the immediate problems. I said all the right things, naturally, and then openly mentioned my being distraught, my utter confusion. I understood, or thought I understood, the objectives of the Revolution. I sympathized with them, to a degree at least. But Fidel was a disappointment. I had known him at the Jesuit school we attended together, and later had believed in him. He had turned egocentric, shamelessly dictatorial, or maybe he always was all of these things. He ran Cuba like a fief. Was I wrong? I wanted to help, but everywhere I went now I drew a blank. Take, for instance, my current efforts to keep my family business from being confiscated. I knew that it would have to go eventually—I was not quite that dumb—but why now? It was running well; my father-in-law was gone and would never come back. Everyone agreed, and yet Government officials whom I had alerted would smile benignly and do nothing. The red tape was incredible and led nowhere at all. I had passed long corridors and waited in scores of anterooms. One waiting room only led to another. I had talked to clerks, who took notes. There was inefficiency and ineptness.

"I tried to find a meaning in all of this," I said. "I was sure there was one, but I was beginning to think that no one really knew what was going on—not even Fidel, not even you, Commander Guevara."

Che Guevara looked at me and said nothing. For an instant, I noted, there was an odd look of, yes, tenderness on his face. He had to be the greatest actor in the world or this dedicated Communist, this controversial man, felt sorry for me.

All the words having been said, we kept quiet for a time, so far apart in one little room. After a minute or so of silence, an aide came in and looked at Guevara. Black, strong, sweet coffee followed, and with it faint daylight through the shades on the top-floor windows of that lonely, tall building in the middle of Havana. Shortly thereafter, like thieves in the night, two fatigues, one crumpled and one neat, and one wrinkled business suit moved quietly through the shades of the corridors in that early dawn, as Commander Che Guevara, his bodyguard, and Tony Navarro left the National Bank of Cuba.

The three men joined the chauffeur already waiting in Guevara's automobile. Che and I sat in the back, the bodyguard next to the driver. Guevara was totally relaxed, but the guard held his Czech submachine gun in such a way that the barrel was not pointing toward me but not completely away from me either— not forward, just sort of up in the air. I was not offended. After all, that was the guard's job, and that type of gun is an awkward thing in cramped quarters. The Cadillac glided silently through the empty city streets in the soft, diffuse light, passing scores of closed shops and an occasional early riser. As we moved from downtown Havana toward the suburbs, Che Guevara was quiet and pensive. He asked a few perfunctory questions of his men, about a building here or a gun emplacement there, but he did not seem to listen to the answers. We reached the Country Club area and the big car stopped in front of my house. Guevara leaned forward slightly on his seat to acknowledge the size of the house and the golf links extending beyond, and smiled softly.

"Tony," he said gently, using my first name, "have you read Kafka's *The Trial?*" The question took me by complete surprise, and the fact that I had not read the book added to my embarrassment.

"No, Commander, I have read *Metamorphosis* and *The Prison* by Kafka, but not *The Trial.*" I thought of saying that I had also read Camus and Sartre, as if it were a kind of cultural quiz, but I knew instinctively that this was not the case. Guevara's had not been a casual question, so I said nothing more.

Instead, Guevara said: "If you haven't read *The Trial,* read it, Tony. Read it. It may explain a lot of things to you. And it may not."

And with a final long look at me, he motioned to the chauffeur, and Commander Ernesto Che Guevara, Founding Father of the Cuban Revolution, looking slightly incongruous in the back seat of a big black Cadillac, disappeared into the morning of a Cuban summer day. Conscious of an experience I would never forget, I watched him disappear with a strange, overwhelming feeling of sadness. Somehow I was sure the feeling was shared.

11

I WASTED NO TIME in procuring for myself copies of Kafka's *The Trial*, in both the English and the Spanish versions. I wanted to be sure no nuance of meaning, no symbolism, was missed, and in the original German, unfortunately, I would have missed the whole book.

For a couple of days, I was immersed in the story to the exclusion of my work, whatever was left of my social life, and even Avis and Alberto. Alberto, in fact, became intrigued himself when I told him that Guevara had suggested I read it, and he was already finding all sorts of hidden meanings on his own.

I, on the other hand, was finding precious little guidance in the book. Alberto asked me for a synopsis, and I wrote one for both of us:

"Kafka's story is a nightmarish recount of the plight of one undistinguished, middle-class clerk confronted with the accusation of an ill-defined crime against society which he doesn't understand or even recall. The 'hero' is tried by a series of phantasmagorical 'courts' holding session in empty, labyrinthian buildings, and the juries are made up of lowbrow, slovenly, grotesque mobs acting without any discernible sense of reason or justice. It is, overall, a singularly depressing story of an innocent man caught up in what appeared to be a totalitarian society bent on destroying him for no reason at all and it ends, in fact, with the man's execution, meaningless and undramatic: a knife stab in a deserted alley by an unknown assassin, without passion or purpose."

I didn't get the message immediately, or perhaps I didn't want to. Whatever I did perceive, I decided not to share with Avis, and I pretended to make light of Alberto's excited comparison between Kafka's fiction and the real-life future for the two of us. But, finally, I gave in to Alberto's dogged intensity.

"All right, Alberto, tell me what it means."

"Boy, are you dumb," Alberto said. "I thought you were the sensitive one in the group . . ."

"Please, Alberto. Whatever it is, I don't like it already," I said impatiently.

"Guevara was simply telling you," Alberto continued, "in a very erudite fashion, I might add, that there is simply no room for the likes of you and me in the new society . . ."

"And, I suppose," I cut in, not supposing at all, "that if we don't do something about it we're going to end up in an alley or some place equally distasteful . . ."

"Very good, Tony," Alberto said. "Very good. I *knew* you had it in you."

I half-laughed at Alberto's delivery, which imitated Julio's humor, but not at the content of his remarks.

"And, also," Alberto went on, "and this fits in with what you told me about your interview with Guevara: that you shouldn't waste your time trying to understand it or make sense of it."

"Alberto, you should have been a priest or an Evangelist," I said. "You'd be good interpreting the Bible for us simple mortals."

However, in the end, little came out of that particular exchange. I was not to be discouraged, and I felt that Guevara's expressed lack of interest in Textilera's fate was good enough for me and, at the very least, meant an indefinite stay of execution. Alberto wasn't so sure, having done a complete emotional about-face and taken over Julio's role of pessimist. Avis didn't bother to conjecture, at least openly, and had simply set for herself a time limit for remaining in Cuba.

Trying to ignore the brooding around me, I proceeded simply to follow the process that had been laid down for me. Guevara's opinion about Textilera was important to Castro by his own admission, and I now had that opinion. Therefore the next clear step was to bring that information personally to the Prime Minister and get a mandate from the highest level which would clear the air and allow me to concentrate on running the mill, paying off a three-million-dollar loan to the National City Bank, trying to get a little money out to my father-in-law, and letting the long-term future take care of itself.

So I repeated the well-learned procedure of telephone calls, messages and visits, and, after one more appeal to Conchita, I was given an appointment to see Castro "some time" on Wednesday.

I arrived at the Agrarian Reform building early on Wednesday and had plenty of time to look around. In looking, I had to admit that the corridors of the ground floor, with people scurrying around like ants, reminded one of Kafka's descriptions of the ghoulish halls—not a very comforting thought.

I went through the routine of the information desk once again, and eventually ended up on the top floor. Conchita was on some sort of assignment away from the office, and the substitute staff advised me rather coldly to find myself a place to wait on a bench somewhere.

"Wait" turned out to be quite an understatement. At the end of the day, I was advised in fairly polite terms that there was really no point in waiting further, since the Prime Minister was definitely not coming to the office that night. I went home disappointed, listened until late to the increasingly dismal news about Cuba–U.S. relations, and returned early on Thursday morning.

I repeated the admission procedure and spent another unproductive morning, even passing up lunch to avoid the briefest absence. During that afternoon, the staff and the "steadies"—those visitors who understood that waiting was their lot and accepted it with unquestioning resignation—began to notice me, and someone even offered me coffee and some of those curled-up, pleasantly oily Cuban crackers. They were certainly a welcome treat.

On Thursday evening I was told again that there was no point in waiting, but this time I ignored it and stretched out on one of the benches with a determination which I was surprised to discern in my make-up.

Sometime during the night—I'm not sure when—I awoke to the sound of loud voices, and although I couldn't see anyone, I was sure that Castro and his entourage had arrived. I didn't dare interrupt, even if the guards would have let me, but I did move to another bench which was located where people leaving the private office couldn't fail to see me.

Throughout the night, I heard sounds of conversation, occasional laughter and, once in a while, the clinking of glasses. Fidel was known to be a steady but controlled drinker of the sweetish and potent Spanish brandy which the Spaniards call cognac to the chagrin of the French, and it could be assumed that a fair amount of it was being consumed during that all-night meeting.

I spent the night in the uncomfortable conflict between absolute exhaustion, both physical and mental, and the awareness that I couldn't afford to be sound asleep and passed by, after all my efforts, by Castro's quick exit. Nonetheless, I surrendered to moments of fitful sleep, and eventually the black quarters began to light up with the soft glow of dawn which would soon give way to the bright Cuban morning sun.

A burst of laughter, the crack of a wooden door opened too suddenly, and a group of men emerged into the anteroom of Castro's office along with a cloud of bluish cigar smoke.

I was instantly awake. I sat up and made a futile pass at my hair, but didn't leave the bench. There were five or six men coming out, still finishing a conversation and showing the signs of a sleepless night. I immediately recognized Fidel and his brother Raul, and, both to my surprise and elation for what it might mean, I discerned the figure of my old labor-leader friend Jesus Soto.

Fidel spotted me on my bench.

"My God," he said, "Navarro, what are you doing here so early in the morning?"

Jesus Soto looked at me and laughed. "Fidel, you've got it wrong. Tony isn't early. He just never left."

Soto knew me well enough to know he was on safe ground. Besides, my rumpled appearance left very little doubt. Fidel walked up to me and said, "Tony, I have to hand it to you. Whatever else you may be, you've got perseverance and the guts to go after what you want. I wish we had more of that in some of our own men. What's the latest in your problem?"

I got up from the bench.

"Fidel," I said carefully, "we all work for what we believe in, in our own ways.

You sent word through Conchita that I should see Che Guevara about the confiscation of our mills, and I've seen Guevara. He doesn't insist on it. In fact, he doesn't care one way or the other. He said it's up to you."

"Listen, Tony, don't worry about your properties," Fidel said, looking at Jesus Soto as if for confirmation. "You won't have any problems. We're both very tired. I know I am, and you should go home and get some rest. Come on, let's both of us go home," and the giant of a man threw his arm around me and steered me toward his private elevator. Soto and the rest of the men stayed behind, still talking, although Soto and I exchanged a parting glance.

At the elevator, Fidel's guards made the regulation move to bar my way, but Castro waved them aside and, with his arm still around my shoulder, we got into the elevator together.

"Did you see the Che at the bank's office?" Castro asked on the way down.
"Yes."

"How was he?" Castro insisted.

"He was fine, Fidel," I answered. "He looked fine to me, and he was very cordial."

"I'll bet he's just like a fish out of water," Fidel chuckled, and nothing else was said till we reached the garage. Fidel got out first, started to get into his car, then turned around and said: "Don't worry, Tony. Go home and get some sleep. You deserve it."

Fidel's big car moved away, with one patrol car ahead and one behind it, and I was left standing outside the elevator in the garage of the building, trying hard to comprehend that, after all the work, all the waiting, all the disappointments, I had accomplished my mission.

I went back to the Textilera Havana office later that morning after only a quick shower, a cup of coffee, and a hurried report to Avis about the good news. She said, "Good, honey, you deserve it," and "Good luck!" as I rushed out.

At the office, I telephoned Alberto with the news and was a little disappointed that he wasn't as excited as I was. I reasoned that his reaction was due partly to caution and partly to a very natural feeling of envy. No matter how much of a friend, Alberto was human, and for him to lose his sugar mill while I kept our textile business couldn't possibly seem fair.

Even so, I was sure that my friend would come around when he thought it out more objectively. Whatever property was *not* taken these days was a victory of sorts for *everyone,* and I would point that out to Alberto at a more appropriate moment. For now, there were more important things to do than assuage his hurt feelings.

I told the good news to those executives on the staff whom I trusted, but I avoided the Assistant Treasurer. He and others in his camp would learn about it through the normal office grapevine, and I only hoped that none of them would be able to interfere with a clear dictum from the top about Textilera's fate.

Finally, I went to see the Interventor and told him all that had happened in the last few days in every detail. He listened attentively and even appeared sympathetic; after all, for a minor official to be confronted with someone who had just spent some time with the Prime Minister himself was pretty heady stuff, and the young man was impressed.

"I am happy for you, Mr. Navarro, and if that is Dr. Castro's decision, I will certainly structure my job around it. After all, we haven't had any problems so far, have we?"

The placating tone amused me. This guy would obviously sway with the wind, whichever way it blew.

"I don't know what the next step will be," I told him, "but I'll keep you informed, and I guess you'll be hearing from the Ministry anyway."

"Yes, of course," the Interventor said. "I have to have some official word from my superiors. In the meantime, I will continue to follow my instructions as originally issued. In fact, I have a letter here from the Ministry which apparently was written this very morning and which asks that both you and I come to see the Vice Minister this afternoon with some figures which I have taken the liberty to request from your staff already."

"No problem," I said. "I'll be back early after lunch and we can go anytime you say. Maybe this is the word we're expecting. One thing I'll say for Fidel. Once he's involved, he certainly doesn't waste much time." It was difficult not to brag openly about my success.

I lunched with the staff at noon, and of course we discussed the new development at length. We decided not to call Burke Hedges until matters had been more clearly resolved. I was much too excited for that kind of a telephone call, anyway.

So at three o'clock that afternoon, the Interventor and I headed for the Ministry for the Recovery of Assets. The atmosphere there wasn't much different from that of the Agrarian Reform building. It, too, had its Kafkian aspects, although the people waiting there seemed to be a cut above those I had seen at the Agrarian Reform offices.

I didn't have to wait long, since I was in good company with the Interventor, and we were ushered into the waiting room outside the Vice Minister's office. To say that I waited impatiently was an understatement; I was at the peak of excitement. Everything I had been working for during the past few long months was going to be resolved right then and there. The man at the top had spoken, and that was it.

We walked into the Vice Minister's office. The Interventor closed the door behind him and approached the desk politely while I stayed where I was.

"The Interventor for Textilera, sir, with Mr. Navarro," he said. The Vice Minister had several men around him and a desk full of papers, and he looked up at the young man for a moment, purposely ignoring me.

The Vice Minister addressed the Interventor in a voice tight with anger. "Let's not waste time," he said. "We don't have any to waste." He reached in a desk drawer, pulled out a newspaper, tossed it aggressively at the Interventor across the desk, and said, "Tell the Hedges family and your capitalist friend there that *this* is our answer. You tell them. I have nothing more to say. You'll get your instructions in writing. Good day."

The Interventor glanced at the paper. His face went white, and he pulled me out of the office. Outside, he silently handed me the copy of the official *Revolucion* afternoon paper.

The headlines were in the very large type used in other countries for announcing wars. They read:

"HEDGES EMPIRE CONFISCATED. $45 MILLION IN ASSETS RECOVERED FOR THE STATE. TAKEOVER SET FOR TOMORROW."

It was final, the paper said. There was no appeal. The Cabinet had signed it. They had proved no wrongdoing but, according to the paper, it was simply "in the interest of the people."

The words were like sledgehammer blows. I read them again. Then I got up, avoided the Interventor's look of compassion, walked to the men's room and got violently ill. It was a reflex action, simply the result of a shock too much to bear.

When I recovered, I went back to say goodbye to the Interventor. He only said, "Sorry," then shouted after me as an awkward afterthought, "I'll see you tomorrow, Mr. Navarro."

Out on the street, newspaper boys were shouting about the confiscation of the Hedges properties. I saw a few people I knew, but no one was unkind enough to stop me. I went into one of the many *bodegas* in the area, subconsciously avoiding the bars where I might have met friends. I bought myself a drink and took it with me to the public telephone.

I called the Treasurer at Textilera and asked him to please telephone Burke Hedges and give him the news.

Then I called Avis. It wasn't easy but, trooper that she was, she took it standing up and even managed a few words of encouragement and said something about a new life somewhere else. That was not at all what I had in mind at that moment, but I let it pass and said that I would be home soon, looking forward to a quiet dinner.

Finally, I telephoned Alberto and gave him the news. There was no reaction, because Alberto and I knew each other too well.

12

WITH THE CONFISCATION of Textilera, my material responsibilities ceased to exist. My ideological responsibilities had ended even before. The confiscation, to be sure, was the last straw; I wasn't trying to fool anyone, least of all myself.

It was one thing—a devastating thing—for Fidel to betray the Revolution. But I was human, after all, and he had now also betrayed me. To save the family business was terribly important, and a personal success if achieved. But my *faith* was more important than that and, once again, it had been dashed. Would I have followed Fidel, even in the face of the confiscation, if he had not violated the renewed hopes of so many of us? I think so, but I'll never know for sure. In novels, motivations tend to be neatly packaged, but in real life it simply doesn't work that way. In the end, however, we are judged by our actions, and I knew then *what* I had to do, though I didn't know *how* to do it. I had never even been a politician, let alone a revolutionist, or counter-revolutionist, if that's what I had to be.

It took several weeks for the take-over of Textilera, although from the very first day armed guards were posted at every door and in every office. I came around occasionally and, of course, I went to all the company meetings, now attended as well by Government officials.

In my relations with the employees, I joined the ranks of the legions who learn, the hard way, who your friends are when the chips are down. On the other hand, I was treated with respect by the "new owners."

A few weeks after the confiscation, we were invited to a reception by our friends, the Brazilian Ambassadors. We were delighted, depressed as we were and tired of well-meaning "condolences." Besides, Avis was definitely preparing to leave Cuba and it would be a good chance to say goodbye. Finally, in my "future," embassies might be important . . .

As fate would have it, this time Castro came to the reception. At one point, he spotted us nearby, broke from his own crowded circle and approached us. Whatever I may have felt, common courtesy dictated at least civility on my part. I was curious about Castro's personal betrayal of his promise, but I knew intuitively that, if I was going to be of any service to myself and my country in the future, it would not do to be openly antagonistic.

"How you doing, Tony?" Castro said, extending his hand. I shook the hand and said, seriously: "You know how I'm doing, Fidel."

Fidel nodded recognition and said, "I know, Tony, and I'm going to tell you something you probably won't believe. *I don't do everything that gets done in this country.* Don't forget that." Then Castro, bowing respectfully toward Avis, turned around and rejoined his friends.

I felt that, as long as I lived, I wouldn't *quite* understand this man. What a tremendous actor he was—or was he really acting? How could he plan such a devastating deception and then take the time to seek out sympathy for his actions, almost to apologize? If Castro didn't do everything that got done in the country, which might well be true, he certainly could *stop* anything from happening if he wanted to. Obviously, he hadn't wanted to. But in the end, I asked myself, what does it matter? It was the *system*, a system that smothered freedom with terror, a system I must now be ready to fight. I was ready.

The next night we had a farewell dinner at home—just family, although Alberto was invited. Paulette had left the island some weeks ago, probably permanently. It was a quiet dinner, full of nostalgic recollections of the fun days with the Batistas and other friends, with very little political conversation. At one point, Alberto said: "You saw Fidel again?"

I nodded. Alberto had heard all about the encounter anyway.

"And the bastard actually told you he had nothing to do with the confiscation?" Alberto asked, rhetorically.

"Yes."

"I think the man is mad," Alberto said. "In fact, I think he was always mad, but cunning as a fox."

"You should know," I replied, with a mild dig which no longer had any sting.

"Yes, I should," Alberto accepted. "Do you think he's a Communist?"

"I never thought he was," I said. "He never seemed disciplined enough for the Party, but times and parties change, I guess. I remember I almost insulted the First Secretary of the U.S. Embassy when he showed me a dossier claiming that Castro *was* a Communist, mentioning that trouble in Bogotá several years back —you know, Fidel bragging about killing some Colombian priests . . ."

"And what about Ambassador Smith?" Alberto interrupted. "He certainly thought Fidel was a Commie."

"My God," I agreed, "Earl Smith told my family, told everyone who would listen, even told Eisenhower officially, that the Castro movement was Communist—and I, smart-ass that I am, went along with those who thought Mr. Smith was crazy, witch-hunting, out of touch with the people."

I paused, tired—too tired.

"He was quite a guy, Smith," I mused. "He was accused by Castro, in print, of having sold out to Batista. *Bohemia* said he did it in exchange for a better deal on a nickel mine. Smith was teed off. He wasn't that kind of man. He showed

me the wire he sent to the State Department. 'There are two accusations I won't
stand for. One is of being a fairy, and the other of being a crook.' State called
a press conference and cleared him publicly, though it really wasn't necessary; it
turned out the nickel contract had been signed by Smith's predecessor . . ."

"Anyway," I went on," what does it matter if Castro was or wasn't—or *isn't*
—a Commie? Why would you care how many stripes the tiger has when he's
coming to eat you?"

"Okay, Tony." Alberto was a little overwhelmed. "We promised we wouldn't
talk politics."

"All right, we won't, but please make me one more promise," I said earnestly.
"I know you've been making plans to join Paulette in the States. Promise me you
won't leave until I have a chance to talk to you again."

"What are you going to do?" Alberto asked, curious, the old nose for drama
sniffing.

"Never mind," I said. "I don't know yet. I honestly don't know; but I figure
if there were ever two people who have a special responsibility in this mess, it's
Alberto Fowler and Tony Navarro."

Alberto thought for an instant, and then he said: "Okay, Tony, I promise. I
can probably find some reasonable excuse to hang around for a while. Is that what
you mean?"

"That's what I mean," I said.

Avis came back from putting the children to bed and sat down, crying softly.
The parting would be very difficult for her, but she had been unhappy for months.
The whole traumatic experience had been too much. She had hardly seen me—
sometimes not at all for days at a time—and when she did see me, I was worried
and uptight. She just couldn't take that life any more. She couldn't stand the
Communist regime. She didn't want it for herself or for her children. The only
answer was to go.

They left the next morning, without any trouble at the airport which I had
halfway feared, and the children, in their innocence, were delighted that they
were leaving "on vacation" and that Dad would soon be joining them.

I returned to a house that now seemed very quiet indeed, and it made me
realize that most of the houses in the neighborhood were just as silent. It was
the kind of thought that brings a lump to the throat.

I spoke briefly to Gisela, the beautiful young mulatto girl who, despite her
husband's confused loyalties, had kept her allegiance and affection for the family.
She said the appropriate things and looked at me so sadly that I had to turn
around quickly to avoid breaking down and embarrassing us both. Still not facing
her, I told her that I'd be back for dinner or would call if I couldn't make it, that
I'd stop by the hospital to see Nanita, who had fallen and fractured her hip, and
that I would then spend most of the day at Textilera, getting ready to move my
stuff out.

Nanita was doing as well as could be expected for someone with a broken hip
at her age. She was conscious and in not too much pain, but sad and lonely. I

hated to add to her sorrow, but she had to know sooner or later that the family had left, so I told her.

Then it occurred to me to talk to the doctors and find out if it would be all right to bring Nanita home with me during her convalescence. I knew enough about medicine to guess that, in fact, it wouldn't matter at all whether Nanita stayed or moved, that the old bones were just brittle and wouldn't heal, and that Nanita's convalescence could end in only one way. If it had to be, however, I was sure she'd rather be with me.

At the office, I first went as a matter of both courtesy and self-interest to pay my respects to the new manager of Textilera. After all, there were still many ways in which decisions taken by the company could affect the Hedges family and me personally, for better or for worse.

The manager was cordial enough, and he appeared anxious to maintain a pleasant relationship for as long as it had to last, which obviously wouldn't be long. The man was a lieutenant in the Rebel Army and, naturally, he wore his fatigues and his handgun to work. He told me frankly that he had had a relatively brief stint in the Army, and that his only civilian job prior to the Revolution had been that of an elementary school teacher in one of the rural provinces. Therefore, his only qualification for the job was loyalty and commitment to the Revolution. It was one more example, I thought, of a well-meaning but unprepared man being given a position of responsibility.

I, in turn, told the lieutenant that I planned to move my personal things to some new offices I had rented, and he granted his permission and wished me well. Toward the end of the brief interview, the Assistant Treasurer came in with some papers to discuss with the lieutenant, and I, for the first time, felt the full impact of being a stranger in my own company.

Back in my own office, my pretty young secretary was waiting by my desk—guarding it, in fact. She was in her early twenties, and she had the hourglass figure that was more characteristic of earlier generations of Cuban women than of the modern girls patterned after the U.S. and the cult of slimness.

Maria Antonieta was openly crying and making very little effort to stop it, and my arrival to clean out the desk naturally didn't help.

"Wherever you're going, I want to go with you, Mr. Navarro," she blurted out, without even saying hello. "I don't care what it is, but I don't want to stay here without you and the family and with these people running it."

I had already thought about that, so I said, "Don't worry, Maria Antonieta, you're coming with me if you really want to. You know the sugar business was my first love, so I've made arrangements with a New York brokerage firm to be their representative in Havana."

Visibly recovering from her crying jag, Maria Antonieta began to smile.

"It won't be a big deal, no big office, in fact, just you and me." If I had intended to discourage her, I sure missed the mark, because the tentative smile now spread all over her face. I was happy that she was happy.

"I know the sugar business pretty well," I said. "Anyone who worked with Julio Lobo has to, and I have the contacts. Maybe some of the owners have changed, but I'll bet I know most of the people running the sugar business today. It shouldn't be difficult."

"I'm sure you can do anything you set out to do," Maria Antonieta said loyally.

"Well," I said, "my heart isn't really in it, but it'll keep me eating and it'll keep you eating. I guess you know my family has left."

"I know." Maria Antonieta's eyes filled again. "Mrs. Navarro, Avis, called to say goodbye, and I've been crying ever since."

"Well, Maria Antonieta," I said, "it won't be forever. At least we have work, and I have my reasons for wanting to stay."

That was as far as I dared to go on that subject, even though I knew I could trust Maria Antonieta completely. We discussed the new offices, the decoration, and the teletype which would have to be installed, and we decided right then and there to go to visit the new place.

My new work was simple enough if one knew the ropes, and fortunately I did. It involved buying large amounts of raw sugar, anywhere from 500 to 10,000 tons, at the going market price and putting together a full shipload for transport to the U.S. refineries. As I had hoped, I found that many of the men I had worked with before were still in the business, which made life a lot easier.

Communications were mostly by teletype, which I enjoyed handling myself, having dabbled at it during the Lobo days, and several times a day I telephoned my old friend Harold Bloomer, the parent broker in New York. The sugar work provided government approval, unrestricted access to the ports, valid reasons for an occasional trip to the States—in short, the perfect "front" if I ever needed it.

To make it even better, a few months later Bloomer's New York company would make a connection with a French manufacturer to supply tinplate to Cuba. That would not only bring additional revenues to my little enterprise, but would also provide access to a few more government ministries.

"The offices," as I called them with a straight face, were in fact one single, long, rectangular room which Maria Antonieta and I managed to break up into little areas for reception, such as it was, i.e., one sofa and one overstuffed chair, the impressive but tiny telex section, and space for two desks. At the back of the room was a filing area with a door to a central section of the building which housed the bathrooms and storage space for the whole floor.

My work at the new office went on successfully and uneventfully. The living it provided, from a fixed salary and a small commission, was at least enough to keep our little household afloat. That household now included Gisela and Nanita, whom I had been allowed to bring home. It was also enough to keep Maria Antonieta and her family reasonably well.

The Cuban government, meantime, was following the preordained path away from any pretense of democracy and into the Soviet camp, and had become a totalitarian, despotic, one-man tyranny in the name of the people—people whom, in truth, the tyrant despised because, somehow, they did not conform quickly enough to the utopic "new man" which he demanded.

For my part, my decision had been made, but I had no political connections who might help me get into the fight against Castro. Alberto, who might have been a source of contacts, couldn't be expected to produce an entree to the underground subculture: his friends had been Castro's allies in the early days, and those who had turned against him were very wary of newcomers.

To my surprise, it was Maria Antonieta—in whom I had finally, if cautiously, confided—who came up with a possibility—two possibilities, in fact. She had two friends, she said, who might be useful: Alberto Gonzalez-Recio and Carlos Solis.

Maria Antonieta explained that Gonzalez-Recio and Solis had been in and around politics most of their young lives, all the way through high school and the university to a deep involvement today. From their earliest years, they had been connected with the political party represented by Tony Varona—a progressive party in social matters but firmly dedicated to democracy.

Tony Varona himself had risen to the position of Prime Minister and President of the Senate during the last democratic regime in Cuba, before the days of Batista. Varona had supported Castro, because Fidel's popularity and apparent selflessness in the latter days of the Batista regime could not be denied. After the take-over, Varona tried, at first discreetly and then openly, to have Castro bring back the democracy he so fervently promised in his guerrilla days. Finally, totally discouraged, Varona left for exile and organized the anti-Castro movement called *Rescate Democratico Revolucionario* (i.e., The Revolutionary Rescue of Democracy) which eventually became well known all over Cuba as simply *Rescate*, or Rescue.

According to Maria Antonieta, her friend Alberto was a leading light of the underground movement in Cuba—young, courageous, respected by his generation, and absolutely reliable. Moreover, and more to the point, young Gonzalez-Recio happened to share one of the offices in our building, in which he and Solis carried on the *pretense* of an import business and the *reality* of one manual printing press and one duplicating machine, hidden in their storage room.

So it happened that hot Indian summer afternoon in September of 1960; Maria Antonieta and I had come back from lunch and were sitting around straightening out files and waiting for telephone calls. Suddenly the back door to our office burst open, and a tall, athletic young man rushed in.

"Tony," he gasped, glancing at Maria Antonieta, "I know all about you and you know all about me. The G-2's coming for me any minute. Here's our latest pamphlet." He shoved some folded papers at me. "It's the original. Don't lose it, and don't let 'em find it. I'll be in touch through Maria Antonieta as soon as I can."

The whole thing couldn't have taken more than ten seconds, and Alberto Gonzalez-Recio was out the front door.

Brushing aside the exultant thought that I was, at last, involved, I tried to concentrate on a hiding place. My first thought was the filing cabinets, but I knew immediately that would be too obvious. A second glance landed on the telex machine and, obviously, that was it. I opened up the little glass cover on the printer and stuffed the papers inside, away from the moving parts. I asked Maria Antonieta to sit there and pretend she was sending a message.

"Just type anything that comes to your mind," I told her, "whatever looks legitimate. You know, something about a boat at some port. And once in a while press the 'answer-back' button and you'll get something back. Those jerks won't know the difference."

Maria Antonieta obediently sat down at the machine and turned it on, obviously praying to her favorite saint. She hadn't hit one key when the front door opened without a knock and with an authority that left no question as to who our visitors were.

One soldier with a submachine gun, index finger on the trigger guard, held the door open. Two plainclothesmen, pistols drawn, rushed through the office without even looking at us, and out the back door which, unfortunately, Gonzalez-Recio had left open. There were several other men outside, and a more composed type, obviously the leader, came into the office and stood there. To me he said, "You know a man called Gonzalez-Recio who has an office in this building, a tall young man?"

"No," I lied, "except that there's a tenant by that name in the building—some sort of import-export business."

The G-2 chief said nothing, and started after his two men. Before he could reach them, one of them came back and said, "We found the machines, lieutenant, hidden in the back room—one press and one duplicator—but our man isn't there. There's no sign of any pamphlets."

"Well, goddammit," the lieutenant said, "the machines aren't there for nothing. They obviously print the stuff and get it out of here fast. But the originals have got to be somewhere. Go back there and keep looking."

He turned back to me and said, "Mr. Navarro, we know you're the ex-owner of Textilera, and we have nothing against you. But you could be tempted. After all, you probably think you'd have good reason." All the while he looked intently at me.

I was more scared than angry, but still I said, "You may be right, lieutenant. I might have good reason. But the fact is that we've only been here for a few weeks and I don't know the man. I may have bumped into him in the john some time, but we've never met. I'm trying to run a sugar brokerage business. The government knows me, including the Prime Minister, and I don't need any problems."

"We know all about that, too, Mr. Navarro," the lieutenant said, and added, "You don't mind if we look around?" Without waiting for an answer, he motioned to one of his men and they both started looking through the desks and the filing cabinets.

Meantime, Maria Antonieta was furiously pecking at the teletype. Once in a while, little bells and buzzers would sound and, even in the midst of the whole thing, I found it hard not to smile.

The lieutenant gave up and came back to where I was standing.

"What's that gadget tied to?" he asked, pointing to the teletype.

"To New York," I said, knowing full well that was a bad word and enjoying it.

"What kind of messages do you send?" he asked me.

"Just regular business messages—sugar prices, arrival of sugar shipments, the usual kind of thing in this business." I hoped whatever Maria Antonieta was typing at that moment would bear me out.

The lieutenant turned to one of his men. "Are these things monitored?"

"Yes, lieutenant," the man answered. "They're all monitored at the central office."

The lieutenant nodded thoughtfully and walked over to the teletype. At that time, thank God, the machine was transmitting the "answer-back" from New York, and no one unfamiliar with the system could make anything out of *that*. The lieutenant nudged Maria Antonieta away and leaned over the machine, intrigued, and actually lifted the little glass cover. This could be it, I thought. I held my breath and put my hand on Maria Antonieta's shoulder before she could gasp, not one second too soon.

But the lieutenant was too fascinated to do a proper job and stared at the gobbledy-gook of the answer-back, missing the folded papers which I, from my angle, could see frighteningly well. The lieutenant straightened up, and I sighed inaudibly, relaxing my grip on Maria Antonieta and leaving finger marks on her shoulder.

"What was that stuff being printed?" the lieutenant asked, "and what's it mean?"

"That's known as the answer-back, lieutenant," Maria Antonieta said, speaking up for the first time. "It just means that New York is ready to receive our message."

"Well, then, who were you sending to *before?*" asked the lieutenant, no fool.

Maria Antonieta looked up at me helplessly.

"What happens, lieutenant," I rushed in, "is that each message is individual. Each time we have to call and get the answer back before we can transmit."

"Oh," the lieutenant said, either convinced or sufficiently confused.

The lieutenant called his men, gave instructions to have the duplicating machines removed and to seal Gonzalez-Recio's office, told us to contact him if we saw or heard from the wanted man, mumbled a brief apology for the intrusion, and left.

Maria Antonieta and I stood there in the middle of the office, looking at each other, expecting the front door to open again suddenly with some typical police afterthought. When it didn't, we fell together in a spontaneous and exuberant hug—a sort of "we did it" celebration. I had passed my first test.

So now the original of the pamphlet must be gotten back to Gonzalez-Recio, who obviously was now a marked man who must go underground.

Maria Antonieta thought she knew how to reach him, so we decided to try to find him, return the pamphlet, and ask him what to do next. Besides, I knew with certainty that this young man would be my contact with the anti-Castro movement.

As we were about to start, it amused me to realize that, in true spy fashion, I was thinking that Maria Antonieta and I should not be seen leaving together. It just might be what the G-2 expected. So I asked Maria Antonieto to go on ahead and told her that I would meet her at Club 21, named after the famous New York restaurant, in the Vedado section of Havana. When I got there half an hour later, she was waiting nervously but safely at the bar.

I greeted the proprietor, Raul Jerez, an old friend, ordered a drink, and slipped the papers to Maria Antonieta under the table. You never know who might be watching, I told myself craftily. Maria Antonieta stashed the papers in the purse beside her and told me that she had already been in touch with Gonzalez-Recio. In fact, she had arranged to get him to my house in about an hour.

That was fine with me, for an hour would be plenty of time to get home, alert Gisela, and clear the house of any visitors. We left the bar and had driven no more than five minutes, lost in conversation, when we stopped short and, after a frantic look at each other and around the car, tore back to Club 21. Maria Antonieta had left her purse at the bar.

As I rushed through the door, probably scared white, Raul was standing right there, holding the purse and looking at it in what I guiltily thought was a suspiciously speculative way. I grabbed the purse, hugged Raul, and took off again. I never did know if he suspected anything.

Maria Antonieta and I had been home for about half an hour when Gonzalez-Recio arrived, wearing a ridiculous raincoat and a wool cap. On a hot, sunny day, it made me wonder if the underground people knew what they were doing, after all. Maria Antonieta rushed over and hugged him, telling him excitedly about the search and the teletype and about forgetting her purse. Gonzalez-Recio smiled and congratulated her on her courage, and I wondered fleetingly if there was more than friendship between those two.

I took Gonzalez-Recio to a small sitting room upstairs at the back of the house, next to my bedroom, and gave him back the pamphlet. I suggested that, under the circumstances, he might want to stay overnight. There was plenty of room and certainly lots of places to hide, and the house itself was isolated enough for his purpose.

Alberto Gonzalez-Recio was grateful for the offer and said to me: "Thanks very much, Tony . . . I guess I'd better call you that."

"Of course," I agreed.

"In fact, Tony, I was hoping you'd ask me to stay, but not just overnight. I know you have the room and I know where your feelings lie, so I'd like to ask you to let me stay indefinitely."

I tried to hide my surprise.

"You may laugh," Gonzalez-Recio continued, "but all my belongings are waiting outside by the front door."

I was thoughtful for a moment. I hadn't expected this.

"I know it's asking a lot," Gonzalez-Recio said, "because it endangers you, too, but I have a feeling that you're ready to take that risk." He looked at me for confirmation, and continued, "I know what you've been through, and you must be ripe to help us out. We badly need places to stay which aren't easy to trace. As for me, I know I'm through. I'm 'burned.' I can't operate any longer. The G-2 has everything they need to go after me. You know the penalty for printing and spreading subversive propaganda."

"I know," I said. I was thinking hard of the risks.

"The point is, Tony, that I won't be going in and out of your house. When I do leave here, it'll be with friends who'll get me out of the country, or with the G-2 who'll execute me. Sorry to sound dramatic, but those are the facts."

I could only manage to say again, "I know."

Then I suddenly made up my mind. Isn't *involvement* what I had wanted, had hoped for? So here it was.

"You're right," I said firmly. "I *am* ready to help, maybe more so than you think. I welcome the opportunity to meet you, and you're welcome to stay as long as you want to . . . as long as it's safe for you."

"Thank you," said Gonzalez-Recio simply.

"Actually, Alberto, it may not be as one-sided as you think," I said, managing a smile. "For one thing, I could use your help with Nanita. She's my great-aunt and I love her dearly. She's bedridden in the corner room with a broken hip which won't heal—she'll never get up again. Gisela, the maid—who is thoroughly reliable, by the way—tries to look after her as best she can. I help when I'm here, and so does my mother when she visits, but a strong man around the house would be a great blessing. Nanita has to be turned occasionally or picked up, and that isn't easy in her condition, even for two people."

"I'll be glad to help," Alberto said.

"Thanks," I said. "But that's only favor number one. The important favor is that I think I can help in the fight against Castro. I want to join the resistance."

Gonzalez-Recio said nothing, but he looked interested, so I continued: "I know about your movement, and I know who the main leader is. I respect Tony Varona as a great democrat and as an honest man who had the chance to be otherwise, but never gave in. I think people will rally round him. I think he's one of our best hopes. I'd like to work for him."

"Before we go any further, Tony," Gonzalez-Recio interrupted, "and since we seem to be on the right subject, you should know that my war name is 'Lorenzo,' and I suggest that from now on you never again call me Alberto or Gonzalez-Recio. We both should try to forget my name—and your servants should never know it—because it's dangerous, particularly since the episode this afternoon . . . I guess they found the machines?"

"Yes, they did," I answered, "and they sealed your office."

"That was very good, the teletype idea," Lorenzo reflected. "It was fast thinking, 'thinking on your feet' as they say; you need a lot of that in our work. I think you're in the underground already, Tony, and don't know it." I smiled, pleased at a compliment from a pro.

"We'll have to find other ways to print the pamphlets," Lorenzo then said. "Perhaps you can help us . . . after we've had a little chat."

Maria Antonieta had been sitting quietly all this time, and at the mention of the "little chat," she decided to take her cue and left the room, ostensibly to check on Nanita.

Lorenzo got up from his chair in the tiny sitting room which led out to a small terrace overlooking the golf links. Avis and I had fixed up the little room as a cozy place to entertain small groups for the very reason of the terrace. It was roofed, the floor covered with white gravel, and it was a great spot to catch the cool evening breeze.

Lorenzo, however, prudently stayed in the sitting room and settled on one corner of the small French sofa.

"Before I can help you," Lorenzo said, "or let you help us, I must know *why* you want to do it, even though I may have my own ideas about it. I also must know how much you're willing to risk."

"I think the second question is answered," I said, "by the fact that I'm here and my family is gone. I'm willing to risk it all. I don't want to be corny, and I hope it never happens, but I'm willing to risk my life."

"Very good, Tony," Lorenzo said, "because that's exactly what you would be doing. In fact, you're doing it right now, just by taking me in."

"I understand that, too," I acknowledged. "Now for your first question. My motives. I think I should make it very clear to you—even if it shocks you—that I don't want to fight Castro because he's a Communist—if he is, in fact, a Communist. Much as I despise that system, that's not my reason." I paused, and Lorenzo waited.

"If Communism could be implanted in our country," I went on slowly, thinking my way, "established by the wave of a magic wand, it wouldn't disturb me that much. I personally would not want to live under that system and I'd just leave. But the materialistic features of Communism, the atheism, don't really bother me. You must understand that I'm not a very good Catholic, despite my education, but I don't think of myself as a bad man. Sometimes the iconoclastic approach of the Communists gives me pleasure when I consider the hypocrites I've known, with chapels in their homes but little charity in their hearts. I don't think Fidel is so wrong when he says Christ would take a hard look at what we've done to His teachings. Not in that, he's not wrong."

Lorenzo was not a philosopher, and less a theologian, and he was probably a little puzzled at my confessions, but he said nothing.

"What I will not put up with, absolutely will *not* tolerate, is the terror which Castro apparently feels is both necessary and justified to establish the system *he* wants for the Cuban people—and I don't care what the damned system is. I will not pay the price to get there. That's my first objection."

Lorenzo hadn't bargained for a speech, but he listened.

"The second objection," I went on, "is that I am for democracy first and last. And democracy, boiled down to one word, means elections—free, secret, universal elections. Whatever the system is, I want the people to be able to change it if that's what the majority wants. It's the ability to change it that counts, not whether it is good or bad, and that principle Castro has openly denounced.

"Finally, Lorenzo, the son-of-a-bitch has betrayed everything I believed in, including himself. It will take years for the good ideas he once professed to have —and with which many of us agreed—to ever be seriously considered again, because he has dragged them down, used them for his own purposes, and made a goddamned mockery of every one of them. If Cuba ever survives him, we may well go back to the Stone Age ideologically, and it will take years, generations perhaps, to get back to the incredible opportunity we once had when he took over. And, to get down to the very bottom of it, I made an ass of myself backing him up, and if you want a personal, selfish reason for wanting to join you, say that I want to redeem myself."

Lorenzo was a little overwhelmed by my outburst. He probably would have been satisfied with any simple explanation, but what Lorenzo hadn't understood was that there was no longer any other way for me.

"Tony," Lorenzo said, getting back to concrete matters after giving me the courtesy of a moment of quiet reflection, "as you know, Tony Varona is in Miami, and I don't think this is the time for you to go there. The man you must meet is our leader here in Cuba. I can and will give you a recommendation, because I think you could be useful to us; but only our number one man can accept you. His name is Max. That's his code name, of course, and you'll be proud to work with him."

"I'd like to meet Max, Lorenzo, if I may. I've heard of him. I guess everyone has."

"I can't take you to him in my condition," Lorenzo said, "and obviously we can't risk having Max come here. He doesn't know you, you don't know him, and there's no reason for a visit. And we can't afford the slightest risk of exposing him."

"What can we do, then?" I asked.

"Let me think about it," Lorenzo said. "I may be able to come up with a go-between, a contact we can trust. I may have a candidate, but I've got to think about it, and I'd like to make a few phone calls."

I looked a little surprised at the thought of using the telephone, which was almost certainly monitored, and Lorenzo noticed it.

"Don't worry about the calls, Tony," he said. "We've had a lot of experience, and if we're going to be caught, it won't be that way. Let me sleep on it. You go about your work with your wonderful secretary tomorrow, and when you come back, I'll try to have an answer."

I agreed, and then decided it was cocktail time. At my ring, Gisela brought us some drinks, along with Maria Antonieta, and beamed her pleasure at serving "company" again, beautiful white teeth gleaming in the café-au-lait face. We enjoyed our drinks on the small terrace with the gravel which slipped and crunched under our feet, sharing the excitement of the moment as well as the beautiful green view.

If you strained your eyes you could see at a distance most of the large houses that circled the golf links, white spots of concrete which appeared when the trees moved with the afternoon breeze.

"I'll tell you," I said to Lorenzo, "I never thought anyone should have left Cuba, but who can really stand in judgment? Certainly not me. They say that money is cowardly, and that's probably right. But it may just be that the rich have the opportunity of mobility which the poor lack, the money to get the hell out of a hopeless situation."

We finished our drinks and I showed Lorenzo his room, where Gisela had already stowed his belongings. I left him to get settled while I drove Maria Antonieta home.

I spent the next day at the office, trying to go about my business as usual, but found myself besieged by the curious but well-meaning tenants in the building who had heard about the "unfortunate episode" the day before.

During the day there was a routine call from the G-2 office, inquiring about Mr. Alberto Gonzalez-Recio, and I repeated our story that I had never met the man and probably wouldn't recognize him if I saw him on the street.

"Look, I'm trying very hard to make a new life for myself in Cuba. I want to help the Revolution, whatever you may think. And I want to stay in my country. I wish the police would appreciate that and let me go about my work. If I hear anything about Gonzalez-Recio, which I doubt, I certainly will call the police. I owe nothing to Mr. Gonzalez-Recio and just want to be left alone."

When the day was over, I left for home slightly earlier than usual (but not *too* much earlier), anxious to hear what, if anything, Lorenzo had been able to arrange for me to meet "Max."

At home, I went directly upstairs, not even checking in on Nanita, although Gisela assured me as I came in that there was no problem there.

Although Lorenzo had been given his own room, I found him in the little sitting room off my bedroom, sipping some rum which I had of course made freely available to him. The minute I came in, the question was in the air, and there was no need to ask it.

"I think I've got it," Lorenzo said. "I've made a few phone calls, cleared you as much as I can—we have code words for that, too—and I think we've come up with someone who knows both Max and you; at least, I think he knows you. He seems to know everyone in your social circle." Lorenzo smiled. "I think it's part of his business."

"Okay, Lorenzo. Who is it?" I asked.

"He's a man . . . in fact, a doctor, called Mendez. Raul Mendez Pirez. Do you know him?"

I couldn't believe it. Dr. Mendez as a contact man?

"Of course I know him, Lorenzo. Who the hell doesn't?"

"Well, sometimes we use Dr. Mendez to get men into the embassies when they get burned, the way I am right now. However," he said as an afterthought, "I don't want to go to an embassy and rot there forever, so make a note of that. I want to go right to Miami, talk some sense into my people, and come back in a different way. Anyway, Mendez knows Max, and he knows you."

As I thought more about it, I realized that it wasn't such a crazy choice at all. Dr. Mendez did know just about everyone: the old society, the new class, and certainly all the diplomatic corps. Yes, it would make a great deal of sense for a man like Max, the head of an underground movement, to make it his business to know a Dr. Mendez who could be a go-between with the ambassadors. And who better than the pleasant, gregarious, effervescent Dr. Mendez?

"May I call Dr. Mendez?" I asked Lorenzo.

"Yes, but you've got to be careful. First of all, don't call from here. That might be too many links in a chain for our G-2 friends to put together. Call him from the outside and say you want to meet another doctor, any specialist. He'll know. I'll arrange for that. It isn't the first time Dr. Mendez has done us a favor, and I see no reason why he wouldn't agree this time, especially since he's a friend of yours."

"Okay," I said. "I'll call the doctor tomorrow."

"Wait till about noon, please," Lorenzo cautioned. "Give me time to arrange things, okay?"

"Sure, okay," I agreed. "I've wasted almost two years already. A few more hours won't matter." Then I gave Lorenzo my open, frank smile, the only one I have.

"Hello, Dr. Mendez?" I called the doctor at his office. I recognized the voice I had heard so often at the embassy soirées.

"Yes, this is Dr. Mendez," the doctor answered. "Who's calling?"

"Doctor, this is Tony. Tony Navarro."

"Oh, hello, Tonito. How're you doing?"

"I'm okay, doctor," I said, "but I have a kidney problem. Came on rather sudden, and I thought you could help me. Did . . . did our friend call you to tell you I needed your help?"

"Yes, he did, Tony," Dr. Mendez answered.

"I understand you know a good specialist. I don't; so many of my friends have left . . ."

"Yes, I know, and it's a shame . . . Yes, I think I know the specialist you mean. But he's very busy, as you can understand . . ."

"So what do you propose, doctor?" I asked.

"Well, even busy doctors have to eat," Dr. Mendez said, "and they have to have a drink once in a while. Tell you what. I'll get hold of him and, if it's okay, let's meet at El Carmelo at 6:30 this evening for a drink. His office isn't too far from here. Call me back at five, and I'll let you know if the meeting is on."

"Okay, doctor, thanks a lot," I said. "I'll call you at five, and I hope we'll meet tonight." As I put the phone down, I got to thinking about this completely new experience for me, and I felt just a little shy about confronting a man like Max. After all, I really had no inkling of what I could do to help in an activity I knew absolutely nothing about.

I had lunch with Alberto Fowler at La Torre in a quiet corner of the penthouse restaurant and filled him in on the events of the past few days. Alberto was of course fascinated by the G-2 raid on my office, and he had known Gonzalez-Recio personally when Gonzalez-Recio's club, the Vedado Tennis Club (which obviously was more than tennis), competed with Alberto's Havana Yacht Club (which was obviously more than yachting).

I asked Alberto again not to make any definite plans to leave. This time Alberto got the message quite clearly and was not only willing to wait but very excited about the whole prospect. Alberto had played the show-off most of his life, I thought, and mostly for other people's amusement. But the fact was that there was some pretty solid material there, material which I guessed would be very useful in our new "job."

13

At 5 P.M. EXACTLY, I telephoned Dr. Mendez's office. The phone rang for a long time, and I began to wonder if I shouldn't hang up. Finally it clicked off the hook and a man's deep voice answered, "Hello, Dr. Mendez's office. May I help you?" It just didn't sound like a servant, and it worried me. I almost did hang up, but before I could decide, the voice said:

"Excuse me, sir, are you Mr. Navarro?"

"Yes," I said, barely audibly, still thinking.

"Well," the voice said, "the doctor left word that it would be all right for you to meet him as planned." Maybe it was a servant after all, but I was still doubtful. Wouldn't that be exactly what they would have someone say if they wanted to catch me? My God, I'm getting paranoid, I thought, and I haven't done a damn thing wrong yet.

"Did the doctor tell you where we were going to meet?" I asked.

"No, sir, I'm sorry," the voice answered. Surely he would have mentioned the place if they were setting a trap. Or maybe not. Maybe they wanted *me* to mention it. Oh, come on, it was just a servant, that's all.

"Okay, that's all right. If you talk to the doctor, just tell him I'll be there. The pain in my back is getting worse."

"Oh, I'm sorry. I'll tell the doctor if he calls in."

"Thank you," I said. "Thank you very much," and I hung up.

I felt kind of foolish for having made so much of it, but this sort of thing was brand new to me. It's only natural that I'd feel a little awkward about it. What the hell, I had started new lives before, so to speak, and I could do it again.

I got ready to join Dr. Mendez and Max at El Carmelo and to face up to whatever came next, but I had to admit that I was worried and a little scared.

I entered El Carmelo, the watering place of Havana society for what seemed like centuries and in fact did cover several decades. It was not a bar in the strict sense of the word, but more like that unique European institution: the coffee

house. Liquor was incidental, even infrequent; the traditional fare was hot chocolate in the winter and ice cream in the summer.

That in itself was merely following a Spanish tradition, since the Cuban winter
hardly justified anything hot, and ice cream would have been the logical thing
to have twelve months out of the year. But no society is logical, so, during the
months of the Cuban "winter," women wore expensive furs and drank hot
chocolate, accompanied, of course, by churros. Churros were a delight for children and adults alike—a semi-sweet cookie batter deep-fried to an outwardly
crusty, inwardly airy consistency. Upon serving, it would be sprinkled with pow-
dered sugar to the customer's taste, and if one was daring or secure enough, it
would be dunked into the wide cup of blistering hot, velvety chocolate.

When I walked into El Carmelo, there were plenty of hot chocolates and
churros in evidence. I understood that Dr. Mendez's intention was precisely that:
a crowded setting for a meeting with Max.

I saw two men at a table who looked to me like plainclothesmen, or what I
imagined plainclothesmen looked like. Two seconds later, at closer range, I was
sure I recognized the lieutenant of the sugar office incident and my heart jumped.
If it is, I thought, my God, I've probably let Max down even before I meet him.
But the man glanced at me with no sign of recognition, so I had to be wrong.
Maybe all G-2 types look alike.

With some amusement I thought: good God, here I am, not even in the
Movement yet, and already I'm seeing Castro agents everywhere!

Sitting at a table toward the back, I could make out the frail figure of Dr.
Mendez surrounded, as usual, by cigarette smoke. His grey hair was pasted down
on his head with a part in it that looked as if it had been drawn by a road surveyor.
Yes, he was having chocolate and churros, and it was only October—a Cuban
October at that.

Well, I briefly pondered as I went toward him, *anything* the good doctor
managed to eat at all was bound to be a step forward. Cigarettes and churros are
better than cigarettes alone. I reached the table, nodded gently to the doctor, who
returned the nod, and sat down.

I had seen a few friends on the way to the doctor's table, but I didn't bother
to acknowledge them. Then I wondered if *that* wasn't unusual and therefore
suspicious behavior on my part. No, I was definitely not a professional at this
game, I thought, and wondered if I was doing the right thing after all. By that
time Dr. Mendez was speaking, almost too breezily, in my judgment. Dr. Mendez
was an amateur, too, I concluded.

"Hello, Tony. What a wonderful coincidence! Have something with me. How
about some hot chocolate?"

"No, doctor, thank you, *not* chocolate. But I'll have a Scotch and water, if you
don't mind," I said.

"*Claro*, my boy, of course." Mendez made the traditional sucking sound, a
little weaker in his case, which immediately brought the waiter.

"Waiter, please, a whiskey and water for my friend."

The waiter scurried off, bobbing his head up and down in the performance which denotes years of service and implies that he knew what you wanted before you asked and is happy to have it confirmed.

"Doctor," I said, lowering my voice, "I think I should tell you that there are two men at a table, in front of you and toward the center . . . toward your right" —the doctor was cautiously trying to find them, but didn't seem terribly concerned, I thought—"and they look awfully suspicious to me. Of course, I'm not an expert . . ."

"You're probably right, Tony," the doctor said cheerfully, "but there's nothing wrong with meeting with your doctor and a friend, is there?"

"No, I guess not," I answered, not completely satisfied. The old doctor wasn't exactly the most reassuring company. He probably wouldn't recognize the *head* of the G-2, let alone simple agents.

"I hope you'll join me later," Mendez said. "You're going to the Brazilian Embassy reception, aren't you?" The good doctor just wouldn't miss one of them.

"I might, doctor, I very well might," I said. "I'm very fond of the ambassadors."

"They *are* nice people, aren't they?" the doctor said, "and they certainly have a good rapport with Fidel. They helped his family during Batista times." Dr. Mendez was recounting the obvious to me. "Both his brothers and sisters were in asylum at the Embassy. But I guess you know that. You seem to be very close to that particular Embassy. Is there any special reason?"

"Not really," I answered. "They're just good people, that's all." I reflected one second. "Unless you mean the daughter. Everyone likes *her,* and I'm no exception. She's a real woman, all right. All female, quite a lady. By the way, they say Fidel is *also* no exception."

I realized I was rattling on and on and decided to cut it short. "Anyway, doctor, *you're* the expert. You know everything about every embassy. You never cease to amaze me. You've been at *every* party I've attended, and I'm sure you're there when I'm not."

"A poor doctor has to earn his living," Dr. Mendez smiled. "Only the international set, the diplomats, can pay my fees these days. I'm not really very good as a doctor, you know—just friendly." And he smiled again.

I was getting tired of the chitchat. I liked the doctor, but he was *so* frivolous, even if, as he said, he made a living out of it. I was ready for something more than frivolity, whatever it might be—whatever, in fact, the "underground" demanded of me. Maybe the good doctor had been a bad choice for a contact? Whoever "Max" was, a man who ran the most serious resistance movement in Cuba might conclude that I was equally superficial and not care to be bothered.

"Look, doctor," I finally said, "maybe this whole thing was a mistake." I leaned over toward Dr. Mendez and lowered my voice. " 'Max' isn't here and it's already seven o'clock." I looked around. "There's no one around or even coming into the place. I'm sorry, doctor, and I don't mean to be rude, but this man has a hell of a job to do and is risking his life every minute. Maybe he just agreed to the meeting to be polite. I don't think he'll take a chance with people like me." I was being kind. I looked around one last time.

"Doctor," I said, "I just don't think 'Max' is going to come. And, frankly, I can't blame him." I looked at Dr. Mendez who just looked back at me, seemingly undisturbed by the implicit slight.

"Doctor, I think we'd better leave," I said, and started to get up to get the waiter's attention.

"Hold it! Wait a minute, Tony! Take it easy," the doctor said.

"Aw, come on, doctor," I insisted. "There's no point to it. I was wrong, that's all. It's not your fault."

"Settle down, please," the doctor said firmly. " 'Max' will not let us down."

"How can you be so sure?" I asked impatiently. "How do you know? How do you know he'll come?"

"Because," Dr. Mendez said, "he's *already* here. *I* am Max."

I was totally unprepared for that. I just sat there and looked at him, unable to say a word. In complete shock and disbelief, I took in the frail figure in front of me with the benevolent smile and tried to put it together with my mental image of the man who was the Castro Government's Public Enemy Number One, and to whom literally thousands in the underground looked for support and guidance.

"You . . . you . . ." I pointed my finger and blurted out, "*you* are Max?" It was too loud and I realized it.

"Please, Tony, not so loud," the doctor said softly. "Remember, I told you that the meeting would be a *social* one. Please try to make it look that way, for both of us."

I felt like a child being reprimanded by a man I was ready to dismiss a few minutes before. That man with the feeble-looking frame, the smoke-riddled lungs and the myopic eyes now towered above me. I got hold of myself, came back to the real world at El Carmelo, and said:

"Doctor . . . Max . . . I'm sorry. What do I call you, anyway?" I felt small and embarrassed.

"Socially, of course, I remain Doctor Mendez. In front of our associates, whom you will meet, and *always* on the telephone when on business, I will be Max."

There was a new assurance in his voice, an authority I was only beginning to understand.

"We will meet regularly at different public places. At each meeting I will tell you where we meet next," the doctor continued. "To begin with, you will be our treasurer, our fund-raiser. You come from a rich family, and you have wealthy friends who can help us, if they haven't all left. And, even more important, those who contribute can trust you. But the way I see it, you won't stay in that job long. At least I hope I'm right, and we certainly need all the talent we can get."

I just stared, and the doctor kept talking: "I suppose I don't have to tell you to be discreet, and you must resist the temptation to share your involvement with friends."

All I could do was nod assent.

"To judge from your reaction just now, I guess I kept it pretty well from *you.*"

Max signaled the end of this speech by a little smile—not really so very different from the beatific smile that I had judged so frivolous in Dr. Mendez only five minutes before.

14

O N THAT MORNING in the fall of 1960 in Havana, I went out to my Mercedes in a business suit. In the back seat I had a light green cardigan, my old desert boots and even a black French beret. I didn't really expect to wear the beret, but I took it along just in case, since berets had become one more revolutionary symbol.

And that morning, for the first time, I was both the manager of a tiny sugar brokerage firm in downtown Havana and the treasurer of Rescate, the largest of the anti-Castro movements in Cuba. I had already learned from Max that there were many other resistance movements, including (1) a well-organized group of Havana University students, the *Directorio Estudiantil*, (2) the Christian Democrats, also young and active and Catholic-oriented, (3) a dissident faction of the original anti-Batista guerrillas from the mountains of central Cuba which now had its own anti-Castro groups up in the same hills, (4) a labor movement which started when the government took over the Cuban Federation of Labor, and (5) a left-leaning group led by the able head of the Havana underground in the Batista days, Manolo Ray, who had defected and gone into hiding. Ray's ideas were so "progressive" that others had tagged his movement as "Fidelismo without Fidel."

There were others—including the MRR, whose leader used the code name *"Francisquito"* or Little Francis, and one called simply *"Unidad,"* or unity, which accepted members of any persuasion, including ex-Batista men whom others rejected—reflecting the strong individualism of the Cuban people, their vocation for leadership, and their resistance to conformity. But Rescate was the largest. Its members were more mature and therefore more effective. And it had a respected leader in Tony Varona, with a proven track record for honesty in the pre-Batista, democratic days when honesty was not exactly in fashion.

My job as treasurer of Rescate was relatively simple. It didn't involve any of the financial complexities of the business world. What it amounted to was soliciting and collecting funds from individual contributors, holding those funds as custodian—which in this operation meant hiding them somewhere—and disbursing them to the operating heads of the Movement according to Max's instructions.

Some funds came from traditional supporters inside Cuba or others whom I would have to develop. We got some smuggled into Cuba from Rescate's headquarters in Miami, and, finally, there were sizable amounts of money blocked in Cuba, either officially in banks or hidden in mattresses belonging to families in exile. To have access to these funds, though, instructions had to be received from the absent owner to the holder of the funds in Cuba to release them to Rescate.

In this connection, I had already suggested to Max that I should make a trip to Miami and call on rich exiles who might have funds in Cuba. They might not be aware of our urgent needs for money—for food, boots, medicine, etc. We had to compensate the farmers for their help or to buy their silence. We had to rent houses in the cities to conceal weapons and supplies, and, most important of all, we had to provide hiding places for our "burned" until they could be safely removed or given political asylum. This was absolutely essential. Finally, the families of these freedom fighters had to be supported. Such were the incredible and not always recognized needs of people who were at war.

Max agreed to consider my suggestion of a Miami trip, and I started making plans since I was sure he would agree in the end. I had the unique position of being a member of a well-known *business* family, a rare animal in an eminently political atmosphere. This didn't hurt me at all with my comrades in the Movement as well as with potential contributors.

Whatever the source, if the funds were in dollars, I'd have to exchange them for Cuban pesos in the black market, in itself a somewhat dangerous operation. But the greatest danger for me at that point was running around in my car with literally thousands of dollars and/or pesos. After all, I could be stopped at any time, and if the money were discovered, the whole operation would be blown sky-high.

On one of my first days on the job, when I wasn't even sure yet how to go about the whole thing, Max sent me out to the Miramar section to collect from one of the large traditional sponsors. It was quite an experience. To begin with, the man was immediately suspicious when I showed up instead of the former treasurer. From behind a prudently half-opened door, he put me through a minor inquisition and then made an unnecessary and indiscreet telephone call to Max to check up on me.

I guess it was worth it, though, because the gentleman handed me ten thousand Cuban pesos in ten-dollar bills!

The money was in two brown paper bags, and I decided to leave it that way. I opened the trunk of the Mercedes, briefly considered the spare tire as a possibility, discarded it as much too obvious, and simply propped the bags in a corner of the trunk. I stopped in at a nearby supermarket and bought some unneeded groceries in *more* brown paper bags.

As I was coming out of the grocery store loaded with the two large bags, I saw the police making one of their frequent surprise checks on automobiles.

My car was locked, of course, but it was only two cars away from my turn to be searched. By the time I put away the groceries and started the Mercedes, I would be *one* car away, and any hasty departure would be too obvious. So—risk a fast getaway? Or take a chance and let them search me?

I decided to play it dumb and straight. Casually, and in no hurry, I put the two large grocery bags on top of the trunk's hood while I opened up the two front doors, ostensibly to let the hot air out. I hoped that I looked like any young husband dutifully helping with the household chores to the policemen who now approached me.

While one of them started to search the inside of the Mercedes, I preceded the second policeman to the back of the car. It was, admittedly, a hell of a chance, but life in those days was full of chances.

Hampered by the bags, I awkwardly opened the trunk and there, of course, were the other two brown bags in the corner. The policeman glanced at them, poked around the spare tire, then turned to *help* me stow the bags I was carrying!

I thought I would fall flat on my face, either from relief or the sudden imbalance of being relieved of one of the heavy bags—but I didn't.

The policeman said, "You've been doing a lot of shopping. Takes a lot of food to keep a family going these days, doesn't it? And a lot of pesos," he added with a friendly laugh.

My God, I thought, a lot of pesos, like those in there. But to the policeman, I said, "Yes, officer, you're right. It's hard for a young family."

"Well," he said, "first, I guess, we've got to straighten out the country. Then maybe, after that, The Horse will make it easier for all of us."

"Oh, yes," I said fervently.

"Aren't you warm in that sweater?" the officer asked, noticing my green cardigan and the fact that I was perspiring, as much from nerves as from any real heat. I had forgotten my "costume" sweater.

"No, not really," I said pleasantly. "It's the right color, at any rate, isn't it?" It was olive green, the color of fatigues, the color of the Revolution. "Besides," I said, "this car has a strong air conditioner. German, of course. I enjoy it, but sometimes it gives me an allergy if I don't cover up."

"Oh, yes, that's true," the officer said, very seriously. One was always on the right track mentioning the perils of air conditioning. The masses weren't used to it yet, and blamed it for all sorts of ills. A complaint in common is a friend-maker.

I got into the car, waved and smiled at the policeman, and took off straight for Max's home to get rid of the damned money, but not so fast as to invite another encounter with the police.

I arrived at Max's home. Poor Max, I thought, he talked about his clients at the parties, and it made a very good front, but he certainly didn't have the time to take care of them or to collect the big fees. He had no great wealth to lose. Castro hadn't taken anything away from him.

Max was happy to see me. He put the money away and said that they'd decide later where it should be used. Then he listened with amusement to my story about the police at the supermarket.

"Well, good," Max said. "I guess you've had your real baptism. It wouldn't do for you to get caught. They have ways of making you talk . . . and without pulling out your fingernails like the Batista boys. Anyway, I'm glad you made it. I knew you would."

"I'm glad you knew, Max. I sure didn't," I smiled.

"In fact, Tony," Max said, "I think now you have to take on another job." I looked up, curious. "My assistant. You're smart, you seem to be imaginative, and you've had business experience—which very few of us have, especially the younger ones." He didn't say it was because they had been involved since adolescence in sabotage or terrorism, but that's what he meant.

"What about the treasury?" I asked, even though I liked the new idea.

"The money within Cuba is drying up anyway," Max answered. "Your sub-treasurer can collect it after you take him around once. And I hear we may be getting some important help from 'the friends' soon, so we won't have to go around begging."

Max had always resented the "begging" part.

"Now it's time for you to meet our top men, Commander Augusto and the rest, because you will be working closely with them. I guess you should have a code, you know, a war-name. 'Tony Navarro' was all right as a treasurer, but now only a few of us should know that. So what do we call you? Have you got a preference, Mr. Navarro, for a name to go down in history with you?" Max asked with a twinkle.

I thought for a moment, but couldn't come up with anything clever. A mundane name wouldn't do to "go down in history." Think of Lenin or Tito being called Joe! I shrugged my shoulders.

"Well, never mind," Max said. "You can think about it later. I guess I don't look much like a Max myself, do I?"

"No, you don't," I answered honestly, ". . . and I don't have to tell you how surprised I was to learn that you *were* Max."

"No," Max laughed. "I could see it, and I have to admit that I enjoyed it."

"Well, you *don't* look like a Max. You look like a grey-haired Valentino. They should've called you the Silver Fox."

"Okay, Tonito, have your fun." Max knew when he was being put on. "I've decided you should make that trip to Miami. You can see any friends who might help, and I think you should meet with your tocayo. He hasn't seen you since you joined, even though he of course . . ."

"Hey, wait a minute, Max," I interrupted. "I think I've got it."

"You've got what?"

"My name," I answered. "You just said 'tocayo' meaning Varona, and that's it, of course. He's Tony and I'm Tony. I'm his tocayo, and that's my name."

"I like it," Max said, turning it over in his mind. "Okay, 'Tocayo,' that's it," and we both laughed.

"So, you go to Miami," Max continued. "We'll pay for the trip—or, rather, you will, Mr. Treasurer. In fact, Tony . . . Tocayo, I've got to get used to it . . . I've been meaning to tell you to take money out of the till for your living expenses. It's perfectly proper. Everyone understands you're not as rich as you used to be. And you have your wife in the States to take care of, and I guess your mother here."

"Thanks, Max," I said. "I appreciate it, and I won't abuse the privilege."

"I know that, Tocayo," Max assured me.

"You're right about my poor wife," I said. "The Hedges family got very little out of Cuba, and Avis isn't even living with her father. She's living in her married sister's garage, literally, with the two children. And I just found out she's selling Avon door-to-door in Coral Gables. She's got guts, Avis."

"She certainly does," Max agreed readily, pondering the point, and added: "A millionaire's daughter! Can you imagine! It's incredible what our friend Castro has done."

"My mother," I continued, "seems to be doing all right. She rents a building in Vedado and then sublets the apartments. She can handle herself okay. In fact, I think she may be involved with some underground group; but of course she thinks I'm still all out for Fidel, so that's fine with me. That's the way I want it. It's safer for her, and it's safer for me."

"Yes, I know your mother well, Tony, and I'm not worried about her, either," Max said, putting an end to the personal conversation. "I'll send Varona a message to expect you . . . that's another thing you'll have to learn about, our radio transmission set-up. I'll give you a private number to call when you get to the Miami airport, and then you can make your own arrangements with Varona. Ah . . . you'd better be ready to meet in the middle of the night. That's the way they work over there, and it's safer."

"I'll take care of myself, Max," I said.

"Yes, take care of yourself, Tocayo . . ." Max hesitated slightly, "because our friends in Florida forget easily, and they don't always think of protecting you if you don't protect yourself. Castro has lots of agents in Florida, and there's no way we can know them all. Remember one thing always, Tocayo. It is *you* who will be coming back, not anyone else. I know from experience, and I don't want anything to happen to you."

Max sounded genuinely concerned. I felt almost a father-son relationship between us already, and it pleased me that the older man, whom I now respected tremendously, cared about me.

I made my arrangements for a trip to Miami, although for government consumption it was "to the United States," and I bought my ticket to New York City. I really had no problem, since my sugar business provided unassailable justification for trips to the U.S.: a claim against a U.S. refiner for reported short-weight, an unpaid bill, a large contract for future delivery, all matters now of direct interest to the Cuban government. American sugar companies which had been expropriated without compensation were suing Cuba in the U.S. courts and attaching sugar cargoes from Cuba, and this made me a defender of Castro's interests in the eyes of the authorities and usually earned me an easy exit from the airport.

Of course I took my files with me, so there was always some element of truth in what I was doing in case I should be questioned on departure or on my return.

I had already let Avis know that I would be arriving in Miami on Friday evening when I got an urgent call from Max to come to see him right away at El Carmelo. I didn't much like the idea of meeting him frequently at the same place, but I figured that he was the expert, so I said nothing and went.

The news was bad. The G-2 had learned who Commander Augusto was, and the orders were to find him and pick him up the next day. There was no question about it. Rescate had several men infiltrated in both the G-2 and the regular police who were able to give us, for instance, the license plates of the cars which the police should pick up each day, so we would know which cars shouldn't go out until the plates could be changed. But this was more important intelligence now, about Augusto.

Max told me that Augusto, the Movement's head military officer, had decided that he must leave for Miami that very night. Not only would he now be useless in Cuba, but Augusto had for some time been extremely discouraged by the lack of support that he and his people were getting from headquarters in Miami and from "the friends" who did not seem to be responsive to the needs of the Movement, so the escape to Miami would serve both purposes.

Augusto, or the Movement, owned a fifty-foot, souped-up power boat, capable of handling fairly heavy artillery, moored at the Almendares River on the outskirts of Havana. Augusto planned to leave around midnight with four of his men and to maneuver around the Cuban Coast Guard in the remaining hours of darkness. They didn't know what obstacles they might run into on their way out of the river, and they thought I might be able to help.

It was a pleasure to meet the legendary Commander Augusto and, for the first time, to be taken into the confidence of the higher echelons of the Movement. Commander Augusto had already become somewhat of a legend within Cuba. It was he who ostensibly provided the ground supplies for the guerrillas up in the hills, and the air drops; he was also in charge of a daily clandestine broadcast from somewhere in Cuba which carried encouraging news under his by-line about the successes of the counter-revolutionary effort and passed out messages and instructions. Naturally, the guerrillas and all the city fighters listened to it daily for guidance.

Commander Augusto was tall, thin, sunburnt—a sort of sturdier John Carradine, or maybe Don Quixote. He talked fast and rather nervously, I thought, but that could be because his situation was a touchy one. His handshake, however, was strong and warm.

"Listen, Tocayo." Augusto knew perfectly well who I was, but my new name came naturally enough. "I'm going out that river tonight with my men, and I've got to know what we'll find along the banks. We know about the old Fortress on the right, near the mouth, with a permanently manned .30-caliber machine gun. That's a chance we'll have to take, but we don't know what else to expect. That's where you come in. You know that area, don't you?"

I thought quickly, and said, "Yes, Commander, I think so. How much time do I have?"

"We want to cast off as close to one o'clock tonight as we can," Commander Augusto said. "It's now eleven o'clock, so you have part of the morning and all afternoon. Let's say we meet back here again at six. Is that okay with you?"

"Yes, sir," I said. "I'll do my best."

"One more thing, Tocayo, or two more things, really," Augusto said. "We know about the gun emplacement at the Fortress, but I'm told that there's something at the Tennis Club—near the baseball stands—that *could* be a large-caliber machine gun. Can you get into the Tennis Club and check it out for us?"

"Yes, Commander, I'm sure I can."

"One last thing, Tony," the Commander slipped on the name, and acknowledged it with a passing smile. "When we move out of the river, we want you waiting in a parked car on the street nearest the coast on the Miramar side. If we have to jump ship and swim ashore, you'll be there, okay? The only thing is, the place may be alive with patrol cars, and it would look more natural if you had a girl with you."

"Good idea," I said. "That's kind of a lovers' lane anyway. Should I bring the girl? I could probably get my secretary, and I can trust her."

"No, Tocayo," Augusto said. "We've thought of that. When you meet us here at six, I'll have Maria with me. She's worked with us for a long time. She knows the ropes, she won't panic, and she's absolutely trustworthy."

"Whatever you say, Commander," I responded.

"Besides, Tocayo," Augusto continued, "we may be doing you more of a favor than you know. Maria is a beautiful girl. My men and I are leaving, but she's staying. I know you're alone in Havana and, who knows, she might be useful in more ways than one." Commander Augusto's laugh was so infectious that Max joined in and, finally, so did I.

"Oh, Tocayo," Max said as I was leaving, "you'll have to tell Lorenzo about tonight, and I know he'll be disappointed not to be going along. Tell him I don't approve of this risky deal, but Augusto's the boss on this job and he insists. We'll soon find a safer way to get Lorenzo out—he's one of our most valuable men and we need him to train men in Miami. Did you know he was the head of our entire sabotage operation for several years? The G-2 would love to have his head, and we can't expose him.

"The reason our hard-headed friend here insists on going, over my objections," Max looked at Augusto, "is that he's got a good boat and he hopes to equip it properly in Miami and use it for raids down the coast. That's a commendable purpose, of course, *if* he succeeds. It would be fine, too, if we could take the whole Cuban Navy over there," he said, looking at Augusto a little sternly. "Anyway,

Tocayo, I will not risk any more men in this adventure, so tell Lorenzo to hold on. It won't be long."

"Okay," I said. "I'm sure he'll understand, but he's getting kind of desperate. I'll have to try to spend more time with him."

I telephoned Maria Antonieta that I wouldn't be back to the office that day. Then I called Alberto. I told him casually that I needed his help and was on my way to pick him up. Scenting intrigue, he promised fervently to be at my disposal for as long as I needed him.

I stopped off at home to see Nanita, and then sought out Lorenzo. I explained the situation to him, and he said, sure, that's okay, but I could tell he was very disappointed.

I changed into my own personal underground uniform—desert boots, green sweater, etc.—thinking, "I might even wear the black beret tonight," and drove the few short blocks to Alberto's house.

Alberto laughed a little at my get-up, and then listened attentively to my story. I told him what his assignment was and the reason for it, but without mentioning names, not even code names. I hesitated a little in telling about the planned escape, but I trusted Alberto implicitly and, besides, to tell the truth, there really wasn't anyone around for Alberto to be indiscreet with even if he wanted to.

I said I needed him for the daytime part of the job, and Alberto eagerly agreed. We came to the conclusion at the same time that the ideal vantage point for observing the river would be the house of Magda Vazquez-Bello, a young, widowed society woman who had stayed in Cuba mainly because she refused to give up the creature comforts her position provided in Havana. Magda was a dear friend, and we saw each other fairly frequently. She wouldn't ask any questions.

On the way to see Magda, I told Alberto about my intended trip to Miami. We agreed that I should talk to Alberto's father in Miami to get the family's agreement to Alberto's risky involvement in the underground. Finally, I would of course talk to Tony Varona and tell him about Alberto's wishes to join the Movement. Only after those hurdles had been cleared would I mention Alberto to Max who, I was sure, would be more than happy for me to have a close friend as a reliable comrade-at-arms.

15

T HE ALMENDARES RIVER flowed from somewhere inland in the Havana province through a great portion of the city of Havana and its suburbs until it joined the Atlantic Ocean at the Havana coastline. The Almendares divided the city and the outlying suburban sections of Miramar and, beyond it, the Country Club section, both bordering on the coast and primarily the dwellings of the wealthy.

Two jaws of land nearly closed the mouth of the river, leaving a narrow, deep outlet, but protecting the small craft, both afloat and in boathouses lining the banks, from the treacherous north winds ("northers") that punish the island's coast every winter. The right jaw of land was pinpointed with boathouses for the pleasure cruisers and with more modest landings and warehouses for the professional fishermen. Closer to the river's exit there was, as Commander Augusto had pointed out, a small old structure which was a fortress dating back to the Spanish colonial days and was now manned by the Cuban Coast Guard. Next to the fort there was an old estate, the home of an eccentric late mayor of Havana, full of quaint Japanese gardens which managed to humanize the craggy, inhospitable rocks of the coast. Finally, toward the very tip of the jaw, there was the end of the playgrounds of the Vedado Tennis Club. And, all around, eternally bathed by the tides of the river, were the slippery, moss-covered, razor-sharp rocks, pierced through by a million nooks and crannies, and inhabited by tiny, lightning-fast crabs and by an occasional small fish caught against its will in one of the small pools between the rocks. The left or outlying jaw as a ship moves out had been barren land for years and was called La Puntilla, a diminutive for "The Point." In recent years, it had been developed and now boasted several apartment buildings, one of which was the home of Magda Vazquez-Bello, a member of our close group of friends.

Alberto and I arrived at Magda's apartment unannounced. She was surprised, but not disturbed, since there were no formalities observed or expected in our relationship; we would often drop by in the evening for a drink. Magda was entertaining a "young gentleman" from the Canadian Embassy for lunch. Everyone always expected Magda, an attractive and resourceful young widow, to get married again, but she never did.

I explained that we had come in for a quiet drink, and also that I had brought my binoculars, hoping that from the backyard of Magda's building I could get a good look at a school of sharks that had been reported seen at the entrance of the river. I had brought Alberto along for the ride to keep Magda company while I went outside, although I now saw that wasn't necessary, and Alberto could just sit there quietly, if that was ever possible.

"Tony Navarro," Magda said, "you're just plain crazy, but go ahead and do what you want. You're probably just spying on some poor girl."

I took my cue and moved toward Magda's back door, to go out to the backyard. As I was leaving, Magda shouted after me: "Please, Tony, whatever you do, don't get me in trouble with my neighbors. They already think I'm some kind of a nut."

"Don't worry, Magda," I shouted back. "I won't. And besides, you *are.*"

Magda turned back to the Canadian and Alberto, and I could still hear her. "What's wrong with Tony, anyway?" she said. "What's he doing?"

"Oh, don't pay any attention to him, Magda," Alberto said. "He's probably into something. Don't worry about it."

"He should have left when Avis did," Magda insisted, "but he probably still thinks there's a chance for this place."

"He's okay, Magda, I promise you," Alberto repeated. *"Don't worry."*

"Well," Magda said, "I'll bet you two guys aren't exactly suffering, alone in Havana," and she gave Alberto a mischievous smile.

Alberto laughed, and the Canadian, by that time, thought it would be proper for him to do so also.

By this time, I was perched on one of the posts that surrounded the backyard facing the river, hoping that some trees around the post would make me less conspicuous to people likely to spot me. I could see the river perfectly well, and both banks. There was nothing visible on the bank nearest me or the left bank going out, unless, of course, there was a gun emplacement on the roof of one of the buildings. The buildings, however, were fairly removed from the water and, besides, those roofs I could see showed no signs of action or anything that resembled guns or other military equipment.

I concluded that the left bank was clean. On the far bank, however, I could see clearly a machine gun emplacement. It looked like a standard .30-caliber U.S.-made machine gun, and there was indeed a soldier, presumably the gunner, sitting nearby reading a newspaper and smoking. I could see the cigarette. A little removed from the gun, there were two or three other soldiers inside a small guardhouse, and farther back was the fort itself, a relatively small structure. The Japanese gardens in the back of the old mayor's home presented no problem that I could see. Finally, the playgrounds of the Tennis Club, the stands and the baseball diamond which were closest to the water, were completely empty at this time, shortly after the noon hour.

At the end of the stands nearest the river, I could indeed see a long, tube-like object sticking out toward the river, but I couldn't make out the details. Unlike the regular Fortress which was immediately in front of me, just across the river, the Tennis Club stands were much closer to the final river exit, and the distance was too much for my binoculars. I could tell, however, that the pipe-like object was not wide enough to be a water main and thus it could be the cooling jacket around a machine gun or even the muzzle of a 40-mm. cannon. The back part of the tube appeared to be covered by something that looked like a piece of canvas. In sum, it could well be a gun of last resort, to be used only if an escaping enemy boat had gotten beyond the Fortress's machine gun range. Any kind of a medium-caliber gun at that particular place would reach out considerably beyond the river mouth and pose a danger. No doubt, I thought, it will have to be investigated at closer range, and I started thinking of ways to do it.

I went back to the apartment, finished my gin and tonic, picked up Alberto, and said goodbye to Magda and her Canadian. As we were going out the door, Magda said:

"Tony, we must plan a nice weekend at Varadero before the northers start, and I think we could all fit in my house there. Will you think about it?"

"Good idea, Magda," I said. "Let's talk about it. Maybe we can get enough of our own group, if there are any left, so we don't have to raid the embassies." That last part I said in very quick Spanish, hoping the Canadian wouldn't understand.

Magda just stuck her tongue out at us as we were going down the short flight of stairs to the street. Alberto and I then drove for a few minutes around Magda's neighborhood, the Puntilla area, to see how close the streets came to the coastline and which one would be more suitable for the role of "riding hospital," which my Mercedes was called upon to perform that night. "Riding hospital" was the term used in underground jargon for a getaway car; I used it advisedly, and Alberto was impressed.

We went under the Almendares River tunnel to the Vedado Tennis Club on the other bank. The club was virtually empty, but the bar was open, so that's where we headed. Standing idly behind it was an old bartender we used to know from the club days. He was reading the newspapers and looked rather sad.

"Hello, Joe," Alberto said.

"Hello, Mr. Fowler. Hello, Mr. Navarro," the bartender said, putting down his newspaper. "Good to see you. I guess I haven't seen you in years. What'll you gentlemen have?"

"Oh, anything at all," Alberto answered for both of us. "Gin and tonic, I guess. How you doing, Joe?"

"I'm not very happy, gentlemen," Joe said deliberately. "As you probably know, the Government's turning over the club to the public starting Monday. Not to give myself too much importance, but I don't like it. I don't like it one bit."

"No, I guess not," Alberto said. "It'll be tough. Can anyone at all come in?"

"Anyone at all," Joe confirmed. "I think there's a token fee of fifty cents or something like that. I hate to think what the club'll be like within a week."

"Well, Joe," I said. "That's the revolution—of the people and for the people."

"I know," said Joe, giving me a "go jump in the lake" look.

"Joe," I said casually, "would you mind if we walked around the grounds for a few minutes? A bit of nostalgia, y'know, with the old club changing so. Alberto used to compete here, and even I played a little tennis once in a while."

"I don't think there'll be any problem," the bartender said, "but let me take you by the guard." Then he walked us toward the back door of the clubhouse, which opened onto the pool, the tennis courts and the playing fields beyond. A *miliciano* guard was sitting by the door, the ubiquitous submachine gun by his side.

"I guess it's all right," the guard said. "On Monday the whole world'll be coming in anyway. It's the conquest of the people." It was hard to tell whether the guard was joking or dead serious. "But," he added, "don't take long and stick to the grounds. Don't go into the locker room. There are guards there, too, and I might get into trouble."

"Don't worry," Alberto said, "and thanks a lot. We'll be back in a minute, Joe." We walked out onto the grounds and directly to the stands and the baseball diamond, stopping briefly here and there, so that we would at least *look* nostalgic to an observer.

I made a phantom serve when passing the tennis courts, and Alberto sprinted a few yards at the track field, now overgrown with grass, and we both went directly to the edge of the grandstands.

The "cannon" was a bent piece of iron pipe—what was left of a post that must have once supported a sign. We had to admit that it was just at the right angle to look like the barrel of a gun, and what we had taken for the protective coating of the guts of the machine was just a rotten piece of canvas awning that once had protected spectators from the burning sun.

We walked back to the clubhouse, said "thanks" to the guard, and gave Joe a hug when he said, "No charge, boys. The Government can pick up this one."

We went on to one of our favorite restaurants not far from the club, Centro Vasco, a famous Spanish restaurant featuring Basque food. The restaurant and its owner and cook, Juanito, were known by two generations of Cubans of all social extractions and by many American tourists.

I ordered my standard fare, a delicious Spanish casserole, made of pigs' feet and tripe, called *Callos*. It was not for the squeamish and much too heavy for a hot day, but even so it was delicious.

Alberto ordered *his* standard fare, *almejas en salsa verde*—tiny clams in a thin greenish sauce with lots of garlic and lots of parsley (presumably thereby green), and also delicious. Both of us had white rice—not truly Spanish, but it was the one concession to Cuban tastes that most Cubans make.

While my casserole was cooling, and a little imported Spanish red wine was breathing, I got up and told Alberto I would make one brief telephone call which should set some minds at rest. I telephoned Max, and when I was sure it *was* Max, I said:

"Max, this is your Tocayo. Sorry you couldn't join us for lunch, but I understand. Before lunch, we went down to the Tennis Club and had a drink with old Joe, the bartender. Do you remember him?"

"Yes, I do," Max said.

"Well, the place is going public on Monday, you know, and I took a nostalgic tour around, especially the playground. It's really kind of a mess over there. I'm sure they'll fix it up, but right now it's pretty awful. Over by the playgrounds there are a bunch of pipes around that could be dangerous."

"Yes," said Max, noncommittal.

"And, Max . . ."

"Yes, Tocayo."

"The pipes are just pipes—nothing more than bent pipes. And so as far as I can see we can plan to join and play baseball. I'm sure they'll clean it, and you and your team will have nothing to worry about, you understand?"

"Yes, Tocayo, I understand," Max said.

"Okay, then. I'm having a wonderful lunch. Wish you were here, and I'll see you at the agreed time later this afternoon."

When I went back and joined Alberto, I merely said, "I put my friend's mind at ease about that gun which wasn't."

Then we relaxed over our food and the good wine. It all took its toll, and we waxed nostalgic and philosophical. Besides, Alberto had already had a taste of the underground and felt part of it. He scraped some of the rich, garlicky clam juice with a chunk of French bread, the true mark of an uninhibited gourmet, and said: "Tony, what in the hell is wrong with us?"

"You mean you and me?"

"No, I mean us. I mean the Cubans, all of us. Why would we let this mess happen?"

It was a good question. I thought about it, sipping my wine.

"Well, Alberto," I said, "I've thought a lot about it, and I don't like my conclusions, but here they are."

"Go ahead. I'll probably agree, and I won't like them either."

"Well," I started, "I guess the first thing is that we Cubans are a very special breed, a hybrid really, a mixture of the old Spanish culture and all that means, good and bad. With a soupçon, a big soupçon," I smiled at my own choice of words, "of the African negroes our ancestors imported. And with a tremendous orientation toward the United States, for both geographic and economic reasons. How's that for beginners?"

Alberto just listened, cleaning up his plate, and I continued, "I can't answer for all of Cuba, but as far as the dominant classes are concerned, most of us didn't know beans about what was really happening in Latin America, and we couldn't have cared less. All we knew, all we cared about, was what was happening here and in the United States . . . and maybe a very small group of sophisticates knew something about Europe."

Alberto frowned a little, bread in mid-air, as if he were about to disagree, but I stopped him.

"Alberto, what do you know about Peru or Chile? What do you know about the social forces and political movements at work there?"

"Nothing, really," Alberto had to admit.

"And yet that's what Latin America is all about, and Fidel and his people knew it. We were just too prosperous, I guess. Many of us were educated abroad at some point in our lives. Foreigners thought we were charming, enjoyed our company, and flattered us, but politically we were illiterates. We were an island in every sense of the word."

"Tony," Alberto said, "I think I've heard that speech before, at the Isle of Pines, centuries ago."

"I know, Alberto," I agreed. "I know. But how else could we have mistaken Castro for the savior of democracy?"

"Okay," Alberto conceded. "I'll plead guilty to that."

"If you want a capsule definition of most of us"—I was feeling my wine, and another half-bottle was on its way—"we, as a race, or as a people, are bright, bubbly, outgoing, charming, generous, intense . . . I could go on."

"Do, by all means," Alberto said, slightly uncomfortable with my self-analysis.

"That's the good news," I continued. "The bad news is that most of us, while not necessarily selfish, *are* self-centered. We're individualistic, incapable of working as a team even against a common enemy. And, as a group, we're intelligent but rather shallow, I'm afraid . . ."

"Good God," Alberto said. "You *are* getting analytical."

"Well," I said, "at least *we* ought to know what is wrong with ourselves and not blame it all on that son-of-a-bitch Castro."

"Okay, you're right," Alberto said, figuring that by agreeing he would end the barrage. He was wrong.

"Alberto," I continued, "worst of all is that we stood by while Castro cleverly took us, one by one, not lifting a finger until *our* toe was stepped on."

"No argument there," said Alberto, who wasn't about to argue with me anyway.

"I guess maybe we were just aristocrats, or thought we were," I concluded. "Aristocrats with material, bourgeois goals. We are the product of old Spain, and those values don't wear well in the tropical heat."

"I guess you've heard that an invasion is being organized," Alberto said, trying to bring in something positive. "Your friends certainly must know about it."

"I know," I said, "and I'm happy about it, if it's true. I also know that the middle classes and even the poor people—whom I respect tremendously because they have nothing to lose—are leaving Cuba, to escape what Castro has made of the damned island. If rich and poor do come back to fight, as you say, it will certainly redeem us all and make up for past sins. May God help them."

"He will," Alberto said.

"As for us personally," I continued, "we now find ourselves in a situation where we not only *can* do something about it, but we—you and I, Alberto—*must* do something about it, to make up for our own mistakes."

"The Revolution wasn't a mistake, Tony," Alberto protested. "The man was."

"Okay, Alberto, we both know that. But for whatever reason, we've got to try to straighten things out. I don't care for a life away from my country forever, but I must also tell you in all honesty that I don't care for execution, either, so we'll do what we can, and we'll be careful."

"All right, Tony," Alberto said. "I've already told you that I'm with you. Call on me when you're ready."

By this time the dishes were wiped clean, the new half-bottle was discreetly down to the dregs, and the bill had been signed in good old Havana tradition. We moved out of the restaurant, floating a bit, waited for the air conditioning to push the hot air out of my car, and drove out to the Country Club. I dropped Alberto off and went home to see Nanita and, just maybe, to take a quick nap before my appointment with Max and Augusto at six o'clock.

When I arrived at Max's, Augusto was there with two men and a young woman. The girl immediately gave me a look of inspection, with a "so this is going to be it" expression, and I could only hope that she liked what she saw.

I looked, too, and saw an attractive small girl with happy green eyes, olive skin, and an astounding amount of loose black hair. It was too long for her height, I thought, and immediately made plans to have it pulled back in a bun.

There was an air of excitement, to be expected from men who were about to try a dangerous escape, carrying with them a fifty-foot boat and little else. Max had already categorized the plan as having no more than a fifty-fifty chance of success, and as far as he was concerned, it was an unnecessary, irresponsible attempt. However, he had put aside his objections and, as evidenced by the nautical charts on the table, was dutifully discharging his responsibilities as head of the Movement and contributing his experience to planning the escape.

After Max greeted me with a smile, Augusto stepped forward and said simply, turning to the girl, "Maria, this is Tocayo," and, to me, "Tocayo, this is Maria." Then, with a big grin on the long face atop a lanky frame, he blessed us in priestly fashion: "May you live happily ever after."

I went to Maria and looked into her eyes as she looked back at me. I kissed her on the forehead and knew all would be well with the world.

Max introduced the two men as simply "Patches" and "El Gallego" (the Galician), and no questions were asked. El Gallego, I learned, was not part of the escape plan. He would, in fact, be part of my action group in the difficult times for those who stayed behind.

I reported my findings about the banks of the river, concluding that, in my opinion, the only real problem was the permanently manned machine gun at the

Fortress. Small-arms fire from the extra guards was certainly possible, but unlikely and less effective.

Augusto thanked me for my assistance, told me that there was no need for me to stay while they finalized their plans, and said, "Maria will be driven to your home tonight shortly after eleven. Is that a problem?"

"No, not at all," I said.

"No problem," Max added, almost at the same time.

"Okay, then, she'll be there. I want you in the car with her at midnight at the place you selected today on the road. About here," Augusto said, pointing to a spot on the map, "nearest the rocks on the left bank going out, from midnight until we have *cleared* the mouth of the river." He stopped. "Or until something else has happened," he finished. "If it looks as if the project has aborted totally, wait anyway and drive back home at three. If the worst happens, start the motor and try to pick up survivors."

Augusto was not trying to be dramatic; that was obvious to me.

"We marked our map where you told us your car will be. If you are absolutely sure that some of us are swimming to shore—but only then—turn on the inside lights of your car and leave them on. In the dark of night, it will be enough to guide us, as we will be nearer to your bank. Don't, for Christ's sake, turn on your headlights. We don't need one more target, and you will be well within reach of the .30-caliber from the Fortress. If all goes well, we'll be pulling out from the boathouse at one o'clock, and we should be dead ahead of you ten minutes later."

"I understand," I said and, with a slight nod in the direction of Max and Maria, went for the door. While it was still open, Augusto had an afterthought and said in a loud voice, "Tocayo, I know you young fellows do a lot of drinking these days." Augusto could not be much older than I. "Tonight, however, you will be doing it for the Movement." He smiled. "Be sure you have at least one drink before you drive out there in the dark. If you should get caught, it must look like a lovers' encounter. Maria doesn't have to drink, though. That way, maybe she'll be able to resist you." Augusto laughed and I smiled back, the tension broken for the moment.

The small group of men, dressed as fishermen, arrived in two cars at the large boathouse on the right bank of the Almendares River, one hour before midnight. There was a strong smell of paint inside the boathouse, because for days the men had been secretly painting the big white sportsman's yacht a dark blue-gray which would make it very hard to see against the waters of the night. The choice had to be made between safety in the open seas and the pretense of being a normal white fishing boat during the first few minutes of the escape. That choice had been made. Nevertheless, the gear and provisions they brought were what would be expected from a fishing party going after *pargo*, the Cuban red snapper. If there was anything unusual, it was only the early hour for that type of expedition; but fishermen and hunters are eager and notoriously meticulous about their preparations.

There were four men and Maria. The equipment was unloaded and taken to the landward door of the boathouse. The smaller of the two cars, which had been stolen earlier in the day for that purpose, would be left where it was with no means of identification except as it related to its unfortunate owner. The other car would eventually be driven away by Maria.

The men were very conscious of punctuality. Their very lives depended on moving out of the boathouse into the river no later than 1 A.M., to allow time for the maneuvers required to avoid the Cuban Coast Guard and still meet the boats coming out from Florida to escort Augusto's boat to Miami.

Augusto and his men loudly bragged about their fishing gear and the carefully provided bait while they were still in front of the boathouse. Who knew who might be watching? At the same time, they carefully concealed the weapons they were carrying—mostly automatic rifles and pistols—under several layers of canvas, camouflaging their shapes on the way to being stowed on board.

The banks of the river were quiet, most lights in the boathouses and the little shacks of the fishermen were already out, and, so far, Operation Escape was proceeding on schedule. At that point Maria climbed into the larger of the two cars and left for my home.

She arrived at the Country Club a few minutes late. Finding me worried and impatient, she reassured me that a few minutes' delay was perfectly tolerable within the departure schedule, and she filled me in on the situation by the river.

We put Maria's car into the garage, waking up our gardener in the process, since he lived in a little room above it. The old man, peering out the window, saw us and waved. He had been with our family for years and was totally devoted. If he suspected any shenanigans, he considered it my business and, as far as he was concerned, whatever I did had to be right. I climbed the short flight of stairs to the attic and got the Walther .385 pistol which the old man had been keeping for me. It was the first time I had carried it since the Revolution began. It would never stay behind any more.

Maria and I took the Mercedes, parked under the porte-cochere at the entrance, and drove to La Puntilla, getting there not really much later than originally scheduled.

I looked at my watch. It was a few minutes after midnight. Taking into consideration the information Maria brought me, I drove around the circuitous little streets, full of dead ends and cul-de-sacs. I realized that I couldn't drive around too long without arousing suspicion. The other private cars parked along the impromptu lovers' lane would probably dismiss us as a Secret Service patrol car. Any *real* Secret Service cars, however, might have other views.

Then I happily remembered Augusto's instructions. I asked Maria to snuggle close to me—not at all hard to take—and I even stopped briefly in the parking lot of a bar in the area to buy a couple of drinks and take them out to the car. There was nothing unusual about that, either.

It was now almost 12:30 and, having obediently gulped half my whiskey, I handed the glass to Maria and drove to the exact place marked by an "X" on

Augusto's map. I turned off the motor, hid the pistol in a convenient nook of
the glove compartment, reclaimed my drink from Maria, and picked up the
binoculars. Having thus disposed of both hands, I was reduced to asking Maria
to move over and put her arm around me—"in the interests of the Movement."
Fortunately, it seemed that the interests of the Movement and her own interests
coincided pleasantly. It was fun, but the underlying tension and fear were right
there with us.

I surveyed the river and found the waters peaceful and the banks empty and
silent. From my position I couldn't see Augusto's boathouse, deeper up-river, not
that I needed to. All-important to the operation was the Fortress, and I concentrated on that. It was difficult to see in the dark, little aided by the few artificial
lights still burning. The little Fortress, however, had a floodlight which covered
its immediate surroundings, and a spotlight which at the moment was on. Its
beam died only a few feet into the black waters of the river, hitting the tops of
some jagged rocks in its path.

The soldier in charge of the machine gun appeared to be snoozing near the
gun, and the gun itself was covered. There was no sign of anyone else around.

I tested the inside lights of the Mercedes to be sure they worked properly,
which they did, and decided there was nothing to do but wait for the action.

I later learned that the men at the boathouse, confident that there was no one
to observe them at that late hour, were going about their chores. They looked
at each other in happy anticipation of an easy exit as they carted the bundles from
the overloaded stolen car to the boat. No one pretended to ignore the danger of
the machine gun at the Fortress, but a fast-moving vessel, making, say 40 knots
through a wide river, had an even chance. That was all Augusto dared hope for.
In fact, he had recited a dozen times the factors he hoped he had going for him:
the dark of the night, a fairly low silhouette, and the least possible motor noise
until actually sighted. From the gunners he expected poor marksmanship in
dealing with a formidable but unreliable weapon. Add to that the natural excitement of soldiers awakened in the middle of the night, the qualms about firing
on innocent fishermen, the fear of what might be firing back—those were the
pluses Augusto was counting on. The negatives he had tried to ignore, and the
unexpected had been ruled out. However, as so often happens, it was the unexpected that took place.

A young man in the uniform of the Committees for the Defense of the
Revolution, the neighborhood spy organization, appeared at the door of the
boathouse, attracted by the noise of the motor being tested. A startled Augusto
nervously explained their fishing plans and even offered to take him along. But
the young man was obviously aware of the real purpose of the trip and, without
a word, turned and started running in the direction of the Fortress.

"Se van, se van!" he shouted. ("They're leaving, they're leaving!") Augusto
probably should have shot the boy immediately, but the profit/risk analysis
proved too time-consuming, and the young man was out of sight.

There was now no choice. Aborting the operation and fleeing by land would be dangerous, leave too many tracks, and mean the loss of a good boat. Staying to fight the troops which would soon be coming, and be reinforced in no time, was probably suicidal. The only answer was to go, and to go immediately.

They cast off in a rush, leaving some of the equipment behind in the boathouse, and moved out into the river, lights out. The element of surprise was now probably lost, but a blacked-out boat against black waters had a fair chance, so they went full throttle, choosing speed over silence. They unpacked the guns and hurriedly made them ready. The hour was 12:45 A.M., fifteen minutes ahead of the scheduled departure. The large boat broke the small river swell at full speed, heading for the mouth of the river.

In the car on the left bank, Maria and I heard the noise of the motor before we saw anything. Straining, I managed to see the moving dark mass and the bits of white from the water cut by the bow in front and fringing the wake of the powerful propeller.

I grabbed the binoculars and shifted my sight immediately over to the Fortress, able to see what looked like a group of excited men running back and forth between the Fortress, the guardhouse, and the concrete platform which jutted out toward the river and was the foundation for the gun emplacement.

The boat moved swiftly in the center of the river. Maria and I squeezed hands, our eyes glued to the windshield, hoping they would make it safely beyond the Fortress. But even before the boat got level with the Fortress, the siren by the guardhouse began to sound—short, screeching blasts incredibly loud in the silent night. Half of Havana must have heard it.

About the same time, the machine gun started firing, flames coming out of the muzzle, piercing the darkness, long before the report of the first burst could be heard; but soon after that the flame and the rattling went together in a frightening display.

The bullets skipped over the water, trailing the boat, and sank into the river behind the moving craft until the gunner adjusted his sights, and then the .30-caliber slugs pounded against the rocks on the opposite bank, splitting off some of the sharp edges with loud cracks.

The boat, so far unharmed, began to zigzag in a desperate effort to avoid the gunfire. The gunner was already angling toward the mouth of the river in an effort to hit the target, and appeared to be aiming at the area where we were parked. The burst of flames came frontally in a direction which surely would have hit us if the road were not slightly raised from the level of the river bank. The men in the boat were firing back, and the figures on the concrete platform scurried away into the darkness, jumping off onto the rocks, shouting curses which could be half-heard through the night. The floodlight was shot away, exploding with one last flash of intense light which highlighted the gunner still firing, a dark lump of a man lying next to him on the ground. Then darkness overtook the platform, and only the flames which accompanied the staccato blasts of the machine gun broke the pervasive blackness.

The boat was at that very moment crossing the line of fire, and we could hear the splintering of wood. If wood was splintering, I thought, flesh was being torn too. I heard a dreadful cry of pain and started to get ready for the rescue, if anyone indeed would survive. As I jumped out of the car to get an open view, two things happened.

First of all, the boat moved very close to the left bank, away from the gun and toward me. I immediately scrambled back and started the motor, concluding that the men would try to leave the ship and jump or swim toward the rocks and the car they knew was there.

Then suddenly the gun went silent. The cursing which reached our ears clearly told us that the machine gun had jammed. The boat veered back toward the middle of the river while, at the Fortress, a handful of soldiers were firing rifles and other small arms at the fleeing craft from the rocks.

I thought for a fearful second that maybe using rifles *increased* their chances of hitting the target. But, whatever the results, the boat cleared the last few yards of the river and disappeared into the dark ocean.

Maria and I hugged each other exultantly as lights went on in many of the houses in the area, and some of the lovers' cars parked in the darkest corners blew their horns out of sheer excitement.

If Augusto followed the agreed contingency plan, Patches, the pilot, would try to fool the Coast Guard—now surely alerted beyond the most pessimistic projections—by avoiding the straight course for Key West or Marathon Key and, instead, would hug the Cuban coast as closely as possible while the cutters and smaller craft were searching for the escaping vessel in the open seas. The cutters were large but slow ships, and it was only the range of their guns that had to be feared. The smaller, American-made torpedo boats, however, could equal the 40-knot speed of Augusto's boat, and those simply had to be avoided or it would be the end of the story.

Some hours later and still in the darkness preceding dawn, they would reverse their course and only then aim for Key West or the Florida mainland. They would have missed their rendezvous with the escort boats from Miami, but, barring extremely heavy seas or a fluke encounter with a Cuban Coast Guard unit, those still alive, I thought, should make it to safety.

There was nothing more that Maria and I could do. Our part of the job was over, except for getting word to Max as quickly as possible. I remembered a public telephone at the bar where I had bought the drinks earlier and decided that it would be the nearest place to go to make my call. I asked Maria if she would be willing to stop for a drink with me.

"I'd love it!" she said instantly. "It seems so . . . so *flat* . . . just to go home!"

So we drove to the little bar, which was practically empty by then. I settled Maria at a corner table and ordered drinks from a sleepy waitress before heading for the phone booth.

When I reached an anxious Max, I quickly told him that everything was all right. I said there had been a last-minute change in plans and some serious difficulties had developed but, as far as I could tell, the boat was on its way. Of course, the rendezvous was now impossible. Could Max let "the friends" know?

Max said it was unlikely any of us could do much now but pray, and he agreed that it would be all right if I gave him the details the next day.

I went back to Maria and slumped heavily in the chair, not even reaching for the Scotch that stood in front of me.

"You're tired, aren't you, Tocayo?" Maria asked gently.

Tired? God, yes, I was tired. But I was also excited. I didn't want this night to end like an ordinary night. I looked at Maria—so young and so pretty, so feminine. The memory of our spontaneous hug came rushing back to me, and I remembered the feel of her in my arms, her yielding warmth. Dammit, I realized suddenly, she *fit*. There was something more there than love for God and country.

I straightened up, took a big gulp of my drink, and said, "Maria . . . let's not go home."

There was no answer for a while.

"Tocayo, look at me," she finally said, and when I did, she was smiling at me, those green, green eyes a little misty. Then she said simply, "Yes."

I got up, tossed a bill on the table, pulled Maria to her feet, nodded to the surprised waitress, and made for the door, Maria's hand still warm in mine.

And so we made love, a wild kind of love with the aphrodisiac of furtiveness and the excitement of a shared danger still with us. When it was over, Maria whispered: "What if I fall in love with you?"

I knew that that question was never a rhetorical one; love is not a faucet.

"Even poor freedom fighters can fall in love, you know." She said it so softly that I almost missed it.

"It's a chance we have to take," I said.

She nodded, but said nothing.

"Maria," I said, "trust me. What has happened has happened. It *had* to happen. In our unique situation, our war, because that's what it is, this is something we can give each other, and I hope it means as much to you as it does to me. And I promise you . . . I won't let you get hurt." And I meant it. But someone is always hurt . . .

It was now daylight, and I decided to stop at Alberto's house to brief him on the night's events, but he wasn't there. He was, in fact, at my house, asleep on the couch in the small sitting room off my bedroom. I woke him up and gave him a rundown which I presumed, wrongly, had been the main purpose of his visit. Alberto listened with interest and without interrupting, rubbing his eyes. At the end, he said: "That's very good, Tony. I hope they'll get there okay. But now I have something to tell you which I'm afraid you won't like."

"What is it, Alberto?"

"I'm leaving Cuba, Tony. I wanted to tell you right away, last night, but I wanted to tell you at my home over a nightcap. So I came over to get you. Let's walk back and have some coffee."

I was surprised and of course saddened, but I respected my friend's wishes and how he had planned to tell me about it, so we walked silently the back way, over the fairways, to Alberto's house and sat down in his study over some coffee.

"Father called me from Miami, Tony," Alberto said, "and, in his bumbling way, he tried his best to use codes, but the net of it is that he thinks I should leave Cuba and come to Florida. He thinks I would be useful in the invasion."

"That's certainly true, Alberto. I hadn't thought of it," I said.

"You're kind to say that. Anyway, Father used such expressions as 'your friend who lives three houses down,' meaning you, and 'his boss,' meaning Varona, and it seems they have been discussing my alternatives."

"Well, Alberto," I said, "they certainly know things we don't, so we should listen."

"I hope you know, Tony," Alberto said, "that I don't fool myself. I know my dad is biased about trying to get me out of here and to Miami. But the opinion of your tocayo, Tony Varona, is another matter."

"It certainly is, and I think you should listen to it. I say that honestly, although you know how very sorry I will be."

"I know, Tony, I know," Alberto said. "Varona told my father, as well as Dad could repeat his words, that my knowledge of the north coast of Santa Clara, because the mill is there, would be valuable to the invasion. Father of course never mentioned the word invasion, but I guess it's clear that Santa Clara will be one of the targets—if not for the main force, then at least for a parallel drive."

"Alberto," I said, "your father's motives aside, it all makes sense. You do know that area better than anyone in Miami. And, after all, old buddy, if I lose you but gain an invasion, I really can't complain." Facetiousness sometimes helps, and we finished our coffee in companionable silence.

Of course I was disappointed, but I did understand the reasonableness of the request, and I wasn't entirely joking when I said I would be deprived of a friend but was still happy for what it meant. The invasion was no longer just a fond hope but a reality, and an immediate reality at that. I too, I thought, would have to get ready for it. In that connection I decided then that I would have to change my plans and that, from now on, Augusto's man El Gallego—whom I had liked immediately—would be my companion. I saw no point in mentioning it to Alberto then. There would be hurt enough in the inevitable separation.

I gave Alberto some messages for Avis and for Varona (verbal, of course) and then we embraced, trying not to give way to unmanly emotion. Without another word, I walked to the door to go home. As I passed by the bed with a packed, open suitcase lying on it, I spotted, neatly tucked in a corner, the 26th of July armband which Alberto once wore so proudly at the Isle of Pines.

16

TWO DAYS LATER, I left for Miami in the early evening. Max had been in radio contact with Miami, and I was happy to know that Augusto and the group had arrived safely. One man had been wounded in the upper thigh, involving an artery and serious loss of blood, adding extra urgency to the trip, but he was expected to live. The coast-hugging strategy had worked well, and the boat was being repaired and armed.

I flew Pan American, which still serviced Havana, and arrived in Miami uneventfully to find Avis and the children waiting at the airport. Even at that late hour, the airport was a mass of people. The Cubans had always been great greeters and farewellers, and the uncertainties of those unsettled days made family unity all the more essential.

Burke Hedges was not there. He had told Avis that he thought he shouldn't see me while I was still "in the other camp," friendly with Fidel and the government; and I agreed with Avis' decision that it would be safer for me to pretend.

Avis had brought some friends along to the airport and I joined them for a quick drink, but I was anxious to get in touch with Varona. As soon as my people left, I called him from a public phone and was asked to come immediately to the "office," which Varona referred to casually as El Palomar, as if everyone knew it. El Palomar was Spanish for the nesting place of doves, but the connotation was more that of a "chicken coop."

I took a taxi to an address somewhere near Biscayne Boulevard, only a few blocks from the waters of the Bay. It was by now past midnight, the streets quiet and the houses dark. The address turned out to be a rather large house, which must be the political headquarters of Rescate. Some lights were on and, through the windows, I could see people sitting around in one of the back rooms, but I didn't go in.

Following instructions, I went around to the back of the house where I saw a strange structure which looked like a tree-house perched on four tall pilings. "Chicken coop, indeed," I muttered, and gingerly attacked the flight of almost vertical stairs which led up to El Palomar. Obviously, there was nothing very clandestine about a structure which sat right behind the Movement's clubhouse, but that was part of the style of the counter-revolutionary movements in Miami. It was assumed that the visitor from Havana who was scheduled to return to the island would receive a measure of protection by at least avoiding the public club and coming directly to the chicken coop.

The slightly perilous climb accomplished, I found myself in a fairly standard office, sparsely furnished and utilitarian, in spite of the rather ridiculous setting. A large sign on the wall read: *"You may not be aware of it, but we are at war, and this is a war office. Please conduct yourself accordingly."*

At first sight, the words seemed ludicrous, here in the heart of Miami, a peaceful city in the world's freest nation. Then I realized that these men, in spite of where they operated, were indeed at war—they were the leaders and suppliers for a tiny island ninety miles away which desperately needed their help.

I had entered the office unchallenged and unnoticed, and I recognized Tony Varona immediately. He was an attractive man in his early fifties, balding, and wearing the large horn-rimmed glasses that were so typical of Cubans of his generation. My first impression was that of strength, and the second impression, even before I heard him speak, was one of dedication and honesty, of candidness.

Varona was sitting at his desk with two men who turned out to be his principal lieutenants. The men were obviously of Varona's generation, and I found out later that they had once been important in his government and in the *"Partido Autentico,"* the political party which had spawned the present underground movement.

Varona looked up and saw me. Immediately he stood up and greeted me with an extremely warm handshake.

"Hello, Tocayo," he said. I was both surprised and slightly touched by the recognition, a beau geste on the part of The Leader.

"Dr. Varona, you already know . . . ?" I said. After all, it was just possible that Varona was calling me Tocayo simply because I *was* his *tocayo;* but no, it wasn't that.

"Of course I know," Varona said. "What do you think—that we're out of touch?" Varona was smiling, but just the same I sensed that even Varona was not free of the "exile syndrome," the frustration of being away from the action and the fear of being considered uninformed and uninvolved.

"No, Dr. Varona, I was just surprised that you knew so quickly . . . and that you remembered. I guess I shouldn't have been surprised. I know very well that everything in the Movement is done at your direction—and I'm very proud that you accepted me." I meant that, and Varona appreciated it. Then I handed him the note I carried from Max:

Havana, 14 de Noviembre de 1960—ARTHUR, TANDI y ELIO—Tocayo ha trabajado extraordinariamente bien y de gran utilidad para TANDI y para Rescate, por eso lo he designado mi sustituto en el FRENTE y lo envio a esa para que les

informe de la situacion en Cuba y de todos nuestros problemas ostentando mi
representacion. Ruego sea atendido como se merece.—MAX.

Havana, November 14, 1960—ARTHUR, TANDI and ELIO [code names for
Tony Varona and others]. Tocayo has worked extremely well and has been of
great help to TANDI and to Rescate; for that reason, I have designated him my
substitute in the FRENTE ["the revolutionary front"] and I send him to inform
you of the situation in Cuba and of all our problems bearing my representation.
Please attend to him as he deserves.—MAX.

"Not only did we accept you, Tocayo," Varona said, "but we need you. We
need you a lot. When you go back, you'll have a new job. I want you to help Max
and to start working with Moreno." He didn't bother to explain who "Moreno"
was, and I didn't ask. I'd find out sooner or later, I supposed.

Varona briefly but thoroughly reviewed everything that had to do with me—
my background, my experience, anything and everything that could possibly be
of interest or concern to Rescate.

He went on to tell me about the guerrillas in the Cuban mountains, the groups
already established and the new ones being formed in the hills of Pinar del Rio
and in the mountain range near the U.S. base at Guantanamo. That led to the
subject of the forthcoming invasion, and Varona told me that *when* the invasion
took place—not *if* it took place—he intended to be there with the first wave. He
didn't know then that the CIA wouldn't let him.

At that moment the back door opened and the lanky, Don Quixote figure of
Augusto walked in and gave me a big hug. Then it was Augusto's turn to fill me
in on his plans to arm his "escape boat" to the teeth and to increase the number
and intensity of the sorties into Cuba as a softening-up maneuver leading to the
invasion. Augusto had signed papers from the major guerrilla groups appointing
him as their representative in Miami and the chief supplier of all they needed
to carry on the fight.

One of these groups hoped that the invasion would land near their mountain
stronghold in middle Cuba. They could not only support the landing and cut
across the narrow island in hours and divide Cuba in two but, in the worst case,
they could offer sanctuary to the invaders up in their hills if retreat and regrouping
became necessary.

The beachhead these brave men suggested for the invasion landing was over
200 miles east of another cove in a flat, swampy extension of Cuba's south coast
where guerrillas could not possibly survive. That strategically inappropriate cove
was called La Bahia de Cochinos—the Bay of Pigs. [See map, photo section.]

Augusto finally got around to telling me who "Moreno" was. It seems he was
in charge of the military operations of the Action Section of the Movement. In
other words, he was the coordinator for the guerrillas, as distinct from the
freedom fighters in the cities, and he had reported to Augusto in Cuba. Moreno,
Augusto said, was a good man with a great deal of courage. He was, in fact, an
ex-soldier, and Moreno, of course, was not his real name. I could have guessed

that, but I just assured Augusto that we, now with Moreno's help, would give him all the support we could.

It was getting near three in the morning, and Varona suggested that I go home to my wife.

"Be sure to say hello to Hedges when you see him, Tocayo. As you know, we've been pretty good friends over the years."

"I may see him, Dr. Varona, but if you don't mind, I believe it would be best if Burke doesn't know about my work with you. He still thinks I'm pro-Castro, and I think that's safer all around."

"You're right, Tocayo. That's a good idea. You can't be too careful when you're going back to the island. Too bad about Burke. It'll be a little awkward for you, but he'll know in due course. We'll drink to it together some day at the Floridita"—and we laughed at the joyful thought of a drink together in a free Cuba some day.

"I will tell Avis, though," I said, "because she's got to know, and, besides, she may be a good contact someday. Also, she may need your help at some point."

"I understand, Tocayo," Varona said. "Please give her my regards. She's quite a girl."

I made a gesture which could pass for a military salute, feeling a surprising tingle as I did so, and started down the stairs. Augusto, a big, broad smile on his face, shouted after me:

"Hey, Tocayo, give my regards to your wife, too, and don't forget to tell her about Maria!"

The bastard. I grinned back and waved as I began the tricky descent.

Out on the street, I waited a long time for a taxi and finally picked up a cruiser with a Spanish-speaking driver. That wasn't strange in Miami, but I decided on caution and limited myself to idle talk. The driver was probably just a good man who had been a taxi driver in Cuba—or the head of a law firm—but just the same, one couldn't be too careful. I was learning.

We soon arrived at my brother-in-law's home in Coral Gables. Dr. Robert Miller, a young doctor not long out of medical school, was married to Avis' sister Helen. They lived in a fairly large house on one of those streets in the Gables with Spanish names, some very phony and funny, the product of the imagination of an early Miami developer who wanted to retain the Spanish influence of "La Florida."

As I said a cordial goodbye to the driver, I saw that the house was dark, but Avis was awake, waiting for me. We spent a little time in hushed conversation in the living room, and then Avis led me through the back door of the kitchen into our Miami home: the Millers' garage.

I loved seeing Avis, and she was happy to have me close to her, if only for a little while. It was incredible what she had been able to do with a simple, commonplace garage—albeit at the expense of the Millers' car living outside. She had literally made the small room into an efficiency apartment. The usual garage accumulation of trunks, furniture discards and garden equipment was discreetly covered by a curtain. A full curtain also concealed the broad garage door, and only an unkind visitor would have noticed the metal rails on which the big door slid.

There were rugs and a coffee table and sofas that doubled as beds, and the overall effect was one of warm comfort. I quietly praised Avis' imagination and good taste at length, being careful not to disturb young Tony and Avisita who were sleeping in a corner of the room.

Augusto or no Augusto, I of course did *not* tell Avis about Maria. There was no point, and women have a way of cutting through justifications to discern a threat. Besides, the relationship was only a natural product of the "war," as Dr. Varona would have put it, and would end with the war. Instead, we talked about Avis' job with Avon and how proud she was to be making at least a small contribution that, combined with Hal Bloomer's faithful help, kept our little family going.

Avis prattled happily on, telling me how kind the people in the neighborhood had been to her, buying the cosmetics that she offered and even helping her to make out their bills which, Avis admitted with some embarrassment, she just couldn't seem to do properly. Helplessness and charm, I thought with amusement —a perfect combination for a successful Avon lady.

My God, I reflected in wonder—Avis Hedges, a saleslady, and making a go of it!

We could have gone on forever, but Avis knew that I had only one day in Miami and a lot to do, and so we went to bed. We hugged each other very closely and made love very quietly, knowing that it would be a long time before it could happen again . . . if ever. Avis must have suffered with that thought, too, but she said nothing and soon all was sleep and silence in the Millers' garage.

I woke up early and let the kids romp all over me in bed for a little while so that they'd remember they had a father after all. I dressed and went to the Millers' living room to start making phone calls while Avis made me some breakfast. From the kitchen, Avis shouted, "Dad called, honey."

"Oh?" I said, putting down the telephone, a little surprised.

"He thought you might want to come to a lunch he's giving for Tony Varona today, if you're interested. He said that last part very pointedly, as you may imagine."

"Yes, I may imagine," I came back. "I wonder if I should go."

"Well," Avis said, "it might be one way to ease the tension between you two. And you wouldn't have to tell him anything, really." She paused as if considering the proposition. "I think it might be a step in the right direction."

"You might be right, honey," I said. "Let's go. You call and tell him."

Bob and Helen Miller were now awake, and Bob canceled his hospital duties for the morning to stay home with us. Bob was already a serious, dedicated doctor, but he was also of a normal American background, and what was going on in Cuba, which now touched him through my involvement, was foreign and terribly exciting for him. He wasn't the outgoing sort, but he loved Avis and me in his way and understood what he knew had been for me a self-searching experience that very few Americans ever have to face. Furthermore, as a doctor, he was ready to help. And so, that morning, he had a pill ready for me which, he gravely assured me, I could take if the circumstances required it and I would be dead within seconds. The sun was shining and it was a beautiful Miami morning, and I just wasn't ready for that kind of help.

We laughed about it, and Bob promised that when I next came to Miami (*if ever* was thought by everyone but spoken by no one), he would have a less terminal pill, one which would only make me violently ill for several hours—long enough to buy some needed time. We laughed about that, too, but nevertheless I made a good mental note of the virtues of the second, less drastic pill.

I began a seemingly endless series of telephone calls to wealthy friends in Miami and in New York to ask for money. I asked for money for the fighters in Cuba. I asked for money to help sustain a ship which would sail each day from Florida to the fringe of the Cuban territorial waters and transmit the "Voice of Free Cuba." In sum, I asked for money to fight our war.

The response was somewhat disappointing, but I understood that demands on my friends came from many quarters. However, if there were disappointments, there were also surprises. Particularly gratifying was a contribution from the Kriendlers of the "21" Club in New York, who really knew the Cubans only as good clients of the restaurant and as occasional hosts in Havana. Still, they graciously made a small contribution to a cause which did not affect them directly.

The morning went by rapidly, with all the telephone calls, and soon it was noon and time for us to go to Burke's luncheon. Burke had not quite adapted to the stringencies of exile life as yet, although he would soon have to, and his home was a fairly luxurious residence on one of the bay islands between Miami and Miami Beach, with pool and dock. His fourth wife, Maritza, who had married him just before the debacle, had stuck by him through the bad times—and would continue to do so through much worse. We arrived and joined a noisy group, mostly Cubans with a sprinkling of Americans, already gathered at the pool where a convenient bar had been set up.

Burke and I gave each other a big Cuban *abrazo*, and it was clear from the hug that the ice was melting and that Burke was happy that I had seen the error of my ways and was finally coming home. The presence of the high priest of the anti-Castro movement, Tony Varona, soon expected at the Hedges' home, would provide a fitting blessing to the return of the prodigal son to the fold.

I was wandering around in the crowd when Varona arrived. I saw Burke greet him at the door and engage him in earnest conversation, and I could easily guess the subject. They drifted to the bar. One or two drinks later, Burke summoned me by whistling at me over the crowd, so I dutifully came to be introduced.

Varona and I regarded each other with straight faces while Burke performed the ritual, and all the right words were said about the folly of my earlier loyalties, my disappointment with Castro, etc. It was brief, with Burke doing most of the talking, and it ended with a warm handshake between Varona and me. The reason why, in the circumstances, I still lived in Cuba—in fact, was going back to Havana that day—could have been a logical question, but no one asked it.

I realized that my father-in-law wanted me to stay with him and Varona for a while, to sort of cement the relationship, and so I stayed. We three discussed generalities but, by and large, the Cuban situation was the central theme.

Several drinks under the tropical sun took their toll on all of us, and Varona, reflecting once again the safety and complacency of exile, threw discretion aside, grabbed me by the arm, and moved me slightly away from Burke, but still within his keen earshot.

"Listen, Tocayo," Varona said, "I just remembered that we forgot to discuss the Matanzas problem last night. We have a man there called Pablo, who's been very useful, but I think he's in trouble. He's a stubborn man, Tocayo, and I want you to . . ."

Burke Hedges, five feet away from us, was the picture of utter bewilderment. His highball glass dangled from his hand, his mouth gaped halfway open, his eyes were wide, his eyebrows raised, and he wore a look of total incredulity. He resisted the impulse for a few seconds, but couldn't hold it any longer.

"Hey, wait a minute, fellows," Burke rushed over to us. "What the hell is all this? What's this about 'Tocayo'?" he asked, looking from Varona to me. "And what about 'last night'? Tony only *arrived* last night!"

"Precisely, Burke," Varona said, no longer pretending, since there was no point to it. "He arrived late last night, or early this morning, if you prefer. That, Mr. Hedges," he laughed a little, "is when men of action like us, who are in the war, work at their best."

I just stood there quietly while the surprised look in Burke's face changed slowly to comprehension—and then Burke Hedges silently embraced me.

After Burke walked away, I took advantage of the moment with Varona to ask about Alberto Fowler. I hadn't wanted to bring up the subject until we were alone, but I wanted to know if it would be all right for me to get in touch with him.

Varona said, quite candidly, that he believed Alberto, at the moment, was undergoing military training "somewhere," and though it was obvious that he knew where "somewhere" was, he wasn't telling.

"However, Tocayo," Varona said, "you'll be able to see him on your next trip to Miami, if there is one. I sincerely hope that there will be no need for another trip. We'll do all we can, and I hope God will help us."

"May God help us, tocayo," I repeated, like an acolyte at a Mass, as Tony Varona walked away toward the crowd.

Later on, when we were alone in the inside bar, just before the party broke up, Burke said to me, commenting on what I had told him about Cuba and about Textilera:

"Look, Tony, what's lost is lost. So be it. Let's not lose you trying to get it back. Pretty soon you'll be 'burned,' as we men of action say." Burke smiled as he parodied Varona. "In fact," he continued, "it may be *already* too late for you. You've been seen with people who are openly wanted. In fact, you just told me you're hiding one in your house right now. And all the Castro spies around Miami probably know you saw Varona today. What are you trying to do, commit suicide? You have a wife, you know, and she's my daughter."

"I'm very happy you care," I said, "and I also know that you know where my duty lies."

Burke said nothing for a few seconds and then replied, "Yes, Tony, I guess I know. May God look after Avis and all of you."

In the car, returning home, I told Avis and the Millers what had happened. They, of course, enjoyed it and were relieved by the reconciliation. At the end, I said, as an epilogue, "You know, I will never know, but I can't help thinking that the old goat knew about it all the time and was putting on the best matinee performance of his life."

I was glad it was over, because the fact was that I loved Burke. He had been more of an older brother than a father-in-law, and I had been uneasy and sorry about the rift.

Back at the Millers, I called Varona to say goodbye, made a business call to Hal Bloomer in New York, placed a token call to the tinplate suppliers in Paris, and was ready to pack.

I wouldn't have had any reason to worry about the trip back, armed as I was with bulky files on both sugar and tinplate, except for two irregular items which I had to bring back to Cuba.

One was a handwritten message from Dr. Varona, formally appointing Moreno as the replacement for Commander Augusto as the head of the military operation of Rescate in Cuba. I didn't know Moreno and couldn't understand why a verbal agreement wouldn't be sufficient, but apparently Moreno was the kind of man who wanted his recognition clear and from the top. And so I had a piece of paper signed by Varona to smuggle into the island.

The second item was one of personal interest. I had my Walther .385 caliber pistol in Havana. I loved that gun; it was less bulky and, of course, less powerful than a .45 but, for that reason, more accurate, and, after all, one doesn't need an elephant gun to kill a human being at close range.

It was almost impossible to get ammunition for that handgun in Cuba, even for the Castroites, and, besides, a civilian wouldn't be allowed to *own* the gun, let alone get ammunition for it. Thus I was saddled with the job of bringing back both a subversive message and some forbidden ammunition.

I had thought that maybe someone in Miami—Varona's men or "the friends" —would get around to coaching me a bit on how to handle such things, but no one had. I was on my own and, in fact, I kind of enjoyed relying on my layman's imagination.

After some pondering, I finally took the little piece of paper with Varona's signature on it and folded it over and over many times, until at the end I had a thick but narrow strip of paper. I cut two holes in it so that it could be passed through by the two flimsy metal prongs of a file fastener. I took apart my sugar file, removed about half of the papers, impaled the folded message, and replaced the top part of the file. In a routine inspection, no one would ever pull the papers so far apart as to reveal the folded message at the extreme left margin, covered as it was by a multitude of dull commercial documents. I made sure that the two ends of the metal prongs were securely held by the tiny metal bands provided for that purpose, and that part of my smuggling job was, I hoped, concluded.

I had plans for the several boxes of .385 bullets I would buy on my way to the airport that late afternoon, so I wasn't too worried, although bringing ammunition into Cuba was the most obvious crime against the Revolution and the most carefully policed.

When I was ready to leave, Avis came to me quietly.

"Tony," she said, "do you have to go back?"

I looked at her tenderly.

"You know I have to go back," I said gently. "And you know why."

"Of course I do," she said. "I guess I do. So—please be careful, for our sake, and come back . . . when you can."

I hugged Avis, kissed the children, said a warm goodbye to the Millers, and set out for the airport alone. I didn't want to risk having Avis seen with me, just in case, so I had asked her not to go along.

At the airport, the immigration, or emigration, proceedings were fairly routine, except that I kept feeling that both the immigration officials and the group of Cubans waiting for arrivals automatically looked upon a passenger returning to Cuba as some kind of traitor. That didn't bother me at all. In fact, I considered it a plus for any agents in the crowd.

The flight was uneventful, and in a little more than an hour I arrived at the Rancho Boyeros Airport, the international air entry to Cuba. Security had of course been tightened, and my briefcase was inspected in one room while my luggage went on to the Customs section.

I satisfied the Inspector, a short serious man in the inevitable fatigues, that I was coming back from a trip basically in the service of the Cuban Government, and showed my files to prove it. He opened the sugar file, and I stood there, half-frightened, half-amused, while he glanced at twenty or thirty pages before concluding, wrongly, that if there was anything subversive it would not be openly available to him in the files. As I had hoped, not once did the Inspector pull the papers sufficiently apart to even come close to the little folded message held tightly by the metal fastener.

He did, however, look into every corner of the briefcase and check every paper I carried on my person. With a pleased grin, I acknowledged the Inspector's tacit approval as he stepped back from the bench, picked up my briefcase and followed a guard toward the Customs Inspection.

On the way, I said to the guard sent along with me, "Listen, compañero," I used the approved term, "before we get to luggage inspection, I need a word with the Chief Inspector in his office."

The guard looked at me with surprise, but obediently cut to the left before we reached Customs Inspection and led me to a side office. Behind the desk in the office, a somewhat older "fatigued" type was sitting, smoking a large cigar and talking to a fellow officer.

"Yes?" the Inspector asked, taking the cigar from his mouth and blowing the smoke toward me.

"That's a good cigar, Inspector. I'm glad to get back to them," I said, guileless as hell and smiling blandly.

"Is that what you're here to tell me?" the Inspector said, firmly maintaining his authority.

"No, Inspector, I'm here to tell you that I have some ammunition with me."

The Inspector cast a quick sidelong glance at his buddy and began to take notice.

"What do you mean, 'some ammunition'?"

"Inspector," I said, "I just want you to know, before I go through the Customs Inspection, that I am bringing with me a hundred rounds of .385 caliber bullets."

The Inspector looked at me, his mouth halfway open. He didn't know whether to laugh at this nut or take me into custody. Finally he said: "And so, Mr. . . ." He looked at the guard, and the guard contributed, "Navarro, Mr. Inspector."

"And so, Mr. Navarro, I suppose you have some reason for bringing these rounds in."

"Of course I do, Inspector. I was asked to bring the ammunition."

"Oh, really?" The Inspector was slightly amused. "I suppose you can tell me who asked you, or is that a secret?"

I was beginning to enjoy myself.

"Yes, sir, of course," I said. "You may ask Captain Jaime Fernandez at the Central Sugar Office, who happens to have a gun he can't readily provide for here in Havana."

"Well, that's very nice," said the Inspector, "but you must know that the Central Sugar Office and, in fact, all offices, Mr. Navarro, happen to be closed at this time. I hope for your sake that this isn't some kind of a joke. If it is, it isn't very funny."

"Oh, I wouldn't think of joking about a matter like this, Inspector. In fact, I have Captain Fernandez's home telephone number, and perhaps, if you don't mind, you could reach him there."

"I'll do exactly that," the Inspector said and, turning around to the guard, he snapped, "Have this man's luggage taken off the line and held for special inspection."

The Inspector dialed the number I gave him, reached Captain Fernandez, and assured himself by a number of discreet questions that he was indeed talking to a prominent member of the revolutionary bureaucracy.

Without a word, the Inspector got up and motioned me to follow him into the Customs area where my luggage had been set aside. The Chief Inspector summoned the Line Inspector behind the counter, who came running and saluted his superior. The Line Inspector opened one of my two bags and, right on top, there were four rectangular boxes familiar to anyone who had ever had anything to do with guns. Excited, the junior man opened one of the boxes and exposed the neat, honeycombed package of the bright copper bullets. He picked up the box and came triumphantly to the Chief Inspector.

"Look . . ." he began, but before he could go any further, the Chief Inspector said, "Yes, I know, stupid. Why do you think I'm here?"

"We caught him, didn't we?" the Line Inspector gloated.

"No, we didn't," the Chief Inspector retorted. "There's nothing to catch. This man is okay. Mr. Navarro is with the Revolution. Send his bags down to the taxi." Then he turned and walked away. The Line Inspector was totally dumbfounded, but dutifully he ordered the porters to carry my luggage out of the Customs section.

I came out of the airport, tipped the porter, and got into the Mercedes which Maria had driven to the airport. I gave her a kiss, pushed her out from under the wheel, and drove off.

A great believer in extrasensory perception and telepathy—and therefore never thinking about what I didn't want to communicate—only then did I allow myself to rejoice in the thought that, along with the one hundred bullets in the four boxes seen and blessed by the minions of the Revolution, I had in those bags four hundred additional rounds of the same caliber bullets for myself and the underground movement.

I was elated as we drove toward the Country Club. After all, how can an Inspector, no matter how thorough, insist on looking through all the luggage of a man who had willingly declared that he was importing bullets for a rightful purpose?

"Okay," said Maria, who had been listening to my thoughts and words. "That's very bright of you, Tocayo, but what if they *had* looked?"

"Well, Maria, that was a chance I had to take, and it wasn't a bad chance as the odds go. If they had found the rest of the ammunition, I'd have said it was all destined for Captain Fernandez, who 'did not want to exaggerate his needs.' And, as it so happens, Captain Fernandez is a good friend, and even though I don't really know where he stands today, I know he would have stood by me and borne me out, rather than turn me in to the G-2. Those are the chances you have to take," I said, beginning to feel like a professional in the *action* section of the Movement.

Maria looked at me and simply smiled.

I looked back at her and laughed out loud, realizing how conceited and pompous I had sounded, but enjoying every bit of it.

"Okay, you wench," I said. "I'm the amateur and you're the expert, but I made it—and, besides, I've been in the presence of the Pope in Miami and he has blessed me. Doesn't that impress you?"

Maria made a little moue and said, wrapping her lips around the word: "No.

When Dr. Varona comes down *here* with us, I may think differently."

"All right, all right," I said, "since you're so smart. What's my schedule"—
I reached over with my arm and pulled her over to me—". . . after tonight, that
is?"

"After tonight," she said serenely, looking straight ahead, "you're scheduled
to meet Max and Moreno for lunch tomorrow."

"That sounds all right to me," I said.

And so we drove on and settled down to "tonight." This was my real world,
and Miami so far away . . .

When I finally reached home, it was very late in the night, and all was quiet.
I found a note from Gisela saying that Nanita was doing as well as could be
expected and that she had been asking for me regularly from the moment I had
left. My mother had engaged a nurse who would be coming in daily to take care
of the injections and the pills, but, other than that, Gisela felt she could handle
the situation. *Mr.* Lorenzo was all right, and Gisela was taking good care of him.
Finally, the little note welcomed me home. I wondered how my mother had
accepted the presence of Lorenzo in the house, but I decided that I'd worry about
that in the morning.

I woke up early the next morning and drove to the office way before my normal
arrival time, even before early-bird Maria Antonieta was there. Some time during
the morning I called Max at his office and confirmed a luncheon appointment
at the Toki Ona, where I was to meet Moreno for the first time. The Toki Ona
was another Basque restaurant, less well known and less crowded than the Centro
Vasco where Alberto and I had had lunch the week before, and it was a favorite
of mine.

It was the more legitimate of the Basque places, smaller and chummier, and
to bear out its authenticity, the apartment building above the restaurant was
almost fully taken by the young jai alai players who had come over from Spain,
lured by the hard and plentiful Cuban currency. There was even a practice jai
alai court right next to the restaurant, not that that was much of a temptation
for anyone who had just finished eating its wonderful Spanish food.

On this day I arrived early, ahead of Max and Moreno, as agreed. The owner
of the Toki Ona greeted me and led me to a table in the back, as I had requested,
which was set for three people. The red wine of the Spanish vintner I preferred
came without being ordered, but I told the owner that I'd wait for my friends
before having my favorite lunch.

I looked over the large room, partially divided by a long central bar, and
watched the crowd—some old friends and some strangers. There were people in
coats and ties, others in *guayaberas* (the traditional Cuban cross between a shirt
and a coat), the new Government bureaucracy, and the officers of the Rebel
Army in their fatigues—a motley crowd indeed.

Max was late, and while I knew that punctuality was certainly not a Cuban
virtue, I was beginning to get just a bit anxious. Just when I was sure that
something must have happened, the headwaiter appeared at my table.

"Mr. Navarro," he said in a low voice, "there are two rough-looking characters at the bar who came in right behind you. Please don't look. I've never seen them before, and they keep looking over here to your table. I wonder—is something wrong?"

"Thank you, Manolo," I said. "Don't worry. I see them, and I'll keep an eye on them. And, for your peace of mind, I'm 'clean.' There is nothing on me even if they are the G-2. This is a social lunch."

The headwaiter straightened up, made a show of pouring some more wine for me, and went back to his chores. At that moment Max walked in through the front door with a man who towered above him and also doubled his girth, if not tripled it. That it was not difficult to do that to Max didn't detract from the man's size and presence.

Max immediately spotted me and brought his companion over. The expected introductions took place: "Tocayo, this is Moreno. Moreno, this is Tocayo."

Above the heavy body, Moreno had a disproportionately small head with fine features. He had a pencil-thin mustache, and had he been blond and Irish, he would have looked remarkably like Errol Flynn. His attitude toward me was one of wary caution—a sort of unsmiling "show me," which made me wonder how I'd get along with him.

"I suppose you've ordered your 'patas' for a change," said Max, referring to my pigs' feet favorite.

"As a matter of fact, I have," I said, and I was suddenly aware of a new self-assurance, undoubtedly a result of my meetings with The Leader. "Won't you two gentlemen join me?"

"I suppose Moreno will," Max said, "but if you don't mind, I'll have a steak, very well done, if that's possible in these unlikely surroundings."

"I'll go along with Tocayo," Moreno said, speaking for the first time and still studying me closely. "I think he knows what he's doing." He didn't have to say that, and my heart lightened.

I passed our orders to the nearest waiter and then said: "Listen, I think you ought to know that there are two guys at the bar that the house doesn't know. They look suspicious, and they're obviously keeping an eye on our table."

At that Moreno looked over deliberately at the bar, turned back, and said, "Yes, I know," and that was all. After enjoying his pause and my concern, he said condescendingly, "They're my men. I told 'em to follow you in here, and I guess I described you pretty well." Then he smiled openly for the first time. "You're not hard to describe, Tocayo. I told 'em if they weren't out in ten minutes, I'd come on in with Max. It's standard procedure, Tocayo, and you'll get used to it."

I was relieved, gratified, and just plain happy that I'd be dealing with such a professional as Moreno appeared to be and undoubtedly was. I didn't know then how bold he was also, but I'd soon find out.

Together, Max and Moreno went on to explain to me the details of the so-called Action Sector of Rescate, from the urban sabotage which Lorenzo had

once headed, to the warfare of the guerrillas in the mountains. They said that
guerrilla action would be continued in the central mountains of Cuba where it
had started; it would be strengthened in the eastern province of Oriente near the
Guantanamo base and, finally, it would be extended now to include Pinar del Rio,
the westernmost Cuban province, adjacent to Havana and a good operations base
for an eventual move toward the capital.

As Moreno and I discussed these matters, we got to know each other better,
and he finally told me of his desperate need for supplies. It was interesting and
touching how this rugged man was capable of describing the needs of the men
in the hills with both passion and compassion. Moreno briefed me on his relationship with the other underground movements, particularly the Christian Democrats, with whom he seemed to have a good rapport.

Right after lunch, they told me, they'd take me to the house in the Miramar
section where the radio transmission and reception equipment was hidden and,
they explained, was used for daily contact with Rescate headquarters in Miami
and, through them, on an "as needed" basis with "the friends." I looked forward
to that.

We were enjoying our Spanish desserts, except for the ascetic Max, when
Moreno said, "Listen, there's a guy we've got to get out, right away—a guerrilla
leader in the Escambray Range, in Santa Clara. He's number one, and Castro's
guys are getting too close. He's a simple man but he's got more guts than I have
—and that's saying a lot," Moreno added without even a trace of modesty. "He
had to come down from the hills and he's hiding in Havana. We've got to get
him out to Miami."

I just looked at Max, waiting.

"Tocayo," Moreno continued, "I think that's a job for you. The only way we
can get him out is through the fishing port of Cardenas, ten minutes away from
Varadero Beach. Now, I'd look ridiculous in one of those plush houses at
Varadero, but you wouldn't."

I must have frowned a little, but Moreno said, "No, Tocayo, don't get me
wrong. I don't resent it. If I did, I'd be on the other side like all of those envious
sons-of-bitches, and you know I'm not. I just think that you and maybe some of
your friends would look right in one of those beach houses, and that's exactly what
we need."

"I'll do what I can," I said.

"I'm sure you will," Moreno came back, "and the Christian Democrats will
help. They've got people to get out, too. Tonight, or perhaps tomorrow, I'll put
you in touch with them. Also, tomorrow morning, when our man has had a few
hours to rest from his trip down from the hills, I want you to meet him. His name
is Edel Montana, and I think you'll be impressed. I *know* you'll be impressed."

Coffee and cigars were brought, chosen, and consumed, except for Max who
stuck to his chain-smoking of cigarettes.

"Max," I said, "you've been awfully quiet. I hope we . . . haven't said anything
out of place."

"Not at all, Tocayo," Max assured me. "This meeting was for you and Moreno to get to know each other, and that's what you've been doing. I'm glad, because you two complement each other and the winner will be the Movement"—he paused, totally serious—"and our country."

"Okay," Moreno said, "let's go. We've got a lot to do. We've got to let Florida know when to pick up the men, and we—you, Tocayo—have to get them to the right place. It won't be easy and it will be dangerous." Moreno looked at me for what seemed a long time and then said: "I know you can do it, Tocayo, and I also know we're going to work very well together."

"Thanks, Moreno," was all that I could manage to say.

Moreno glanced quickly toward the bar without any sign that I could detect, and yet the two bodyguards got up immediately and walked out of the restaurant. On our way out, I shook hands warmly with the headwaiter as I settled our check.

As we emerged into the bright Cuban afternoon, I noticed with some comfort that the men who had been at the bar were now standing, deceptively relaxed, at each end of the building which housed Toki Ona, one foot propped up against the wall. Their right hands rested over the buttons of their jackets, comfortably near the bulges on the left sides of their coats.

Max, Moreno and I left Toki Ona in my car, followed by the two bodyguards and a chauffeur in an old black Cadillac that Moreno must have bought with gangster movies in mind. We moved out of the center of the city, past Vedado and Miramar, and even beyond my home at the Country Club.

About a mile away from my place, we came to an area that wasn't yet totally developed, and there were still a few empty lots around. It was in that section that I was directed to pull up in front of a large corner house across from an empty lot. The house was fronted by a semi-circular drive which rose from the street, and I drove up to the front door. The second car stayed behind on the street.

"This was Augusto's home," Max said to me, "and this is where we have our radio. In fact, Tocayo, it will be interesting to see if you can find it."

The door was answered by a pleasant-looking black woman and we went in. I looked carefully around the house for the hidden radio—in every room, in every closet, the fake fireplace, everywhere. I thought I had a pretty good imagination, but I finally had to give up.

Max led me into the master bedroom and over to the large main closet, full of suits and dresses, with double-tiered shoe racks along its length. He reached down, removed a pair of shoes, twisted a section of the wooden cleat which keeps the shoes from sliding off—and there, behind the closet, was a small area with all the typical equipment of a radio transmitting and receiving station, including even a table and chair for the operator.

Max and Moreno laughed at my surprise and restored the closet to its normal condition.

The maid brought Max an envelope with the decoded message of that morning's communication with Miami. It wasn't always possible for Max or someone else from the Movement to be present at contact time, they explained to me, and so the radio operator would leave the messages with the maid.

That day's message contained, as hoped, instructions for getting a group of men out of Cuba through the north coast near Varadero Beach. The pick-up would be three days later at Cayo Arenas (Sandy Key), about an hour by motorboat from the port of Cardenas which, in turn, was about two hours away from Havana and immediately adjacent to the Varadero Peninsula. Contact would be made at midnight on the open ocean side of the sandy key.

The group to be smuggled out, the message said, would include Lorenzo, which made me very happy, and the guerrilla leader Montana, and there would be room for two more. Max told Moreno and me that he'd like to send two corporals from the telegraphy section of Castro's army who had been helping us for months and had reason to believe they might be suspected. The Christian Democrats were interested in their escape, too, and would provide help.

Max turned the operation over to Moreno and me and left us making plans while he was driven back to his office.

17

MORENO AND I STARTED OUT that morning to meet with and arrange for the escape of Edel Montana. I had gotten word by radio from Commander Augusto and from "the friends" in Miami that it was absolutely essential to have Montana in Florida as soon as possible. Not only had he become a legend—and therefore a natural rallying point as a guerrilla leader—but his knowledge of the southern coast and hills of the Santa Clara Province was crucial. It wasn't difficult to guess that it all had to do with the invasion.

After all, it was common sense that, whatever beach or coastline was selected as the main entry point for the invasion, there would have to be a secure area to retreat to in case of need, and that could only be one of the mountain ranges on the island. That way, a certain degree of success or staying power could be salvaged even from a defeat at the beach. From a mountain stronghold, a sufficiently large group could still manage to cut the island in half, leaving the Communists only Havana and adjacent provinces, with a lot of opposition even there. If no overt help then came from the Soviets, the democratic forces would gradually move in and put an end to the civil war. Of course, I didn't know all of this for a fact. I was only guessing—wrongly, as it turned out.

I left my house early, picked up Moreno at his apartment directly across the street from the U.S. Embassy, a building by the name of Olan Towers, and went on to fetch a reporter from *Newsweek* magazine at the Hotel Nacional.

The reporter turned out to be a pleasant, smart young man named David Reed, and he was anxious to get a story of the *new* Cuban underground for his magazine. He had, of course, been thoroughly cleared, so Max said that it would be all right to have him along for at least part of the mission. Moreno, true to form, didn't approve, but he went along with Max's orders. Reed proved to be a bona fide, straightforward reporter, and whatever misgivings had been entertained were unfounded.

Moreno and I drove by the entrance of the Nacional about 9 A.M. to pick him up. I introduced Reed to Moreno who responded coolly, and we were off toward the center of Havana. Finally we parked in front of one of Havana's principal department stores, El Encanto.

We went into the store, keeping an eye on the street entrance. When we were sure that we weren't being followed, we quickly ducked through a side door to the street, where two of Moreno's men were waiting in the by-now-familiar black Cadillac. The whole thing reminded me of early gangster films, but I came to the conclusion that there are just so many ways of skinning a cat and eventually there are bound to be repetitions.

The Cadillac twisted around the Havana streets for about fifteen minutes and finally stopped in front of a small, seedy apartment building in an area well known as a red light district. Fortunately for the aesthetics of the surroundings, the whores and pimps who would people it in a few hours were still sleeping off their night's work. The unlikely Cadillac sat there with Moreno's henchmen, while Moreno, Reed and I walked through the front door and toward the back of the building where the doors to two apartments could be seen. Moreno knocked at the door on the right, and it was immediately opened, at first cautiously and then all the way. The man who opened the door was obviously another one of Moreno's "staff," so he discreetly put his gun back somewhere inside an oversized coat.

At that point, the door to the bedroom opened and a man appeared. He was young, in his early thirties, with a crew-cut and a wild look in his eyes, and he had a submachine gun tucked between his arm and his chest, at the ready. I stared, fascinated, at the legendary Edel Montana, for obviously that's who it was. David Reed was staring at him too, as fascinated as I was.

Moreno crossed the room to greet Montana, while I quietly briefed Reed that Montana, a simple farmer, had made quite a name for himself as one of the most respected guerrilla leaders in the mountains, as even Che Guevara would admit. That the Castro Government also recognized it was attested to by the fact that the troops had been sent up to the mountain to get him, outnumbering his group of about 200 men by ten to one.

During the skirmish, he and four others had been cut off from the main group and had decided to try to break through the Castro lines. All four of Montana's companions were killed or wounded, and only Montana survived to reach the relative security of the home of some friends on level land. There, as he recovered, or partially recovered, from his wounds, he realized that the anti-Communist fight in Cuba was doomed without help from the outside.

Eventually, he had made contact with Rescate couriers, who instructed him to come to Havana where he would be provided a hideout until someone from the Movement, probably a man called Tocayo, got in touch with him with plans to get him to Florida. Montana had asked only that his identity as the founder and leader of his guerrilla group be respected, and that he should be allowed to come back to their rescue as soon as possible. Both requests were granted and, in fact, fitted in perfectly with the plans of Augusto and Varona for the guerrilla support of the invasion.

Reed and I sat in the little back room with Montana, while Moreno went back to the living room with the guard. Reed, like all good journalists, smelled a story and began firing questions at Montana.

Montana, a farmer all his life until he became involved in the fight against Batista and later against Castro in the mountains he loved and knew so well, was practically illiterate, but he was naturally bright and a born leader. His responses were unsophisticated, and his convictions were strong and clear. Reed was clearly taken with him, and his eager questions literally tumbled over themselves.

"Why are you fighting Castro now?"

"Because he's a son-of-a-bitch and a traitor."

"Didn't you support Castro in the fight against Batista?"

"Not really. I never trusted him. I was fighting my own fight, but I did think . . . at the very beginning . . . that he might be the solution."

"What about Guevara?" Reed asked. "You must have known *him* fairly well."

"Well," Montana said, "he was a Communist; but he fought the common enemy and he fought in my mountains, so that was okay with me. At least you always knew where you stood with the Che. He never pretended. And I know where I stand now. He's the enemy, and I'm fighting it."

The man was sitting on the edge of his bed, skeletally thin, answering the questions with lowered eyes, his machine gun resting awkwardly on the pillow.

His right pants leg was slit from the knee, showing a bloody bandage on his ankle. He had gunshot embedded in his back, which Moreno had forced him to show us, and there was a nasty red bullet graze which parted his short hair in the wrong place. He could manage a shy half-smile once in a while, but mostly his face was serious, even sullen.

"All right," Reed said, "but why exactly did you break with Castro?"

"Look, mister," Montana came back, raising his eyes, half-surprised, half-angry, "where the hell have you been for the past two years? If you don't know why I broke with Castro, there's no point in talking."

"I know something about it," Reed excused himself, "but you know reporters have to ask questions, even if they know the answers."

Montana's shy smile recognized the apology, but his voice was still angry.

"Well, Mr. Reporter," he said, "do we have a democracy in Cuba, or didn't you know we were promised a democracy? Or maybe it doesn't matter in your country whether we have a democracy or not."

"Of course it does, Señor Montana," Reed said. "So now, why are you going to the United States?"

"Because we need help, and we can't get it here."

"Well, what do you want from the U.S.?" Reed continued, hitting at the sore points. "Why should we care what happens in Cuba? What is it you want, anyway—money?"

Montana was visibly upset, but containing himself, and I began to wonder whether the interview had been a good idea after all. I looked pleadingly at Reed, but the reporter had his journalistic facade on, asking fighting questions but without seeming to be involved in the fight.

"The U.S. should help . . . because you're a democracy—a big and powerful democracy. We've always looked to you as a model, but maybe you don't know this. Perhaps your own revolution happened too long ago and you have forgotten . . ." Montana paused, looking straight at Reed. "No, we don't want your money. All we want is guns to fight our own fight. My men will provide the guts."

Reed then dropped his facade and smiled openly, breaking the tension immediately: "Okay, Mr. Montana, enough nasty questions. I just had to get the answers in your own words. Believe me, I personally wish you success. After looking at your wounds, I guess I don't have to wish you *luck.*" At that we all laughed.

I realized that the interview was ending, but I still had my own question to ask of this impressive, unassuming man. Therefore I said: "Mr. Montana, tomorrow, when we mount our show, our pretense, in order to get you out to the keys safely, we won't have time for serious talk or philosophy, and I've been wanting to ask you, simply, if you're not afraid of what you're doing now and what lies ahead tomorrow. I think Reed's readers would like the answer, too."

I waited to give him time to think, then encouraged him: "After all, hiding in a city, hunted, is very different from being out in the open in the mountains you know so well. Here, you're alone. There are no buddies on your side to fight with you, and there's no clear enemy to fire at. This is a sordid kind of danger, sort of sick and helpless. If you're caught, you're in enemy territory, and your chances of surviving are very small. I know you're a brave man, but isn't this a different situation? Aren't you afraid? I ask you because I must confess that at times I am."

Montana didn't answer immediately. It was an honest question and he gave it honest consideration. Then he said: "No, Tocayo, I guess I'm not afraid. Of course, I prefer my kind of fighting, the kind I know, but I'm not afraid. Long ago I accepted the possibility of death; but, besides that, I am protected."

There was a tone of amusement in Montana's voice. Reed and I exchanged glances and looked at Montana curiously. Montana smiled, said. "I guess you want to know how," and started to unbutton his shirt.

As a Cuban and a Catholic, I patiently got ready to be shown, once more, the large gold medals with elaborate images of patron saints that the Cuban farmers wear around their necks. They were fiercely superstitious about these medals, to which were attributed almost divine powers. I had run into the medals and the beliefs hundreds of time. But this time I was wrong.

From the end of a long, thick cord, which reached below his belly and into his crotch, the guerrilla leader fished out a nicely polished, ready-looking hand grenade.

"They'll never catch me," Montana said to his astonished audience, "and, if they do, I won't go alone."

There wasn't much to say after that. Reed and I got up to leave, but, before joining Moreno, I instructed Montana briefly on the next day's trip to Varadero and gave him a package of sports clothes to wear. We walked out to the car, where the street showed the beginnings of the noontime prostitute action.

Moreno dropped me and the reporter at my car, still parked near the department store. I left Reed at the Hotel Nacional, reminding him to use discretion and to remember security when he wrote his story. Then I drove over to bum a drink from Magda at her apartment in La Puntilla.

Magda was alone, and seemed glad to see me. She told me excitedly about the shoot-out at the river a few nights ago and how the bullets whistled by her windows—which was probably bending the truth a bit. I was properly interested and concerned, but volunteered nothing. I realized again, as I had on other occasions during my "career," how very human it was to want to share exciting experiences with friends, and how, as a result, plans of the underground were innocently betrayed.

I asked Magda if I could borrow the keys to her house at Varadero Beach. I told her I'd be using it for one night only and please not to ask for details.

"I don't need to know the details," Magda said. "Don't you think I can guess? I'm a grown woman, you know. Varadero is very convenient if you don't mind driving two hours to get there. Please just don't leave the place a mess."

"I won't, Magda, I promise," I said.

"By the way, when is Avis coming back?" It was a good female association of ideas. "Didn't I hear she was expected back?"

"You may have, Magda," I answered simply. "I think it'll be soon, but I don't know when."

I encouraged the rumor of Avis' return. It gave me an extra degree of credibility with the Government, because here I was staying in Cuba and trying to make a success of the Revolution and, furthermore, Burke Hedges' daughter was coming back to join me.

I gave Magda a goodbye kiss on the cheek, ignored her parting look, which was amused and knowing at the same time, and went alone to the Toki Ona for a quick lunch—or as near thereto as a Basque restaurant could provide.

After lunch I picked up El Gallego to fill him in on the plans for the "Varadero Exit," as I called it, and we went on to meet Raquel, the Christian Democrat representative who would also participate.

It was an incongruous group that met that afternoon at Raquel's large and pleasant home in Miramar. Raquel de Ville was in her early twenties, attractive, with short brown hair and brown eyes—smart, feminine, but dedicated. She really had no business in a man's fight, but a man's fight is a woman's fight, too. She came from a relatively well-to-do family, had been educated at the Sacred Heart, which was *the* school for those families that could afford it, and had graduated from the University. Her social and religious upbringing aside, Raquel was a dedicated anti-Castro activist, and a staunch and active member of the Student Directorate. She also worked with the Christian Democrats, an older group that was well-structured internationally and, although disclaiming leadership from the Vatican and at times openly challenging its positions, was still basically Catholic enough to satisfy her most cherished principles.

Then there was El Gallego. No one really knew who El Gallego was, or *why* he was. Physically, he was the typical Spaniard—curly black hair, a strongly chiseled face with a permanent five o'clock shadow, and friendly dancing eyes that would have suited a gypsy. He was about my height, with the lean body of a bullfighter. I had the feeling always that if you threw a cape at him, anytime at all, in any place, he would grab it and swing it around his body in a perfectly executed *veronica.* I didn't know his family, and never would, and El Gallego's front, if it was a front, was vaguely that he was a free-lance, itinerant commercial designer. The only thing I knew for sure, and he only told me this when pushed against the wall for details of his background, was that he had left Spain after fighting Franco's Rightist regime. How strange, then, that here he was fighting the extreme Left of Castro's Communism. But his courage and loyalty had been tested and proven, and that had been enough for Max and Augusto, and it was enough for me.

Raquel was in charge of collecting the two servicemen Max wanted to get out of Cuba. There were rumors at the time that large units of the Cuban Navy were ready to defect, provided only that the much-touted invasion was in fact a reality. Raquel would also provide the two or three extra women we needed to complete the "Varadero Exit" charade of a young people's beach party, and their loyalty was essential—not only to this particular venture, but to the Movement itself.

Mine was the responsibility for the operation, but most of all I had to provide the raison d'être of the escape: Edel Montana and my permanent house guest, Lorenzo, two of the most distinguished leaders of the resistance, each in his own field.

We agreed that El Gallego, Maria and I would be the only members of Rescate to participate, and there would be only Raquel from the Student Directorate. We would use two cars—my Mercedes and a sportier car, a Chevrolet; no large black Cadillac would be suitable for this junket. The men would be provided with fake ID cards. No weapons would be carried, since possible discovery at a checkpoint would be a dead giveaway. I, however, intended to stash my pistol away in the special cranny of my glove compartment, and if I had to, I'd think of some plausible excuse. Finally, the pick-up hours were coordinated to the minute, in itself quite an undertaking in Cuba. When El Gallego and I left, Raquel was already busy on the telephone.

Shortly before noon, the two cars bearing a dozen men and women, the girls on laps, arrived noisily at Magda Vazquez-Bello's beautiful beach house in an isolated section of Varadero Beach. We had brought drinks and things to cook, and the girls happily set about making lunch. They were all young, probably Sacred Heart products like Raquel, and they were pretty and full of life.

Lorenzo, El Gallego and I looked our parts quite adequately. The two servicemen, however, had that fish-out-of-water look of soldiers in civilian clothes, and farmer-fighter Montana was nothing less than a sight in slacks and sports jacket easily two sizes too large.

While the girls were busy with lunch and the prospective travelers were readying their minimum gear, I left El Gallego in charge and wandered out toward the beach—the incredibly beautiful Varadero Beach.

Magda's place was toward the end of the peninsula which formed the famous beach, and I could look over the long expanse of talcum-powder-white sand which started high up at the green line of sea-grapes and sea-oats swaying in the breeze and extended two or three hundred yards into the sea. At high noon, the sun ruled over it all, a little overwhelming in its pervasive brightness, bringing out the sparkles of the wet sand and the foamy ripples of the waves, and intensifying the blues and greens which succeeded each other, ever deeper in hue, as they progressed toward the dark blue waters of the open ocean, seemingly so still in the distance.

On this day, the wide stretch of sand before me was virtually empty of people, and I remembered a melancholy Brazilian song I loved, *"As Praias Dessertas,"* the deserted beaches, and a pang of sadness came naturally with it. I forgot for one moment what I was there for, and my mind went back to the image of the Varadero of years ago.

I peopled the sand with the old gay crowds, groups greeting each other as they passed, warm sands under their feet, making quick dates for meeting later in the day—the budding, thrilling romances of young boys and girls, sparked by the heat, the sun, the semi-nude bodies, the sensuous movements, the happy noises, and the floating excitement of it all.

And the appropriate cells of my brain brought back the smells, recalling the unmistakable aroma of sea water, of the delicious little tree oysters which tanned fishermen would peddle all over the beach—the best hors d'oeuvres ever invented —of the distant, slightly acrid aroma of the rum daiquiris reaching you from any number of seaside houses as you walked, of the pungency of cigars which even the tropical breeze could not totally dissipate, and of the human smell of fresh, clean perspiration from the exertion of healthy bodies at play.

Then there were the welcome pauses in the cool shade, under thatched-roof little oases where groups would gather for a breather, inevitably engaged in heated discussions on the merits of the crews and swimming teams from the various clubs which converged at Varadero to compete each summer. The American tourists, too, would come, and in no time at all would be at home in the mad, wonderful party atmosphere which prevailed for several months each year at what was reputed to be the most beautiful beach in the world.

Abruptly my reverie ended, and the happy crowds faded to the few little figures which I could actually see on the beach, while the beach itself remained there, unmoved by the changing ways of human beings.

I turned back to the house and observed, to my satisfaction, that the goings-on were perfectly in keeping with a normal beach party arranged by people still unconcerned or irresponsible enough to enjoy it.

Luncheon was being served, and the two servicemen, a little more at ease with the girls' encouragement, were talking about their work. They had been helping by relaying intelligence to the Movement and by intentionally delaying orders which would have sent the Cuban Navy's PT boats out to shoot down anyone fleeing Cuba in whatever boats they could find. In Miami, they said dramatically to impress the girls, they would be needed to establish telegraphic contact with the resistance forces inside Cuba and would eventually come back to join the guerrillas in the hills and to guide the air drops of food and weapons to sustain them. "Communications, after all," they said, "are the life force of a revolutionary movement." The girls were duly impressed.

After lunch, I made one quick trial run to the port in my car, taking Maria with me. I wanted to know exactly how long it would take in the Mercedes at normal speed by the main road, which I had already decided would be better than the old country road, which offered no particular advantages. I also wanted to meet the fisherman who would take the men out to the first key, where they would all eventually gather and make one single trip to the final destination, Cayo Arenas, a good hour away from their first rendezvous.

I knew we had a fairly tight schedule to meet. I, or someone, would have to make four round trips from Varadero to Cardenas, and the fisherman, in turn, would have to make four round trips to the middle key meeting point, about ten to fifteen minutes from the dock. Although the car and boat trips could run concurrently, it was still very tight. It would all have to be accomplished within three hours, between nine and midnight, and there was little leeway for error. I timed the one-way run to Cardenas at fifteen minutes, just about what I expected, and we met the fisherman, who turned out to be an old member of the Movement.

The provincial head of Rescate had given the fisherman complete instructions. He was ready and had no questions to ask. I drove slowly by the docks, stopping briefly for Maria to inspect the oceanside bar where the men would wait for the exact time of contact. She reported that the bar looked perfectly suitable. After that, we returned to Varadero, taking the old road just in case, for some reason, it became necessary to use it. The "test" had taken less than one hour altogether.

Back at the beach house, we went over the plans for the escape once more. During the fake party we would stage that evening, part of the group would slip out at appointed hours to the nearby port town of Cardenas, not more than fifteen minutes away by the regular highway or twenty-five minutes by the old country road. The choice of road would be made at the time of departure.

Two couples at a time would ride to the port: two of the girls, one of the men who was to be picked up at the keys, and the driver—either El Gallego or me. The car would stop at a small park by the water's edge and the "fugitive" whose turn it was would step out alone, walk to the dockside cafe, order a drink and pay for it immediately, await the exact moment, walk out and be met within seconds on the street by a fisherman. The clothes the fugitive wore would be in keeping with an early morning fishing expedition in a small motorboat, and, of course, all the fishing gear would be in evidence on board. After greeting each other normally, the two men would then go together to the docks and get into the skiff which would make the trip to a mid-point between the shore and Cayo Arenas. There the traveler would disembark and wait for his fellow travelers while the fisherman would return to the mainland for the next trip.

Once the four trips were completed and the men were reunited, they would travel together in the motorboat to Cayo Arenas, would be dropped on its north shore, facing the open Atlantic, and would be picked up there by a large, fast, adequately armed boat provided by the Movement or by "the friends," and take off for Florida.

If anything went wrong before boarding the skiff at the dock, there was an alternate meeting place within the town where members of the Movement were stationed, with enough guns to overcome a patrol car or put up a stiff resistance against a larger contingent. If serious trouble arose and bluffing was useless, the alternate meeting place would be given as the "place of residence" and, on arrival there, the orders were to fight it out. There really was no alternative. I had agreed to the plan when it was proposed. To go out that way was better than being executed.

The afternoon passed quickly. We all took naps, in turn, to be both relaxed and alert for the job ahead. When evening came, we staged a party, drinking— or pretending to drink—dancing, and walking in couples on the sand.

It must have been convincing because, while we were putting on our act until it was time to make the first trip, someone spotted a patrol car. It was right outside the house, headlights out—and full of armed men. Everyone froze, which was, of course, the wrong thing to do. The car played its searchlight back and forth over the porch while inside we sat motionless.

Then I started singing—anything to break the telltale silence—and motioned the others to join. Two of the government men, carrying submachine guns, got out of the car and came to the front door. They looked us over disapprovingly; it was obvious what they thought of the party, and I breathed easier. I didn't mind a little disapproval, as long as they bought our act.

"The young gentlemen are having a good time, no?" one of the men asked, for some reason addressing the girls. No one answered. We all just stood there, probably looking like a poorly staged tableau.

"Well," the spokesman said, still seeming to single out the women, "you might as well enjoy it, because these *señoritos* have little time left."

"You're right, lieutenant," I decided to answer. "Having fun is exactly what we're doing."

He gave no reply.

"Wouldn't you like to join us in a drink?" I threw out desperately, hoping they wouldn't notice Montana in his ill-fitting sports coat.

The leader ignored the invitation and said, "We can't do anything about you *yet*, but don't stay up too late. The ladies," he nodded pointedly, "might catch cold, and that's against the morals of their society." With that, he swung around and left, followed by his partner.

It took a few minutes of disbelief before it could sink in. Then there were some nervous ripples of laughter, some long-drawn signs of utter relief—and the unmistakable sound of one of the girls being sick in the bathroom.

After things calmed down, I reflected that it was probably just as well that the police had come when they did. They weren't likely to come back, so better now than when the trips were under way.

It was, in fact, about time to start the shuttling, and I decided that I would take Lorenzo first and use Maria and Ráquel as the more experienced of the girls for the first trip. I told the others to keep on partying, but to be sure that the men stayed sober. The Mercedes then took off for Cardenas.

We arrived at the port too early for the first meeting. Rather than going to the bar, Lorenzo thought it would be fun (and not a bad cover) if we took a coach ride. We agreed, and hired one of the horse-drawn open coaches standing at a corner of the seaside park. It *did* relieve the tension, and we enjoyed the clippity-clop of horseshoes on the cobblestones of the narrow streets which bordered the bay, their serpentine patterns conceived hundreds of years before.

Five minutes before meeting time, we got out of the coach and Lorenzo and I said goodbye. The Revolution had brought us together, and we had become very close. He was a good human being, and I loved him. I was never to see him again.

Lorenzo crossed to the bar while we went back to the car across the park. From there we couldn't see inside the cafe, but we saw Lorenzo clearly when he left and joined the fisherman at the corner. Then the two men moved together toward the docks. I waited a prudent time and started back to the beach house with the two girls. One down.

The second trip was made by El Gallego in the Chevrolet, since four successive trips to Cardenas by the same automobile was probably not the smartest move to make. I decided that Edel Montana should go on this trip. The truth was that I cared first for Lorenzo as a dear friend, next I knew the importance of Montana to the Movement, and only after that was I concerned with the two army men. Therefore I wanted to get Lorenzo and Montana out to that key as soon as possible, before something could go wrong. Although some of Raquel's girls clamored to go this time, El Gallego again opted for the two veterans, Maria and Raquel, so off they went with him and Montana. Forty-five minutes later, El Gallego and the two girls were back at the beach house. They reported that it had gone like clockwork.

"Did you find out anything about Lorenzo?" I asked, not really expecting that he had.

"No, Tocayo. Sorry," El Gallego replied. "We weren't supposed to have personal contact with the fisherman, so we didn't. I think it's safer that way."

"Sure," I said, "I was just curious."

"I'm sure your friend is safe," El Gallego tried to reassure me. "Otherwise, we would have heard."

I sent El Gallego for one more trip in the Chevrolet with one of the servicemen, this time with Maria and one of the four girls in Raquel's group. That trip was also successful and uneventful, and El Gallego and the girls were back in even less time than the previous trip.

For the fourth and last trip to Cardenas, it was again my turn. I took the second serviceman and Raquel and another one of her "wards," and I used the Mercedes because I figured that enough time had elapsed since the first trip. Besides, I felt more comfortable with my own car.

The trip over was without incident, although it was getting late in the night. While no formal curfew had been established, it was increasingly frequent for cars to be checked out by the police and the volunteer "civic citizens" any time after midnight. We dropped the second serviceman within a block of the cafe, which was still open and fairly crowded.

The girls and I relaxed in the car a good block away from the cafe, diagonally across the park. At least Raquel and I, the "veterans," relaxed. The other girl was petrified with fear and excitement, her eyes glued to the cafe in the distance. I even turned on the radio to hear some local music, something I never would have thought of doing on the first trip. I rolled my window partway up, turned around and rested my head against it, waiting at ease for the meeting time.

All of a sudden, the quiet night was torn by the loud, flat, dry sound of gunfire. I straightened up, turned off the radio so sharply that the knob came off in my hand, and started the motor. There were some thick, leafy trees between us and the restaurant, but we could see the figure darting through them toward the car. Of course we knew who it was, so I slowly eased the car in his direction.

Bullets whizzed overhead and struck sparks off the concrete sidewalks, but none came near the Mercedes. I grabbed my pistol from the glove compartment and took a shot at one of the pursuers, but I couldn't tell if I hit him. In two more seconds, the serviceman had wrenched open the back door of the car. He was no sooner inside than I gunned down a side street, hoping that no one had gotten a good look at my car.

I raced out of there, trying to think. The exhausted serviceman managed to tell us that he had had the bad luck to be recognized by an ex-Army buddy now with the G-2. Of course he was questioned, and had panicked. Aware of his faked ID, he had bolted out of the restaurant hoping to get back to the car. The three G-2 agents had fired at him, but more for show than from any serious hope of hitting him. After all, desertions from the Army were frequent and not that big a deal these days, and the G-2 men apparently had not connected the escaping man with earlier trips to the keys by a number of "fishermen."

I forced myself to slow down, and drove apparently at random up one quiet street and down another, thinking hard. The serviceman had to make it to the key that night or he'd never get off the island. Besides, the escape group would be waiting for him—and the delay was dangerous for them.

My instinct told me that the fisherman must have seen what happened at the cafe and had probably hurried back to his little house on the shore, so I took a chance and drove there. But the middle-aged man who opened the door was wearing a business suit. He saw my doubt and said, quickly: "It's all right. I know what happened. The fisherman is here in the back of the house." Then he extended his hand to me and said, "I am Pablo."

Pablo was head of the Movement in Matanzas, where both the port of Cardenas and Varadero Beach were located, and I had heard Max mention his name many times.

"I think you're safe here for the moment," the older man said. "They don't bother much with deserters. But don't stay any longer than you have to."

"I am very grateful for your help," I said. "I'm Tocayo."

"Yes, I know, Tocayo," Pablo said. "Max has told me about you, and I'm very happy you're with us. As for helping you, it's my job—one of the most important ones. Good people are essential, and right now it's over there"—Pablo pointed toward the ocean, toward Miami—"where they belong."

I thanked Pablo, told him how highly Max and especially Varona regarded him, said goodbye, and left the serviceman to be disguised as a fisherman and to make another attempt from a small private dock near the house.

By the time the two girls and I started back for Varadero, it was way past midnight, and what had been only probable became inevitable: a roadblock had been set up midway between Cardenas and Varadero, with an improvised wooden barrier and a blinking light, and the police car itself parked at the side of the road. Quickly I considered the additional and perhaps unnecessary danger of a chase to the girls, plus the fact that the car and I were clean, and pulled the Mercedes over beside the policemen.

They were not regular police, but *milicianos*, complete with the inevitable submachine guns. One of the volunteer soldiers walked up to the car, while his partner remained behind, and looked in at me, sitting with two girls.

"Hey, chico, what goes on here?" the soldier asked. "Isn't one enough for you? What are you, Superman or something?" He wasn't referring to the noble American Superman, but to a legendary character in the Havana after-hours life, a big black man of allegedly incredible sexual prowess who delighted and awed the American tourists with private "showings" nightly in the capital.

"No, officer, it's not that," I said, with an almost honest smile. "We're having a party down at the beach, and we're expecting more men than we can handle." I said "expecting" because I had a sudden vision of the soldiers deciding to escort us and finding only El Gallego and me with an unlikely group of six young women. The soldier didn't seem convinced and curtly ordered me out of the car. As he went about searching me, the extra girl in the back seat suddenly called out the window, to everyone's surprise.

"Listen, big boy," she said in a loud, coarse voice which she apparently thought appropriate. "I don't really care who I go to bed with. Listen," she repeated, the way drunks do when they think they're losing your attention, "I'd gladly go with one of my own, with one like you, big boy, for five pesos, rather than with any of these rich señoritos, for much more. Whatcha say? Are you interested?"

The soldier looked her over with the standard glance of fake disapproval men give women whenever money is mentioned beforehand in these transactions, and said, "No, thanks, you're not that good. Anyway, I'm on duty." Then, being, after all, a Cuban, he had to add, "Maybe some other time."

The distraction had worked, and after a casual glance at my ID and car registration, he waved us on.

We managed to hold our laughter long enough to get out of earshot; then we exploded, exuberantly congratulating the frightened little "whore" on the back seat. Her performance was incredible, especially since I knew that this particular girl was a devoutly religious member of the strict lay organization of the Daughters of Mary.

Back at the Varadero house, we found El Gallego almost sick with worry. But we were safe, thank God, and everything was okay. El Gallego forgot his bad moments and was soon roaring with delighted laughter at our story of the girl's roadblock performance which, of course, he had her reenact several times.

We all enjoyed some honest-to-goodness drinks and finally, dead tired and relieved of the tension, retired to our respective corners for some well-deserved sleep—and the Varadero orgy never really happened.

18

I AWOKE EARLY the next morning very anxious to get back to Havana. I stretched and looked around the little beach house. My God, I thought, all this "feminine pulchritude" around me. My friends would never believe it. In fact, my friends would never believe any part of this whole experience. I shook El Gallego awake and then blew reveille, using my hands as a horn, for the benefit and amusement of the girls.

After showering, toothbrushing, face painting, and so forth, we had some coffee and rolls and got ready to leave. We all took one last look at the incredible beach, more beautiful than ever in the early morning, and split up into the two cars, driven, respectively, by El Gallego and me.

El Gallego's veneer of self-assurance was, as usual, shining brightly, and he blithely promised that nothing at all would happen on the way home. While I wasn't about to rely on El Gallego's mystical powers, I really didn't expect any trouble. It was early morning, and we would be on a broad, well-traveled road, since it was a much more beautiful drive out of Havana than the old and monotonous central highway. I carefully locked up Magda's beach house and blew a kiss to it. Then the two cars took off for Havana.

There were no problems on the road. We had agreed that if one of the cars was stopped, the other one would continue on because somehow one man and three girls seems easier to explain than two men and six girls. However, the two or three patrol cars we met paid absolutely no attention to us, and we arrived safely at Raquel's house. We left all the girls there, including Maria who said that she wanted to get to know Raquel better, and El Gallego joined me in the Mercedes.

We didn't stop to telephone Max or anyone else but decided that the important thing was to get to the radio to find out if the men had made it safely to Miami. If they hadn't—well, then we'd have to come up with something.

I didn't plan to stop at my own house, but I drove by it because it was on the way, and I was happy to see that it was quiet, with the driveway empty. Always

I dreaded the possible presence of an ambulance, or even worse, thinking of Nanita. We went on to Augusto's old house where the radio was.

It was no more than 9 A.M., the beginning of the day in Havana, and there was practically no traffic on the streets of that outlying suburb. I hoped that the radio operator who normally came to the house in the early morning would still be there to make contact with Miami, but if not, I knew where to reach him.

The Mercedes reached Augusto's house, climbed the inclined semi-circular ramp from the right side, and stopped at the front door. I got out, walked around to the passenger side, and asked El Gallego to wait. At the white wooden door, I gave the light, rhythmical knock used by the Movement. There was no answer. I repeated the knock, still using my knuckles rather than the brass knocker, and suddenly the little round peep window swung open.

A portion of the familiar face of the mulatto maid peered out at me, brown eyes wide with horror. She stuck her lips partially through the aperture and, carefully, without a sound, mouthed the word "PO-LICE." As I stood there, petrified, the brave woman repeated her warning. It was only seconds, but the utter desperation in her eyes, all over what I could see of her face, moved me into instant action.

I jumped off the steps, jerked open the passenger door, shoved El Gallego under the wheel and whispered, "Come on, man, let's get out of here!" Even the battle-seasoned Spaniard was so rattled that he fumbled the starter. Frantically wishing that I had time to get under the wheel myself, I reached over and started the car for him, urging, *"Coño,* let's go!"

The Mercedes, in the hands of a stranger, literally leaped off the plateau at the head of the ramp, raced down the incline, cut across the grass that fringed the sidewalk, bounced over the curb, and took off wildly in no particular direction. We heard shots behind us, felt one and then a second hit the back of the car, and heard the unmistakable whizzing of bullets through the air.

"Dios mio! Dios mio!" was all El Gallego could say, and he kept repeating it till we were well out of range of the guns. We got out of the neighborhood fast. I directed El Gallego around a circuitous route to shake off any pursuers, then headed straight for my garage. The damned thing was locked, but the gardener came running with the key, and we were safely inside in seconds.

Behind the closed door, we inspected the car for damage and readily found two bullet holes on the back panel near the rear window. The holes were clean, and the slugs, apparently almost spent, hadn't gone clear through and were probably embedded somewhere in the padding. I found a hammer and slightly dented the area around the holes so that they'd look less like bullet holes and more as though I had backed into something. I asked the gardener to do a fill-up job with some putty and patch it up with some extra paint I had around. It couldn't possibly match, so I figured that I should consider a complete repaint job, after the two recent incidents. Somebody somewhere must be looking for a metal gray Mercedes. I'd have to check it out with Moreno.

As I walked into the house, Gisela was crossing the hall, and I looked at her

*Brazilian Ambassador Vasco Leitao Da Cunha (white jacket) and his wife
Nininha (far right) at a Havana reception. The Brazilian Embassy had
provided refuge to Castro's relatives during the difficult Batista times, and the
Ambassadors were highly regarded by the new government.*

*Havana woos Fidel's sister, Emma Castro (second from right). "Castro's
young sister was already there, and Avis and I spent a few moments with her.
She was pleasant and friendly, and not at all political . . ."*

Fidel to Avis: "You won't believe me, but I don't do everything that gets done around here." We didn't believe him.

"Tocayo"; Castro accepting adoration; David Salvador, head of the Cuban labor movement. Salvador later defected, was jailed, released, forgotten. © A. Chiong, LIFE MAGAZINE c. 1959, Time Inc.

Helping to solve textile labor's early problems. Jesus Soto, later head of the Cuban labor movement (seated, center), "Tocayo" and friend. © *Andrew St. George, LIFE MAGAZINE c. 1959, Time Inc.*

First Revolutionary President Urrutia. Would not tolerate Communism. Would not last long. Castro mounted a TV "show." "Urrutia found refuge in our textile mill."
© *Andrew St. George, LIFE MAGAZINE c. 1959, Time Inc.*

"Dr. Manuel Antonio (Tony) de Varona. Prime Minister of the last freely elected Cuban Government, later leader of anti-Castro movement 'Revolutionary Democratic Rescue' (Rescate)." "Varona told me that when the invasion took place . . . he intended to be there with the first wave. He didn't know then that the CIA wouldn't let him."

(Above). Dr. Raul Mendez Pirez:
"Behind a beatific smile . . ."

"El Gallego." "I had the feeling always that if you threw a bullfighter's cape at him, any time at all, in any place, he would grab it and swing it around his body in a perfectly executed Veronica."

The real hero:
Ernesto Perez Morales,
alias "Moreno," military
head of "Rescate"
in Cuba. Executed by the
Communists September 26, 1961.
"He was a monument to
something I never quite
understood."

"Lorenzo," "Maria,"
and "Tocayo":
before the fall.
Some would die.

The terrifying home of the G-2 and "The Library" behind a gracious facade on La Quinta Avenida (Fifth Avenue). "Life at the Library became a hell-like continuum of day-night which was broken, paced, measured only by the succession of knocks on that wooden door which electrified each man with fear . . ."

"Captain Padilla (center), former Chief of Castro's prison, shown in refuge at the Brazilian Embassy, where he was assassinated, reportedly on Castro's orders."

U.S. citizen Captain William Morgan, of the Revolutionary Army, supervised Castro's executions at El Paredon, defected, was betrayed and caught. "It took two volleys and two coups de grace to finish him off." © Jean Raeburn, N.Y.

The fake ID card from Castro's police which was the beginning of the end. "Second Lieutenant of the P.N.R. (National Revolutionary Police)."

Rescate Democratico Revolucionario
(RESCATE)

Expediente No. 31

Carnet No. 0031

Presté mi JURAMENTO el día

DICIEMBRE 1960

Firma

Rescate Democratico Revolucionario
(RESCATE)

CERTIFICAMOS: que ANTONIO NAVARRO V.

es MIEMBRO DEL CONSEJO DE DIRECCION

de esta organizacion y en tal virtud rogamos a todo miembro civil o
militar de la misma, en Cuba o cualquier pais por donde transite, re-
conozcan su condicion y presten su mejor cooperacion.

Miami, Fla. U. S. A. 23 de JUNIO de 1961

HONOR, DEBER, VALOR.

Por el Ejecutivo Central

Sec. General   Sec. Organización

And the real card: one of the leading anti-Castro movements.

(Above and left). Political asylum at the Brazilian Embassy. Triple bunks and then some. © *Antonio Navarro,* TIME MAGAZINE, *August 11, 1961.*

"I'm coming to get you out, Tony. The invasion is coming. There is absolutely no way the Communists can stop us. . . ."

"It was three months and seventeen days before the Bay of Pigs invasion. . . ."

Uneasy haven.

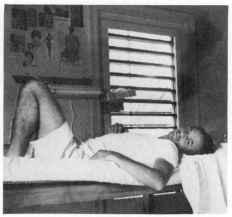

Uneasy boredom.

inquiringly. In answer, she opened her right hand and waved it from side to side in the traditional symbol for "so-so."

"But she's alive?" I asked.

"Oh, yes, caballero," Gisela answered, her frown scolding me for the thought.

"Is she asleep?"

"Yes, she is."

"Let her sleep. I'm off again anyway. When she does wake up, tell her I'm back from Varadero and I'm okay."

"Very well," Gisela said.

"And, Gisela?"

"Yes, caballero?"

"Tell her I love her a lot."

"Oh, yes, caballero," Gisela smiled her beautiful smile. "I always do."

Caballero, which literally means "gentleman," indicates the head of the household. And since there is only one caballero per household, I was it in what was left of *mine*.

I telephoned Max immediately. The first thing he said was, "Thank God."

"Right, Max," I came back, "but you don't know the half of it."

"I can imagine it, Tocayo. Why don't you come right over here?"

"Okay, Max, but please, first, just tell me about Lorenzo and the rest . . ."

"They're okay. They made it."

"See you soon, Max," I said, and hung up.

In less than fifteen minutes, El Gallego and I were in Max's office. Moreno was there, too, and the warmth of his mute handshake surprised both of us. Together, he and Max filled us in on the take-over of Augusto's house the night before.

The G-2 had finally connected Commander Augusto with his real identity and, more importantly, his relationship to Tony Varona, and had followed the lead to Augusto's home—with Fidel Castro himself at the scene. Besides the maid, there were two members of Rescate in the house at the time, and the G-2 had taken them.

"But they're my men," Moreno said. "They won't talk."

"As for the maid," Max went on, grimly, "they had left her there as a cover for a couple of their agents who had been planted as a trap for anyone who might appear at the door. God knows how she managed her warning to you, Tocayo. I can only guess that the men were asleep, but you can bet she's paying for it."

"I'll find out where they've got her," Moreno said, and there was no doubt that he meant it. "If it's the last thing I do, I'll get her out safely."

"Please, Moreno," I said, "count me in. I owe her my life."

"You're in, Tocayo," Moreno answered briefly. Then, muttering something about it being a pleasure to show those "damned *Nangaras*" (Commies) a thing or two, he abruptly walked out, slamming the door.

Max didn't know if they had found the radio. In any case, it was certainly not available anymore, and we were out of touch with Miami. Moreno had posted men in the neighborhood, posing as itinerant gardeners and ice cream vendors, to observe the goings-on and to warn any members of the Movement who might be approaching the house. But they hadn't been able to warn us, and they also missed a young man, just back in Cuba after training in radio and demolition by the CIA, who had come to report to Augusto. He wasn't as lucky as we had been.

Then it was my turn to report on Varadero. I told Max about the courage of Raquel and her girls, the unfortunate and unpredictable identification of the second serviceman at the port cafe, the half-hearted shoot-out by the agents, and the meeting with Pablo, a distinguished and valiant man.

"And, at his age," I added on the subject of Pablo, "the Movement should be proud to have him." As soon as I said it, I realized that Max was at least as old, so I hastily ended my report by saying, "Now, tell me about our guys. You said they were safe."

"They are," Max confirmed, "but Augusto had to wait and cast off at the very last minute, which was dangerous. The men had been held up so long because of our serviceman's problem that Augusto's crew was about to give up. Anyway, when they did get off, they set course straight for Marathon Key in Florida at full speed, not even bothering with any zigzag tactics. And they made it."

Satisfied, I changed the subject.

"What about the raid on Augusto's house?" I asked. "Were you able to tell them about that?"

"Not really," Max answered. "They seem to know that we're cut off, but they don't know why. They may well be trying to reach us by radio, because it's very difficult on the telephone, as you know. We'll have to get word to them somehow, and we *must* get hold of a transmitter, one way or another."

"Maybe I can do it through Avis," I said. "Husbands and wives have a way of communicating with each other that beats any code. That's why they're so good at charades." I realized from his look that Max hadn't the slightest idea what "charades" were, so I hurried on. "Don't worry, Max. I'll let 'em know, but what about the radio?"

"That, Tocayo, is Moreno's problem, and he's working on it. I suggest that you and El Gallego go after him right now. He'll be holding court at either Toki Ona or La Roca. After all, he just left, so he can't be far ahead of you."

Since it was on the way, El Gallego and I took a taxi first to La Roca, a more plush and touristy eating place than Toki Ona, but Moreno wasn't there. In fact, the restaurant was almost empty; not even American tourists have lunch at 11:30 in the morning. The only customers, if one could call them that, were a couple of *milicianas*, two young women with that unmistakable sullen look but, still, rather pretty, dressed in fatigues with Sam Browne belts and .45 automatics in holsters which seemed incredibly huge and unmanageable around those hips.

They looked at me with obvious disdain, for their own reasons. I stared back at them and couldn't resist saying, with a big, broad smile, "Are you boys having a good time?" I was out the door and into the taxi before they had a chance to recover.

We tracked Moreno down at Toki Ona. There he was, in a corner of the half-empty restaurant, "holding court" indeed, as Max had said. Moreno's two most trusted bodyguards, two loyal Sancho Panzas, who looked the part even if the master didn't, were at a nearby table, so obvious that a child could have spotted them. There was a younger man at Moreno's table, busily taking notes. Sitting around other tables were five or six other men who, I later learned, were there to discuss their problems with Moreno.

Moreno, quite simply and incredibly, was conducting the day-to-day business of a counter-revolution: discussing who was in trouble, who needed money, and what guerrilla group had to have equipment to go up to the hills, while perhaps someone was asking for a special escort for some good reason, or a false ID card, or a good contact inside the Government.

Moreno asked me to join him at his table, while El Gallego discreetly drifted over to some friends at a table nearby. I repeated the account of the "Varadero Exit" and our experience at Augusto's house that morning. Moreno already knew about the Augusto house episode from Max, of course, and I was surprised and, at the same time, comforted by the fact that Moreno wasn't afraid but simply angered to the point of explosion by the Government's raid the night before.

I mentioned my concern about the Mercedes' exposure and the almost certainty that information about it had been "circulated" to the Havana police. Moreno took note, looked over at his "secretary" and nodded toward the telephone, at which the younger man went directly to the phone booth. I kept on filling in details and answering Moreno's questions until, in less than a minute, the "secretary" came back to report that the Mercedes was *not* on the list of the Havana police that day. Moreno nodded and turned to me.

"Nevertheless, Tocayo, we'd better have it repainted, repaired, and the plates changed. Where is it?"

"In my garage."

"I'll have a man there this afternoon. Call your people and tell 'em it's okay to let him in. He'll mention my name."

"Thanks, *viejo*," I said.

Moreno told me that he had plans for Augusto's house and that he was also working on rescuing the courageous mulatto maid. He had arranged to obtain another radio transmitter/receiver which, he said without a ripple of emotion on his face, would be taken from the Cuban Navy radio unit that afternoon. It wasn't as good as Augusto's, but it would do. Nothing this man could do could impress me any more, and I asked him if I could stick around for a while and watch the proceedings.

"Sure, Tocayo, stay," Moreno said, a little amused at my reaction. "Stick around and have some coffee—but, half-gringo that you are, you probably want your noontime drink. Just ask the bartender over there. Be my guest."

I laughed openly and did, in fact, move over to the nearby bar for a gin and tonic, turning around to watch the improbable scene.

I sipped my gin and "ersatz" tonic, that lousy local product which only vaguely resembled Schweppes, and pondered the whole situation and the reason for the existence of a Moreno at all. Watching him in his corner, gruff, fully in command, even a little gross, I realized how very like the G-2 agents Moreno was. It was said that he never fired at a Castro agent unless his own life was in danger. Also, he seemed to get information, or whatever he wanted for the Movement, from Castro's units. It was that, perhaps, more than anything else, which made the man not only valuable, but unexplainable to men like me and even Max.

Before I finished my drink, I thought that I had the answer to Moreno's personality, or what would have to pass for an answer. The intelligence community, I concluded, was set apart from the rest of the world. There was a camaraderie, fragile on the surface, but deep-rooted. These men trusted each other, indeed sought each other out on either side whenever it was possible to do so, and would spare each other's lives if at all possible. Theirs was a profession, not a philosophy, and which side they were on at a given time was an accident of fortune. In a funny way, I thought, they are like the professional ballplayers in the major leagues. They play to the best of their ability for whatever team they are with, and they take pride in their personal accomplishments, but the fanaticism, the unswerving devotion to the team, the rah-rahs, all that is left to the spectators. The only exception were the Communist agents. To them only, professionalism was secondary to politics.

Once when I had remarked to Max about Moreno's seeming unconcern for danger, he had pointed out that Moreno was just as afraid as anyone else, really, but his outward composure was a combination of his training, his fatalistic attitude toward life and, most of all, his well-thought-out need to inspire fearlessness in his men if the job was to be done.

At that moment, the telephone at the rear of Toki Ona rang, the bell shrilling through the still, almost empty, restaurant. The call was for me.

"Bad news, Tocayo," Max said. "I'll pick you and Moreno up in about ten minutes. We can talk better in the car. El Gallego can join us, if you wish."

"We'll be waiting."

Fifteen minutes later, we were riding in Max's car through the crowded streets in the center of Havana, and by then the most important part of Max's bad news had been told: Pablo, of the Matanzas province, was dead. The car stopped at a red light and Moreno, sitting next to the driver, automatically rolled up his window. It was by now second nature because of the number of instances where conversations overheard by the occupants of one car standing next to another at a traffic light had promptly been reported, complete with descriptions and license numbers.

The rest of us followed Moreno's lead, and Max's car turned into a small oven in a matter of minutes.

"They caught the fisherman," Max continued his report, "and he talked. The military, especially the Commies, who are strong in that province, were able to tie the real-life Pablo, who was pretty important in the provincial government, to *our* Pablo."

Max stopped for a minute to control his voice, and then went on. "They tried him, summarily, for treason, and he was executed today, less than an hour ago. They don't bother with even minimum formalities in the provinces, those bastards."

I had never seen Max so distressed, but of course Pablo had been a close personal friend from the old days. But scarcely had we started to offer some comfort when he was himself again. Max was made of stern stuff, and he went on to give us the details that he had gotten somewhere from someone—God only knows how.

"They spared the fisherman," Max said. "He got thirty years in exchange for his information. He was poor and illiterate. I only wish that I could hate him." His voice broke again, but he went on. "Pablo was condemned for being what they called 'intellectually culpable' in assisting the escape of the enemy, and there was never any hope. One of Castro's men had been killed."

"Well," Moreno said, "there's nothing we can do about it. Pablo was a good man. He did his duty to his country as he saw it."

Moreno seemed to know that I needed some kind of absolution, although I had kept to myself that I felt personally guilty for Pablo's death. His comment sounded terribly sincere. It was his credo.

"That makes it even more important for us to get busy on Augusto's house," Moreno said and looked over at Max. "I was going to, anyway. You and I," he said to Max, "will discuss it this afternoon, and then I'll take it up with the two of you"—he turned toward the back—"tonight, at my place."

"I'm afraid there's more news, Tocayo, and it's not good," Max said.

"Yes? I'm ready, Max."

Without turning around, Max said: "The fisherman identified you. At least he said he had met an elegant, city type, and he mentioned 'Tocayo.' He also described your car as a gray Mercedes."

I said nothing. The circle was closing.

Moreno turned around and said, "That settles the car matter, doesn't it, Tocayo? Have you told your people to expect a man this afternoon?"

"No, I haven't," I said, "because I'm going there right now myself. But in case you're speedier than I think, I'll call ahead anyway." I was making a pitiful attempt to make light of it.

Moreno smiled his almost Asiatic smile and said, "I'm speedy, Tocayo."

I smiled back, and Moreno, as if he had read my thoughts, said, "Tocayo, don't blame yourself for that Varadero incident. You're an amateur, but you're getting there, and I couldn't have handled Varadero better myself."

El Gallego and I took a taxi home from a nondescript corner in the center of Havana where they dropped us, and Max and Moreno went on together someplace.

As soon as I got home, I called Maria Antonieta, who was understandably puzzled by my prolonged absence, and who had any number of "important problems" to discuss with me. I told her to run the business as if she owned the shop (which she *could*) and said that I had other things to take care of. "By the way, they're things *you* got me into," I reminded her. I hung up on her indignant protest, poured myself a cup of coffee which I didn't need, and briefly planned how to phrase my important phone call to Avis.

"Honey, how nice to hear you!" Avis answered the phone. "Are you all right?"

"I'm fine, dear. I miss you very much and hope to see you soon, but right now I want you to do me a favor. Will you deliver a message for me?"

"Of course, honey," Avis said. "What is it?"

"You remember my boss," I said—"not the sugar boss, but the other one right there with you."

"Yes," Avis said, with a little hesitation.

"You're sure you know, darling?" I insisted. "He's quite a fun guy. You remember, I spent most of the *night* with him while I was there."

"Oh, yes," Avis said, this time firmly.

"Okay, then, I want you to get a message to him."

"Sure, dear. What is it?"

"Well," I began, haltingly, "remember the last time we were at the Brazilian Embassy?"

"Uh-huh."

"And you remember the nice man we talked to about the, uh, confiscation . . . and someone took a picture of you and him?"

"Yes, Tony. I remember *clearly.*"

"Well," I went on, "then please tell my boss that that very nice man paid a personal call to his brother-in-law's home." I waited for her reaction.

"I understand perfectly," Avis said, and I knew she did.

Avis was okay, I thought, with a rush of pride. She hadn't mentioned Tony Varona and she hadn't mentioned Fidel Castro.

"Good, honey. Don't call my boss directly. Call his brother-in-law. Tell him what I've told you and that I'll call you back in a few days because there's no way I can get hold of him now. Understand? *No way I can get hold of him now.* And when I do call you back, I hope to have some good news. Tell him I'm interested in a property, an apartment house, over there, and wonder if he would consider going in on it with me. I have a specific place in mind, and when I call, I'll give you all the details, price and everything. Okay, dear?"

"Yes, of course, honey," Avis said, but I could tell that she hadn't the faintest idea what I was talking about. It was my fault—I had piled it on too fast.

"Look, never mind. Forget the last part. We'll get to that the next time. Just tell him about our friend from the embassy and about his visit."

However, I couldn't resist going a little further.

"Avis," I said, "also tell him that one of my best associates just died."

There was nothing Avis could say to that, so I continued: "You'd better make notes of this. Tell him he handled our business over there where Magda Vazquez-Bello has a little house—at the beach. Tell him my friend was killed in . . . in an accident."

"Yes, dear." Avis was more than a little confused. "I'll do my best to let him know."

"That's all I want, darling. Thanks a lot. The first message is the most important, and I'll be calling you again soon. Good luck, dear—I can't wait to see you again."

"Bye, honey. I love you," Avis said.

I hung up, knowing that I had gone too far, and guiltily aware of having burdened Avis unfairly. But there had been no breach of security, only a little bit of confusion. She'd be all right, but I'd be sure to keep my messages simple from now on.

Avis sat looking at the phone, somewhat bewildered, but also excited to be a part of something important to her husband and, in fact, to her adopted country. She carefully dialed Augusto's number (which I had left for her marked "for emergencies only" and which she never thought she'd have to use). Her heart was beating uncomfortably fast as she listened to the distant ring, acutely aware that what she was doing was important—and dangerous.

A man's voice finally answered: "Yes?"

"Look . . . you don't know me . . . there's no need for you to know me, but —I have a message from Cuba."

"Yes?"

"It's for Augusto, Commander Augusto."

"Oh? What's the message?"

"Tell him Fidel Castro personally raided his home in Havana."

"*What?*"

"Well, that's the message. Fidel Castro has raided his home in Havana."

"Look, lady, this must be a joke, but why don't you try it on the Cubans?"

"I'm sorry. Maybe I have the wrong number. Is this 361-3610?"

"Yes, it is."

"Well, then, that's all I can do."

"Wait a minute, lady. Can you tell me who the message is *from?*"

"Uh . . . well, it's from Tocayo."

There was silence, and then, in a different tone: "What's your address?"

"2503 Alhambra Circle."

"I'll be there in ten minutes."

The doorbell rang in less than ten minutes, and Avis opened the door to a young man who took one astonished look and blurted, "My God, *Avis*. I can't believe it. You're 'Tocaya'!"

"My God, Junior," Avis mimicked, hugging him enthusiastically. "I can't believe it, either. You, working with Tony!"

Junior, as Avis had known him all her life, was Patches—the navigation expert who had successfully brought Augusto's party to Miami through that bullet-ridden escape out the Almendares.

They sat in the Millers' living room for an hour, going over and over the message about Fidel Castro and the raid.

"We heard something on the phone about the radio being cut off, but we had no idea what had happened. We've been trying to make contact ever since, but no luck."

"There were two other messages," Avis began, "but I'm afraid I didn't understand them. Something about a man being killed, someone who works with Tony and is in charge of Varadero Beach? It makes absolutely no sense to me, but Tony seemed to think you'd know."

"Oh, my God," Patches said. "That's got to be Pablo, our man in Matanzas. And he's dead. Well," he sighed, "what's the other message?"

"That one was even worse," Avis answered. "It was something about some real estate that Tony and you people were going to buy jointly. But then he said to forget about it and he'd call me later on and give me the price he thinks you should pay. I'm afraid, Junior, that that one was a total loss."

"Maybe not," Patches said thoughtfully. "It could be that somehow he's going to tell us about transmitting again . . . maybe the frequency. Yes—it must be the frequency. They'd have to change *that*. Thanks a lot, Avis. You've been a great help—more than you know. And let's keep in touch. Tony's doing a good job for us down there. You should be proud."

"I am," Avis said.

That night in Havana, El Gallego and I paid a visit to Moreno in his apartment at Olan Towers, driving over in my almost-new Mercedes. By the time I got home that afternoon, it had already been painted dark green and equipped with a new set of license plates! That Moreno was really something.

Olan Towers was a medium-sized apartment in Vedado, near the Malecon and the ocean. It was typical of Moreno that he would live directly across from the U.S. Embassy, and typical also that there was a .50 caliber machine gun right in front of the entrance to his building, placed there by the Government to be ready for the ghostly ships of the invasion which, presumably, one day would break through the fog and appear within yards of the waterfront.

Although there was an elevator in the building, El Gallego and I climbed to Moreno's third-floor apartment. He was there with a girl whom he introduced as his wife and who, I thought, could probably be just that. She was a pretty peasant girl, innocent and childlike, obviously devoted to Moreno and completely bewildered by the goings-on around her. They couldn't all be Marias, after all. And this one had reason to be bewildered: the bedroom was littered with stacks of military maps and a collection of guns. The open display was testimony to Moreno's supreme self-confidence—as if no one but friends would ever come calling.

Moreno explained the plans for the next day when we would go to "liberate" Augusto's house from the G-2, and what would be expected of El Gallego and me.

It would be a dangerous operation—we all knew that—and the danger was not talked down by Moreno, but simply recognized as fact. We discussed the most appropriate time to move, opted for a low traffic period, discarded siesta time because of the possible presence of too many husbands in the neighborhood, and finally settled for 11 A.M. as zero hour.

19

AT ELEVEN O CLOCK the next morning, a black Cadillac was driven up to Augusto's home and parked at the street level with the motor running, as a heavy but agile man got out and quickly climbed the small ramp to the front door. When the peep window opened, Moreno said something and showed what must have been an acceptable police ID card.

A man opened the door and stood there, a .45 automatic loosely in his hand. Moreno yanked the guard outside and pushed him against the door, taking out his own pistol. As the guard yelled, another one rushed from inside the house, submachine gun at the ready. When he saw the scene beyond the door, he aimed at Moreno's chest and shouted, "Drop it or I'll kill you!"

Without moving or lowering his gun, Moreno shouted back, "Look in front of you, you bastard!"

The second guard peered across the driveway and the lawn and, from the brush and the tall grass of the empty lot across the street, he saw five figures rise abruptly. I was one of them, my Browning trained directly at him, and I shouted, "Hold it, man, hold it. You haven't got a chance!"

The second guard had no doubts about the outcome. At Moreno's command, he tossed his machine gun out on the lawn and put his hands up. "Please, I'm not a Communist! Please, I'm not a Communist!" he began pleading, and he kept repeating the phrase over and over again until Moreno told him to shut up.

Moreno, another of his men and I took the guards into the house, while the rest of the men remained in position. There was a third agent inside the house, but his hands were already up by the time we reached him, and Moreno curtly but not unkindly told them that he had no intention of killing them. In fact, he was almost friendly with them.

He took their G-2 ID cards, told them that he understood their predicament, and said that the cards would be returned to them if they agreed to pretend that nothing had happened after he left. If they didn't, the cards would be mailed to the head of the G-2 with the information that they had let themselves be taken without a fight. The men agreed immediately, and almost eagerly answered his demand to tell him where the mulatto maid was being held.

He locked the three of them in the bathroom and cautioned them not to try to escape through the window or to break through the door. If they did, he reminded them casually, his men were still outside and ready to shoot.

Only then did Moreno go to the main bedroom's closet, muttering, loud enough to be heard, a crude Moreno-like prayer, peppered with curses. He triggered the hidden lock and swung the fake wall around, and then snorted more than sighed with relief. The radio gear was there!

"We're all poor, dumb humans, after all," he said, as we carted the heavy pieces out the door and into the trunk and back seat of the Cadillac. Two other cars appeared seemingly from nowhere, packed everyone in and took off again in a matter of seconds.

A few blocks away, we stopped and restructured ourselves. Moreno, El Gallego and I were in the Cadillac with the radio gear. We left the others and followed, as usual, the least likely approach to my home. The garage was conveniently open, the Mercedes by the porte cochere, so the Cadillac drove right in and the door closed behind it.

Moreno said there was no other solution but to set up the radio transmitter in my house. I tried to think of all the possible hiding places there. The equipment would have to be used every day, of course, so it had to be fairly accessible. Finally, I hit on the elevator well as the perfect place.

Moreno agreed immediately, and we loaded the heavy equipment into the elevator cab and down to the cellar. There, we tripped the switch in the "guts" with a long wooden stick provided ad hoc by the gardener, the elevator cab rose from its nest, and we carefully packed the transmitter/receiver and all its accessories in the well around the big spring. After boarding up the only other entrance to the cellar, we brought the cab back down and went upstairs.

Even Moreno seemed a little excited after our successful mission, and the three of us went to the little living room where Gisela, bless her, had already set out the rum and the ice.

"Well, we made it," Moreno finally said.

"We sure did," El Gallego said excitedly, and then, a little embarrassed, looked at Moreno and said, "You did."

Moreno laughed heartily, the first time I had seen him do so, and said, "No, my friends, we all did it. This was one project that needed teamwork, and teamwork was what we had."

El Gallego and I grinned at each other, pleased by the unaccustomed compliment.

"All I can say," I said, "is that I was as surprised as those poor bastards must have been. Obviously the government had the trap set, but it sure as hell wasn't expecting so many rats."

Everyone laughed at that, and I said, "Moreno, are you really going to return the ID cards to those jerks?"

"You bet I am," Moreno said. "That's three more friends I have on the force for when I need them."

And that, I thought, was the simplest statement of Moreno's philosophy.

While we were having a drink together, I took my pistol from my belt and, with the other two watching, went out to the little terrace, kicked aside the gravel in one corner, laid the pistol on the floor and covered it up neatly.

"What are you doing, Tocayo," Moreno joked, "burying it?"

"Yes, smart-ass, that's exactly what I'm doing. Just because you leave your guns around all over the place doesn't mean I have to be crazy, too—and, anyway, if I ever have to get out of this house in a hurry, it'll be through that terrace, so that's a good place for the gun to be."

Moreno nodded approval, and we finished our drinks in easy camaraderie, as if we hadn't just pulled one of the most important coups in our underground career.

As we were finally leaving my house, Moreno said, "Just so you don't feel too smug, Tocayo, the day's not over, and we still have two jobs to do. One is to ferret out the radio operator, who's probably hiding in some dark corner by now, and tell him that he'll be operating from your house. You'll find him a quiet, reliable man."

"Okay," I said. "That's obviously your job, so what's the other one?"

"The other, my friend, is that we must go this afternoon and get two pounds of plastic dynamite which we will keep until someone comes for it. We'll be the middlemen, see? We get it from the provider, and the men in our Action Group get it from us. After seeing your house and your brilliant talent for hiding things," Moreno smiled, "I think this is the place to keep it overnight."

"Okay," I said. "I'm afraid I'm almost beginning to enjoy all this."

We all left in my car, and Moreno directed me to one of the fringe areas around Miramar, not far from where Maria lived. Moreno got out, made a brief visit to one of the small houses, and came back with the package of explosives. We stowed it carefully in the coolest spot in the car and went on to a very late lunch at Toki Ona—so late, in fact, that some American tourists were already coming in for dinner.

At first the uneasy thought kept nagging me that there was enough dynamite outside in my car to blow up the whole damned building—but I soon put the thought out of my mind with the aid of some wine.

I took a few minutes to telephone my office, and Maria Antonieta scolded me. I hadn't been there for *days,* and sooner or later someone would think it odd, including our neighbors in the building, some of whom *could* be secret members of the Neighborhood Revolutionary Committee, couldn't they? She was right, of course, so I promised to come in some time the next day.

We finished our "lunch," and I delivered El Gallego and then Moreno home. Before I dropped off Moreno, he told me that someone would call me the next morning about the dynamite. His password would be Moreno's name, and he would mention the "candy" I was holding. As he got out of the car, Moreno added, "Be careful, Tocayo. That stuff is pretty ticklish, and it has a bad temper."

I went home, took the package up to my room, and took a good look. I had been told it was officially known as C-4 plastic dynamite, a type of nitroglycerin. It was an amorphous mass in a cellophane bag, with the consistency of putty, sort of melon-colored. It was almost pretty, for God's sake. It looked like a paste made from some tropical fruit, and I even fancied that I could see the grains of sugar. In fact, we had a dessert in Cuba called *pulpa de tamarindo,* made from the acidy fruit of the tamarind tree, and it struck me that the stuff looked very much like it.

Again I had to rack my brain to come up with yet another safe hiding place. Not the elevator well—too much heat and the danger of sparks. A bureau drawer? I'd rather keep an eye on it. So, what the hell: I put it under my pillow. Not the cleverest idea, but it would have to do. Without a detonator, it should be safe enough.

The uncomfortable lump under my head kept me awake long enough to marvel at how, in such a short time, I had gone from an innocent industrial manager to this predicament. Finally I fell asleep.

"Tocayo?"

"Yes," I answered the telephone. It was eight o'clock in the morning.

"Moreno said you had some candy for me."

"Right," I said. "Where shall I meet you?"

"Come over to one of the little coffee shops near the Havana Yacht Club, just a few minutes away from you, the last kiosk nearest the entrance to the Club. My buddy and I will be there having coffee. I know your car. Just drive by and pick us up."

"Okay."

"And, Tocayo . . ."

"Yes?"

"Can you make it right away? Someone could be listening."

"I'll be there," I said. I got in the car quickly, thinking, in passing, that if "someone could be listening" just happened to be a fact, I had had it anyway. I had never been comfortable with that kind of phone call, and decided to mention the subject to Max. Maybe we could get it across to the irrepressible Moreno. I drove toward the Havana Yacht Club, passing the interminable series of little coffee shops that lined the Avenue, which everyone called Las Fritas. Geared to a very active night life, at that hour of the morning they attracted only a few patrons.

In the last one I spotted two young men, one of them black, dressed in the mod garb of the day. I slowed down, almost but not quite stopping, and they immediately put their coffee cups down and got in with me, one in the front and one in the back.

I handed over the package immediately, happy to be rid of it, and asked, out of curiosity, what it would be used for. The black man, who seemed to be the spokesman, said, "Mr. Tocayo, we're going to take care of some Communists tonight at the Blanquita. You just be on the lookout, and you may hear it."

All I could think of to say was "Good luck," and so I did.

"Thanks," the black man said. "I think we will have it."

By that time I was coming around by the Country Club again, and I stopped to let the men out where they could catch a bus or a taxicab, or however they intended to travel with that package on their hands. The black man left his partner on the sidewalk and came back to the car, to my window, and whispered, "Mr. Navarro, I know who you are, but don't worry. I won't tell anyone."

I was of course surprised but also intrigued.

"How do you know?" I asked curiously. "I'm sure Moreno didn't tell you."

"No, Mr. Navarro. You see, I am the son of Don Pedro, and he knew you very well. He calls you Tonito."

I was trying to understand, and the young man added, "My father has told me a lot about you. In fact, Mr. Navarro, I saw you myself a couple of years ago at the Isle of Pines when I was helping my father on a job."

"Oh, my God," I said, "of course. Don Pedro. He's part of my childhood memories. How is your dad?"

"He is very old, Mr. Navarro. He has aged very quickly. I don't think he'll be around very much longer."

"I'm sorry to hear that," I said. "Does he know what you're doing?"

"Yes, he does, sir."

"Does he approve?"

"I can only tell you what he said to me the last time we talked about it. Dad has always been, I guess you'd call it, a philosopher, in his modest way. He said, 'Those who remain with Castro today, my son, are not those who were the servants in fact like myself, but those who were the servants in spirit.' "

Deeply moved, I shook hands warmly and repeated a very sincere "Good luck."

"Thank you, Mr. Navarro. I wish we didn't have to do these things, but they'd do it to us without blinking. They're selling our country to the Reds. We don't want any more dictators. Someone's got to stop them." Then he turned away.

I watched him join his partner, and took off for the Country Club.

At the house, I found Moreno and, as promised, the radio operator. Seeing this small, neat man carrying his bulky black briefcase gave me the immediate idea that he could pose as a doctor or a male nurse calling daily on Nanita. It was a good cover and was unanimously accepted.

We timed the routine of getting the equipment from the elevator well in the basement to the second floor and decided on four o'clock each day for transmission time. It remained for the operator to test the equipment after its trip and determine from the "crystals" he had what frequencies would be most suitable for the transmitter's new location.

The best frequency range would be between 7.29 and 7.33 megacycles, and it was agreed that I should get that information to Avis somehow as soon as possible and tell her we would try to make contact the next day.

Moreno and the operator left, and I was alone with my thoughts. I called Maria Antonieta at the office to tell her once again that I wouldn't be coming in. She obviously had given up anyway, because this time she didn't even go through the litany of the dangers of my continued absence.

I called Maria and asked her to grab a cab and come over. By now it was routine for her to spend most of her time with me, going back to her own home just often enough to keep up appearances. Oh, by the way, she was now wearing her hair in a bun.

I wanted her with me now—not only because I needed the softness of her company after the strain of the last few days, but also because it was necessary that she learn the routine of the daily radio transmission. She just might have to take over at some point.

She arrived in time for lunch, which Gisela served us on the small upstairs terrace. I always wondered about Gisela's reaction to Maria, but I needn't have worried. Gisela was intelligent enough to understand what was going on and to realize that Maria was an important part of it. Feeling more relaxed than I had in days, I left Maria with her coffee on the terrace and went to pay a call on Nanita.

I tried to spend whatever spare time I had with Nanita. Although her lucid moments weren't too frequent, she always seemed aware of me, and I think it was good for her. We'd talk mostly about the past, both because she enjoyed recalling the early years, and because I, on my part, was curious about my ancestors and I appreciated the knowledge that she, only she, could pass on to me.

Nanita enjoyed relating the experiences of her youth, her romances, and the suitors she *could* have married.

"Tonito, your grandfather was such an exciting man," she would say. "I think you will look like him some day. He had a crew cut, very military, but of course in the old days it was gray. Quite a figure of a man . . . Did you know that he fought with Buffalo Bill in the North?"

I would say an unnecessary "yes."

"You know, I think he exaggerated a little, but I like to believe he knew Buffalo Bill . . . such a great figure . . . and I know for sure he was involved in gun-running during our war, our war of independence from Spain. As a young woman, I thought it was all so thrilling . . . I never married, you know. Oh, I had chances . . . well, one chance anyway, and I turned him down. He was such a handsome figure of a man. A bird in the hand . . . but I guess I was too young. And I liked my brother, your grandfather, so much . . . looked after his children . . ."

Her voice would trail off, and I would sit quietly. After a few minutes, she would begin again.

"Your grandmother died early, you know, in Atlanta. I didn't like her side of the family. They were noble . . . and we were never allowed to forget it . . . and they were Spanish. They were Spanish. My brother . . . was a true Cuban. He was not very rich, but he was a Cuban."

"Nanita," I would say, "I loved my grandfather, your brother, and I want you to know I am now fighting for the same freedom he once wanted for his people."

"Men always talk about freedom . . . and life goes on . . . and here we are again. You talk about freedom now. There is no real freedom in this life. Maybe in death, but that's not very . . . not very pleasant." She looked almost like a little girl when she said that, displeased with the prospect.

I would listen until she tired, slowed down, and eventually fell asleep—and I think I enjoyed those conversations as much as the old lady did.

On this afternoon I spent a long time with Nanita, and it was getting dark when I got up to leave. I squeezed her hand gently, feeling the faint pressure in return, and went back to the upstairs sitting room where Maria was quietly waiting, sketching. I asked her tactfully to go and spend a little time with Gisela, and when she was gone, I put in a call to Avis.

"Hello, honey. Are you all right?" Avis asked.

"I'm fine, dear, and I'm going to be fine, so please don't worry."

"You know I'll worry, but I'm glad to hear your voice."

"Avis, remember that piece of real estate that my friends and I want to buy?"

"Of course, dear. What about it?"

"Well, it's a seven-story building. That's important, Avis . . ."

"Yes, I know."

". . . and I think we should pay somewhere between twenty-nine and thirty-three thousand dollars for it. You know, in that range. I leave it up to my friends to find the right place. Okay, honey, that's it."

"I understand, and I'll let them know. Will I be seeing you soon?"

"I don't know, dear. You'll see me as soon as I can manage it. Business is getting a little difficult."

"Well, you know how I feel about it, but it's up to you. You know best . . . I love you. Did you hear me? I love you."

"Yes, dear, I heard you, and I love you too. Goodbye."

"Goodbye, my love."

Just as I hung up, there was a loud noise, a blast—strong, even though obviously far away. The plate glass window overlooking the fairways shook with the pressure and the wooden frame creaked. It had to be a bomb—very likely *the* bomb. Thank God Avis didn't hear it, I thought. She'd have worried even more.

Maria came running from downstairs.

"Did you hear that?"

"Yes, I did," I said, "but don't worry. It's only a bomb. I have the feeling you'll be hearing lots of them. During Batista's last days there were ten or twenty every night, and pretty soon nobody really cared. They used to make book on how many would blow before midnight, remember?" I tried to sound casual.

"I remember," Maria said, "but it scared me then and it scares me now. One thing I don't like is bombs."

I laughed, put my arm around her and led her to the couch for a quiet drink.

The next morning I awoke early, turned on the radio for the news, and went down to the front door for the morning paper. Sure enough, a bomb had exploded in the men's room of the Blanquita Theatre last night, minutes before the beginning of the plenary session of the International Communist Youth Movement. No one, fortunately—the newspaper said—was in the rest room at the time, but a young *miliciana* who had been guarding the door was seriously injured by the blast.

I put the paper down. These were the things, I thought, that simply had no justification except for other, equally unjustified, tragedies created by the other side. Life went on and, as the newspaper had stated, the Communists had gone on with their meeting, and it had been a "huge success." Counter-revolutionary elements were suspected, and "proper measures would be taken to bring the criminals to justice . . ."

I thought of the millions who had been killed over man's history in wars which were meant to bring happiness to mankind. The dead were now just numbers, if that, and yet life had once been so precious for each single individual . . .

I didn't have time to philosophize on the inhumanity of man toward man, so I said goodbye to Maria, told Gisela to be sure to tell the doctor about Nanita's new symptoms when he came by, and took off for a meeting downtown.

I met El Gallego and one of Moreno's men, as agreed, at a small photographic studio on Galiano Street, one of the main arteries of downtown Havana. With its tiny waiting room, studio and darkroom, it looked no different from any other little photographic studio in the world—but there was a difference.

When our turn came, instead of being given a comb and mirror, El Gallego and I were handed shirts to change into, complete with police lieutenant's insignia, and regulation ties to go with them. The photographer took a couple of shots and then handed us ID cards to sign. They already had the Chief of Police's signature and all the particulars filled in, including fingerprints.

I pondered the question, and finally decided to use my own name on the card. In the end, it didn't really matter, because Moreno intended for us to use the cards only as a last-resort, quick identification to get in or out of buildings. Specifically, what he had in mind was the rescue of Augusto's mulatto maid from the women's jail. We couldn't do anything about the two Moreno men captured at the house because they were being held at a maximum security prison. The young CIA-trained man who had gotten through Moreno's protective dragnet had already been executed. Any association with the CIA automatically brought the death penalty or the maximum sentence of thirty years' imprisonment. Therefore the maid was our only target.

The photographer, who turned out to be a member of the police force infiltrated by Rescate, said that our cards would be delivered to us in a day or two, as soon as the photos were finished. I left El Gallego and went to meet Moreno at Toki Ona, where we were to confer over lunch with one of the heads of the Christian Democratic Movement just back from Miami. The Christian Democrats and Rescate jointly planned to establish guerrilla operations in the eastern province of Oriente, so some coordination was necessary.

I arrived at the restaurant first and was seated in the customary corner. Not far from me, I noticed a table of young, athletic, good-looking men, obviously Spanish—the accent reached me clearly—and obviously *pelotaris.* I always enjoyed observing their hands, remarkably large and calloused, for these young men, from early childhood, were trained to become jai alai players by playing handball with bone-hard balls, using only their bare hands.

Then Moreno came in, followed, as usual, at a discreet distance by two of his men, and I would have bet all the money in the world that there were at least two others outside the building—and that I would win.

Moreno sat down with me, and we talked about our first attempt to contact Miami with my transmitter that afternoon, and the crying need for such contact, without which we were literally flying blind. Moreno brought up the subject of men who were "burned" for one reason or another and had to be gotten out.

"There's one in particular," he said, "a young guy named Carlos, who needs a good hideout. How about it, Tocayo—can he take Lorenzo's posh accommodations at the palace?" He grinned at my expression. "In fact, Carlos says he's a friend of Lorenzo's. He knows your secretary, too—says he's often been to your office building."

"Oh, yes," I said. "I think I remember him. Anyway, if he's a friend of Maria Antonieta's, he's got room and board . . . at the palace, you rat."

"Thank you, your Highness," Moreno joked. "Carlos thanks you, Max thanks you, and I thank you."

Just then I noticed three men and a woman approaching our table. Two of the men wore beards, and the whole group would have looked menacing except that the woman was Raquel. On second look, there was something vaguely familiar about one of the bearded men, but I couldn't tell exactly what.

"Hello, Tocayo," Raquel said when they were within earshot. "Or is it okay to call you that?"

"I guess it's okay, Raquel," I said, "in spite of Matanzas."

"Yes, I heard," Raquel answered, kissing me on the cheek, Cuban style.

One of the bearded men kept looking at me with a knowing little smile and said, over our handshake, "How do you do, Tocayo," so significantly that he *had* to know who I was. Then Raquel said, "And this is Laureano. If you try hard enough, Tocayo, I think you could guess the last name."

Oh, my God, I thought—Laureano Batista, Julio's brother.

"Okay, okay, you've done it to me," I said, looking at Laureano. "Now I know why Julio told me his little brother had some unfinished business here."

Laureano laughed and gave me a hug, and we all sat down at the round table. One of the other two men was Javier (a war name), the Christian Democrat who was meeting with us to plan the Oriente Province operation, and the second bearded one was a young European who had a little difficulty with Spanish. His real name was Hans but, being a Swiss, he was well known in underground circles as "El Suizo." I never quite figured out what he was doing here with us. I only knew he was a writer, an expert in racing cars (which was his front vis-à-vis the Cuban authorities), and knowledgeable about firearms. He was also a long-time friend of the Batista family, in itself a good credential.

Moreno and Javier got down to business, arguing aggressively about their respective capabilities and knowledge of the mountainous Oriente region. Regarding the forthcoming invasion, they did agree that it was necessary to provide several guerrilla nuclei as a diversionary tactic to distract Castro's forces, as well as a number of parallel mini-invasions. They also agreed that the invasion should come at some spot on the island readily accessible to an established guerrilla focus in case retreat was necessary, and it was unanimous that that could only mean the town of Trinidad in the mountainous area of the central south coast of the island. Everyone knew, however, that the final decision was not ours to make but was, instead, the province of the high command and, even more likely, of "the friends."

The heavy decisions of the "holy war" settled, Laureano began to regale us with some of the experiences his group had had during several lightning raids to the north coast of Cuba over the past months. With relatively small groups, great mobility, and carefully planned telltale tracks left behind at each camp, they had been able to make the Communists think that massive infiltrations were taking place, and some of Castro's platoons had even surrendered to them, creating a problem for the in-and-out invaders.

I wished Laureano and his group well and took off, leaving Moreno to complete the details of the joint military operation.

Half an hour later I was home, opening the front door to the radio operator. Shortly before four in the afternoon, a larger group arrived, including Moreno and Max, and they had Carlos with them, prepared to stay. As with possibly incriminating phone calls, I wasn't comfortable with gatherings of that size, even if this one was justified by the first attempt at establishing the absolutely essential contact with Miami. But then I decided that the underground agent's frame of mind must, sooner or later, resemble that of the veteran automobile racer: after so many laps safely completed, it just couldn't happen to him, even if it is happening all around.

In any case, I showed the men in, with a special greeting for Carlos. I showed him to Lorenzo's old room, feeling a little like the man who brings a new puppy home to use the basket of one recently lost.

Carlos and I helped the radio operator bring the gear from the basement hiding place to the second-floor room we had set up for transmitting. I wanted Carlos to learn the routine, since he, being in confinement, would certainly be available to do the job. We set up the antenna on the upstairs terrace next to Nanita's room, and Carlos had the chance to meet Nanita, who was perfectly lucid at the time, graciously charming to Carlos, and apparently quite aware of the goings-on.

At 4 P.M. exactly, the operator started the beep-beep on the selected frequency range, 7.29 to 7.33 megacycles, with all of us crowded into the room. For a long time, the operator shifted frequencies under our tense faces. The men looked at me but said nothing. I had promised that Avis would understand. Maybe, I thought, it had been too much to expect. My God, it would be tragic if contact could not be made. Everything depended on that now. A few more unbearable seconds and, finally, very weak at first, then stronger, a return beep was heard. There was a general sigh followed by applause. It meant a lot.

After relaying the code and an immediately agreed change of frequency to avoid detection, communications were established, and the era of my radio "station" had been born.

Everyone was excited, so we took turns sending brief individual messages to our friends and associates in Miami. Max mentioned the need to get several men out through the north coast, and Moreno stressed the urgent need of his men, particularly those in the Pinar del Rio ranges, for minimum supplies to survive under the intensified Communist persecution. I was even able to get a personal message relayed to Avis.

When it was all over and the group was leaving, Max said, "Tocayo, I'll need you tomorrow afternoon at three, with your automobile." Moreno looked questioningly at Max, but Max said, "Sorry, Moreno, it's just a special meeting. It's nothing you have to know about, and it would be better if no one else knew."

"Okay, Chief," Moreno said. "I just wanted to give you protection."

"Thank you, my loyal guardian," Max said, "but this time I don't think I'll need you. At least, I hope not."

So at three the next afternoon, I parked my car in front of the relatively tall building where Max had his regular professional offices. I was always wary when I came to the office because I was more than likely to meet people I knew in the waiting room or the elevator, and forever afterward I would have to remember, when I saw them again socially, that I was supposed to have been sick. This time, however, the waiting room was empty; Max had canceled all afternoon appointments.

He came out of his office and greeted me warmly, as if we didn't see each other every day of our lives, and we went directly down to the car. Then he gave me an address in Miramar.

"Tocayo," Max said, putting a restraining hand on my arm, "all you have to know about this meeting is that it's a reunion of the top men or coordinators of the most important underground movements on the island. We've agreed that we can be more effective if we work together, regardless of any political differences we may have. It's important because, above all, we're expected to provide support to the invasion." Max stopped. "And an invasion *is* coming, Tocayo. Our country may be free after all. I have to attend the meeting even though our position, as you know, is quite clear and pretty solid."

"I understand," I said, "but what . . . what about the revolutionary front? I thought that was all set in Miami, and I thought Dr. Varona was to be the head."

"You're right," Max said, "but that's in Miami for political purposes. The arrangement they're considering here is at the working level, at the Cuba level.

Anyway," he added a little impatiently, because it bothered him too, "it won't change anything as far as we're concerned."

"Okay, Max, whatever you say," I answered, and drove off.

Right after crossing under the Almendares River, one of the Mercedes' tires went flat and I had to stop. I wanted to find a taxi for the rest of the trip, but having a car at hand was important to Max. Fortunately, we were near a garage, so we limped our way toward it. Max felt that a slight delay wouldn't do any harm since, as he said, the men might be leaders, but they were still Cubans. The tire was fixed in less than fifteen minutes, and we headed on toward the meeting place.

As we approached the house, we saw that something was very wrong. There were several patrol cars on the street and a good number of policemen, some standing on the lawn in front of the house, some going in and out of the front door. There was also an ambulance halfway up the drive to the garage.

I froze and, with only a sidelong glance at Max, I kept going, past the house and the policemen.

"Looks bad," Max said. "I think we'd better avoid my house and go to yours, Tony." Max must have been rattled, to call me by my real name. When we got home, Moreno was already there. The man was incredible. Knowing only *when* the meeting was, he had managed to find out where and why. Not only that, but he even had an interim report on what had happened.

"What happened to your meeting, Max," and there was just a trace of I-knew-I-should-have-gone-with-you in Moreno's voice, "is that the police were at the house next door looking for someone else entirely. Nothing to do with you or your friends in the summit meeting. That's what they're calling it, y'know."

"Go on, please," Max said, trying very hard to be patient.

"The host of the meeting has a daughter, a little girl, who just happened to be playing with friends next door. Maybe the agents scared her, or maybe she thought something funny was going on in her own house. Whatever, she ran home to tell her parents."

Max and I hung on and waited.

"Unfortunately, she was seen by one of the government boys, and he followed her on a mere hunch. They're dumb, my old colleagues, but not *that* dumb."

"Please continue, Moreno, just please continue," Max said, with an authority which was understood clearly by non-com Moreno.

"Well, sir . . . Max, the rest is simple," Moreno's shrug meant the inevitable, "and sad, very sad. I'm sorry. There was some shooting, one of the leaders was wounded, the police squad next door was alerted, the men in the meeting were outnumbered beyond hope—I have to give them that—and they were captured unharmed. That's no great deal, though. For the leaders I see no mercy."

It was a major blow to the Cuban underground. We of Rescate were stunned to realize that three or four of the principal anti-Castro movements were now left without leaders precisely at the time when they were needed the most. The invasion could be jeopardized. Max was deeply disturbed, trying to assess the damage, but still he found it possible to say to me, "You know, Tocayo, it's a good thing that even an expensive German car can have a flat tire."

We laughed dutifully, but it was no time for jokes and Max knew it. Except for a crazy coincidence, Max and I could have been captured with the rest. And now, until the resistance movements involved in the raid could restructure themselves, a much greater burden would be placed on those who were left.

The Communist government made the most of the successful raid. They painted the clandestine meeting as totally inspired by forces outside Cuba, which of course it wasn't, and the raid as the result of their excellent intelligence, which of course it wasn't either. It had been pure dumb luck. Whatever the public relations ploy, the practical outcome was sordid and violent. Three of the leaders were executed forthwith: "Francisquito," the fabled and respected head of the MRR Movement, "Rafael," the head of "Unidad," and Commander Sori Marin, ex-Minister of Agriculture of the Castro government and judge of the early public trials. One or two others would follow later.

The whole episode, the proximity of it all, shook me up, and added to the worry about the Varadero fisherman who had "fingered" me. The Communists' ruthlessness ran true to form. Those men were the best stock of leaders of a future Cuba, but because some of them disagreed with Castro only in his *methods* and some criticized only his *subservience* to the Soviet masters, they still were not allowed to live another day. It convinced me then and forever that, when the Communists are winning, no quarter would be granted.

Even as I continued with preparations for the forthcoming invasion, now taken for granted on both sides of the fence, and was kept busy with the more immediate objective of getting "burned" men off to Florida, the possibility of a direct attempt on Castro's life began to haunt me—a retaliation for wanton killings and the only way, in my mind, back to sanity for Cuba.

It wasn't only frustration. Castro's charisma was such that, in effect, he *was* the Revolution. Remove him from the scene, and the scene would be very different. I never believed in the so-called Communist "machine," which would presumably continue no matter what; Cuba simply didn't have one. I was positive —so positive that thinking of ways to kill Castro became an obsession.

I thought again about my early amateur plot to strafe the dais at one of the outdoor public gatherings, but I knew that an earlier suggestion along the same lines had been turned down by Rescate's high command in Miami—and therefore probably by "the friends"—because the lives of innocent people in the square would be in jeopardy. So that was out.

But then another opportunity presented itself, or at least it seemed to me like an opportunity. The Communist Party announced a night meeting to take place at the Blanquita Theatre, by then the accepted locale for indoor affairs. It was a huge structure, the largest in Havana, and it stood with its back to the Atlantic Ocean. The stage, then, which became a dais for meetings, was separated from the ocean only by several inches of concrete wall.

And so I conceived the idea that a well-armed, ocean-going craft—say a PT boat—could come over from the Florida keys and approach the Cuban coast in the dark of night, just behind that concrete wall. With the proper equipment, they could blast the wall with armor-piercing shells, and four or five well-aimed rounds could put a quick end to the Communist dominance of the island.

As a layman in higher-caliber military weapons, I took to studying all the U.S. books on artillery I could get hold of. I figured that a 106-mm. recoilless rifle, with an effective range of 1,100 meters and a bursting area for the shell of 40 feet around, would do the job. Or maybe even a rocket launcher with a range of only 275 meters, since the distance between deep water and the wall was just within that range. Both weapons were a regular part of the U.S. Army arsenal, I knew, and could be mounted on any big yacht.

I took my plan to Max. He wasn't very encouraging, but at least he agreed to pass it on. In due course, word came back that the plan was "indeed imaginative," but that "the friends" considered that "to make a martyr out of Castro" at this particular time would be "counterproductive."

So much for that, I don't like killing any more than the next guy. I wasn't surprised, we all knew the CIA helped only those who played the game strictly their way. Others were left to their own devices *at best.* We were among the chosen ones. (Maybe).

Instead, word was promised in the next few days giving instructions for a sortie from Miami by water which would deliver weapons, medicines and money to supply the guerrillas in the Pinar del Rio province, who were considered an essential distraction to protect the invasion forces. But, of course, there was no word about the *date* or the *place* of the invasion—not even to us. In fact, we *never* had word.

The underground activities continued to accelerate on what an outside observer might have characterized as a collision course with disaster. Moreno was busy traveling back and forth from the hills, supplying the guerrillas in both the easternmost and westernmost provinces as the Castro forces concentrated on trying to wipe out the guerrillas in central Cuba, where the forthcoming invasion was most likely to land.

I, in turn, assisted Max in his overall responsibilities, acted as liaison with Moreno, supervised the daily radio contacts, and managed to put in a brief appearance every other day at the sugar office. And all the time I looked over my shoulder for the G-2 men who I knew some day would come.

Then I got a jolt. My faithful Maria Antonieta told me her family had convinced her that she was in danger working for me. They thought she ought to leave Cuba, and she had reluctantly agreed. She was so upset about telling me that I tried to make light of it, saying that I'd probably have to close the office soon anyway. But it was one more thing to worry about, the loss of my "front."

One day toward the end of the year, near the second anniversary of the Revolution and that unforgettable weekend on the Isle of Pines, I set off from the Country Club to join Max at a routine meeting at El Carmelo.

As I drove into the parking lot, the old attendant limped over to me, as he always did, but this time he had more on his mind than the usual friendly greeting.

"Mr. Navarro," he said quietly, "I may be talking out of turn, but in our business we hear things, and I want you to know that I wish you well, if y'know what I mean. And what I want to tell you is that there are some men here who don't look right to me. I've never seen them before, and they aren't our type of clients, if y'know what I mean. Three of them stayed out here; they're over there now." Following his discreet nod, I saw a small cluster of men in one corner. "The other two went inside. I thought you should know, *por si acaso*, just in case," and he smiled a knowing little smile, showing missing front teeth, and limped away.

"Thank you very much, my friend," I said, almost to myself. I got out of the car, every sense alert, and walked with what I hoped was nonchalance into the restaurant. Before I could get to our regular table near the back, a waiter stopped me and guided me instead to a table in the middle of the room.

Startled at first, I decided to go along and sat down in the chair he drew out for me. The waiter said: "Good evening, Mr. Navarro. May I bring your usual Scotch?" Then, without indicating "there," he added, "I don't think you want to sit back there today."

Our usual table was empty, a very sober-faced waiter near it, and right next to it sat the two plainclothesmen, if that's what they were—and they sure looked like it. My mind was racing. They must have seen me come in and had made no move. So if they didn't want me, they must be waiting for *Max*—and a current of fear started welling somewhere around the pit of my stomach.

I finished my drink, gave the waiter a tip and squeezed his hand tightly, and unhurriedly left the restaurant. The parking lot attendant prudently stayed away, and I drove off, went around the block, down to the side of the nearby park, and parked, motor running, where I could see the entrance of the restaurant.

I was still thinking. The police agents might have a photograph of Max, or maybe they were just acting on a tip about our Carmelo table. No, that didn't seem likely. But Max was never late, so either the old codger smelled a rat or—chilling thought—the order for his arrest was general and he was in trouble somewhere else.

This possibility was so real that I had to do something, so I drove off, circling the park to avoid passing in front of the parking lot, and headed straight for Max's home.

As I approached the park in front of Max's house, my heart sank. The park was alive with uniforms—on the sidewalk, sitting on the marble benches—and there were two patrol cars parked at each end of the block, obviously there to head off anyone who might be coming to Max's house.

I wondered if I should turn off at the corner or keep going and take the chance of driving past the patrol car ahead of me. I chose to keep going and, like any innocent motorist, I glanced at the police with normal curiosity—and no one stopped me. They either had Max already, I reflected, and were waiting for company, or they were in fact waiting for Max himself. One thing was sure: this was no coincidence. They had Max's number and they were going after him.

I drove directly home as fast as I dared. I told Carlos what had happened and warned him that he might well have to find another hiding place if things were as bad as they looked. After that, I tried calling Max's office, not really expecting an answer, and I got none. I hesitated, then took a chance on telephoning Max's home on the remote possibility that the G-2 might have given up the raid as a false alarm.

I stayed on the phone only briefly, not long enough for a phone check to be run, but long enough to hear the unmistakable military voice that answered. I said absolutely nothing and hung up. Finally I decided to try Moreno at his apartment and found, to my unbounded relief, that the good doctor was indeed there, safe and sound.

We agreed that Olan Towers was not the most prudent place for Max to stay, and Moreno's boldness, admirable as it might be, didn't help make the place any safer. Therefore we decided that I would pick up Max and take him home with me.

In less than twenty minutes, I was at the front door of Olan Towers. Max was waiting and, in a mild attempt at ironic wit, he was actually leaning on that stupid .50 caliber machine gun which sat there unattended. I grinned at him and shook my head. "You're really something, Doc," I said as Max climbed into the car.

Despite the problems, Max seemed to be in a good, relaxed mood—or, perhaps, I thought, it was more a resigned, philosophic mood. I didn't have to wait long for the reasons. As we retraced our path back under the Almendares River, I asked Max about the raid on his house.

"I don't know, Tocayo. It could be a betrayal, of course, or maybe somebody had a hunch, like checking a whole list of suspects. And that sure as hell might include you. Maybe they do have some intelligence on me, or they might even consider it a false alarm and drop the whole thing. But obviously I can't take a chance until we know what really happened. Staying with you for at least a few days makes all kinds of sense."

"The Navarro hotel is more than happy to have you, Max," I said.

"I know, Tocayo, and I'm grateful for it. Who was going to tell us it would come to this when we first met at some foolish embassy soirée? I've forgotten when or where."

"You're right, Max," I said. "It does seem like a million years ago."

"Anyway, Navarrito, it's a time of great changes," Max said, calling me by my real surname in the diminutive for the first time *ever*. "I have some more news for you—good or bad depending on your point of view."

"Oh?"

"You will be the new coordinator for Rescate in Cuba," Max said seriously, fixing his eyes on me. I didn't look away from the road, but I was surprised and probably showed it.

"It has nothing to do with the raid on my house, Tocayo, although that probably makes it more imminent. I'm being recalled to Miami. They apparently believe that I am burned, and also that I can be of some help with the invasion. They need direct, firsthand information on our organization here and on whom we can trust the most in each province when the time comes. I got the word this morning by courier."

"Well, Max," I said slowly, "I'll spare you the part about it being an honor, but I want you to know that I will miss you very much."

Max, touched, purposely ignored the remark and continued: "Actually, Tocayo, it makes a lot of sense. You speak English fluently, and that will help our credibility with 'the friends.' And you aren't a professional or a politician, really, so no one will resent you. I've already checked with Moreno, and he accepts you gladly. Moreno, as you know, was delighted with the recognition from Varona that you brought him. And, finally, Tocayo, let's face it—you've learned a lot."

"Thank you, Max. We'll do our best, as you know, but I'm afraid we don't have much time. I don't want to be dramatic, but the way I see it, either the invasion comes soon or the end comes soon anyway . . . for all of us."

"I hope not, Tony," Max said, very seriously. "If it's up to me, you won't stay here much longer either. I haven't forgotten about that helicopter last week, and your code name is blown. It's irresponsible to expose you any more. As for the end, I'm afraid you're right, at least as far as I am concerned."

I didn't quite get that oblique remark.

"Well, it's time for me to go anyway, it seems."

Something important was disturbing Max, and I couldn't pretend not to notice it. I stopped the car by the curb on Miramar's Fifth Avenue.

"Okay, Doc, what is it? What's wrong?"

"I will tell only *you*, Tonito," Max said, "at least for the time being. I am dying of cancer."

There was a great long silence.

"It's cancer of the lungs—what else?" And Max smiled a wry smile, flicking away his cigarette.

20

MAX AND I ARRIVED at the Country Club, and Gisela, not surprised by my news that there would be one more boarder for a while, helped me to set up the radio room as a bedroom for Max. In fact, her attitude was as if she expected him and many more before the whole thing was over.

That night we all dined together on the upstairs terrace, including Maria, who had arrived in the early morning with every intention of staying. It was a pleasant dinner, or as pleasant as it could be. From the outside looking in—if anyone in fact ever bothered to look any more—it probably seemed like any other dinner that had taken place on that same terrace in the early days. But what a fantastic difference in the guests. Happy as I was to have them, I couldn't help thinking that probably not one of them would have been there that night in the normal course of events—but nothing was normal now.

After dinner, Carlos and I enjoyed our cigars while Max reestablished the chain of cigarettes that had been briefly interrupted by the food. When Carlos retired to his room, Maria excused herself to go somewhere, knowing that Max and I would want to talk alone.

The night air was getting damp, so we returned to the small living room for an after-dinner drink.

"For one thing, Max," I said, enjoying my Montecristo and some aged dark rum, "you can help a lot with Nanita—if anyone can help, that is."

"I'm afraid not very much, Tony," Max admitted. "I guess you've made peace with that notion."

"Yes, I have," I said. "I'd just like to make her last days as pleasant as I can."

"Of course, Tocayo," Max said. "You know I'll do what I can—while I'm here, that is, because I guess I'll be leaving on the next boat with Carlos and the others. Unless—could we find out if my name's on the airport list?"

"Sure. We'll check it out tomorrow, but I'm not very hopeful. We'd better tell Miami that there'll be another passenger—a very important passenger." Max smiled at that.

"Okay, Tocayo, you do that," he said, and relaxed in his chair to sip his liqueur.

After a few moments of comfortable silence, the old doctor mused out loud.

"You know, Tocayo, there's one thing I'm proud of. Funny how you can be proud of such little things."

"What's that, Max?"

"I'm proud of the fact that I diagnosed my own illness, you know? I only had to have it confirmed."

I was a little embarrassed and said nothing. Then Max continued, "Maybe that proves I'm not such a phony doctor, after all."

"You've never been a phony anything," I managed to say.

"Thank you. That's nice to hear. But, you know, many people never thought I was a good doctor, and now they'll never know I was a good anything else."

"You're wrong, Max. Everyone will know. If nothing else, I'll tell them."

"Well, somehow it doesn't seem to matter very much," Max said. "What does matter is that my forthcoming yachting expedition will be a one-way trip. I'll never get back to see my country free after all, and that's what really hurts."

The next morning, Moreno set the wheels in motion to find out if Dr. Raul Mendez' name was on the "wanted" list at the International Airport. It would take a little time, maybe a couple of days, because names could be added to the list almost every day.

I made a quick swing by the sugar office during the morning and found that Maria Antonieta had made her plans to leave that weekend. However, she had a cousin who would be willing to come by the office occasionally to sort of help out if I would like. It was more than clear that my business activities were grinding to a halt. I'd have to do something about it—it was my only front— but I also decided to "worry about it *mañana.*"

I picked up El Gallego, and we met Moreno at La Roca for lunch (where I was pleased to note there were no female Communists this time throwing their weight around). Moreno reported that the guerrillas on all the mountain ranges were doing well. He mentioned a pall of expectation about the invasion that seemed to have settled over Havana, affecting Communists and anti-Communists alike. El Gallego agreed, and they exchanged stories where members of the G-2 and other repressive forces had been unusually cordial and had actually gone out of their way to let people know that, whatever they were forced to do, their hearts were not really in it.

After lunch, El Gallego and I headed for home and broadcast time, leaving Moreno behind because it was just imprudent to have so many Rescate officials together at any one place these days.

At the usual time of 4 P.M., my radio was on the air, and we made immediate contact. Miami was ready with information about the next escape. It would take place two nights later, after midnight, and the site would be a key on the north coast of Pinar del Rio.

Everything was recorded, including the names of the passengers on the boat's return trip to Cuba, and the supplies, weapons and cash which it would also carry. Before closing the contact, I had the operator tell Miami that Max would also be coming, since it was doubtful that he would be allowed to take the plane. There was a moment of hesitation from Miami, and the confirmation of acceptance was transmitted.

Moreno's participation in planning the escape was essential, and this presented a problem. It wasn't considered prudent for him to come to my house, and we certainly couldn't discuss it on the phone. In the end we decided to have the message fully decoded, and El Gallego and I would take it to Moreno at Toki Ona when we met for dinner that night. Traveling with such incriminating documents was dangerous, but exceptional circumstances required exceptions, and Max decided that it was all right to go ahead.

To make the decoded messages as inconspicuous as possible and easier to conceal, I rolled them up and snapped a rubber band around them. There was a special glove compartment in that particular Mercedes, on the driver's side, where I thought the rather bulky roll of papers might fit. There was a hole in the cardboard sidewall, and I managed to force the roll in there. It didn't go quite all the way—part of it jutted out into the glove compartment—but it couldn't be seen with a casual glance. Although, unlike later models, this compartment had no door, you'd either have to lean down and peer in or grope with a hand to know it was there, so I figured that it was safe enough for our short trip. In fact, it was a pretty good hiding place.

We set out for Toki Ona, and I was surprised that Moreno wasn't there. It wasn't like him to be late. We waited for him for a while and then decided to go ahead with dinner, but still he didn't show. I called home, but there hadn't been any word from him.

We decided that something must have come up to detain him and he wasn't coming at all. In that event, it was probably best for us to go on home and try again in the morning. I didn't relish the idea of running around Havana with incriminating papers near curfew time. I also decided that El Gallego might as well spend the night with me so that we could get an early start in the morning.

We left the restaurant and traveled at a fairly fast pace back out of Vedado through Miramar's Fifth Avenue, and eventually started up the road from the Havana Yacht Club to my home, a broad and beautiful road which at one point forked and surrounded the Country Club links from both right and left, only to meet and become a single road again.

As I was driving up to the fork, I noticed a line of cars ahead of us, bumper to bumper, which could mean only one thing: a roadblock for routine searching. El Gallego and I looked at each other, naturally thinking the same thing, as we inevitably approached the last car on the line.

My mind engaged in a risk-analysis which weighed, among other things, the dangerous papers in the compartment and the possibility of their discovery, as well as the unthinkable consequences of arriving home followed, or even escorted, by a patrol car without Max and Carlos having had any warning.

Consulting El Gallego with a quick glance, I backed away from the queue, veered, and took the lefthand path of the fork, away from the roadblock, stepping hard on the accelerator. It was inevitable, I guess, that the patrol car at the front of the line gave up the search and came after us instead, at full speed.

I saw the patrol car in the rear view mirror and again made the risk-analysis: run for it, or risk a search. I chose to run for it and gunned the motor, but I soon realized that the souped-up patrol car would overtake even the Mercedes on a straightaway, and at that point, unfortunately, there was no place else to go.

Concentrating as I was on that dangerous roll of papers, I almost forgot something. It was a sickening thought to remember suddenly that both El Gallego and I were carrying those false identification cards. Dammit, why hadn't we gotten rid of them? Or why have them on us tonight? Overconfidence, I guess, or that damned feeling of divine immunity.

El Gallego took his card out and slid it under the rubber matting under his feet. Too obvious, I thought, and said so, but I couldn't think of anything else to do with *mine* except move it to an inaccessible pants pocket and hope that I could get rid of it somehow. At that point the patrol car cut in front of the Mercedes, forcing me to pull to a stop in front of the Country Club fence. It was December 7, 1960.

The men from the patrol car jumped out and approached the Mercedes in a body, machine guns pointed in our general direction. The group of six men appeared to be a mixture of volunteers, that is, fanatics who had come along for the thrill at no pay, plus bona fide members of the Havana police force. They acted wary and, at least at first, were probably as frightened as we were.

"What's going on? What are you running from?" The fat mulatto in a regular uniform approached the car at the driver's side and shouted at me, almost hitting me with the barrel of his gun. I attempted an answer, but without much assurance.

"We're tired and we didn't want to waste time waiting on line. There's nothing wrong in going home a different way."

"Oh, really?" the policeman said skeptically. "And *where* is home?"

"Oh, beyond the Country Club over toward the water in the Biltmore section," I waved vaguely in the wrong direction.

"Listen, men," the mulatto said, addressing his squad, "I'm your leader, and I tell you what to do. Understand? They look very tame now, but they were running away, and I know they're big fish. I just know it."

There was a general rumble of agreement from the "troops."

"All right, get out, so we can search the car."

"This is it," I thought, but I obediently got out of the car and walked around to the curbside with two of the men prodding me with the points of their guns. Flashlights came out, and some of the men searched the Mercedes, starting, of course, with the trunk. That part was all to the good—the trunk was "clean."

What I kept dreading was a shout of triumph that would announce the discovery of the roll of papers or El Gallego's ID card. But none came, and I realized then that El Gallego's all-too-simple solution had been the right one, at least for the moment.

There were cries of "Nothing here!" and I knew they'd be searching our persons next. That stupid card would surely ruin what otherwise might have been given up as a false alarm, and I knew I had to get rid of it. I casually slipped my right hand into my pants pocket, palmed the card, withdrew it cautiously and let it slide down my pants leg to the thick grass. I held my breath while the little plastic card hit the grass and slipped in between the blades.

"*Hold it!*" The head policeman came from behind me, flashlight flashing at my feet. "He dropped something!" he shouted. The men immediately forgot the car, forgot El Gallego and rushed over to me, at the same time cocking their machine guns, and I figured that this time it really was the end. I said nothing, and the head man picked up the card and looked at it under the light.

"What's all this?" he asked, shining the light into my face. "You a member of the force?"

I didn't answer. It was obvious that the head man was puzzled, wondering about the possibility that I really *was* an officer of the revolutionary police.

"It's a fake, isn't it?" he shouted. "Of course it's a fake!" He pushed the flashlight right into my eyes. "Isn't it a fake?"

I gathered all my thoughts in a fraction of a second until I said, very deliberately and louder than necessary. "Yes, it's a fake."

"You see? I told you!" the leader said to his men, and then turned back to me. I held on to my composure and offered no further explanation, which seemed to disturb the policeman. He stood there, waiting for me to explain, I guess, but I was silent.

At that point, one of the "volunteers" in the group, older than the rest, with a just slightly less disreputable appearance, motioned to the head man and pulled him aside for a private conference. Seconds later, the volunteer in turn pulled me aside.

"Señor," the man said, "you are obviously not an ordinary man, and that is not an ordinary card. I think I understand why you are acting the way you are. However, I also am a secret member of the G-2, and you can talk to me."

My God. I had stumbled into something that might save my life.

"Look," I said to the man, "I appreciate what you've just said, and I'm grateful for your help. Please tell your fat boss over there that I do have an explanation, but that I will talk to no one but Commander Diez-Arguelles."

It was immediately evident that my mention of the number two man in the Havana police had been the right thing to do. The older volunteer went back to the head of the group for another conference, and all I could hear were some final words from the fat mulatto: "Okay, maybe so, but in that case we'll take him right now and I'll take him myself."

The mulatto then ordered all the men but two back to the patrol car. Those two he indicated were to join El Gallego and me in the Mercedes, and he himself got behind the wheel.

I sat in the center of the back seat, El Gallego to my left, to my right a policeman holding a cocked .45 automatic against my side. He was also able to control El Gallego from his position. Next to the mulatto driver, the other policeman sat—or, rather, knelt—holding a submachine gun with the barrel resting on the back of the seat, trained directly at my chest. That gun was cocked, too.

Thus the Mercedes made its precarious way back to downtown Havana, followed by the patrol car. It was obvious that the group was excited about their "catch," and they were taking no chances.

At one point at the beginning of the procession, I couldn't resist saying, "Come on, sergeant, or whatever you are, is all this display necessary?" Flippancy is a good cover for fear. "Don't you think it's a little dangerous, just in case we *happen* to be innocent?"

"Look," the head man said, turning his head around, the way careless drivers often do, "that's the way it's going to be, whether you like it or not. Count yourself lucky that it hasn't been worse," he paused, "*whoever* you are."

I resigned myself to the trip, praying that there would be no sudden stops or other dangerous jolts, and taking some comfort that at least Max and Carlos hadn't been involved. As we drove on, I glanced at El Gallego. He was terribly quiet. I could see, and almost hear, his knees knocking together—which surprised me, knowing El Gallego's record of bravery.

Then it dawned on me that he was ahead of me. El Gallego, the veteran, was aware of our acute danger and already concerned with the future, while I thought of nothing but the present emergency and my reaction was one of a strange calm.

For the rest of the trip, I distracted myself by observing the few cars on the street at that hour, wondering if any one of them could be Moreno's Cadillac coming to the rescue, and groaning inwardly at the way the mulatto sergeant was torturing the gears of my precious Mercedes. Trying hard to concentrate on such minutiae, I was almost able to ignore the reality we were facing.

In another ten or fifteen minutes, we arrived at the main police station where Commander Raul Diez-Arguelles had his office.

"Navarro, you are just plain crazy."

"Now, look, Raul . . . I mean Commander . . ."

"Dammit, Navarro, call me whatever the hell you want, but give me an explanation. You have implicated *me*, you know!"

"I will if you'll calm down and quit calling me Navarro."

"All right, Tony, all right. Let's have the story. I guess you understand that you've gotten me into a lot of trouble."

"Yes, I'm sorry about that, Raul. But the point is that those hoods you call your police were about to kill me right then and there."

"And they probably had good reason to . . . Okay, go on."

"Well, I just had to buy some time and I couldn't think of any other way to do it. I do have an explanation for that damned card, and I do want to tell it to you and to no one else."

"Why me, Tony? Why me? That's straining a remote friendship, don't you think?"

"Probably, Raul, but please consider that what's at stake is a little discomfort or embarrassment for you versus my life, Raul—my life."

"Okay, Tony, granted. However, the whole police force will be talking about it, and maybe even higher up. And they'll all be laughing because you turned out not to be a secret agent after all, but a joker with a fake ID card and a story. The story had better be good, because the crime is important, and, believe me, dancing and singing with me at the Brazilian Embassy is not going to get you out of it. Besides, as you know, you have more than enough family credentials for being a counter-revolutionist, and that, my friend, is bad business."

"I know, Raul, and I won't get you into any more trouble. The card is a fake, as everyone in the world must know by now. I wish that I had never accepted it."

"What do you mean, *accepted* it? Accepted it from whom? Do you realize you're impersonating an officer on my force?"

"I do, Raul, and that, I'm afraid, is another story. I don't know how they got the card. That, I guess, is your problem."

"It sure as hell is, but get on to how you got it."

"Well, the only way I can tell you is by confessing to a few other things you'll probably like even less."

"Okay, go on."

"Well, I have a friend who is involved in the underground, in the counter-revolution—more than I thought, I guess."

"Yes?"

"I . . . ah . . . well, I knew he needed help, and for a while I let him stay with me at home."

"You mean you were hiding him at your house."

"Yes, I guess that's right. But I didn't do it very long. Once I found out more what he was about, I asked him to leave."

"Your loyalty to the government touches me."

"All right, goddammit, Raul, loyalty or not, I just couldn't afford to get into trouble. And here I am in trouble anyway."

"Yes, you are. And now you're also guilty of harboring an enemy of the Revolution."

"Well, anyway, I'm no longer harboring him, and I didn't know how involved he was when I *did* harbor him."

"And he gave you the card? Is that the story?"

"That's not the story, Raul, that's the truth. He gave me the card, or he got it for me, and he told me it would be official. You know damn well that sort of thing was done in the old days, and I'm sure it's being done today."

"I hope not, Tony, but I won't vouch for it even if I am the sub-Chief of Police. The force is too big, and anything can happen."

"All right, then, so I saw nothing wrong in accepting it, and it would enable me to carry a gun, and that I was very interested in."

"Why?"

"Because I live in the Country Club area, as you know perfectly well . . ."

"And no one else does?"

"Because, I might add, no one else has the guts to stick it out with the Revolution."

"Okay, Tony, I won't argue that. Your record is pretty good in *that* respect."

"Well, in any case, my house is isolated and I have a great-aunt, almost a grandmother, who lives with me and is very ill, and I'm just worried."

"There is no street crime anymore since the Revolution, Tony."

"Come on, Raul. I may be in deep trouble, but I don't have to accept that."

"Okay, I was just kidding, but let me tell you—you *are* in deep trouble."

"Can you do anything to help me?"

"Can you and will you give us information on your friend?"

"Yes, I will. He's brought me nothing but trouble after all the help I gave him. I may not agree with the Revolution in many things, but I don't agree with him either. Yes, Raul, I'll tell you what I know about him."

"No, Tony, don't tell me. All I can do—and that's a lot—is to agree that I know you, that I think you have behaved correctly in the past, and that you are doing so despite your family. That much I can do. Beyond that, I have to turn you over to the regular authorities, and it is to *them* that you'll have to tell your story, and it's up to you to convince them."

"Do you think I have a chance, Raul?"

"Frankly, it looks pretty flimsy unless, perhaps, you can produce your friend and he confirms it, but then he'd be executed anyway. I'm sorry, Tony, but I've got to be honest with you. You should be happy if all you get is a big jail sentence. It could be worse, and it may well be. There's nothing I can do for you beyond what I have done. Even I can't afford any further involvement. If the Jesuit training you received hasn't all worn away, you'd better start praying. Good luck."

A guard escorted me out of Diez-Arguelles' office to where El Gallego and part of the patrol guard, including the mulatto sergeant, were waiting outside. The guard announced that the two prisoners—it was the first time the word was mentioned—would be taken to a nearby G-2 processing center. In plain words, a G-2 "first instance" jail. The patrol car contingent said goodbye to us, visibly satisfied at having made a worthwhile haul.

They took us to a huge, outwardly elegant building on the periphery of the presidential palace's plaza, approximately halfway between the palace itself and the Morro Castle which loomed in the distance across Havana Bay. The imposing building had been, in fact, the Ministry of Foreign Relations under Batista and now was one of the main police stations in downtown Havana, which "rented" one of its wings to the Army's intelligence service, the G-2.

Inside, it was bleak, even dirty, with nothing left of its onetime elegance. The whole impression was ominous.

I immediately conjured up visions of *The Trial* again, reflecting on how soon indeed Che Guevara's predictions were coming to pass. I wished I didn't remember so well the hopeless and tragic end of Kafka's novel. In fact, we were both filled with forebodings on that early morning. Although we didn't share them, El Gallego and I both had thoughts of truth serum injected in our veins, and doubts of our ability to hold our tongues and protect our comrades.

The guards led us toward the G-2 wing, far enough ahead of us that, for the first time, we were able to talk to each other. El Gallego whispered hurriedly: "Did your friend help, Tocayo? Did he? What do you think they're going to do with us?"

"He helped to the extent that we're alive now, Gallego. I'm afraid he can't do much more than that. And what that means," I said, stealing a look at the guards to check their proximity, "is that we'll go through the regular G-2 investigation, and God knows what that *really* means. By the way, call me Tony. Forget Tocayo . . . you know why."

We continued our walk down the hall in silence, and I mentally reviewed the various techniques of brainwashing I had heard of and concluded that even the roughest brainwashing might not be so bad compared to *other things*. What I didn't want to think about—and, for that reason, did—was the frightening possibility of the procedure—which had always terrified me—whereby most of the blood is drained from the bodies of prisoners in admirable, selfless "donations" to the Government Blood Bank allegedly made by the unfortunate victims just before their execution. The image of a weak, milk-white man being tied to the wooden post for support before the volley that would shatter him into oblivion refused to go away.

We finally reached the G-2 wing and went down a flight of stairs to a catacombs-like area with dim artificial light where, behind unusually thick bars that looked much too strong for the needs, there were two cells, side by side, which, as it developed, held common and political prisoners alike. It was, in fact, nothing more than a police station, and the G-2 merely shared it.

Our cell was small, maybe ten by ten feet, empty but for two fixed granite benches, both occupied by sleeping bodies, and one toilet in the far corner, of the depressing, all-purpose variety, with no-slip places marked for your feet, no bowl and no seat, and no privacy.

The cell next door was relatively quiet. Dawn was perhaps the only time when some sleep was possible in the G-2 catacombs, and dawn was happening, somewhere outside.

We came to realize that the lights were always on and that day and night blended imperceptibly except for the changing of the guards and the wave of young terrorists, caught at or suspected of sabotage, who were herded in from midnight until dawn. Those night hours, too, saw the arrival of the refuse of any large city—the drunks, the perverts, the aimless. Later, these sediments of the city broth were released, once more to ply their lonely trades.

The political prisoners, as it turned out, were transferred to the main G-2 headquarters in Miramar for further investigation by the higher echelon or, if guilt was obvious, to the Cabana Fortress across the bay to await a rubber-stamp trial and a jail sentence or the firing squad. Thus, the cell population swelled and ebbed, sometimes straining human comfort and certainly dignity. On the particular dawn that El Gallego and I arrived, we were lucky; only two men shared our cell.

At the clanging of heavy keys and bolts, done with a gusto for noise that only the Cubans know, one of the men on the benches awakened and said, "Welcome," more sadly than ironically, I thought. A few words were exchanged. The man was a political prisoner and had been there for many days, which was rather unusual.

El Gallego and I told him only that we had been apprehended on "suspicion." He looked at us knowingly, but merely said, "You fellows look beat. You need some sleep. I'm bored and slept out, so I won't mind sleeping on the floor." My protests went for naught, and as the man got up from his bench, he said, scratching himself lazily all over, "Booked on suspicion, huh? Oh, yes, of course, suspicion . . . amazing how many suspicious people have been taken out and shot since I've been here." And then he smiled and went directly to sleep on the floor.

I thought, what a contrast between the generosity with material things and the mental cruelty which prisoners imposed on each other. But that, of course, was all part of the Master Plan, one more way to break a man's spirit.

We didn't immediately take advantage of the vacated bench. We were too tired and too keyed up to sleep and, although we didn't say it in so many words, we were both sure that one and maybe both of our cellmates were stool pigeons, planted there to draw us out. I needed some time to think, to come up with a plan, a follow-up and confirmation of the "plausible" explanation I had given Diez-Arguelles. Then El Gallego and I had to "synchronize" our stories—we were bound to be questioned separately, and there couldn't be any discrepancies. But before tackling that problem, I had one immediate, urgent task to perform.

The G-2, with the inefficiency that would characterize their performance to the end, had failed to search us for papers, although they thought, of course, that they had searched the automobile. As a result, I still had in my pocket a little notebook filled with telephone numbers—not the truly important ones, to be sure, but enough to implicate people who shouldn't have to be implicated.

There are, of course, many ways to jumble a telephone number (reversing the order, for instance, or adding one constant number to each digit), but I had just never got around to it and was always going to do so the very next day. Again the divine immunity syndrome, and so now the notebook had to be destroyed. But how? Tearing paper was sure to awaken the sleepers if, indeed, they really were asleep. So, probably, would flushing the toilet with that high water tank with its long pull-chain. I concluded that there was nothing to do but eat it.

In true spy-film style, I started chewing the nasty little papers. After gagging for a while and managing to get down only a few little pages, to El Gallego's great amusement, I decided that I'd have to risk the flushing operation. I did, and no one stirred. Then I found a few more pages that I had missed in my haste and some other papers in my pockets, and these I crumpled and tossed up into the high tank. For all I know, they're probably still there.

A bit shaky, I shoved El Gallego away a little on the too-short stone bench, lay down as best I could, and tried to think.

Our crime—or, actually, my crime, since El Gallego's card hadn't been found —was, on the surface, relatively minor. "Minor," in the Cuba of those days, was anything you didn't get shot for. Impersonating an officer, of course, could have very serious implications, no doubt about that. Still, I doubted that the government would have me killed for that crime alone.

El Gallego, at any rate, seemed a safe bet for eventual release, since they had nothing on him, really, except that he had had the bad luck to be with me at the wrong time.

But, below the surface of the minor crime—unfortunately, not deep enough—lay the crux of the matter: the compromising papers in the Mercedes. Their discovery would condemn both of us, without question. The certainty gnawed at my mind while El Gallego snored on the cold bench, and I mentally reviewed the cables.

One, I recalled, was drafted in exquisitely minute detail. In the first place, it was addressed to me by my war name, instructing me clearly to collect certain men from certain places (spelled out by addresses where names were not known), transport them to a point on the coast of Pinar del Rio, longitude and latitude given, and, at a certain hour of a certain day, following the exchange of certain agreed signals, also spelled out, deliver them to a waiting boat. As if that wasn't enough to provoke cold sweat, there was more.

In turn, I was to receive four tons of weapons (shipping list included), plus a certain amount of money for the Movement—and all that was sitting at this very moment inside my car, which, in turn, was held by the police. Why on earth the papers hadn't been found when the car was searched I couldn't figure—inexperience, maybe—but it was too much to ask that a sober, daylight search would miss them also. Even accidentally, suppose that someone dropped something on the floor and, in stooping to pick it up, just happened to look up into the glove compartment . . . I shook my head violently.

I finally decided to try to get some sleep, so I scrunched up in a precarious fetal position on as much of the bench as I was allowed, but sleep wouldn't come. I thought for the first time about Max and Carlos and how terrible it would be if the G-2 found them in my house, unaware, and I blamed myself for my selfishness in not thinking of them earlier. I finally said a stumbling prayer and surrendered to sleep.

Our two companions in the cell were awakening. They had slept so long and so soundly that I wondered if perhaps they had been drugged, and I started again to worry about truth serums and esoteric sedatives. But, no, the men were just bored, apparently, and had no reason to wake up any sooner.

We still didn't trust them, so we kept our distance and stuck to our story that we were in for "suspicion," period. During the morning, the two other men talked to us about their common problems in a friendly, spontaneous manner, but we were still suspicious. They talked about executions in detail, with a shocking mixture of morbidity, relish and, one would have to say, sadism.

They pointed out names scratched on the walls of the cell—men, they said, who had recently been marched out to their deaths. Indeed, I remembered some of the names recently reported in the Communist press as having had the "full impact of revolutionary justice." The men insisted, patronizingly, that El Gallego and I had really nothing to worry about unless, of course, something *concrete* could be proven against us. I cringed.

El Gallego, as a trial balloon, ventured to mention my false police card since, after all, the G-2 already had it in their possession. The other men exchanged knowing looks and said, "Well, for *that* he won't get more than five or ten years." I said nothing, but I was ready to settle for that sentence right then and there.

The men went on to explain that they were actually members of Castro's police force in a kind of house arrest in their own police station. There were about thirty of them, they said, in the same situation all over the station. The story seemed plausible. It was a known fact that Castro distrusted the police force, for these young men were his own rebels turned policemen; they knew him too well, having fought Batista along with him, and they wouldn't go along with Castro's double-talk as naively as the civilian *milicianos*.

Nevertheless, El Gallego and I never quite opened up. Too much was at stake. We did eventually get rather friendly, but the two policemen didn't stay in the cell very long. They were moved shortly afterward, destination unknown, and when they left, El Gallego and I quite sincerely wished them good luck.

That day, or what passed for day in that place, was spent in fretful slumber, broken at some point by a meal of cold black beans and rice, plus a worm which El Gallego found and enjoyed waving at the guards. For me, on and off, there were fantasies of a white roll of paper and how it would come to be found. With midnight came people. Among the debris of the common offenders were several drunks, falling, cursing, and getting sick. From their profanity, which opened up new areas of the language for me—and I'm no prude myself—one could gather that some were pro-Castro, some against him, and some just in favor of getting out of there as quickly as possible. They were much bolder than El Gallego and I, for the simple reason that no one was likely to have *them* executed.

One terribly thin old man with a spotty beard was given a forced shower on arrival, which didn't help much. He was apparently a regular and specialized in a litany-like harangue that sang all the glories, military and otherwise, of the Cuban triumvirate: the great Fidel, referred to as "The Horse" in the endless singsong, brother Raul, and Che Guevara. It was difficult to say anything good about the cruel, smooth-faced little brother with the shifty eyes who, it was said, "carried his inferiority complex like a sword," but still the old man some-how managed. Once in a while the litany also included the singer himself, making it thus plain to all that a great injustice was being perpetrated on a well-known Liberator and revolutionist by obliging him to share a prison with the likes of those counter-revolutionary "worms" and despicable "sellers of the Fatherland."

"Long live The Horse because he saved us from the oppressors and marches against them like the avenging angel with his brother Raul by his side in case he should fall but he will never fall because we are all with him and he is with us . . . Long live Che Guevara, that great Argentinian who came to our help, and we will together defeat the Yankee imperialists . . . Fidel, do it well, and send the Yankees to hell! Long live the Revolution . . . Long live Fidel Castro who came down from the hills . . ."

The guards apparently were highly amused by the shrill stream-of-consciousness chatter, and if it stopped, they would quickly start the old man off again with a "Viva Fidel," "Long Live The Horse," "Viva Raul," etc., much like the push given the blades of a fan to get it going. Another drunk finally hit the old man full in the mouth after a grotesque fight, and they moved him, bleeding, to the cell next door, followed all the way by applause.

The cells were filling by then. A very young boy was brought in, with curly blondish hair matted under an incredibly dirty cap, ragged clothes, and a cherub's face that should have been smiling. Instead, he was sullen and full of scorn, openly insulting the guards who showed him in. Still there was a certain dignity in his defiance. Word went around the cell that he was a young terrorist, caught in the act, and even the drunks kept quiet. The penalty, they knew, was death. The poor kid had been found with a package of explosive jelly. He told us, after some prodding, that he had found the package on a rack where he usually kept his sack of marbles and opened it out of curiosity. He was about to eat what he thought was mango jam, he said, when the police arrested him. "Those lousy, dirty pigs, those sons-of-bitches, murderers, like Castro."

I remembered very well that the explosive did, in fact, look like a jam, but the smell is characteristic and overwhelming, and there is definitely nothing succulent about it.

One of the guards had overheard the boy's semi-whisper. "Listen, you little bastard," the policeman said, "telling that crazy story won't help you any. Do you think we're stupid? Didn't you see the fuses right there in the package?" The boy looked up and said softly, "You mean those little pieces of string? I thought they were just to tie the package," and he lowered his head and sank back into silence.

He was just a kid with a tall tale, a child from a very poor family who fought maybe because his brother fought, or his father—or, who knows, perhaps even he understood what it means not to be able to have an opinion on a street corner. The guard moved away, saying as he left, "Go ahead. Tell all the lies you want. It doesn't really matter. You've had it. Even if you tell us who gave you the package, you've probably had it . . ."

It was obviously a come-on to get the boy to talk. The men tried quietly to get him to lie about his age—and he did look awfully young—but he proclaimed to all that he was already seventeen and proud of it. Being underage might have saved him.

Early the next day they came for him, a disheveled, slovenly group of soldiers which resembled a squad only in the number of men. There was, however, some attempt at officialism, and one of the uniformed men proclaimed that he was a lawyer and would read the sentence. They marched the boy away as he kept cursing and shouting "*Viva Cuba Libre*" over and over again, and they must have taken him to an inside patio somewhere within the G-2 wing not far away. We waited in the cell, not daring to talk to each other, but simply anticipating what we all knew we would hear, and just wondering when.

Soon we heard sharp, unrecognizable military commands, and one last high-pitched curse. Then came the blast—a loud blast which reverberated off the walls of the old Ministry building and shook the men in the cell. I waited tensely for the single shot I expected to hear, but it didn't come. After a few seconds I spoke. "Those bastards," I said under my breath, and the others kept quiet.

Suddenly there was the sound of raucous laughter that kept coming closer to the cell block. Finally, the door burst open to reveal the soldiers joking and laughing, and two of them virtually carrying the young boy, very quiet and very pale. They shoved him into the cell, and before they left, one of the guards said, "I've got to hand it to you, kid. You've got guts. You never talked. Too bad you're on the wrong side and won't get to grow up."

The boy stood in the middle of the cell, totally still, surrounded by the staring men, and then suddenly he rushed to the catch-all toilet and got miserably ill, in every way.

Late that night they came for him again. One of the men, a lieutenant, asked him, "Are you really seventeen?"

The boy said, "Yes."

"Too bad," the lieutenant said. And they took the boy away. The men left behind in the cell waited for him, but he never came back.

By then, El Gallego and I had been there for two days and were getting used to things. We were sleeping on the floor, covering ourselves with newspapers against the cool nights and trying to avoid globs of stepped-on food and other things spilled by the drunks. We had given up our bench rather than argue for it with the other prisoners, and I had a sore hipbone.

The food continued to be lousy and cold, and had to be eaten with our hands or with improvised newspaper spoons, if one felt like eating at all. I did not, but even so I felt surprisingly well, and even reflected that for a hypochondriac—which Julio Batista always accused me of being—I was getting along splendidly without my pills. The mind, however, was another matter. There was time, too much time, for thinking. Since the men were afraid to talk to each other, silence was broken mostly by the clang of the big bolt on the door, by a drunk's soliloquy, or by the quiet sobbing of a prisoner, a sound which brought your own plight to you vividly.

Soon explanations would have to be given. Our turn would come. I reviewed our situation in my mind over and over again, and always came to the same conclusion: the ID card I *might* be able to explain away, but there could be no explanation for the papers in the car. Beginning to show the effects of strain and unrelieved anxiety, I worried constantly that, through telepathy, I might suggest the hiding place to my captors. I believed in the whole spectrum of extrasensory perceptions, and I now felt compelled to discuss the subject with El Gallego.

"I'm worried, Gallego," I would say. "And the more I worry about it, the worse it gets." El Gallego, however, was not much for parapsychology, and said so.

"Well," I insisted, "maybe you won't transmit it, but I might. You know," I said, warming to the subject, "I discovered a long time ago that the best technique for thought transmission is not to concentrate too intensely on the object but, rather, to think of it in flashes, in the midst of ordinary thinking. And that, Gallego, is unfortunately what I find myself doing."

"Come on, Tony," El Gallego said soberly. "You're going to drive yourself crazy." For a Spaniard given shamelessly to myth and superstition in lighter moments, El Gallego was behaving very sensibly, but not enough to stop me.

"You see, Gallego," I continued, "it's a little like the way the light from a lighthouse pierces darkness much better with flashes than it would with a steady beam. That's precisely what happens when you try to avoid thinking. Have you ever tried *not* to think about something?"

El Gallego was beginning to understand.

"That, my friend," I concluded almost triumphantly, "is exactly when you transmit the best."

"Well, then, for Christ's sake," El Gallego said, "get yourself all thought out," and he grinned. "Or maybe these guys have such thick skulls they won't be very receptive."

El Gallego was doing his best to cheer me up, and I smiled back at him and put my arm around his shoulder.

It was interesting that, once in the cell, El Gallego had been calmer than I. The reverse had been true on the way to jail. Perhaps El Gallego felt that he was truly less implicated at this point, but that didn't quite explain his inner peace while I had a mild typhoon in my brain. I asked him about it, and he just said he had "good lawyers" as he pulled out a bunch of medals pinned to his undershirt. El Gallego had simply placed himself in the hands of God. But it was different for me. I was, after all, an agnostic, or thought I was; and an agnostic, in the end, is nothing but an atheist without the courage to admit it and face a pointless world. On the other hand, I was now more human and humble—and afraid.

"Could I have one of your . . . your . . . lawyers?"

"Sure you can." El Gallego smiled warmly. "You can see I have many." Detaching two of the medals and one of the small safety pins, El Gallego freely shared his protection.

The next morning an Investigator, a lieutenant, was appointed to the case of the "Revolutionary Government against Antonio Navarro and a Companion of Spanish Nationality," and the man arrived at our cell.

He was a youngish man, but not one of the smart adolescents whom the Revolution seemed to have catapulted to responsible positions before their time. He was neatly dressed in civilian clothes, and he had a pleasant face. He struck me as a career man in the Intelligence Department, but I made up my mind that I would not allow myself to be lulled into complacency by any encouraging signs. I couldn't afford it, and it was probably all a ploy, anyway.

The Investigator said a polite "good morning" to us, the two men whose case had been assigned to him, and then directed a guard to bring me along to a small waiting room near the cell block, but totally independent and private. The show, I thought, was on. Right off, the Investigator started, severely but not uncivilly.

"I hear that the Mercedes you were driving was a stolen car," the Investigator said. "What do you have to say about that?"

The reference to the car made my heart jump. I watched the man sitting before me for any indication that they might have found the hidden cables. If they had, maybe I should pretend that it was indeed a stolen car. But there were no such signs that I could see, and I had to answer.

"Here is the registration to the Mercedes, made out in my name." I stretched my arm across the table. The Investigator looked at the little card without surprise. It was undoubtedly a routine question, probably the first one always asked and probably one which often led to the truth. Right then, I began to realize the simple, rudimentary, almost amateurish nature of their technique, and the image of the infallible, Gestapo-sharp G-2 began to blur. On the other hand, this was only the beginning.

"Mr. Navarro," the Investigator said, "the charge against you is very serious, as you know, and there is no question about it since we have the evidence. But the Revolution does not want . . . I personally do not want . . . to commit an injustice, and I understand from my superiors that you have an explanation which at least must be examined."

I then told the quiet, measured man across from me my "story."

"Lieutenant," I said, "some time ago, I agreed to harbor in my house a childhood friend who seemed in some kind of trouble. The nature of the trouble was never made clear, and I remembered the saying about 'a friend in need.' " To test the mood, I smiled feebly, but the Investigator did not. Instead, he said, "Go on, please, Mr. Navarro."

"Well, I took him in on the strength of our old friendship and the fact that both his family and mine were away. At least, he told me his family had left." I paused. "By the way, my wife left because she was worried about the situation at one point. Lieutenant, I don't pretend to agree with the Revolution in all it has done, but I have no intention of leaving and therefore I am arranging for my wife to join me again in Havana." I really had taken the trouble to go through the motions of requesting visas and permission and so forth, so I knew that the assertion would hold up if, as I expected, the G-2 were to check it out.

"I wish you well with your wife, Mr. Navarro. Please go on."

"Anyway, Lieutenant, it seemed logical for my friend to join me in my lonely house and to help protect it, for it stands in a neighborhood of empty houses, abandoned long before by their owners who were incapable of adjusting to the Revolution." I was making my point, I hoped, subtly; and, after all, it wasn't that far from the truth. "So, my friend wanted to repay me for my help in some way, and he offered to get me appointed to the police force, you know, honorary, so that I might legally carry a pistol or, at least, have one at home to protect the house and my ill grandmother who lives with me."

"Very interesting," the Investigator said.

"I wasn't too clear on the arrangement," I continued, "and had my doubts, but I went along with it anyway—foolishly, I guess."

"Yes, Mr. Navarro, I believe it was foolish on your part."

"At any rate," I went on, "my friend brought me a police shirt and took my picture wearing it. I was rather flattered, Lieutenant, that I was given your own rank."

The Investigator said nothing, but his eyes smiled a little.

"Very soon after that," I continued, "I began to suspect more and more what my friend was about, although he seemed to come and go at will, not at all like a man in hiding. Anyway, about that time, I finally asked him to leave my house because I didn't want to become involved in whatever it was he was doing. He understood, and he left, and I haven't seen him since."

The Investigator furrowed his brow as if he didn't like that part of the testimony, but still he remained silent.

"Weeks later," I said, "in fact, the very day I was arrested, Lieutenant, a total stranger delivered the police identification card to me. He had called first and made a date to meet me in my friend's name. I could see immediately that the card was false, although we have to admit that it was cleverly done, including the signature of the chief of police."

I knew perfectly well that the card couldn't have been produced without the help of someone inside the force, and that the signature of the chief was probably real. I also knew that the Investigator realized it only too well, and in spite of everything, I enjoyed the perverse satisfaction of confronting him with the proof of infiltration. If the lieutenant recognized my dig, he didn't show it and continued taking the notes that presumably would become his report.

"Mr. Navarro," the Investigator said with increased intensity, and I sensed that the question would be crucial, "would you be willing to give us the name of your friend, and would you describe him?"

I pretended to consider the question for a few seconds and to struggle with the implicit betrayal. Then I said: "Lieutenant . . . yes, I would . . . I certainly would. After all, he got me into all this trouble, and I don't owe him anything beyond the help I already foolishly gave him."

"Well, then," the Investigator said, betraying eagerness for the first time, "tell me about him."

"All right," I said. "His name is Alberto Gonzalez-Recio."

The Investigator made a note of the name, and I had the feeling that there was some recognition, but I couldn't be sure.

"Will you describe him, please?" the Investigator said.

"He is tall, athletic build, fair skin, crew cut, well known in sports circles."

"What else? What does he do?"

"All I know is that he was enrolled in the University—law school, senior year. That should at least be a good lead for you."

"It might," the Investigator said. "Do you know his address?"

"No, I don't, Lieutenant," I said. "I'm sorry, but I don't. I never went to his home. However, with what I've told you, and if the G-2 is half as efficient as they say it is," the Investigator looked up briefly from his pad and went back to his notes, "you shouldn't have any problem finding him." As I said it, I conjured up in my mind, as I looked placidly at the Investigator, the image of Lorenzo sunning himself happily in Miami.

"We shall see," the Investigator said, and then, as if that subject had been sufficiently explored, he asked:

"Mr. Navarro, do you have any weapons in your house, or anything else incriminating? You may as well tell me, because you must understand that the house will be searched, and surprises would do you no good at all."

I thought of Max and Carlos, mentally wishing them safely away, and I thought of the arms cache in the elevator well and the Walther pistol under the gravel, and poor Nanita and Gisela. But, to the Investigator, I said the only thing I *could* say:

"All I have, Lieutenant, is a hunting gun, a 12-gauge Belgian Browning."

"Do you hunt?" the Investigator asked, and I realized that I had found common ground.

"I did, Lieutenant. I hunted a lot . . . once," I said, with well-structured nostalgia.

"Anything else?"

"Well, I've had a .385 automatic pistol for years, and I could never bring myself to turn it in or throw it away, but I hid it so well I honestly don't remember where." The Investigator looked up from his pad quizzically. "I know it was wrong, Lieutenant, but that was one of the reasons I was happy to get the card." I figured I had to cover myself for the pistol, just in case they found it. There was little I could do about the hidden weapons in the cellar except perhaps to pray to my new-found "lawyers."

The Investigator rose, indicating that the interview was over, thanked me politely, and said he would see me again in a few days.

"Oh, Lieutenant," I said.

"Yes, Mr. Navarro?"

"You haven't asked me, and it may not matter, but there are some people in the government who might vouch for me, or, at least, who know me."

"I don't think it would matter, Mr. Navarro," the Investigator said. "The

evidence will have to stand on its own, and that is what you and I must examine."
Then he paused. "Who are these people?"

"Well," I said, "Jesus Soto, the head of the Cuban Confederation of Labor,
has known me for many years. He knows my 'trajectory' with the Revolution."

"Uh-huh."

"And even Guevara, Lieutenant . . . and, of course, the Prime Minister himself.
They know me."

I was pulling out all the stops, but also taking a chance at annoying the
Investigator with my name-dropping. Hell, it was worth the gamble.

"Very impressive, Mr. Navarro," the Investigator said, "but I'll be more
impressed if I find that all you've told me is the truth. Believe me, your situation
is very serious. It will not be resolved with 'padrinos.' "

He said goodbye and told the guard to escort me to the cell and bring El
Gallego back with him. As a result I had to pass El Gallego at the cell door
without being able to tell him one single thing or give him the slightest clue.

I sat down on one of the benches and again reviewed the whole thing in my
mind, going over my chances. If they didn't find the papers in the Mercedes, if
they didn't find the weapons in the cellar, if El Gallego didn't slip and somehow
mention the name "Tocayo," if the Investigator, in checking the G-2 files, didn't
come across the reference to the Mercedes in connection with the Matanzas
incident, which, God forbid, might even lead to a confrontation with the jailed
fisherman—if none of these things happened, I might come out all right. But,
I reflected sadly, that sure was a lot of "ifs."

As to what actually happened while I was in jail, waiting for what I now
thought inevitable, this much I know.

One morning, Gisela answered a ring at the door, and the Investigator and two
other G-2 agents brushed past her without a word, looked around the foyer,
taking in the elegant staircase and the door to the small elevator, and then moved
on through to the back. They wore civilian clothes, but they looked uncomfortable in them and walked like soldiers, and Gisela knew immediately who they
were.

"What's your name?" the Investigator asked.

"Gisela, sir."

"Okay, Gisela. How many people live in this house?"

The question was loaded. Gisela knew it and almost panicked, but she held
on to her calm.

"Well, sir," she said carefully, "Mr. Navarro, of course, and Mrs. Navarro, but
she's away right now."

"Yes, we know that," the Investigator said. "Who else?"

"Mr. Navarro's great-aunt. They call her Nanita. She's very old and very ill.
She's in the corner room upstairs."

"All right. Who else, Gisela?" the Investigator said, looking sternly at her as
he motioned to his two men to search the upstairs floor.

"Nobody else, sir, except me, of course. My husband . . . has left me," the maid said. "And, oh, yes, the old gardener who lives over the garage."

The Investigator made a note on his pad.

"Gisela," he said, "Mr. Navarro told us that there was a man living here with him—a young man—and that he was hiding."

"Oh, no, sir, no one else lives here," the maid said. She had thoroughly cleaned the room in the twenty-four hours since Max and Carlos had left, alerted by Moreno, and she knew that they wouldn't find any traces.

The Investigator smiled and insisted, "Didn't anyone ever stay here over-night?"

"Oh, yes, I suppose so, once in a while. Sometimes I go to bed and I don't really know what goes on, but nothing permanent, no, nothing like that."

The Investigator changed the subject. "How about weapons, Gisela? Did Mr. Navarro have any arms around?"

"No, sir, not that I know of . . . I don't think it's legal."

"No, it isn't, but did he?"

"No, he didn't, sir," Gisela said shakily.

Just then the other two agents, coarser and rougher than the Investigator, came down the stairs. When Gisela saw one of them carrying my Browning shotgun, she put her hands to her face as if to hide. She had seen the gun in my closet and, knowing nothing about guns, simply assumed that it shouldn't be there. Therefore she had hidden it—but not well enough.

"I guess we've got your boss now," one of the agents said, triumphantly waving the gun at Gisela.

"It's all right, Gisela," the Investigator reassured her. "Mr. Navarro had told us about the gun." Turning sternly to his men, he said, "Anything else upstairs?"

"No, Lieutenant," one of them answered. "There's a real old lady up there. I think she's dying. She asked about Navarro."

"And what did you say?" the lieutenant asked.

"I told her," the man answered.

"All right. Search outside for weapons or plastic," the lieutenant ordered. "Check the gardener and come right back. We'll go down to the cellar."

One of the agents left through the front door in the direction of the garage, and the other went through the back, obviously to obey the "search outside" order. In five minutes they were both back. "Nothing," they said.

The Investigator told Gisela to take them down to the cellar in the elevator. She hesitated, for she knew that *something* was down there. She had been aware of the recent activity between the cellar and the radio room upstairs, and she was afraid of what they might find. But she had no choice. Silently, she joined the men in the elevator.

The elevator cab clunked softly on the cellar floor. Gisela turned on the bare bulb and held the door of the elevator open while the men got out and looked around. There was nothing to see but the boarded-up door in the far wall and a few wine racks and, of course, the elevator machinery behind the cab. The high-voltage elevator guts were contained by a chicken-wire fence, but the trigger switches were in plain view, clearly marked "1," "2," and "C" for the two floors and the cellar. Resting against the wall beside the wire fence was the long wooden pole which had to be poked through the wire fence to trip the switch.

One of the G-2 men picked it up and turned it over in his hands, obviously wondering what it was for, since there were no other tools lying around the immaculate cellar. He idly stuck it through the chicken-wire and touched some of the bare wires connected to the switches, childishly fascinated to be touching something safely which, he knew, would give him a violent shock if he touched it with his bare hands.

Gisela saw him playfully aim the stick at the switch marked "1" and suddenly she knew, with absolute certainty, what was in the cellar—and where. The radio gear *had* to be in the elevator well. There was no other place it could be. At that moment, the stick connected with the switch and tripped it, sparks flying.

Gisela gave an involuntary little cry and let the door slam shut as the cab shook, the motor hummed, and the elevator started to rise.

"Listen, stupid," the Investigator shouted at the agent, grabbing the stick from his hand and tripping the "C" switch, "are you crazy? You want to leave us stuck down here?"

The elevator made grinding noises, the gears resenting the sudden switch, and then settled back to the floor. Gisela said, *"Ay Dios mio,"* quietly to herself, and leaned back against the wall to keep from fainting.

"Can you imagine!" the Investigator said. "The captain at headquarters would just love it, and the whole force would hear about it." Then he threw the wooden stick violently at the offending agent. The guilty man caught it and let it slip out of his hand sheepishly. It fell inside the wire fence, coming to rest against the motor.

"Come on, let's get out of here," the Investigator said, and they all went back to the main floor. At the door, the Investigator said, "Gisela, you're very loyal —so loyal, in fact, that you almost hurt your beloved boss. We *know* you had a man hiding here, but don't worry about it. We already know all about him. You should reserve your loyalty for better things."

"Yeah," one of the other agents said. "Why should you want to help an oligarch, anyway, a señorito? The one you should be loyal to is the Revolution because it's helping you, the working class. But I guess you're too dumb to realize that."

"Mr. Navarro has always been good to me," Gisela said, looking at the floor and starting to sob.

"Well," the agent said rudely, "you won't need *him* anymore. If you just want to be a servant all your life, you'd better find somebody else, because you can be sure he won't be around."

Gisela started to cry openly and just stood there.

The Investigator shook his head and said, "Aw, come on, for Christ's sake. Let's get out of here." And the three men left as they had come, without saying goodbye.

"Can't you tell me if you've finished your report?" I asked.

"All I can tell you is that I am about to do so," the Investigator answered.

"Can you tell me if it's . . . favorable?" I asked—I *had* to ask.

"Mr. Navarro," the Investigator said, "you have a beautiful home."

This man sitting in front of me in the little interview room just *couldn't* be so callous if he had found the radio and the weapons, and my spirits lifted a little.

"Thank you, Lieutenant. That's very kind of you to say so. As you probably know, we inherited it from my wife's grandfather. I could never have afforded it."

"Yes, we know that, too, Mr. Navarro."

"Did you see my great-aunt, Lieutenant? Was she all right?"

"I didn't see her, but my men did. She is alive, Mr. Navarro."

"Thank you, Lieutenant."

"You'll be happy to hear," the Investigator said, "that your maid is very loyal to you, although I expect that's no surprise."

"Gisela is one of the family," I said.

"So loyal, in fact, that she almost spoiled your story about Gonzalez-Recio."

My heartbeat quickened, but I said, "I don't know what you mean, Lieutenant. There's nothing to spoil. That story is true."

"Okay, Mr. Navarro," the Investigator said. "Don't worry. We have other ways of checking it out."

"Did you find my gun?" I asked, not specifying *which* gun.

The Investigator's eyes lit up.

"Oh, yes, Mr. Navarro. A beautiful Browning." I breathed relief inside. A sporting gun was less damaging. The shotgun the Investigator found was the one I bought to replace my beloved Belgian "blond" which had been confiscated. "It was well hidden, but we found it."

"What do you mean, hidden, Lieutenant? It was in my closet, in plain sight."

"I told you your maid was very loyal," the Investigator said.

"Lieutenant," I asked impulsively, "will you accept the gun? I know you're a hunter, and I'm afraid I won't be using it for some time."

"Thanks, Mr. Navarro," the Investigator answered. "I really can't. Thank you. I'm sure you understand."

I waited, prayed, for some assurance from the Lieutenant that, yes, I might be able to use the gun for hunting sometime, but no such assurance came.

"Mr. Navarro," the Investigator said, "whichever way the report goes, and whatever the reaction to it from my superiors, you are to be moved over to Fifth and 14th tonight. That is all I can tell you."

I knew that "Fifth and 14th" was the name in the jargon for the G-2 headquarters, once a luxurious home in the plush section of Miramar where the broad Fifth

Avenue crossed 14th Street. Many embassies were in that area along with the dread G-2's main prison.

"Is that necessary, Lieutenant?" I asked weakly.

"Everyone must go through headquarters, Mr. Navarro," the Investigator answered, "and I think you'll find the men there quite different from me—a little smarter, I'm afraid."

I shook hands with the Investigator for the last time, feeling a little as if I might be losing an ally. Then a guard took me back to the cell and brought El Gallego back to the interview room.

After an hour or so, nearing noon, El Gallego came back, a little shaken, but with a light in his eyes that I thought could only mean matters were going well for him, and, apparently, they were. He was no longer afraid to talk, at least in the relative privacy of the cell, and he told me that the questions they asked him seemed harmless and he was able to answer them easily. They did tell him, he said reluctantly, that they were sure I was conspiring heavily, but nothing more than that.

But against El Gallego, they actually had nothing. His story, which paralleled mine somewhat, had been difficult to check out because of his personal habits. He could explain his association with me because, as a draftsman, he had assisted with the decoration of my new offices and because, he told them, he was working on a scheme for me to sell Cuban sugar to Spain, but even that didn't explain our apparent intimacy. Still, there was nothing concrete against El Gallego— nothing, that is, as long as a centimeter of rubber carpeting stayed put on the metal floor of a German-made car being driven around town those days by the G-2.

The worst moment came for El Gallego when the G-2 checked the address he had given them. Very much of a Bohemian, El Gallego lived anywhere, often with me, but his official residence was with an old Spanish uncle and aunt in downtown Havana. These poor old people, frightened to death by a terror only a Cuban could know, insisted that they had never heard of him when they were questioned by the G-2. El Gallego tried to explain, as tactfully as he could, that the old people were simply scared. The Investigator naively couldn't see why *anyone* should be scared and why they should be likened to Batista's men who tortured prisoners brutally, pulling out their fingernails, puncturing their eyes with red-hot picks, and perpetrating other atrocities. This was the party line which Castro fed the masses daily to overshadow the Communists' "cleaner" handling of enemies—the firing squad.

"Haven't I always been civil to you and Mr. Navarro?" the Investigator had asked. "Have I subjected you to any of these things you feared?"

"No," El Gallego had said, "you've always been civil to us. Too bad the people on the outside don't understand it. But," El Gallego said, "don't worry about it, Lieutenant. In time, perhaps *everyone* in Cuba will learn about the G-2 treatment from *personal* experience." The irony went over the Investigator's head, but El Gallego's gypsy wit was satisfied.

El Gallego was finally permitted to talk to his relatives on the phone. Reassured by his voice and some soothing words from the Investigator, the uncle and aunt gave in and agreed that El Gallego was indeed a dear, if somewhat wayward, relative. God knows, I thought, El Gallego was *that,* but he was also a good draftsman, a connoisseur of military equipment, a dedicated anti-Communist, and a good human being. So, since the G-2 knew that they could recapture him any time, he was officially released that night, turned loose on the street after a standard "no hard feelings" speech from the Investigator over a beer at the nearest bodega. I was now alone.

In a corner of the cell, I sat on the floor, away from the other inmates, and dared to hope that maybe, now that El Gallego was out, perhaps he could get to Moreno. Moreno and his men would try to rescue me, I was sure, even though it would be a risky effort indeed. I wasn't sure at all that it could be done, or even that they ought to attempt it, considering my present status. If I was only sentenced to five or ten years in prison, then the risk of human lives was not justified. But if the cables were found, the sentence would be death, and perhaps it would still be foolish or selfish to jeopardize other lives—but I couldn't help hoping they'd try it anyway.

Such were my thoughts when a guard approached the bars of the cell and announced to me, now officially, that I would be moved that night to headquarters at Fifth and 14th.

21

T HEY CAME FOR ME about midnight, and when they mentioned the words "Fifth Avenue," they evoked misty memories of New York and the stores and the parades. However, the memories were so distant and the contrast so shocking that I cast them aside and got myself ready for the trip. They loaded another prisoner with me into the back seat of the smallest four-door French automobile I had ever seen—probably an early Peugeot beaten out of recognition. It was the G-2's standard procedure to use private cars which had been confiscated or commandeered from prisoners and suspects to go about its daily business. It could well be, I thought, that other unfortunate men might at that very moment be riding in my Mercedes.

They put one man, a plainclothesman carrying nothing but a pistol, in the back seat with the two of us, while the Investigator himself drove the car and had next to him a big *miliciano* in uniform with a submachine gun which could only be held upright, and even then the muzzle was lodged in the felt roof of the tiny automobile. As the odd little group of men moved through the quiet Havana streets, late at night, I thought how ridiculous the whole thing was, how very like a comic opera, or a Broadway show spoofing Latin American revolutions back in the days when they were still funny.

I considered, vaguely, making a break for it—just opening that little French door at a stop and running like hell. I felt fairly sure that the machine gun could not get working in time, but the pistol surely could unless the other prisoner, just a kid sitting in the middle, understood and was willing to help. Without outside help, I concluded, it was really impossible. It might have been worth the try in a desperate situation, but, surely, my situation was not desperate. After all, it was almost certain that I was going to G-2 headquarters just to be properly booked, and that then I would be immediately released. A getaway attempt under those circumstances not only was a great risk, but probably an unwarranted one. My concern, therefore, was more that perhaps Rescate's men would pick this opportunity—the transfer between the two jails—to rescue me. If the attempt failed, it would certainly indicate to the guardians that I was more important than they had supposed and would make the G-2 take a second look at every fact and at every piece of evidence, including, certainly, my car.

And so the group rode down the lonely roads with *both* the Investigator and me fearful, only for different reasons, of the approach of any car. Only one, in fact, came at all near the Peugeot. It was full of men in uniform who looked over the little car suspiciously, while the men in the Peugeot looked back at them just as suspiciously, and we eventually went our different ways. Outwardly, there was nothing more than an anxious glance from the Investigator at the crowded machine gun beside him, thinking perhaps how much his life depended on that awkward piece of steel.

We finally arrived at Fifth and 14th. Our guards parked the Peugeot on one of the side streets which flanked the large house, and with me and my fellow prisoner a few feet ahead, we all walked into the building and over to what was obviously a waiting room. No guards stopped us; no one took notice or said hello.

The Investigator left us in the room, walked out and closed the door. I wasn't worried. In fact, I felt even a little cocky, responding to an inner feeling of superiority vis-à-vis the other prisoners waiting there, like myself, to be booked. I at least knew the ropes. I had survived the questioning and, evidently, also the searches that went on as part of the investigation. I would probably be released that same night, or the next morning at the latest. Certainly the Investigator would tell everyone who counted that Navarro was all right, that he was just passing through as a routine, and that he should be treated accordingly. After all, I was absolutely sure that the report had been favorable.

But what if the Investigator forgot to mention those facts in his rush to get back. What then? These careless people could lose a written report, or ignore it. That possibility soon became unbearable to me, and I got up and knocked on the waiting room door through which I had entered. I would find the Investigator and remind him of his obligation to set the record straight for the new men who might not know my case and to tell them personally about the favorable recommendations the Investigator had made. The Investigator was a good man, and he would understand my logical request.

"Yes?" the guard said, opening the door and letting me into the other room. There was nothing friendly in his voice. In fact, I hadn't heard quite that tone since I was first apprehended on the Country Club road.

"I'd like to talk to the Investigator—y'know, the Lieutenant who brought me here."

"The Lieutenant is gone," the guard said curtly. "You just go back to the room and wait. You'll be booked soon enough. There are others in there, you know."

"I know," I said, "but my case is different. The Lieutenant must have told you."

"The Lieutenant told us nothing," the guard said.

"But he must have," I insisted, getting desperate. "Mine is a special case. I was investigated already and I was *cleared.*" I took a chance on the certainty. "I'm only here for a routine booking before release."

"Listen, mister," the guard said, using the barrel of his gun to push me back through the door, "I know nothing of what you're telling me. No one in your category is cleared unless *we* clear him in this office."

My mind was swept with apprehension. In one instant, all my conclusions—all my illusions, really—had vanished. I realized that I was entering G-2 headquarters almost as a new case, with no good marks in my favor, and the bad ones, which were so obvious, against me. Evidently only minor offenders were released from the G-2 branch office. All the questions would be asked again and all the searches would again be made, and these men seemed colder, less involved, more alert. Here, I sensed, guilt was assumed. This was really pushing my luck much too far.

I went back to the waiting room and slumped on a bench, hope ebbing and making way for despair, the same despair which stared back at me from all the other eyes in the room. One older man, in a coat and tie which contrasted with the dress of everyone else, was sitting very straight, very stiff, obviously paralyzed with fear, his back pushing against the edge of the bench and the wall behind it, as if he hoped in that way to leave that horrible room, mentally at least, and to get away from some kind of dread contagion in the air. When two guards came through the door opposite the entrance, the older man somehow knew instantly that they were coming for him, and every muscle in his body and his face became tense.

"No!" he screamed, springing to his feet, even before they reached him, "not me! You're making a terrible mistake!" The guards ignored him and grabbed him by the arms, one on each side, and literally carried him toward the open door at the back, the man all the time shouting, "No, please, no! You're wrong! You're wrong!" As he was disappearing through the door, everyone in the room clearly heard him say, "I have the same name! I just have the same name! Don't you understand? The one you want is my son!" Then, in agonized tones, he cried out, "Please, son, forgive me. I'm so afraid! Let me out of here! You really want my son!" Finally the door closed behind him.

About three in the morning, over two hours after I arrived, a middle-aged black man came into the room, grumbling to himself about the hours he had to keep, pointed a finger at me and had me follow him out the back door to have my photograph taken for the files. There were other men waiting by the improvised studio, which was nothing more than a dirty white screen for a background and a beat-up Leica grossly soldered to a stand. The black man took the photos of the men, one by one, with a little sign for each which he hung around their necks. Some signs carried the old byword "suspicion." The others read "active conspirator." My last trace of hope disappeared when my time came and I found that I was in that last, definitive category. The Investigator must have rendered, after all, a condemning report, or his "superiors" didn't believe him. Or, I tortured myself into thinking, they had in fact found the papers and were keeping me around only long enough to see what other members of the Movement they could catch, based on the information they would extract from me in who knows what ways. In the midst of my depression, my embattled mind still allowed that strange intrusion of trivia, an escape-valve from madness, and found time to notice how odd it was to see a Leica performing such a sordid, inelegant job, how really un-Leica it all was, and how some of my friends would have loved to see this photograph of me—dirty, unkempt—with that sign under it.

More guards came by, took my belongings from my pockets, and gave me a dark blue denim jacket which, they said, I was to wear all the time I was at Fifth and 14th and "wherever else I might go."

"Unfortunately," one of the guards joked, "it isn't bulletproof." Very funny, I thought. Deeper inside, however, it increased my anxiety. Dear God, I don't want to die.

Then came the beginning of what was to become a dread ritual in the dark, gloomy prison: the constant knocking on wooden doors at all hours for all kinds of reasons. This particular time the knock had to do with determining which of the various improvised cells had room for one more unfortunate man—me. They finally came to one known to everyone as "The Library" for the simple reason that it had been the library of the original house, and the room still bore the usual paneling trademark of its once noble purpose. Now, however, it housed twelve frightened men who, at the knock on the door, had all sat up straight in bed, eyes wide open, the unmistakable look of terror turning slowly to relief when it was clear that it was only me standing there looking for a bed. It was by then about four o'clock in the morning. The one bright center light had been mercilessly turned on for the tenth or twelfth time that night after as many sudden, jarring rappings at the door, and I could see the room clearly.

The Library was not small; it had a large window looking out toward the entrance of the house, but it was boarded up almost to the top. Still, by standing on the top bunk and stretching, one could manage to see a little of the outside, a bit of sky, but one also had to be ready to jump down the minute the ominous knocks announced one more visit, which at any time could be *the* visit every man dreaded. At the other end, the room was cut off from the hall by thick wooden boards over which also one could see, from a ceiling-high crack, the guards come and go with the Czech machine guns in hand and, on Sundays, an occasional glimpse of poor women asking after their dear ones. One such woman, I later learned, had kept coming every Sunday after everyone in the building knew her boy had been executed. Men, of course, no longer came to inquire lest they, too, be taken.

In a tiny room to one side of the Library, with no door, there was a toilet, of the all-purpose variety now familiar to me, and a crude, improvised, incredible shower. For most of the day there was no water, and in spite of honest efforts on the part of the prisoners, a foul smell permeated the room.

With the door locked behind me, I stood there at the entrance surveying my new home and my new group, not knowing exactly what was expected of me. One of the men, without leaving his bed, motioned me with his head to one empty bed in one of the corners which I had not noticed.

"He might as well take Little Joe's, right, boys?" The man looked around amusedly at the other prisoners. "Unless, of course, he has scruples."

I knew that was my cue.

Someone else said, "Poor Joe's only been dead for one day and already the bastards have taken everything he left behind—cigarettes, comb, everything—except, of course, his toothbrush. You'd think poor Joe died of something contagious."

"Yeah, lead poisoning," another one said. They all laughed, and still another one continued the fun, saying very seriously: "Well, y'know, around here lead poisoning *is* contagious."

There was more laughter, though a little strained. Then the first man spoke directly to me: "Whatever your name is, you might as well take Little Joe's bed over there if you're not superstitious. If you are, there's nothing but the floor."

"Look, guys, cut it out," I said, finding some strength. "My name is Tony, and I'm not a newcomer. I've been through all this already. I just came over from the other place."

The first man interrupted me.

"Okay, okay, so you're a veteran and we're lying," he said, looking around at the men. "You'll find out soon enough."

As the sadistic merriment subsided, I would find out from one of the men, who seemed younger and softer, that Little Joe had been accused of setting fire to a department store in Havana. On television, Castro had asked for exemplary action. Joe was tried, condemned to death, and shot—all in the course of forty-eight hours. He was still in the Library when the rubber-stamp sentence was published in the papers. That day the fatal knocking on the door was meant for him, and he was taken to La Cabaña and killed at dusk. There, indeed, was his toothbrush, stuck through a knothole in a board of the bunk over my head. Scribbled in pencil on the nearby wall, I read: "Goodbye, Mother. I die for my country. Please forgive me for your grief. I will miss you wherever I am." It was signed, "Your son, Joe."

"You're in for 'suspicion,' aren't you?" a mocking voice said as the bright light was turned off by someone who happened to pass by in the outside hall. I said nothing, laid my head back on the pillow, and tried hard not to think.

By the time morning came, I had been accepted as one of the group of unfortunate inhabitants of the Library. The grim, hurting jokes abated, and I ceased to be a novelty to be appraised and teased. The men had too many worries of their own. Morning was distinguished from night by a little light through the cracks and that ribbon of open area at the top of the boarded-up window, and also by the outside noises: increased shuffling in the hall beyond the wall, the stereotyped, shouted commands of any garrison, and the increasing sound of horns from the awakening street traffic.

I woke up, or, rather, shook off the twilight of thought and dream, and allowed reality to fill my mind, unwanted as it might be, as I took in the room with the aid of a tenuous and filtered dawn. I looked at the toothbrush still there above my head, thought about it for a moment, grabbed it and walked the few steps over to the sink in the bathroom to brush my teeth. For me, always fastidious and shy of unnecessary personal contact, it was a sacrifice and an unspoken tribute, in the only way I could make it, to a brave young man, a tiny bit of immortality. Some of the other men noticed it, said nothing, but looked at me differently from then on.

When I came back to the main room, breakfast had been brought to the Library, and one of the men handed me a cup of *cafe con leche* and a slice of dry, hard French bread. The coffee was hot and sweet and it really wasn't bad, and I was thankful—I didn't quite know to whom—for being alive to enjoy it. Someone else handed me a cigarette and I, a cigar smoker who looked down on cigarettes, took it anyway and pretended to enjoy it to acknowledge the kindness with which it had been offered. Again, in all this I found the generosity in material things which I had noticed before among men sharing a common tragedy. The Library group, I found, had established a "cooperative" which was managed with great mock seriousness by one of the two Nicaraguans who, for reasons never clearly explained, were part of the group. The "kitty" they had established was used for milk, cigarettes, sweets, an occasional cigar and, every few days, maybe a newspaper—always, of course, *Revolucion*, with reports of the local happenings and news of all kinds of Soviet successes on the front page (the U.S., apparently, just didn't ever have successes any more). These little extras were shared freely and equally. It didn't matter that you hadn't been able to contribute to the fund, and no one embarrassed you by asking why.

I, for one, had spent at the other place what little money I had and was now flat broke. Some of the other members of the group, especially the young ones, had really never been other than broke most of their lives. The Library, I thought, was truly a cross-section of the Cuban people. Whoever had said, from the safety of the U.S., that only the privileged classes were against the Castro government should have made a survey of that little enclave of men who shared both fear and hope, regardless of class.

The Library cell included one older man, conspicuously well dressed, trying hard not to look uncomfortable in his unlikely surroundings; two young men, clean-cut, from one of the predominantly Catholic-inspired movements, who probably came from well-to-do families; a Captain in Castro's rebel army who had risen from a farmer-soldier fighting Batista to become one of Major William Morgan's closest aides and, as such, possibly had enjoyed some measure of financial well-being; and the two Nicaraguans, exiles from their country, whose status, social or otherwise, was difficult to determine. Along with me, these people constituted a sub-group which, to strain the adjective, was "privileged" in the Library society because of our upbringing. The balance of the group was obviously poor, with the weatherbeaten, shy faces of farm workers looking back at you with an open honesty hard to reproduce in urban society. Yet in those faces, perhaps even more than in those of the more sophisticated, the proud, rebellious, in-dividualistic Spanish strain was clearly in evidence.

Life at the Library became for me a hell-like continuum of day-night that was broken, paced, and measured only by the succession of knocks on that wooden door which electrified each man with fear at the first sound, to subside only when it was clear that they wanted someone else. Life just crawled between knocks, and since they followed no particular pattern, you had nothing to go on, and each one could be for you. It was not kind or brotherly, but all the men, poor wretches, were happy when it was not for them and they would be spared until the next glaring light and the next startling knock.

As far as anyone knew, there was no physical torture actually used—not the Batista kind. The guards who came to the door were rough and unsympathetic, but no one was beaten or manhandled, and, considering the circumstances, one might say that they were even courteous, although it was a cold, foreboding courtesy. The thing was that everyone knew that at any given moment these courteous men would open a door that led to an improvised courtroom where three bearded men, sitting as judges, would read a sentence already written; they, in turn, or their minions, would courteously open another door, and there would be the firing squad, once more to perform their routine job that, for only *one* man, would be so terribly final.

"There is nothing clean or courteous about death," the Nicaraguans would confirm. "We know that from our country, and it's the same here. And whether the executed man is a democrat or a Marxist, it's all the same—a shattered body lying awkwardly on the ground, oozing blood, agonizing in pain, twitching like a dying animal. No, there's nothing pretty about death."

The Catholic boys would cringe, wishing that they didn't have to hear these things, and the Nicaraguans, like dogs smelling fear, would go after them: "What are you priest-mongers worrying about? You shouldn't mind dying. You're going to Heaven for a family reunion, aren't you? Didn't you like your grandparents?"

I would intervene and pacify matters. Even the Nicaraguans seemed to respect me for some reason and would leave the boys alone. To sign off the conversation, I would say something I believed in: "Look, fellows, as far as I'm concerned, I'd rather live without fingernails any day."

That would bring a laugh and usually end the discussion. On one particular day, I picked up *Revolucion* and pointed to an item in order to change the subject.

"Son-of-a-bitch," I said, holding up the newspaper and hitting the page with the back of my hand.

"What's wrong?" someone asked.

"Look at this. They're showing off that damn hospital again."

"What hospital?" one of the Catholic boys asked, forgetting his own problems.

"Mazorra, of course," I said. "Mazorra" was Havana's principal hospital for the mentally ill. It was out by the airport road, halfway to the city. Fidel had made it into a showcase for the many visitors from the Socialist countries who trooped through Havana, and also for the well-meaning, starry-eyed friends from the West.

"It's really nothing, I guess," I said. "It just bothers me."

The others said nothing, waiting.

"That hospital was a pigpen," I went on, "like most mental hospitals anywhere. No one really sees a mental hospital unless you have a sick relative, and it has to be a close relative for you to brave it."

"And now?" someone asked.

"Well, I guess it upsets me for a personal reason, too. The bearded doctor who runs it, Commander Ordaz, was born and raised at Textilera. His father was the doctor there for my father-in-law who, by the way, had paid his way through medical school. Two weeks before the end, the doctor went up to the hills to join Castro and somehow he came back with the biggest goddamned beard I ever saw." The men laughed. "Fidel appointed him head of the mental hospital, and they decided to make it a model. It's now the cleanest place in the world and all the nuts you see there are 'recovering'; the real bad ones have been sent away. So now it's a standard visit in the tourist routine, and they show them photographs of what it *used* to be like, a snake pit just like all the other snake pits. It just pisses me off."

"Forget it, Mr. Navarro," one of the Catholic boys put in. "No one really believes it."

"The hell they don't," I said, pointing to the newspaper. "Here they are showing it to some U.S. reporters. I think Fidel is the greatest showman, the greatest PR man in this generation, maybe in this century. The blend of Marxist and Jesuit training has to be the biggest thing going. I think if Castro hadn't made it in what he's doing, he could be in the White House selling Kennedy or Nixon to the Americans. Whatever I may think about that bastard, you couldn't find a better man for the job."

Give the Devil his due, I thought, and it wouldn't hurt either if there was an informer in the group. At any rate, the Nicaraguans and the Catholics would forget their argument—at least until the next day.

From the experience of those who had been at the Library the longest, everyone knew that when your time came your immediate destination was one of just a few possibilities—although when the time *did* come, you went along in a daze, mind turned off, half-hearing the feeble encouragement your buddies managed to offer as you walked away. Once through the door, you either went to be questioned and came back, or were taken to La Cabana Fortress to await trial—which could take months—or you went to trial immediately, and that other door leading to The Wall would almost mercifully end the ordeal. That last procedure, I had been told, was the way Little Joe had gone to meet the Maker of this, to him, incongruous world for the crime of trying to reshape it "closer to his heart's desire."

I wondered why I hadn't been called as the days went by, and I thought that perhaps my files had been lost or, much worse, that the papers had been found and they needed me alive to confront the other members of the Movement when they arrested them. I understood full well that the knockings were in themselves a subtle form of torture. The anticipation and anguish they created continued undermining our will, driving us to the point where *anything*, just so it was definite and final, was preferable to the nerve-ravaging uncertainty. The knocks were always urgent, hard and loud, no matter what the object and no matter what the time, and their devastating effect was aided, ironically, by the prisoners themselves. It all contributed to shut out the possibility of rational thinking. The end result was that the pitiful men caught in the carefully planned pyschological trap were no match at all for the bright-eyed interrogators at Fifth and 14th and their Soviet advisors. The system worked.

One of the Nicaraguans would invariably follow whoever was called to the door, strumming an imaginary guitar and singing in mockingly sorrowful tones, *"Ayudame, Dios mio!"* ("Help me, dear God!") To me, mockery in the face of death was very hard to take, and I hoped that my nerves would hold out until my turn came. The fact that I was in prison for one thing, but fearful of another, made the waiting unbearable.

At one point the newspaper reported the arrest of a group of men and women caught with radio transmitters and messages for the guerrillas. I recognized none of the names, but that of itself was irrelevant. I would not necessarily know *real* names. One of the Nicaraguans, not the guitar-strummer but the other one, whose feelings toward Castro were still not clear, said after reading the newspaper report: "Those are the truly guilty ones, not the other poor bastards up in the hills. They're the ones that feed them weapons and make the fight possible. They're the ones who should be executed."

A cold chill went down my back. This was the real torture at G-2—terror hanging like smog, soaking us, the room, the beds, a terror made up of little things, of casual remarks. Was it a carefully thought-out plan out of a Soviet textbook, or was it simple sadism, perhaps unconscious? I didn't know, but it certainly worked. There was no need for pulling fingernails.

I realized that I was beginning to care less whether I lived or died, and maybe that, too, was part of the plan. My only real concern was now for my family— my young wife and two children, practically babies, all terribly dependent on me, now to be left alone in the world, and my parents, growing old with no means of support. For once in my life, I could say honestly to myself that it was others that mattered to me the most.

I had no taste for the expected heroics at the end. Going to my death did not appeal to me at all. My spirit was not *that* broken. I had risked my life every day in the underground for the past several months, knowing that at any minute I might have to shoot it out with our enemies. In retrospect, I had almost enjoyed that; it had been an exhilarating feeling. But an execution was quite another thing. To know exactly when and how you are to die is a cold, passionless prospect. And perhaps in the lack of passion lies the whole difference and horror of planned death. No passion on one side, only fear and helplessness. No passion on the other, only blind obedience from the soldiers, perhaps unspoken terror and a sick stomach. And, at the end, twelve round black dots facing you with twelve fellow human beings behind them, joining in cutting down a life just like theirs, a life they did not make and do not own, with which they share a destiny for a short time on a tiny planet. Better a thousand times, I thought, to die carrying a gun in battle, whatever the odds, screaming your heart out like a rocket.

One of the poor farmer boys in the cell said to me: "Señor, I confess that I'm scared. I don't want to be shot. I'm too young, and I'm not sure I understand exactly what I'm dying for, or even that I will die the way they say you have to die—like a brave man." He was only a youngster, an honest youngster, with all pretense dropped.

"What do you mean, like a brave man?" I asked for lack of anything else to say.

"You *know*," the boy said, "the final speech and all to the firing squad. I can't think of anything pretty to say that . . . that anyone would be proud of, later, when it's all over."

"Forget it," I said. "You don't have to say anything. It's what you've done for what you believe in that counts." I saw the mixture of gratitude and fear in the boy's face and added, "But forget it, son. You're not going to be shot." Then I asked God that maybe just this once I might be right. I patted the young man on the head and went to my bunk and sat down. Did I know truly what I myself might die for? I wasn't at all sure. Not all the men with Castro were ruthless Communist liars and murderers. Some were poor fools in good faith—"useful fools" is the Marxist term for them—still duped as I myself had been for a long time. And, conversely, not all the men fighting Fidel could be said to be good, and one could not be proud of them without exception.

Could one, then, face death for a cause as cloudy as that? The answer, I knew, was yes. The problem was in being *too* objective, seeing both sides—a defect in my make-up and in that of most liberals everywhere when dealing with the Communists. One cannot afford to be objective for the simple reason that *they* are not. *You* see the good points of their system, the bright possibilities of a new, more human world, the end of the exploitation of man by man, and what could be more wonderful than that? They, however, pursue their goal unswervingly, with "blinders" on. Ultimately they drop you, when you cannot follow them to the brutal repression (which you never believed ever *really* existed) to which they must resort in order to stay in power, or when you will not share their unconcern —in reality their contempt—for the freedom and the rights of individual men. I guess that one has to live through the experience to understand it, I thought. It's too bad you could not bottle it in Cuba and distribute it elsewhere in the world. It might spare us all a lot of sorrow.

Life at the Library went on, dreary hours passing into unstructured days interrupted by the knockings on the door and the abrupt flashes of light without any real reference to the time frame on the outside. Sometimes the knockings were only the whim of a guard passing by in the hall outside and led to nothing but the shock and the instant fear, never dulled, no matter how many the repetitions. At other times it was for real, and one of the men would be taken away from his fitful sleep. Not knowing *which* it would be was the key to the terrible psychological game.

The two Nicaraguans in the group were somewhat of a mystery, and they were the jolliest, probably because they were fairly certain that Castro would never go so far as to have them shot. As they told it, they had been sent to Cuba originally as representatives of the *Sandinista* guerrillas, the anti-Somoza movement in Nicaragua, and they came to enlist Cuban help. Unfortunately for them, their plans called for a democratic revolution in their country against the Somoza dictatorship, but Castro had other ideas. Self-determination and elections are, for the Communists, something you talk about when out of power and repress when you are in power. The resulting conflict in objectives led to Castro putting the two men away at the G-2 headquarters, and when I arrived, they had, by their own admission, been there for fifty-two days. They were intelligent, progressive thinkers, and I came to consider them to be basically good men who, not having yet succeeded in overturning the Rightist Nicaraguan dictatorship, did not understand just how careful you have to be when you go about ridding the world of tyrants. In Cuba, they were finding out. Changing a Somoza for a Castro was no bargain.

The Nicaraguans continued to argue religion with the two Catholic boys, and most of the time I enjoyed the discussions. The Catholics were pitifully outclassed, being fresh out of parochial schools where no one had ever seriously challenged their beliefs. They were nice kids, softer than the rest of the group and, except for religious discussions, talked mostly about their girls. In fact they would spend many of the daylight hours perched at the top of the boarded-up window peeking out to see if they could see them pass by the building. They had obviously enjoyed a fairly easy life, but, outwardly at least, they were taking their present situation with strength and dignity. That was admirable when you consider that one of them was *already* condemned to thirty years' imprisonment on one count and his life was at stake on another. At best, he would be in his middle fifties when he came out, and no girl would wait that long. Every night they would say their rosaries almost furtively lest they might be seen and possibly kidded about it, but I saw it and realized how it reflected what went on inside, and it made me think a good deal about my own situation.

The days went by relentlessly, as relentlessly inside Fifth and 14th as they did in the distant outside, and soon it was Christmas Eve everywhere in the world.

"Oh, guard," one of the Nicaraguans said, "aren't we going to have a Christmas tree? Please, guard? The library is *always* the place for the tree, you know," and he looked up at the guard, who was hunched over, snickering, a latter-day Quasimodo.

"Shut up and get back to your bed," the guard said. "A Christmas tree is a Christian tradition, and an Anglo-Saxon one at that, alien to our culture. We don't need those phony symbols." He looked around to see if there was any reaction to his pontification, which quite obviously he only half-believed himself.

There was no reaction, and he continued, "We *will* celebrate the day of the Revolution next week, however, if you pious men are still alive." He laughed and banged the door shut.

It was Christmas Eve, and I felt very much alone. It might be the last Christmas of my life. I wondered why people didn't measure age by the number of Christmases. It was such a special time of each year. "I am so many Christmases old . . ."

I lay back on my bunk while a few of the younger men attempted to start some Christmas carols in defiance of the guards. They failed to get any support, and again the room was quiet—more oppressively quiet because of each man's personal thoughts. I reached for a pad I kept under my mattress and wrote, slowly, looking up from time to time at the rusty springs of the top bunk, trying to put the words together:

> "Christmas alone
> With memories hanging heavily
> Like leaded tinsel.
> Memories of green and red
> Alcohol and laughter
> Love and you.
> Gay loud people
> Blurry faded people
> Wax mannequins melting . . ."

The pencil dropped from my fingers and tumbled to the floor. Even in our circumstances, sleep brought merciful relief to the pathetic men in the Library. Outside, at the far edge of the sound horizon, faint carols could be heard.

Among the loners in the group, Captain Gomez was clearly a man's man: a quiet, strong type with a reputation for heroic deeds in the war against Batista which had preceded him even there. The Library group, in fact, was proud to have him. He was one of Major William Morgan's top aides and had been indicted with him for conspiracy against their former chief, Fidel Castro. Everyone knew how Fidel felt about what he considered a personal betrayal, and all the men hoped for thirty years for Captain Gomez as the lesser of two evils in the trial just then in progress.

Major Morgan was almost a legend in Havana. An American who took up the fight against Batista, he was feared and respected in the hilly area of central Cuba during the war, the Escambray range of mountains. After victory, Morgan learned, along with everyone else, that Castro was not about to share his power with anyone. Still, Morgan stayed in government, somewhat conspicuously on the sidelines. He did, however, help Che Guevara with the early executions at La Cabana, and he apparently believed in their justice. About that time he also helped abort an anti-Castro conspiracy by pretending to go along with it, much to the amusement of Castro, who naturally televised the whole thing nationally and had the conspirators condemned to thirty years or executed, depending on their age and degree of involvement. A side benefit for Castro from this operation was that he thus managed to "compromise" Morgan by having him universally blamed for these deaths which he did not anticipate and perhaps did not condone. The conspirators, after all, had never hurt anyone or fired a gun in anger, and they were hoping for a bloodless overthrow of what they considered Castro's madness. Morgan, in fact, was a simple, affable gringo, maybe an adventurer, but never a Communist. He finally had had enough of Castro and was taking off to the hills to start a guerrilla movement anew when someone tipped off the G-2. He was apprehended along with a group of friends which included Captain Gomez. Morgan had a following in Cuba among fighting men, and Castro could not railroad his death sentence through the kangaroo courts as he did with lesser figures. An elaborate trial was held, but all in Cuba could predict the result before it started, so well known by now was the vindictiveness of the Maximum Leader of the Revolution.

Captain Gomez had been with Morgan from the modest beginnings up in the hills in pre-Castro days, and was now with him at the end. The Library group quite naturally bombarded him with questions about the war, about the last conspiracy, and about the trial. I took him into my confidence further than I had most of the others, and we discussed mutual friends whom we had known in the hills or in the urban underground. I even confided to Gomez that my concern for the fate of my Mercedes went beyond the mere worry about the G-2 drivers stripping the gears—a rather foolish reason I had given to the group generally. As a consequence, I was able to ask Gomez, my top bunkmate, to help me be on the lookout for the automobile through the crack in the Library's window board, in case the G-2 should ever bring the car into the patio of the building.

Everyone attributed Gomez' taciturn behavior to his worry over the trial, and everyone understood that quite well. One week after my arrival, one of the knockings turned out to be for Captain Gomez. The Nicaraguan jester never dared sing his lament for the Captain, for he instinctively knew that it would be inappropriate. Gomez was gone for most of the day, came back in a darker mood than ever, and went directly to his bunk. The men respected his privacy and could only wonder about the trial proceedings. That night the evening newspaper found its way to the Library through the courtesy of the guards, who were always happy to provide it when the news was bad. Major Morgan, as expected, had been condemned to death. Various others had drawn sentences from thirty years on down. Captain Gomez had been acquitted. The men couldn't quite understand it, but it really didn't matter. They sang, and jumped up and down, and congratulated the captain on his good luck. After all, the world may disagree with Castro, but if he has you shot you're dead, and that's that as far as *you* are concerned. Gomez appeared to be surprised at the news, and only said that he was sure he was to be tried for other charges, and he did not seem happy.

The next day *Revolucion* carried the full story. The key to it read:

"Major Morgan was convicted largely on evidence supplied by his former aide, Captain Gomez, who confirmed many of the charges of gunrunning to the Escambray Mountains and of masterminding the major revolt within government, which were brought against him by the military prosecutor."

One of the Catholic boys had read the newspaper aloud. I looked at Gomez, and the captain looked back, and neither of us spoke. No one else in the Library said anything.

I had talked with Captain Gomez a lot in a few days, and I thought I could tell what Gomez would say should he elect to speak. But Gomez did not speak. Yet, in my mind's eye, I could see the sad, wise look on the rugged face and I could hear the words:

"Look, my new friend, I know I am an informer—a pitiful thing to be. A history of bravery under fire denied forever. But I have a wife and I have children, and I've been fighting for nine years. Nine years out of my life and out of my wife's life, and *all* the life of my children. Morgan was going to be shot, anyway, and I was going to die, too, unless I talked. Well, I couldn't help Morgan and they couldn't kill him more than once . . . His memory, also, would not be hurt, not by my contributing further evidence of a courageous stand against tyranny. So why shouldn't I live? . . . I don't care any more for honor, and I'm tired of death . . ."

That's the way I heard it. Maybe I was wrong. No one would ever know. Captain Gomez was taken out of the Library that same day, accompanied by complete silence.

The day after that, one of the boys half-shouted to me from the window: "Hey, Tony, I can see a Mercedes-Benz coming up. It's the right color and the right model. Could it be yours?"

I jumped up to the boards and, sure enough, she was going by, full of bearded men. I wished for Superman's X-ray vision so that I might look through the car and into that glove compartment, although I knew that those cables would not, could not, still be there; and if, by a miracle, they had been missed so far, how long would it be before one of those bitter, resentful men reached in to see what the "privileged classes" kept in their glove compartments? I got back down from the bunk, worried. Almost immediately after, the Library contingent was told by a newcomer that a group of men and women had just been brought in and were awaiting questioning. Apparently it was a big thing. They had, again, found transmitting and receiving radio equipment. This time, however, their physical description, as far as it went, checked much too closely with my own group who, by now, I thought, would probably have inherited just such equipment from El Gallego. I gave in to despair and lay down on a corner bunk, brooding.

That night was worrisome for everyone. I was so tense that I probably wouldn't have slept anyway, but most of the other inhabitants of the Library didn't either. A noisy group of people paraded for hours on the street outside the building in the early evening hours, right under the Library windows, separated only by a narrow strip of garden. The young men and women outside carried banners and apparently had their official cheerleaders, all well organized by the Party. They sang *"Paredon, Paredon!"* ("To the Wall!"), and things like "Death to the worms," meaning, of course, the frightened people inside. They kept singing and marching and screaming, and there seemed to be no end to it. Even though everyone knew the whole thing was planned by the Communists, the men in the cells inside did not think that the G-2 needed any encouragement to perform their duties, and they both feared and hated the whole show.

At one point, one of the guards performed the knocking ritual on the door, opened it and said: "Do you guys think we should follow their advice out there, or should we continue to be generous with you?" The smile that should have gone with the remark wasn't there. Someone from a corner told him to go to hell. The guard shrugged his shoulders and closed the door with a bang.

Eventually the parade moved on, perhaps to torture other poor men elsewhere, singing:

> *"Fidel, Fidel;*
> *Que tiene Fidel?*
> *Que los Americanos*
> *No pueden con el?"*

Freely translated, that meant:

> "Fidel, Fidel;
> What has he got,
> That the Americans
> Simply have not?"

It was sung to a sort of Conga beat to which they danced as they finally faded away. Communism in the tropics.

Early the next morning, before dawn, there was a sudden, demanding knock on the door and it startled everyone, some men literally jumping out of bed. I felt instinctively that it was for me, and I was right. I was being called in for questioning. The Nicaraguan followed me to the door with his make-believe guitar and his *"Ayudame, Dios mio"* performance, but it must not have seemed very funny, for no one joined in. They had all seen how terribly worried I had looked that day.

I could tell immediately that the questioning here would be nothing like that at the earlier G-2 branch office, where an almost friendly attitude had prevailed. They escorted me through the halls which crisscrossed among other cells like the Library, and led me to a small room which, in earlier days, must have been a maid's or chauffeur's room at the back of the house. It was completely paneled with white acoustic tile, and it looked very much like a control booth in a sound studio. The only furniture was a simple, school-like desk. On one of the straight chairs behind the desk sat a trim, shower-neat young man with a blue-black beard, closely shaven, all the cleanliness standing out oddly against the party-line sloppiness of his comrades everywhere. He looked cold and acted cold, and I couldn't get rid of the feeling of a hospital in the air. A man in a white jacket would have looked just right in the setting, and maybe one was due at any minute, I thought, going back to my imagery of injections and blood-drawing. I tried to forget my thoughts and look composed. The guard who had escorted me motioned me to the chair before the desk, while he himself took the empty one next to the Interrogator, brought out a pad and pencil from the drawer, and got ready to take notes. These were obviously no ordinary guards.

I must have overacted my relaxed attitude, because the Interrogator's first words to me were a curt "Sit up straight!"

"I expect yes or no answers," the Interrogator said, *"only."* I nodded in resigned assent.

"Is your name Antonio Navarro?"

"Yes."

"Do you have an alias, a war name?"

"No . . . Am I supposed to have one?"

"I believe it is obvious that *I* ask the questions."

"Yes. Sorry. No, I don't."

And so it went, going over the territory which the Investigator at the G-2 branch had already covered, although I thought I detected *some* recognition of that earlier interrogation. When they got to the matter of the faked police card, I tried to explain that yes or no answers would not be satisfactory, since they would not tell the whole story, but I was ignored and told bluntly to shut up and stick to the rules. I took some private comfort from the fact that it didn't seem logical for the Interrogator to spend so much time on the police card if they had indeed found the papers and thus had more than enough to hang me. On the other hand, I thought, the incriminatory cables had not been *dated*, as far as I could recall, so the G-2 could have found them and perhaps were not sure if they belonged to me or to the man I admitted hiding and befriending, Gonzalez-Recio. If the latter were true, they might not have a clear case against me.

After a while a pattern emerged, and it was, I concluded, to establish the degree of *willful* involvement on my part with the anti-Government activities of Gonzalez-Recio. At one point another man entered the cubicle. He, too, was neat, and there was something foreign—not American, but perhaps European— about him. I was not a physiognomist, but it did not take a great deal of studying to conclude that the new face was Slavic, from Russia or, possibly, one of the East European satellites. I had the impression that he was not supposed to be there, but had come in anyway for some special reason. He had in his right hand what appeared from a distance to be some kind of letter, and he seemed excited—for a Slav, that is. He motioned the Interrogator to step outside. They both did, and were back within a minute.

"Mr. Navarro," the Interrogator said, "we understand that you correspond regularly with the U.S. Government. Is that correct?"

I was surprised by the question, but I stuck to the rules of the game.

"No," I said firmly. I felt safe on this one. I had no such correspondence, unless —my God, unless they had *just* found the roll of cables and they were talking about the daily radio and "the friends." They were, after all, the U.S. Government, weren't they? I started perspiring and I felt my face turning red. I struggled for composure, but my reserves of play-acting were reaching the end and I felt weak, lost.

"No?" The Interrogator grinned sadistically. "And what, then, is this?" It was a single sheet of paper, not a roll of cables. It was the same letter I had seen before. It was pushed in front of me and I looked at it. Sure enough, there was the emblem of the U.S. Senate on the letterhead. I recognized it immediately. Even in the gravity of the situation, I might have laughed, but I didn't.

"Officer," I said, "may I depart from the yes-or-no?"

"Go ahead."

"Sir, have you read this letter?"

"It's in English," the Interrogator said, avoiding the question and the admission of ignorance.

"I'm sure your colleague here has read it," I said, looking up at the Russian. "Anyway, if *anyone* has read the letter, you will have noticed that it is signed by Senator William Fulbright of the Foreign Relations Committee."

The two men standing in front of me nodded briefly, while the guard kept looking at his notes.

"The matter, gentlemen, is quite simple," I continued, encouraged. "In fact, I think it is ironical. I had written Senator Fulbright, whom I have never met, to congratulate him on statements he had made about the Cuban Revolution which showed that he at least was keeping an open mind while others simply criticized what was going on in our country, what we were doing." I paused, feeling a sudden urge to be sincere, no matter what. "I was one of you then," I said.

I stopped and found my common sense and, after looking at and past the Russian agent, settled on the Interrogator and said: "I mean, what you were doing then, Officer."

There was a moment of silence, and I said: "May I read from the letter?"

The Interrogator closed his eyes briefly in assent, and I said, "After my letter to him commending him on his public statement in July of 1959, Mr. Fulbright said the following," and I read, in Spanish, what Fulbright had written:

"Coming from a man like you: a Cuban, on the spot, but, as you say, uninvolved, your approval of my position, Mr. Navarro, is most rewarding, particularly when you consider that my constituents have not always agreed with my views on Cuba."

At the bottom of the letter, I noticed that an annotation had been pencilled in by the G-2: "Collaboration with the imperialistic powers."

I looked up from the letter and made it clear that I was through. The Interrogator said nothing. The Russian spoke for the first time, the grammar perfect, the accent thick.

"Why was it important for you, this approval from the United States?"

"We are very close to the United States, sir," I said firmly, "in many ways. I have to admit that, at that time, I thought it was important."

The Interrogator remained silent—a damning silence from the Soviet viewpoint. The Russian looked at him briefly, grabbed the letter abruptly from my hand, and marched out the door.

The Interrogator was aware of his loss of position and lost no time in reestablishing what he considered his proper relationship with me. I meantime realized that the letter from Fulbright had been taken from my files at the sugar office, something the earlier Investigator had not made reference to, and that therefore a new dimension had been added to my process. The Interrogator, however, returned to a more central theme.

"How long have you known Gonzalez-Recio?" he asked.

"On and off for most of my adult life," I answered.

"Did you know what he was doing when you took him into your home?"

I vacillated: "Not . . . completely."

"What do you mean by that?"

"I mean that I knew Alberto was involved in something political, but I didn't know how deeply."

"In other words, you knew that Gonzalez-Recio was conspiring against the Revolutionary Government when you offered him assistance?"

I thought about the question for a few seconds. My intuition told me that you come off better with these people if you are mildly guilty but repentant and contrite than if you are absolutely and confidently innocent but arrogant and critical. It was perhaps a play on their own insecurity. I didn't care what the psychological mechanism was; besides, it was too late for complete pretense.

"Yes," I said, "I knew. Perhaps not at the very beginning, but I began suspecting it with time, until finally I asked him to leave our house. I would be lying to you if I pretended that I knew nothing about it. I think that would be a foolish course for me to take, and I won't take it."

I couldn't tell what effect my remarks had behind the cold mask of the Interrogator which at times sparkled, reflecting God knows what conclusions. The man was not a fool.

"Mr. Navarro," he said, "are you familiar with the new law dealing with counter-revolutionary activities?"

"I know about it, sir," I answered, "but perhaps I am not familiar with the details."

"Well, let me tell you," the Interrogator said, "that it is provided in that law that anyone who gives comfort and assistance to the enemy, to those engaged in counter-revolutionary activities, will be considered to be as guilty as the man he protects and will suffer the same punishment as would be accorded to the primary guilty party, if caught."

"I understand, sir," I said, truly shaken.

"Do you know what Gonzalez-Recio is wanted for?" the Interrogator asked.

"No, I don't," I half-lied, expecting a recounting of crimes.

The Interrogator kept quiet for several seconds and then, suddenly, he said, "Mr. Navarro, guard, the session is over."

I was taken out of the presence of the "clean one" by the guard and into the inside patio on the way back to the Library. Everything being relative, the guard seemed more accessible, and I took a chance in questioning him. I was terribly worried. As we walked slowly, I asked: "Did you know Gonzalez-Recio?"

"Not personally, Mr. Navarro, but we in the department know about him, especially by his war name of Lorenzo."

"Was he very involved?" I asked, dreading the answer.

The guard held his right thumb and forefinger out, slightly separated, as if he were measuring something.

"Mr. Navarro," he said, "we have a file that thick on Gonzalez-Recio."

Although it was not unexpected, my spirits sank. I knew perfectly well that Lorenzo had been for many months the head of the terrorist activities of the Movement and that a G-2 dossier on him must indeed exist.

"Sergeant," I said, "you seem to be a good man. You haven't gone out of your way to be unkind. How does my case look to you?"

"Not good, Mr. Navarro," the sergeant said briefly.

"Would it be, do you think, many years?" I asked, blood rushing somewhere where it made me very hot and, I felt, tell-tale red.

"Mr. Navarro," the guard answered, "you'll be lucky if *it's only a matter of years.*"

I returned to my cell by mid-morning at the lowest point since I was caught out on that lonely road, ages ago, it seemed. I was almost sure now that they had found the cables and were just playing a game to see how far I would go with my farce, to what inconsistencies I would fall prey, before confronting me with the full blast of the evidence. Even if they hadn't found the papers, the Interrogator had made it clear that I would be just as guilty as Lorenzo for "aiding and abetting" him, and just as severely punished. I would have settled for any sentence right then and there, even thirty years, if there had been an obliging Mephistopheles around to arrange things.

I went directly to my bunk without a word and lay there quietly for a long time. In that room of desperate men, I was alone. There was no one to turn to anymore —no one except, perhaps, God. And so I prayed. I had twenty years of agnosticism behind me, and I prayed. It's hard for a man to make peace between intellect and emotion. At times, when I had the courage and the sun was shining and everything was right with my world, I had acknowledged to myself that agnosticism was only the coward's way out, that I really was an atheist and, when driven to it by a friend whose intellect I respected, I would admit it. The difference was that agnosticism at least left you with hope, and I now desperately needed not only hope; I needed certainty. I asked God, wherever He was, *if* He was, to please remember my wife and children, so helpless and so deserving and so innocent of my own wrongdoings in religious matters—if wrong it was, indeed, to grope for a meaning and to reject the facile answer.

The two Catholic boys had been watching me for some time, isolated in my bunk, and they knew that I was deeply troubled. One of them came over and handed me a little medal on a chain. He said, "Wear it," and went back to his bunk. I accepted it silently and thought that El Gallego's "lawyers" now had company. Maybe there was safety in numbers—or in faith.

Dusk came and night came, and I sat on my bunk and no one disturbed me because, despite the curious, unmeant sadism of poor wretches thrown together, there was a limit that everyone respected. Later in the night, the quiet was disturbed when twice the power failed and the brash, merciless lights went out all over the building. The guards outside the Library shouted orders and ran back and forth, apparently expecting an attack. The inmates jumped from their bunks because they knew, most of them from personal experience, that a machine gun fired from a passing car at close range would go through wooden boards like paper, and it would be ironic indeed to be killed by their own people. The blackout lasted for two or three minutes the first time and was repeated half an hour later.

I considered the possibility that it could be my Rescate buddies coming to rescue me, and I daydreamed myself out of the Library, kicking the door, hitting the guards, and rushing outside to meet my friends, bullets and shouts of anger and pain following me out the gates toward the big black Cadillac which surely would be there. But the lights came back on, all was quiet again, and that awful reality was there to be faced. If it had been some kind of attempt, it had failed and would not be repeated. I looked up at Little Joe's toothbrush, which had become a symbol to me, and sank into deeper depression. Every once in a while I reminded myself that, after all, I always *knew* that a violent death could lie at the end of the road. Sleep just wouldn't come. I thought of the simple prayers of my childhood and repeated them quietly: ". . . pray for us now and at the hour of our death." Perhaps that Man up there I had so often denied when the going was easy might forgive me and change the course of events which now seemed so obvious, so inevitable. And, finally, I slept.

Avis drove her brother-in-law's car to the Miami International Airport just after sundown. She was responding to my call a week before, asking her to meet the Pan American flight on that day when Niniña Leitao Da Cunha, the wife of the Brazilian Ambassador to Cuba, was arriving. She parked the car at the lower level and took the escalator to the area where a crowd of Cuban exiles were greeting an addition to the ever-growing contingent in Miami. Spotting the Brazilian Consul to Miami, she started toward him. As she walked through the crowd, she saw Tony Varona and a group of men, all obviously members of Rescate. Avis intuitively tried to avoid them, but it was too late; *they* had seen her.

"Tocaya! Tocaya!" several people shouted above the crowd. "Good to see you! Who are you meeting?"

Avis heard it, made a lightning judgment that the whole thing had to be bad for her husband, with Varona there and all the spies around, and she walked right by without a sign of recognition. At least Castro's spies might not tie it in to her and to the Navarro name. Avis would do anything to protect me, but apparently my friends were not as careful and were prepared to toss caution, *my* caution, to the winds. In Miami, it was easy to forget.

Avis met Ambassador and Shra. Leitao Da Cunha and received from her an envelope I had sent. The ambassadors were going to stay at a hotel in Miami Beach and would then go on to Rio de Janeiro, where Vasco Leitao Da Cunha would become Foreign Minister of his country. Avis kissed the ambassadors; she was very fond of them, particularly Vasco, who was her image of a true gentleman and a true friend.

Then Avis drove back to the Miller home. She had already opened the envelope and found that it included some personal notes from me, but also some information that she was to convey to Varona and the Rescate group. The information, at least in Avis' estimation, was not terribly confidential or compromising. She knew that I would never misuse my Brazilian friends to that extent —not unless I *had* to.

When Avis reached home and was about to call the Rescate office, the telephone rang. It was Shra. Leito Da Cunha.

"Avis, I have some very bad news for you."

"What is it, Niniña?"

"Tony has been captured by the G-2, and he's in jail."

"Oh, my God."

"I'm sorry, Avis, but I had to tell you. We just heard about it from the Embassy in Cuba. The call was waiting when we arrived."

"Can't you do something about it?" Avis asked, not knowing what to say, unable to think, hoping against hope.

"No, we can't." Niniña was surprisingly definite. "We can't because he, unwisely, has taken the liberty to involve us. He has mentioned the Brazilian Embassy, and this is something we cannot accept."

"But he's in *jail,* " Avis said, not understanding the cold reasoning of the other woman.

"I'm sorry, Avis. That is his problem."

Avis managed to say: "What do you think will happen?"

"I'm very sorry to tell you this," Niniña answered, "but from what I've heard, I'm very much afraid that he may be executed. Why . . ."

But Avis had hung up, not wanting to hear anything more. She burst into wild, uncontrollable sobs of utter anguish which brought Helen running.

"Avis! *Avis!* What *is* it?"

The Millers comforted Avis to the extent they could, and then together they called Burke Hedges. Apparently Varona already had the news and, through him, Hedges had learned of it.

"Avis, please, dear," Hedges said. "Everything will be done that can be done. Do you know the name Moreno?"

"Yes, I do, daddy," Avis said.

"Well, we have word—Varona told me—that he intends to rescue Tony when they transfer him from one jail to the other. I don't know exactly what that means, but everyone respects Moreno a great deal."

"Yes, I know," Avis said.

"Well, apparently Tony will be moved between jails or finally to La Cabana for . . . whatever his sentence will be."

"Oh, dad, they'll kill him!"

"No, they won't, honey. Whenever they move him, Moreno will act."

"Is that all we have to go on?"

"Yes, dear, I'm afraid that's all, except that I have told them that if it's a matter of money, all that I have is available to keep Tony alive."

"Thank you, daddy. I must hang up now. I don't feel very well."

Avis cried quietly for a while while her sister and Bob Miller sat with her, unable to offer any reassurance. They, too, were very worried. Avis wiped her tears away, went back to the phone and called the Brazilian ambassadors again. She got Niniña.

"Hello, Niniña."

"Yes, Avis." Her sobbing voice was recognized.

"Could I please talk to Vasco?"

"I'm sorry, Avis, but he has just left. Miami was only a stopover for us, and he has gone ahead to assume his new duties."

"Oh?"

"Yes, Avis, he is going to be the new Chancellor."

"Oh, Niniña, I'm so happy for you," Avis managed to say. "He certainly deserves it. He's a wonderful man."

"Thank you."

"Niniña," Avis said. "You must understand. It's my husband. Do you think I could call Vasco in Brazil?"

"That's up to you, Avis," Niniña said. "Of course you can call him if you wish, but I don't know what he could do. I'm afraid that Tony has gone too far. I'm very sorry for you."

"Goodbye, Niniña," Avis said. Then she hung up and sank into her chair, sobbing.

The morning after my first question session was unusually quiet at the Library. Conversation between the men was only the essential at breakfast, and even then it tended to be somehow hushed. I knew that the interrogation had gone poorly for me, and I had confided my misgivings to the Catholic boys. They in turn were protecting me discreetly by keeping the others from the usual joking and carrying on. Sitting alone in a corner, I had gone over my problem a thousand times, and my conclusion was always the same; in fact, it could not be otherwise. The best assumption was that they had not found the cables, but that I had confessed to helping an enemy of the Revolution. It would suit the Government to make an example of me, and my tie to the powerful Hedges family was an added bonus for the Communists. In their place I would do it, I thought. I would apply the full rigor of the new law against counter-revolutionaries, showing all my opponents the risk they were taking when they contributed money to the anti-Castro movements or allowed their houses to be used for hiding men wanted by the Government. These activities were a serious problem for the Communists, and a well-publicized trial and stiff sentence would be a great help. For me it was all a foregone conclusion. And that was the *best* of the alternatives. There was no point even thinking about the worst one—but of course I did.

Late in the morning a harsh knock came, and the guard said loudly: "Navarro!"

I sprang to my feet. It was an odd time for questioning, and an odd day, New Year's Eve, two years from that other fateful eve on the Isle of Pines. I wasn't thinking too logically any more, but it *had* to mean that I was being transferred. And *that* could only mean La Cabaña; that's where the more official trials took place, and that's also where The Wall was. To be sure, the guard shouted impatiently: "Bring your things!" The men in the cell understood and gave me a handshake or a pat on the back that tried hard to be encouraging. The guard cut the goodbyes short and urged me through the door, which he closed with a hard bang. He did not motion me toward the back of the house where interrogations took place, but toward the front. At the front office, the same office which saw my arrival a fortnight before, a non-commissioned officer pushed toward me a printed sheet of paper which was lying on the desk and said: "Are you Antonio Navarro?"

"Yes, sir."

"Sign this."

"Shouldn't I at least read it?" I asked half-heartedly, actually managing to grin. "Even if it's my sentence, I would like to know if I'm really important or just a run-of-the-mill worm."

"What's the matter with you, anyway?" the sergeant said, straightfaced. "You're being released."

"Look, mister," I said, eyes flooding more out of self-pity than anger—I was too worn out for anger. "I've been through a lot. Only a sadist would enjoy a joke at my expense."

"Okay," the sergeant said, turning impatiently away. "Read it for yourself." I picked up the paper and read to myself:

"The Intelligence Service of the Cuban Rebel Army, not having found sufficient evidence to substantiate the charges brought against prisoner Antonio Navarro, hereby decrees that he be granted his immediate freedom, regretting any inconvenience . . ."

I read no further. It was true; I was a free man. That is an easy thing to say, but, oh, the meaning to me at that particular moment. What a wonderful feeling to be able to walk about at will, or not to walk at all, to be free of fear! For the moment, I just stood there with my mouth wide open, totally disbelieving.

Why was I being released? At the very least, I had impersonated an officer and given shelter to a fugitive from justice. Politics aside, that was enough mayhem even outside a police state like Cuba. Had I simply talked my way out? Or did I have friends in government who had interceded in my behalf? Jesus Soto, the labor leader? Was Moreno really that powerful? Or could it even be Guevara? Had they let me go in order to follow me and eventually apprehend the whole group? Were they, incredibly, willing to give a second chance to a man who had shown some support for the Revolution, despite his position? Could it be that some members of the G-2 saw the handwriting on the wall, anticipated the forthcoming invasion and its success, and were already hedging their positions? Unlikely. Or, finally, was it some sort of a miracle? I unconsciously raised my eyes to the high ceiling of the old house as I considered this last possibility—that somebody up there cared after all. "Tony Navarro, we are giving you a new year you never expected. Use it wisely." Who knows? If nothing else, Tony Navarro would be less arrogant and more tolerant of human weakness, if that is what the need for a faith was.

"Sergeant, I take it that this is absolutely serious." I still could not believe it.

"Of course it is, Mr. Navarro," the guard said softly.

Who could resist the overwhelming happiness of a man rescued from the very brink? My first reaction was to hug the sergeant, and so I did. The man was shocked, and shied away from the contact, but he still managed to smile. I guess they're human, after all, I thought, and are glad to have one less crime on their consciences.

"Sergeant," I said, impersonal again, "may I be allowed to go back to the Library and collect a few things I left there? You see, I never quite believed that I was leaving this place."

"Granted," the sergeant said, also recovering his professional status, "provided, Mr. Navarro, that you don't tell the men in your cell what has happened. It's against our rules."

"Of course, sergeant, I understand."

I went back to the Library, walked in without knocking, looked terribly serious, and picked up my few remaining things. The men looked at me, and it was obvious that they were worried. I ignored them, but shook hands briefly with one of the Catholic boys. I wished that I could tell the young man that his medal had saved me, whether or not I myself believed it, but all I could manage under the scrutiny of the guard who had accompanied me to the Library door was a conspiratorial wink which no one else saw, and I hoped that it would tell my young friend and the others the whole story.

At the door I paused for a second, looked over my friends for the last time as if I were commanding their attention, and then I walked deliberately to my old bunk, reached for Little Joe's toothbrush from the knothole in the board, put it in my pocket, and walked out. I took the few steps that separated the Library from the rest of the building with the greatest composure while my heart pounded away in my chest. At the front office, I took off my denim jacket, and the guards handed me a handkerchief tied into a pouch with my belongings inside. They looked at me oddly, I thought. One of them casually cocked his rifle, and I read all kinds of things into that gesture—a shot in the back, the whole thing a cruel hoax—but kept walking. I reached the porch within view of Fifth Avenue. Five more cautious steps, a quick, nervous meeting of the eyes with the last guard, and I walked out of the door of the G-2 and into the world.

22

I WALKED INTO a bright noon, a New Year's Eve noon, and onto the shimmering sidewalks of the center island of the Avenue, with flower beds that shouted back their colors. It was a good feeling, but I felt the urgency to get away quickly and looked around for a taxi, but there was none. I started to walk on the broad cement sidewalk, away from the terrible building, slowly at first, then faster— then I ran. I ran openly, shamelessly, rushing by the flowers and over the hot bright cement as if it burned my feet. Disheveled, with three weeks' growth of beard, in dirty clothes I had slept in all that time, I ran aimlessly and wildly down a perfectly peaceful street on a warm, sleepy, holiday afternoon.

I finally waved down a taxi. The driver looked intently at me as he stopped, but eventually decided to take a chance on the apparition and pick me up. I sat on the back seat of the rickety taxi, simply moving *away*, without directions having been asked for or given, in a sort of silent understanding.

Then I looked for the first time at the bundle of my belongings. It was a pitiful little bundle. I thought, one is born with less than that and one goes to the grave with less. It had cards and a wallet and notebooks—or what was left of them after my paper-eating episode. As I dug through it, I realized that my passport wasn't there and I wondered if, in fact, I had had it with me the night I was arrested. At the bottom of the mess, I spotted a card—a plastic-covered card—and I couldn't believe it. It was the fake police identification which had started the most terrible twenty-four days of my life. What kind of people are these G-2s, anyway? Are they just inept and overworked, or are they incredibly stupid? My mind wasn't up to sober analysis. I pondered what to do about my passport. I knew I would need it, and in quick succession gave the utterly confused driver contradictory orders: Go back to G-2! No, don't go back! Find a telephone booth! No, don't! Finally, common sense prevailed and the taxi set course for my Country Club home with a sigh of relief from the driver. Maybe I would send someone later to pick up the passport. Perhaps it was the G-2's way of being sure that I wouldn't leave the country.

As the taxi moved swiftly over the upper blocks of Fifth Avenue, the old me began to be reborn.

"I bet you think I don't have the money to pay you," I said to the driver.

"Oh, no, sir," the modest man answered. "I can tell you have a problem, but I know you'll have the money."

"Wrong," I said. "I am absolutely broke."

"Your problem looks big," the driver said. "I'll take you where you're going, free."

"Thank you, *sir,*" I said, smiling, "and a Happy New Year to you. You'll get your money when we get home."

We arrived slightly past noon.

"I knew it," the taxi driver said, "I just knew it," as he turned into the semi-circular driveway. I touched his back in a mute gesture of gratitude as I got out of the cab and walked cautiously to the front door, ready, at this point, for anything. There was no need for concern. Gisela answered the bell immediately. We hugged each other quietly, and she cried freely.

I said, "Nanita?" and Gisela pointed upstairs and said, "Please go, caballero. Please go."

I started to run up the stairs. "Please take care of the taxi driver," I said. "And, Gisela, take care of him well."

I found Nanita unconscious, and though I did my best to bring her back, to tell her that I was there, as lovingly as ever, by her side, it was useless.

Gisela came back to Nanita's bedside and told me the story. The G-2 had come back a second time and had found nothing that time, either, as far as Gisela could tell. But Nanita had asked them about me, and the agent in charge had said to her:

"Look, old lady, your little Tony isn't coming back. In fact, he'll be executed —especially if we don't find what we're looking for."

Nanita had looked at the man, Gisela said, very lucidly, her sunken eyes full of horror and grief. And the man had added: "Better forget him, old lady. He couldn't have cared for you, anyway, to abandon you the way he did. *Asi son los ricos.*" ("That's the way the rich are.")

I became desperate and wanted, above all else in this world, to have Nanita know that I was here before she died. I thought of calling Max, but that was much too dangerous. Besides, hopefully, the old doctor was already in Miami. I called my mother. She was relieved to hear me. She had been trying to help me with whatever connections she still had, and hadn't been able to be around Nanita much, although she was aware of her condition.

"Mother," I pleaded, "can't someone give her a shot, to bring her back for just a minute? She *can't* die without knowing I didn't abandon her!"

"It's too late, son," Mother said. "We tried. All we can do now is wait for her death and pray to God that her lot in the next world is a better one."

"Thank you, Mother." I put the phone down.

Even in the midst of my sorrow, I realized full well that my duty lay with the living, and so I decided to go and find Moreno. I kissed Nanita on the cheek, said a soft goodbye which would never be heard, and took time for the fastest shower of my life. At last in clean clothes, I picked up the second set of keys for the Mercedes and went to look for my Walther pistol. I found it undisturbed, still sitting out there al fresco, under the gravel, and put it under my belt behind my back. Then I picked up one of my Basque berets, hugged Gisela tightly and said, "Please, if she wakes up . . . you'll tell her, won't you? Tell her I'm safe and that I never really left her." Gisela nodded, knowing that words would only bring tears.

I went out the door to walk the ten blocks or so to a taxi stand. Before I turned the corner, I took a long look at the quiet, gracious house I had enjoyed so much and which would never be the same again.

I found Moreno at his apartment at Olan Towers, after walking around the area for half an hour to make absolutely sure I wasn't being followed. Moreno embraced me like a lost son and filled me in on the happenings. Preparations for the invasion had accelerated. Max had left for Miami as scheduled, and the Movement was being run in administrative matters by one of Max's lieutenants, and in the military by Moreno. The escape operation off the north coast of Pinar del Rio had been postponed when Miami learned of my arrest, for fear that the cover would be blown. However, as far as Moreno knew, the hidden cables hadn't been discovered, or else the G-2 was cagier than anyone could believe. That the papers might still be in the car posed a continuing threat, and that problem would have to be dealt with immediately.

As I had thought, Moreno had in fact made plans to rescue me, either from the G-2 directly or when I was in transit between Fifth and 14th and La Cabana. The power failure at the Library had been engineered by Moreno, but it never went beyond that.

We agreed that after certain problems were taken care of, such as the papers in the Mercedes and the weapons in the Country Club house, I should go into asylum at an embassy. He said that I was now definitely burned, and I had to agree. We also agreed that I had been a lucky man—so far.

It was by then about 1:30 in the afternoon. Before making specific plans, I asked Moreno if I could call Avis from his phone, and Moreno nodded, adding, "Tocayo, maybe I didn't get you out of the G-2—you didn't give me a chance —but I can assure you that I know for an absolute fact that *my* phone is not tapped. Trust me."

"Moreno," I said softly, "we've gone through a lot together, but you never cease to amaze me. I never doubted you would come for me." Then, dramatically, I added, "On *your word* alone, I accept as gospel truth that your phone is 'clean.'"

I dialed Miami, and the answer came immediately.

"Oh, honey . . . oh, honey . . ." was all Avis could say, and she started crying. It had been a long journey for her from the uncontrollable sobs which the Millers had heard when she first learned about my capture and the tears of that moment, almost mixed with laughter.

"You bastard!" she said. "You bastard! I forgive you all your shenanigans. But I don't forgive you this scare. Come home, honey! *Please* come home!"

"I will, darling, I will," I said. "I promise. But first there are a few things I have to take care of."

"There is nothing you have to take care of, Tony, nothing except you and me," Avis said, very seriously.

"I know, Avis. You have my promise. Tomorrow I will pay a visit—a long visit, I guess—to Vasco's friends. I think that's the best thing to do."

"Oh, yes," Avis said. "Thank God."

She then told me hurriedly what had happened in Miami—the help and understanding from her father and the Millers, how she had felt guilty at the airport when meeting Niniña, because they had called her by the "wrong name."

"I know, honey," I said, "but don't torture yourself. By that time I was already very much in jail."

Avis told me about the cool reception she had had from Niniña, who seemed to be worried about her country being compromised.

"But then," Avis said, "I took the bull by the horns and I called Vasco at home. He's a very important man there now."

"Yes, I know," I said. "What did he say?"

"He couldn't have been nicer. He asked me what I wanted him to do, and I told him. He said he'd do it gladly, and for me not to worry."

"What did you ask him to do, Avis—can you tell me?"

"I don't know if I can tell you, but I will anyway. I just asked him to say that he and his government were interested in you and that he should somehow get that message to the top man."

"Do you think he did?" I asked.

"I don't know," Avis answered.

"Well, honey, *I* think he did, and do you know what? I think you saved my life. I hope you won't be sorry," I replied, laughing.

"Oh, honey, how *could* I be sorry?" Together again, if only by telephone, we hung up.

Moreno and I quickly mapped out the short-term strategy. The day was running out and there was much to be done. Moreno said, "We know that the G-2 tactics are to leave you alone the first day out, maybe two. They figure you'll be too scared to try anything and they mean to give you a false sense of security before they start tailing you again. It's standard KGB policy in Russia."

"Well, then," I said, "our strategy should be exactly the opposite. We should do everything we can during the first day's free ride. Agree?"

"Absolutely."

"Right. Let's get started. The first order of business, I would say, should be the papers in my car—if they're still there. After that, we'll worry about those weapons in the elevator, if we're still around to worry."

"Let's go," Moreno said. He arranged for me to ride with him in his Cadillac, and provided a second car that I was to use after the attempted rescue of the papers. I would do this job alone. I had insisted that I would not involve Moreno any further, for the Movement now needed Moreno more than ever. It had already been determined that my Mercedes was being kept in the main police station in the old "Colonial City" in downtown Havana, one block from one of the oldest cathedrals in the New World.

The cars stopped at the cathedral square. One was parked and left there for my getaway, and the Cadillac dropped me and took off. Moreno was to rejoin me at exactly 4 P.M. at the Country Club house, unless he heard from me to the contrary.

The main Havana police station had been a fortress in the Spanish days. It still had the turrets and the large hewn stones and the walls and a cobblestoned inside patio where the confiscated automobiles were kept. That's where the Mercedes would be if not in use.

I put on my beret which, along with my grown beard, gave me the proper look of a dedicated Revolutionist. The guards by the stone pillars at the entrance looked casually at me, one more slovenly compañero, and ignored me. I walked inside the patio and there was the Mercedes.

I stood by the driver's door, invoked El Gallego's "lawyers," and started to let myself in with my extra set of keys. The guards looked. I had been so damned scared all along that nothing could scare me any more. However, I was careful to make no moves that could appear hasty, and the guards looked away, distracted by a female form that happened to be passing by.

With my heart in my mouth, I reached into the glove compartment. Incredibly, unbelievably, the roll of cables was there! In three weeks of frantic driving, apparently no one had reached a hand deeply into the compartment. I grabbed the precious roll, put it into my pocket, got out of the car and closed the door. Then I walked nonchalantly over the polished cobblestones which slipped under my desert boots and right past the guards, who gave me a military salute. In my pocket were the lives of many men.

Rather than leaving the area immediately, I surrendered to my old queer relish for danger and walked into a corner bodega halfway between the police station and the cathedral. I ordered a double rum, straight, took it with me into the smelly john, closed myself in, and proceeded to tear the cables into the smallest pieces I could manage. Then I threw them into the bowl, feeling a devilish elation as they grudgingly floated to their doom in the chugging whirl-pool of water—all of this accompanied by swallows of sweet, burning rum, which immediately had a decided effect on a stomach subjected to forced absti-nence for so long.

I floated out of the cafe, truly free, no longer worried about the damage I might do to others, and looked the guards at the station straight in the eye—that is, to the extent it could be done from a very safe distance. The car, my beloved Mercedes—to hell with it. It had done its noble job. The risk-reward equation was loaded the wrong way. It's probably still there, God bless it, racing around loaded with frightened men.

I walked back to the car parked in the square. My next move was to pick up Maria, to be with her one last time and to have her look after Nanita while I did what I still had to do. I had telephoned her from Moreno's and was to meet her at a bodega near her home, but, even at a slow pace, I'd be much too early. I had allowed too much time for my encounter with my old friend, the Mercedes.

I decided to go ahead anyway and wait at the bar of the bodega. Selecting a corner of the bar next to the wall, I sat on the well-worn stool, my back resting against the wall, and I ordered a Scotch-and-water, a wonderful Scotch-and-water, the first in what seemed like years. Following as it did a recent double rum, it placed me in a cozy twilight of perception where I could shut out the noises of the store and the street and lose myself in the sheer enjoyment of my freedom.

I was in a mood as I sat there, my elbows on the old mahogany bar, moist and dark wood steeped in the acrid spillings of a thousand daiquiris and worn smooth by the rolling of dice and the boisterous banging of the chunky leather cups. It was all part of being alive, the smells, the feel. I put down my thoughts on a little piece of paper because I knew that my increased awareness of being alive wouldn't long survive the everyday demands of life itself. I wrote:

"Have you seen the flies on a dark, wet counter in a dirty bodega when you are playing dice and they get in the way? Have you seen the sun play and scatter on their wings, the elusive, shifting colors moving over the tenuous surface? Of course you haven't. Why the hell would you, normally? Well, that's the prettiest damn sight I have ever seen, and I see it now for the first time. How could I have missed such simple beauty . . ."

My drink finished, I walked across the street to a little neighborhood church, filled with the need to give thanks to someone. Maria would wait at the bodega when she arrived—no problem.

The church was empty except for an old woman in a far corner by the bank of little flickering candles wrapped in wine-colored glass. I dropped into the very last pew, just enjoying the silence and the faint odor of incense. How peaceful it was. No one would be knocking on any doors . . .

A priest came in from a side door—the traditional roly-poly Spanish priest, like so many I had known in my youth. He came over to me, his face stern, and said: "Young man, that's no way to sit in the church, sprawled out like that. It isn't proper, not pious. I should show more respect if . . ."

I sprang to my feet, instinctively angry, and grabbed the surprised priest by the shoulders. It was a quick reaction of pent-up fear and anger, but it didn't last long. Realizing that the poor man had no way of knowing the background, I relaxed my grip, but left my hands on the priest's shoulders.

"Look, Father," I said, "I'll tell you what I think. I think if I were to *lie down* on this bench, God would still welcome me here today. You have no way of knowing."

The priest didn't have to know why. He sensed that there was a good reason, and he was moved by what he piously wanted to recognize as the beginning of a conversion, sure to lead me eventually back to the lost path.

"Stay as long as you want, my son," he said kindly, "and stay any *way* you want. There's really no one here to be shocked, anyway." He looked around. "God never gets shocked—only we foolish humans."

However, I couldn't stay, so I said goodbye to the old priest and saw the satisfaction in his eyes at having witnessed what he knew was the return of a prodigal son.

"In your prayers, Father, say something nice about a woman called Nanita." I promised to come back some day, and he blessed me. As I was leaving the church, Maria was coming in. She had been told that she would find me there, and we embraced quietly on the church steps.

We got into my borrowed car and went off to pick up El Gallego. He was already waiting, anxious to see me for the first time since we had parted what seemed light-years ago, and we hugged each other too. After all, it was a return from the dead. Then the three of us headed for my home.

We had agreed that Moreno shouldn't show up at the house unless it was absolutely necessary, and that he shouldn't be seen with me in public until it was all over. Those rules didn't hold for El Gallego, since we two had already been linked together by the G-2. It was El Gallego, therefore, who would help me carry the weapons and the radios and the maps from their hiding place in the elevator well and out the kitchen door to the back of the garage. Moreno would come at an appointed hour, checking for police and joining us only long enough to transfer the equipment to his car. Maria would stay behind. Not even the G-2 would question the presence of a girl friend, and Maria's links to the Movement had ended when Augusto's group left.

As I approached my home, I had an odd, uncomfortable feeling. I wondered if I was feeling the vibrations of the presence of the G-2. Maybe they had come to check on me sooner than expected. I was wrong.

As we approached the front door and Gisela came to meet us, I knew.

"Nanita is dead, caballero," she said. "I am so terribly sorry."

"So am I, Gisela," I said. "I'm sorry for both of us."

Neither of us cried. As we walked in, I asked her softly, already knowing the answer: "Did she come to? Were you able to tell her?"

"No, caballero. She never woke up."

"Okay," I said. If I lived a thousand years, I would never forgive them for sending Nanita to her Maker believing that I had forsaken her. Moreno would find out for me who had told her the cruel lie. The story was not yet ended.

I went up to Nanita's room, where Gisela already had candles burning, leaned over the frail body and gently kissed Nanita's forehead for the last time.

Then I went to my room for a suit, a shirt and a tie, and came downstairs. Moreno had given me some money which I gave to Gisela for my mother. It was to be used for the funeral and for other family needs.

"Gisela," I said, "tell Mother I'm safe. I'm sure she knows what it's all about. I probably won't be coming back, but I'll be all right. Tell her—and I tell you —that I'll contact you when it's safe. Thank you for everything you've done."

El Gallego and I addressed ourselves to the job of carrying the gear from the cellar to the car in the garage. I purposely asked Gisela and Maria to stay out of it; if later questioned, they could deny any personal involvement. The moving of the heavy equipment took us a good half hour, and it was getting close to the time for Moreno's brief appearance.

While El Gallego and I were both in the garage, with the door closed and the lights on, stowing the equipment in the trunk, Fabian showed up silently at the back door. Fabian was the war name for one of the leaders of the Directorio Estudiantil, the student movement (to which Raquel also belonged) that was giving the Communists so much trouble.

Fabian ran a portable TV station which broadcast anti-Castro propaganda from a different site each day. The Communists were closing in on him and he was looking for help from Moreno. He was also a man of courage and a great shot, and Moreno had brought him along for the ride. He came from a distinguished Cuban family and we had been friends from the old hunting days. "Today the pigeons might be shooting back," he said, laughing, when we greeted each other.

His arrival, in fact, took us by surprise, and El Gallego and I reflected with discomfort that it could just as easily have been a G-2 agent who had shown up, absolutely unnoticed by the old gardener posted on the front lawn, or by Maria and Gisela in the house. Just as well, I thought. Then Moreno himself came and asked to ride with me in my car. El Gallego would go along, too, and so would Fabian.

Moreno hadn't been able to find a good house for the equipment and a future transmitting station, and he was bitter about it.

"We do the things we do," Moreno said, "and when we ask people simply to contribute a house, they turn us down. We're trying to save our country, their country, and they won't even do that much."

"I know," I said. "It's sad, isn't it? But it's also probably human nature. We can't ask everyone to be like us and, frankly, no one, Emilio, could be like you."

Moreno looked up, startled. It was the first time I had ever called him by his first name. It was the beginning of goodbye, and we both knew it.

While Moreno, El Gallego and Fabian piled into the car, I rushed back in, kissed Gisela, and told Maria to meet me at the Almendares Hotel in downtown Havana at exactly 10 P.M. Back at the garage, the gardener opened the door and we drove out, Moreno beside me, the other two in the back. Fabian, a pistol lying on his lap with an extra long clip protruding from the handle, was ready for action.

The chances we were taking were great, even for our group. To be caught with the radios, the weapons and the maps was, of course, bad enough. For El Gallego and me, after our round with the G-2, it was unthinkable. And for Moreno— now known as "The Lion-Hearted" all over Cuba—to be with us was simply foolhardy, even irresponsible. We all knew it, but the equipment had to be moved and there was no one else we could trust. It was essential to the operation and, besides, we were together again on what could be our last mission.

Rather than risk going directly to Olan Towers, which I had reluctantly accepted as the best interim hiding place, we decided to take a well-paved country road that led to a rural area and took us in a direction completely opposite from the Towers. That particular road eventually joined the central highway leading toward the Hedges textile mills. The idea was to reach the central highway and then turn back and reenter Havana as if we were coming from the provinces.

I drove quietly. Moreno and Fabian were silent, but El Gallego was excited, chattering away. It was about 6 P.M. and beginning to get dark, although that orange ball of the Cuban dying sun still had some time to go before it was finally swallowed.

Fabian was the first one to see the *miliciano* on the road, and the waving flashlight.

"Roll your window up!" Fabian said. "Gain time!" I didn't hesitate.

The soldier stood in the middle of the road and motioned for us to stop. Moreno and I looked around, and the same thought crossed our minds: the man couldn't possibly be alone. There were bushes on each side of the road, and there was a narrow dirt road just off the highway where a patrol car could easily hide. I slowed down, looked at Moreno, and said, not as a question but as a statement, "I'm going to stop." Moreno looked briefly back at Fabian for confirmation, and just nodded.

I brought the car to a full stop a few feet away from the soldier, who immediately moved toward the closed window by the driver's side and motioned for me to roll it down. I looked at Moreno quickly.

"No other way," was all he said, then, "Roll it down slowly." He reached for his army .45 automatic, cocked the gun as it rose, and, without really aiming as the window went down, pulled the trigger, once, twice. The large bullets fanned my face as they whizzed by, and the noise seemed to explode inside my right ear. But the man in the road had a round hole over his right eye, red starting to gush softly for an instant, and the body folded back to the warm asphalt of the country road.

Mesmerized by the shots, I hesitated an instant before I pressed the accelerator—one instant too long. Ten yards ahead, in a ditch to the left of the road, two more soldiers stood up and started firing.

I shouted, "Get down!" and slammed the accelerator to the floor as we instinctively dropped below window level. I zigzagged the car as well as I could from my awkward position, as Fabian emptied his clip toward the soldiers. I thought we had made it when I heard *"Ay, Dios mio!"* from the back seat. El Gallego had been hit. I glanced back at the soldiers, still shooting though out of effective range, to see if I could spot a patrol car. There was none, thank God.

Fabian took care of El Gallego while I kept driving. Tearing off his shirt, he saw that the bullet had entered the left shoulder blade and probably shattered it. There was no exit hole; the bullet must have been half-spent when it hit. The

wound was bleeding heavily, and I agreed with Moreno that there was no way
to apply a tourniquet. El Gallego was in shock, but he tried to make light of it,
saying: "They'll never believe it. Not in Galicia, they won't. Not of me." Then
he slumped back in Fabian's arms, almost unconscious.

"A doctor before anything else," I said shortly.

"Then, my friend," Moreno said, "we must get rid of you. If it gives you any
comfort, you're probably one of the most wanted men in Cuba. They may not
know it's *you* they want, but they have several pieces of a puzzle and, stupid or
not, someone's going to put it together."

I knew that Moreno was right, so I drove on, trying not to think about the
dead man. I kept telling myself that we had no choice. We drove toward the city,
taking short cuts, no longer going the long way that we had originally planned.

Moreno directed me to a house in an outlying district where some of his men
lived. This peripheral suburb was a kind of underworld that harbored petty
criminals as well as some who were not so petty. It was a hodgepodge of humanity
where privacy was respected and no questions were asked. But it wouldn't do for
too long as a hiding place for anyone truly wanted for political reasons, and it
would make no sense at all as the site for a radio transmitter.

I drove the bullet-riddled car to an automobile repair shop which Moreno
sometimes used as a front for his men and where changes were frequently made
to Rescate's fleet of cars. El Gallego was able to walk, so Moreno directed Fabian
to take him to a doctor whom Max had recommended as absolutely trustworthy.
We moved the guns and the radio gear to another car, and Moreno asked me
to join him.

I gave El Gallego a parting hug and a kiss on the cheek, tasting the cold, salty
sweat. El Gallego was too weak to do more than squeeze my arm with his good
hand as he painfully made his way from the shop, the blood concealed under the
oversized jacket. I wondered if I'd ever see him again.

In the new car, Moreno and I resumed our trip to the city. He had arranged
for two of his men to be waiting in the basement garage to help carry the
equipment up to his apartment. It seemed a very risky solution, but we couldn't
think of another. Moreno, his typical nonchalance now slightly frayed at the
edges, reassured me. He told me that his men had "reserved" one of the two
elevators in the building by putting an "out of order" sign in the lobby and that
they were holding the cab at basement level.

When we reached the center of town, Moreno stopped the car, reached in the
back seat for my small valise, handed it to me, and said, "Now go! Get lost, and
don't show yourself anywhere till you get to the embassy! And," he paused for
a second, "God bless you. It's been good being friends. Only a crazy situation
made it possible. At least I have Fidel to thank for that."

"So do I, Emilio," I said, and got out.

I looked at my watch. It was 7:30 P.M., and the city was beginning to make
New Year's Eve noises. Remembering Fabian's advice, I got on a bus with my
little bag. I rode all the way to the end of the run, got out, walked a few blocks

and boarded another bus, to ride back again downtown, after making sure that there was a different conductor. Fabian told me he had once used that ploy for seven days straight. I kept up the routine until it was time to meet Maria. The hotel bordered the park in the center of Havana, where most buses either started or ended, so that I could gauge my time pretty well. At a few minutes before ten I arrived at the crowded porch of the Almendares Hotel, and Maria was already there, having a cup of coffee at a sidewalk table, *her* little bag by her side.

It was good to see her. I sat down to have some coffee with her and cautiously told her most of what had happened, leaving out the shooting. It would be better if she didn't know about it. Half an hour later, we unhurriedly walked into the hotel. I was a little worried about checking in, because the Communists were keeping an eye on hotel guests, but we were lucky. This was a small, second-class hotel that catered mostly to transient merchants, and no one much cared who came and went. I used a phony name, of course, and wrote in "Sr. and Sra.," and the desk attendant didn't bat an eye or ask any questions. We had luggage, after all. Payment in advance was all that was required, and I paid.

And so we had a room on the second floor of the Almendares Hotel on New Year's Eve. We both knew that this could well be the last night we would ever be together again, but we didn't discuss it. We made love quietly, almost because it seemed the thing to do, although I think we both might have preferred just holding each other, trying to capture, to freeze in time the moment, the sharing of affection under strain—everything that would soon be a memory.

As we were falling asleep, we heard the crowds outside in the park, marching and chanting, over and over again, the hymn of the Revolution: *"Adelante Cubanos."* At some point someone, a drunk or a fool, started to sing "Auld Lang Syne" in English, but was quickly shouted down by the crowd. The year 1961 and the third year of the Cuban Revolution had been ushered in.

We slept until eight o'clock the next morning. I asked Maria to stay in bed while I got up, bathed, dressed in the suit and tie I had brought in my bag, gave her a kiss which pretended to mean "so long" rather than what it really was, and took off. First checking the lobby for possible agents, I hailed a taxi and rode past the New Year's debris to a point near the Brazilian Embassy.

I arrived within sight of the Embassy before ten o'clock and dismissed the cab. Immediately I sensed something unusual going on, with people scurrying and someone in the distance, some guard, shouting an unintelligible order. Then I saw an armed guard at the gate unhurriedly, almost deliberately, raise his automatic rifle to his shoulder and fire several bursts toward the narrow garden at the side of the building away from me. I heard a cry of pain, and I saw a man drop from the tall side fence onto the sidewalk.

A group of men from the garage behind the main building were shouting and throwing rocks. I moved cautiously nearer until I could see a man lying on the sidewalk, rolling from side to side in pain. One of his shoes was still hanging on the fence he had been trying to climb, caught there as he was blown off by the bullets.

The guards rushed over, picked the man up and put him in the back seat of a patrol car which moved over from its normal parking space at the embassy entrance. An officer from the patrol car directed the operation and, after the car took the wounded man away, took over the post at the gate, along with a sergeant.

The scene had shaken me up, but I was beyond the point of no return. I had to go through with my plan, so I walked up to the head guard, a lieutenant. He immediately moved in to stop me.

"What is it? What do you want?" He looked at my coat and tie, which seemed to reassure him.

I was determined to seem unconcerned.

"My name is Navarro," I said. I was taking a chance, but I figured that I had to use my right name if I was to get in. "I'm a frequent visitor here. You surely must have seen me before," knowing full well he never had. "I'm here for a late breakfast with the Ambassador's family."

"The family is out for the weekend," the lieutenant said. "You didn't know?" Then there was a frightening pause. "How come you didn't know?"

All I could say was a lame, "I guess they forgot to tell me. They aren't very reliable, are they?"

The lieutenant studied me for a while, sorting out his doubts, and finally said, "The First Secretary is here."

I knew the secretary, Gustavo Pflucker, a Brazilian of German origin and a good man.

"Navarro, did you say?" the lieutenant asked.

"Yes, Navarro. Tony Navarro."

The lieutenant glanced at the sergeant, who grabbed what appeared to be a list of names from the drawer of a makeshift desk by the entrance. I didn't like that. It sure as hell wasn't a guest list.

"Navarro," the sergeant repeated, looking down at his papers. "Full name Antonio?"

That does it, I thought. I looked at the distance from the gate to the front door. There was no way I could possibly rush it.

Just then someone shouted from inside the house: "Tony, is that you?" It was Pflucker. I darted by the surprised sergeant and reached the front door Gus was holding open. Confused, neither soldier made a move in the few seconds it took me to make my dash, and I ran into the embassy never knowing if my name was really on that "wanted" list.

Despite the fact that it was a holiday, part of the staff was there. They all seemed to know about my ordeal and welcomed me back. Some confessed that they had enjoyed picturing my last stance at The Wall. Did I do a pirouette, to show my dancing ability to the very end, or did I perhaps sing "Babalu" for the firing squad? Very funny, I thought. But I was glad we could joke about it and even happier that the Embassy officials didn't know—would never know—what my real job had been with Rescate. It was better that way.

The First Secretary, who had been my host many times at Embassy parties, asked me jokingly if I had "come for breakfast."

"Gus, you are absolutely right. I have come over for breakfast, I have come over for lunch, and I have come over for dinner—today, and for a long time."

Although they all laughed, they weren't really surprised, for they had been expecting this to happen. The only surprise was, in fact, my sudden release from jail.

Gus said, "We're happy to have you, Tony. You know where your quarters are. I'm afraid they won't be as much fun as our parties."

"I only hope," I said, "that they are *safer* than your parties."

"Tony," Gus said, "your friend Raquel called last night. I don't know her that well, but I think she was trying to tell me that you would be requesting asylum. She seemed very concerned."

That piece of news worried me too. I hadn't expected our people to know. Much as we all trusted her, Moreno would never have told Raquel until he was sure I was safe within the Embassy. He just wouldn't take that chance. And I didn't think Fabian would either.

The First Secretary of the Embassy invited me, this time seriously, to have breakfast, but added: "Tony, registration proceedings will take a little time, particularly on a holiday, but you don't really have to wait for them. You can sign the papers after breakfast. I suggest we get it over with and join our guests in the garage."

Then he looked out toward the back of the house, where things had now calmed down.

I also looked. It was a building I knew so terribly well. Through the office window I could see most of what had once been the Embassy's garage. At the gate, peering over the wall, were the same anxious faces Julio and I had seen there so many months ago. Were they the same, always there? It was a disquieting thought.

"Mr. Navarro," a servant said, "there's a young lady to see you."

For a moment I forgot that I was safe—legally at least in Brazilian territory —and the rush of adrenalin began to well up in my body. No one but Moreno and Maria should know I was there.

"Who is it?" I said, more harshly than I intended.

"A young lady called Raquel," the servant said.

Raquel! Of course! I guess if anyone would figure out where I was, Raquel would. Probably no one *told* her.

"May I see her?" I asked, turning to the First Secretary.

"Yes, of course, Tony. You certainly may, while you're still being processed. Even at other times some exceptions can be made, but not many. You should have no contact with your country other than official."

"I understand," I said, and walked to the front office where Raquel was sitting. She rushed into my arms and started to cry.

"Look, dear," I said, "there's no reason to cry. I'm all right. I'm alive."

"I know," Raquel said, "but I have bad news."

"What is it? Is El Gallego dead?"

"No, he's all right. He's going to be all right."

"What is it, then?"

"Moreno has been caught," Raquel sobbed.

"Oh, my God."

"He was caught with everything," Raquel said.

"But how can it be?" I said, hitting a desk with my fist as hard as I could. "Everything was arranged. I just saw him last night."

"I know, I know," Raquel said through her tears, "but listen, Tocayo. You know Moreno. After he left you, he went on to get Augusto's maid out of jail."

"He . . . *what?*"

"He didn't tell you. He didn't want you involved any more. But he was determined to get the maid out, and he did—but they must have followed him. They were waiting for him when he got home. It's almost as if he had a premonition."

Moreno's words came back to me: "If it's the last thing I do, I'll get her out."

"Yes," I said softly, almost to myself. "Moreno would. He wasn't the heartless bastard he pretended to be. He cared." I realized with a shock that I was thinking of him in the past tense. "Did . . . did they kill him?"

"No," she said. "He's badly wounded, but he's alive."

"How do you know all this?"

"Some of his men told me. I was trying to reach you. It was a big thing, Tocayo, a terrible thing."

"Do you know what happened?"

"All I know is that he got to his place last night and his men weren't there. They were *supposed* to be there, but I guess they'd been caught before Moreno got home." Raquel was crying harder, but I couldn't wait.

"Tell me." I shook her by the shoulders.

"I . . . I'm sorry. I should be stronger."

"No, you shouldn't be stronger. You should be just what you are—human. We all should be. But please—tell me what you know."

"He took the elevator to his floor and they were waiting for him—two G-2s. He knocked both of them down and bolted out the door. But they managed to get to the balcony and yell to some other agents in the street. They chased Moreno for two blocks, firing at him with machine guns, and he shot back when he could. They say it sounded like a war."

"Good Lord."

"They got him with two bullets in the stomach. He hit one of the three men who chased him. They took him, thinking he would die." Raquel was breaking up. "They took him to the emergency hospital, and I guess that's where he is now. They've taken all his best men, the ones who could help him, the ones who tried to get *you* out."

"What about his family?" I asked routinely, but really worrying much more about Moreno and the desperate situation of the Movement now.

"They took his wife when they came in to wait for him."

I said nothing. What can you say when the house of cards crumbles? The organization was lost. And Moreno? Moreno was more than a man. He was a monument to something I never quite understood.

"Raquel," I said gently. "There's nothing you can do about it, and you shouldn't even be here with me. Don't you see that? Go back and keep up your work if you can. One way or another, we'll keep on fighting, but this is a terrible blow. It will take us months to get going again. And the giants are gone. The Maxes and the Morenos are gone."

Raquel cried openly, and I pulled her to my shoulder.

"I'm afraid it's time to go," the First Secretary said, coming quietly into the room.

Raquel kissed me goodbye and walked to the front door. As a guard was closing it, she turned and said, "Tony . . . I can call you Tony again, can't I? . . . You've regained your faith, haven't you? Never mind how I know. I know."

I looked at her without answering. I didn't know what to say. She stood there in the doorway, and somehow the presence of the guard was not an intrusion in the intimacy of the moment.

"Tony," Raquel said.

"Yes, Raquel?"

"Now that you've found it, don't lose it. Please don't lose it, Tony." And the guard closed the door after her.

I picked up my small canvas bag and started toward the garage.

"Will it be a long time?" I asked Gustavo.

"It depends," the Brazilian said. "Sometimes it's quick—two or three months. At other times Fidel may have a pet peeve. The rebel captain who ran the Havana prison for Fidel, and defected, has been here for over a year—Captain Padilla. Castro has sworn he'll never leave alive. You'd better think in terms of at least several months."

I looked out the window at the worn faces. Meanwhile the phone rang, and a servant announced that it was Mrs. Navarro, calling for me.

"May I answer?" I asked.

"You may," Gus said—"this time."

"Darling!" Avis said on the telephone. "You made it! Thank God!"

"Yes, honey. Even I'm beginning to think He had something to do with it."

"Oh, I'm so glad! I know we shouldn't be talking, so take care and goodbye. I hope to see you soon, but there's someone here who wants to say hello."

"Hello, you son-of-a-bitch," the voice said. "So you finally chickened out?"

There was no way I could fail to recognize Alberto's voice.

"Listen, you bum. It never felt so good to be a chicken—a live chicken."

"Seriously, Tony, we're so happy you're safe. Avis told me, and she didn't think we should call you, but I don't give a damn. I know you're beyond hurt now."

"I hope so, Alberto," I said. "It's going to be an entirely new life, but anything beats the old one."

"Tony, let me tell you plainly, because I don't care any more who hears me. In fact, I hope they do hear me. We're beyond that point now. The invasion *is* coming, and it's coming soon. There is absolutely no way the Communists can stop us."

"Good luck," I said, and I felt tears welling up.

"We'll need luck, Tony. But let me tell you that we've got everything else."

"I hope to see you, Alberto, and Avis . . . some time."

"Let me tell you, Tony," Alberto said, "and I'm telling Avis, too—she's right here with me. I have a personal objective in this. Making Cuba free again is what it's all about, but I have a personal objective."

I could hear Avis crying in the background.

"I'm coming down there to get you out," Alberto said, "to get you out, Tony. To be together again . . ."

"Thanks, Alberto," I managed to choke out. "Goodbye and good luck."

It was high noon, January 1, 1961, three months and seventeen days before the Bay of Pigs invasion.

EPILOGUE

Alberto Gonzalez-Recio, alias Lorenzo, and Carlos Solis were killed in action during the aborted Bay of Pigs invasion, April 17–20, 1961.

Ernesto Perez Morales, alias Emilio Moreno, alias The Lion-Hearted, was executed by the Communist Government's firing squad on September 26, 1961.

Dr. Raul Mendez Pirez, alias Max, died of lung cancer in Miami, Florida, in 1963.

Major Raul Diez-Arguelles was killed in action in Angola in 1977, still in the service of Fidel Castro and the Cuban Government.

Captain Ramon Padilla, Warden of the Isle of Pines Prison under Fidel Castro, who later defected and sought political asylum, was murdered inside the Brazilian Embassy in 1962, allegedly on Castro's orders.

Hans Tanner, alias El Suizo, took his own life in the United States in 1976.